BERLIOZ

Louvre

BERLIOZ

Courbet

BERLIOZ

THE MAN AND HIS WORK

W. J. TURNER

VIENNA HOUSE
NEW YORK

This Vienna House edition,
first published in 1974,
is an unabridged republication of
the work originally published by
J. M. Dent & Sons, Ltd., London, in 1939.

International Standard Book Number: 0-8443-0096-9
Library of Congress Catalog Card Number: 72-93826

Printed in the United States of America

CONTENTS

BOOK I (1803–21)

BOOK II (1822–30)

BOOK III (1831–43)

BOOK IV (1843–69)

LIST OF ILLUSTRATIONS

BIBLIOGRAPHY

BIOGRAPHICAL

Hector Berlioz, sa vie et ses œuvres, Adolphe Jullien. Paris, 1888
Berlioz intime (nouvelle édition), Edmond Hippeau. Paris, 1889
Berlioz et son temps, Edmond Hippeau. Paris, 1890
Deux pages de la vie de Berlioz, Michel Brenet. Paris, 1889
Hector Berlioz et la société de son temps, Julien Tiersot. Paris, 1903
L'Histoire d'un romantique (3 vols.), Adolphe Boschot. Paris, 1908–13
Hector Berlioz, Studien und Erinnerungen, Richard Pohl. Leipzig, 1884
Hector Berlioz, sa vie et ses œuvres, J. G. Prod'homme. Paris, 1913
Berlioz, Arthur Coquard. Paris, 1909
Berlioz, Léon Constantin. Paris, 1934
Berlioz, J. H. Elliot. London, 1937
La Vie amoureuse de Berlioz, Étienne Rey. Paris, 1929

BERLIOZ'S LETTERS

Correspondance inédite de Hector Berlioz, Daniel Bernard. Paris, 1879
Lettres intimes, avec un préface par Ch. Gounod. Paris, 1882
Les Années romantiques, 1819–42, correspondance publiée par Julien Tiersot. Paris, 1919
Lettres à Mme Estelle F. (*Revue bleue*). Paris, 1903
Briefe von H. Berlioz an die Fürstin Carolyne Sayn-Wittgenstein. Breitkopf & Härtel. Leipzig, 1903
Briefe hervorragender Zeitgenossen an Franz Liszt (La Mara). Breitkopf & Härtel. Leipzig, 1895. (Two volumes containing sixty-one letters from Berlioz)
Lettres inédites d'Hector Berlioz à Thomas Gounet, publiées par L. Michoud. Grenoble, 1903
Correspondance inédite (*Revue bleue*). Paris, 1917
Autobiographie inédite (*Revue bleue*). Paris, 1919
Nouvelles Lettres d'Hector Berlioz (*R.M.I.*, 1905), ed. by J. G. Prod'homme
Les Lettres de Berlioz à Auguste Morel, ed. by J. G. Prod'homme. Paris, 1912
Lettres inédites de Hector Berlioz (*R.M.I.*, 1913), ed. by J. G. Prod'homme

BOOK I
(1803–21)

CHAPTER I

PARENTAGE

Louis Hector Berlioz was born at five o'clock in the evening of Sunday, 11th December 1803, at La Côte-Saint-André, a small town in the department of Isère, in the province of Dauphiné, France. The official announcement of his birth made on the following day reads as follows:

> Du lundy vingtième jour du mois de frimaire, à onze heures du matin, l'an douze de la République française. Acte de naissance de Louis-Hector Berlioz, né hier dimanche dix-neuf de ce mois, à cinq heures du soir, fils légitime du citoyen Louis-Joseph Berlioz, officier de santé, domicilié à la Côte-Saint-André, et de Marie-Antoinette-Joséphine Marmion, mariés, etc.

The month 'frimaire' was the third month of the republican year (21st November to 20th December) and it was the twelfth year of the first French republic.

The paternal grandfather of Berlioz (born in 1747, died in 1815) was a lawyer in the Parliament of Dauphiné and afterwards a magistrate; his was an exceptionally vigorous, forceful character. Berlioz's father, Louis Joseph, was his second son, born on 9th June 1776, and he married in the year 1802 Marie Antoinette Joséphine Marmion, born at Meylan near Grenoble in 1784. He was a doctor of medicine but also a man of some property. In 1803, when Berlioz was born, his father was twenty-seven and his mother eighteen years old. Berlioz was the first child; a sister, Anne Marguerite, known as Nanci, was born in 1806, another sister, Adèle, in 1814, and a brother, Prosper, in 1820. Edmond Hippeau in his *Berlioz Intime*, published in 1883, was the first to make generally known the fact that there was a younger brother whom Berlioz does not mention in his *Mémoires*. He also had another sister and brother who both died in childhood.

The father of Berlioz was a boy of fifteen in 1791, when the French Revolution broke out, and it is worth remarking that he and his forefathers belonged to a part of France, Dauphiné, which was one of the most liberal and least fanatical provinces. Protestants were always numerous there, and it was at Vizille, in 1787, one year before the famous summoning of the States General, that the French Revolution actually started. Grenoble is the principal town of Dauphiné, and at Grenoble the revolutionary spirit was most active. Berlioz's grandfather had been a lawyer in the parliament of Grenoble, and he shared the views of the great philosophical school of the eighteenth century. His son (Berlioz's father) was brought up, says Edmond Hippeau, 'on the ideas of Condillac, Voltaire, Rousseau, Montesquieu, Diderot, and d'Alembert, and all their works were to be found in the library of the young doctor.' Nevertheless, according to Berlioz *père*, the grandfather was on the list of notorious suspects during the Reign of Terror.

The province of Dauphiné is situated between Savoy and Provence, and Berlioz's family originally came from Savoy. In my opinion there are definite Italian characteristics in Berlioz and this is not surprising, for the Italian influence, which is clearly visible in the houses and buildings as well as in the people of Savoy, also extends to Dauphiné, where the buildings, says Edmond Hippeau, have an Italian character although they are constructed in stone, never in wood as in Savoy. In language also, according to the same authority, the Dauphinois are profoundly Latin, speaking a patois which derives from the Roman Provençal. Stendhal,[1] who was also a Dauphinois, says that the spirit of the peasants of Dauphiné resembles that of the peasants of Tuscany. In his *Mémoires d'un Touriste* he has defined the character of the people of Dauphiné as follows:

They reflect a considerable time before they act, hence their superiority over the peoples surrounding them. 'Peoples' is too emphatic: but the fact

[1] Beyle, Marie Henri (1783–1842), author of *Le Rouge et le Noir*, *La Chartreuse de Parme*, etc.

is that the populations of Lyonnais, of Provence, and of Savoy in no wise resemble the sagacious inhabitants of Dauphiné. . . . There is one trait which makes their character particularly pleasing in the nineteenth century, that is their complete lack of hypocrisy, I mean passive hypocrisy; as for that active form of knowing how to live in the world, they are greater masters of it than any one else, the Parisians always excepted. But, in short, it is quite contrary to their nature to be duped.

It is interesting to find that in a letter written to Hiller in 1831 Berlioz makes a remark which is exactly in keeping with Stendhal's definition of the Dauphiné character:

I believe it is necessary to reflect a great deal on one's project, and when all preparations have been taken, then to strike such a blow that all obstacles are smashed. Prudence and force, these are the only two ways in the world of attaining success.

Other writers give a less pleasing picture of the character of this people. I will quote two proverbs mentioned by Boschot because they are amusing in themselves. The first is a malicious saying: *Le Dauphinois, fin, faux, courtois.* The other is: 'In Dauphiné if you wish to drink a good wine with an honest man you must bring the wine and the honest man.' Such proverbs do not tell us much since they are of universal application, and Berlioz himself applied the last to the people of another country.

It is curious that Stendhal elsewhere compares the Dauphinois to the Normans. This reinforces my opinion that Berlioz, as his portraits show, belonged to that tall aquiline racial type that is common in Northern Italy. In physique he is certainly more like a North Italian or a Norman than a Frenchman of the centre or south, and in no respect does he resemble the type classified by anthropologists as the small dark Mediterranean race. It is also noteworthy that Berlioz had reddish hair as well as a boldly marked aquiline profile. In Venice and throughout Northern Italy we often find this type of colouring, and it generally goes with very fine, rather long, aquiline features quite different from the wider, more flat-faced, fairer German and Slavonic blondes. Those familiar with Stendhal's writings, who thus know his incessant comparison of the Italian character with that of the French, will have no difficulty in seeing in Berlioz's music and his writings that he is absolutely Italian and not French in character, according to Stendhal's differentiation.[1]

Unlike many eldest sons Berlioz had no animus against his father, with whom he was almost always on the best of terms and of whom he writes invariably with much affection. It was in his mother that he found his first antagonist, and from this fact alone we might infer the respective characters of his parents. His father was a man of more than average intelligence and of exceptional character. He was distinguished among his profession by having had a technical memoir on chronic diseases crowned by the Medical Society of Montpellier, which was one of the most important in the country. But his character was still more distinguished. Berlioz *père* was sane, serene, equable, just, and affectionate. When someone spoke to him of the way in which his ideas had been borrowed, if not stolen, by his colleagues, he said: 'What does it matter so long as the truth prevails?' Another remark is equally characteristic: 'All the resources of medical dietetics will fail before the disorders produced by the passions in our animal economy if morality does not succeed in making man master of his soul.' Brought up on eighteenth-century rationalism, living in his early youth through the French Revolution with which his own sympathies were strong, Berlioz *père* could hardly have been narrow or conventionally minded unless, indeed, he had been born by nature a fanatic. But his temperament was the exact opposite of a fanatic's, so that Berlioz had the good fortune to be brought up in a free atmosphere. There is a truly charming story of how his father, who supervised his early lessons in Latin at the local seminary, was hearing him read a passage from the *Aeneid* one day when the boy was so overcome with emotion that he stammered and could not go on: 'That is enough for to-day my boy, I am tired,' he said, closing the book and pretending not to notice anything. The Abbé Jacquier relates that Berlioz

[1] It is amusing that Berlioz had no high opinion of Italians or Italian music and a very poor opinion of Stendhal's writings on music.

père was mayor of La Côte-Saint-André in 1817, and describes him as 'independent, disinterested, good, kind, faithful, and an indefatigable worker'; and another witness describes him as 'of a melancholy, inquiring, gentle, and good nature, delighting in solitude and dividing his life between study and the management of his estate.'

His mother was the storm-centre of Berlioz's home-life according to his own account, which, however, is not to be trusted in every detail. Her maiden name was Marmion and she came from military stock. Edmond Hippeau states that those who knew her depicted her as a most sympathetic character. She was blonde, tall, beautiful, and distinguished, with a fresh complexion. She often complained of her health, but her husband would chaff her on her healthy appearance; she was fond of receptions and her house was one of the most frequented in the town; games were played but no music. She was religious and gave her son a religious education. In his *Mémoires* Berlioz describes her religious convictions as *fort exaltées* and says that for her 'actors, actresses, singers, musicians, poets, composers were abominable creatures marked by the Church for excommunication and, as such, predestined for hell.' On the face of it this is an exaggeration, since I am unaware that the Catholic Church has ever excommunicated poets, composers, actors, or musicians as such. In fact it could hardly have done so, since it has used all these in its own service since very early times. But Berlioz is not speaking literally; he is no doubt trying to give a vivid impression of his mother's intense piety. It is odd, however, that he seems unaware that without being particularly devout or pious and without having any religious belief in the dogmatic sense, many individuals have a distaste for public performances, public exhibitions of personal skill or ability, and this applies to performances so diverse as public scientific lectures, public political speeches—in fact all exhibitions in which there may be an element of 'showing off' or of domineering or flattering the crowd when it is there to admire, to be flattered, or to be bullied.

But Berlioz was far from indifferent, either as a boy or as a man, to his religious education. In 1848, when writing his *Mémoires* in London, he says:

I need not say that I was brought up in the Roman Catholic Apostolic faith. This charming (now that it burns nobody) religion made me happy for seven whole years, and although we have been on bad terms for a long time I have always kept a tender memory of it. I find it, too, so sympathetic to me that had I had the misfortune to have been born in the bosom of one of those schisms hatched under the heavy incubation of Luther or of Calvin, certainly I should have hastened at the first awakening of leisure and the poetic sense to have made a solemn abjuration of it to embrace the beautiful Roman faith. . . . I made my first communion the same day as my elder sister and in the convent where she was a boarder. This singular circumstance gave to this first religious act a softness which I recall with tenderness . . . I thus became suddenly *holy*, but holy to the extent of going to mass every day, of communicating every Sunday, and of going to the confessional to say to the director of my conscience: 'Father, *I have done nothing*.' 'Very well, my son,' the good man would reply, 'continue as you have begun,' and I followed his advice only too faithfully for several years.

Berlioz's father was a truly enlightened man, not merely a man with 'enlightened' or 'advanced' theories, for although he had lived right through the great period of the French Revolution with which he was in sympathy he did not try to bring up his son in some completely new-fangled way, but allowed the boy's mother also to exercise her influence and to give him the traditional religious education of the women of his country. He even went so far, Berlioz himself tells us, as to supervise his reciting of his catechism—'an act of probity, of seriousness, or of philosophic indifference,' adds Berlioz, 'of which, I admit, I myself should not be capable with my son.' It is worth adding here a description written by Berlioz *père*—in a *livre de raison* in which he was accustomed to jot down all sorts of notes—of his own father; we shall see that Berlioz resembled both his father and his grandfather in some ways:

My father was of medium height, well proportioned, and muscular; he had a good figure and an expressive face. His habits were always very methodical. He was excessively sober and scrupulously religious; he had never examined the reasons for his belief and would have thought it wrong to wish to do so. He had little education, but a more than ordinary good sense directed him in all circumstances. He held aloof from public functions, was economical and augmented his fortune by good management and perspicacity, but was not avaricious. His conversation was lively, but he would suffer very little opposition. He was severe with all his children until they were twenty years of age, when he showed himself only as a tender father and a friend. He divided his fortune into four parts, giving one to each of us (there were four children to become adult, but one died in early manhood) when we married. The fourth part was ultimately given to me. . . . I was seventeen when the Republic was proclaimed. The misfortunes of my father (under the Terror his property was confiscated) moderated my republican effervescence; but when conditions became less stormy the fine words of liberty and equality, which were ceaselessly dinned in my ears, the triumphs of our armies and the reminders of Athens and of Rome made me rave like many others, and many times I must have sorely tried the patience of my father.

My father intended me to become a lawyer, but I could never overcome my repugnance to the commentaries and glosses on the laws, the importance at bottom given to forms, the numberless subterfuges of red-tape, and the rapacity of the pack of lawyers who surround the temple of Themis. For three years I studied successively mathematics and law, gave myself up to drawing and music, cultivated literature, and without a master took up the study of the English and Italian languages. At twenty I turned to medicine with a decided bent. I took a course of botany with Dr. Villars and of chemistry with P. Trousset. But I learned the art of healing without any oral lessons and without demonstration. I dissected and studied at Grenoble and I had only been, on two occasions, three months in Paris when I was admitted as doctor in December 1802.

After having been a witness of so many important events I can, without presumption, believe myself capable of giving some salutary advice to my children and of indicating to them *the manner in which they should behave if they have the misfortune to witness a new revolution.* I recommend them to guard against enthusiasm. The sang-froid of reason is one of the most precious qualities in all circumstances of life, but it is still more so during political crises. Let them refrain from rancour or persecution in religious matters. It is for God alone to punish the crimes of thought and opinion. If we believe our brothers to be wrong let us pity them as unhappy men and help them if they need help. In political discussions beware of innovators. Never dispute—a too heated discussion clarifies nothing; it produces or increases animosity. Discuss coolly with those capable of cool discussion the subjects which divide opinions, but keep an imperturbable silence with all others.

At all times of life avoid seeking 'places.' There is no man as happy as he who preserves his independence; neither money nor honours make up for the loss of liberty. However, accept with devotion public duties which you believe yourself to be able to fulfil in a manner useful to your country.

It will be seen that in a certain passionate wilfulness Berlioz resembled his paternal grandfather, but he also had the sceptical intelligence of his father, although he had more of his mother's temperament. His father's mother was the daughter of a doctor, Antoine Robert (1720–63), from whence we may trace his father's inclination to the study of medicine, but there is little available evidence of any hereditary source for Berlioz's musical ability apart from his father's amateurish interest in music, mentioned in his *livre de raison* which I have quoted. This 'little' resolves itself into Berlioz's account of his maternal uncle Félix Marmion, an officer in Napoleon's army, whom he describes as 'gay, gallant, a great amateur violinist, and a very good singer of comic opera.'

CHAPTER II

LOVE AND ROMANCE

Berlioz's maternal grandfather, whose name, he says, 'is that of the fabulous warrior of Walter Scott (Marmion),' lived at Meylan, a village in the country between Grenoble and the frontier of Savoy. It is mountainous country, and the Marmions' white house surrounded with vineyards and gardens looked into the valley of the Isère; behind were rocky hills, an old ruined tower, and the huge mass of Mont Eynard, 'one of the most romantic spots I have ever admired,' says Berlioz in his *Mémoires*, and he adds: 'predestined to be the theatre of a romance.' This is a reference to Berlioz's first love, which plays such a curious part in his life. A Madame Gautier had a villa at Saint-Eynard where she resided in the summer with her two nieces, the younger of whom is the Estelle described by Berlioz in a famous passage in his *Mémoires*.

This name [Estelle] alone would have attracted my attention; it was dear to me on account of the pastoral of Florian, *Estelle et Némorin*, which I had taken from my father's library and had read secretly hundreds of times. But she who bore it was eighteen years old, had a tall and elegant figure, large eyes full of fire although always smiling, a mass of hair worthy of ornamenting the helmet of Achilles, feet, I will not say of an Andalusian, but of a thorough-bred Parisian, and—rose-coloured lace-up boots! I had never seen such boots before. . . . You laugh! . . . Well, I have forgotten the colour of her hair (which, however, I think was black), yet I cannot think of her without seeing simultaneously the gleam of her eyes and of her little pink boots.

Seeing her I had an electric shock; and I loved her, that is all. An infatuation took possession of me and never left me. I hoped for nothing . . . I knew nothing . . . but my heart felt a profound sadness. By day I hid myself in the fields of maize or the secret nooks of my grandfather's orchard like a wounded, dumb, suffering bird. Jealousy, that pale companion of the purest of loves, tortured me at every word any man addressed to my idol. I can still hear with a shiver the noise my uncle's spurs made when he danced with her. Everybody at home and in the neighbourhood made fun of this poor child of twelve years overcome by a love beyond his powers.

She herself, who was the first to be aware of it, was much amused by it, I am sure. One evening her aunt gave a party and they played the game of prisoners' base; in order to form the two enemy camps it was necessary to divide into two equal groups; the gentlemen chose their ladies; I was purposely made to choose mine before everybody. But I did not dare, my heart was beating violently; I lowered my eyes in silence. Every one made fun of me; when Mlle Estelle taking my hand said: 'No, I will choose! I take M. Hector.' Oh, what misery! She also laughed, cruel that she was, looking down on me in all her beauty. . . .

No, time does nothing . . . other loves do not efface the first . . . I was thirteen when I ceased to see her. . . . I was thirty when, returning from Italy over the Alps, my eyes were dimmed on seeing afar Saint-Eynard and the little white house and the old tower. . . . I loved her still. . . . I learnt that she was married and . . . all that follows. That did not cure me at all. My mother, who teased me sometimes about my first passion, was perhaps wrong to play the following trick on me. Several days after my return from Rome she said to me: 'Here is a letter I have been asked to give to someone who is to pass here presently in the diligence from Vienne. Go to the mail office while they are changing the horses and ask for Madame F—— and give her the letter. Look at her closely; I am sure you will recognize her, although you have not seen her for seventeen years.' I went, without any suspicion of what this meant, to the station of the diligence. On its arrival, with the letter in my hand, I asked for Mme F——. ''Tis I,' said a voice. 'Tis she! echoed in my heart like a heavy blow. Estelle! . . . still beautiful! . . . Estelle! the nymph, the hamadryad of Saint-Eynard, of the green hills of Meylan! It is the carriage of her head, her splendid hair, her dazzling smile! . . . but the little pink boots, alas! where were they? She took the letter. Did she recognize me? I do not know. The carriage started; I returned tingling with emotion. 'Ah,' said my mother, examining me on my return, 'I see that Némorin has not forgotten his Estelle.' His Estelle! wicked mother!

The experience related in this passage, one might say, is not an uncommon one, but, as in every experience, it is the degree of feeling which is important. A difference in intensity can so alter an experience as to make it a different experience and not merely a quantitative difference. After all the Atlantic ocean is only water, and wherein does it differ, except in quantity, from a bucket of sea-water? Even in science what seems like a mere quantitative difference can utterly transform one thing into another with no physical resemblance whatever to the first. So

I warn the reader against taking this early episode in Berlioz's life as mere high-flown 'romantic' description of a very ordinary experience which everybody knows about. We shall find later that Berlioz behaved with regard to Estelle in a way that is so extraordinary that I do not know of any similar conduct in the life of any man. But it is as well at this stage to clear our minds about the use of the word 'romantic,' as it is a word universally applied to Berlioz. It has many meanings, and the Oxford Dictionary tries to separate them distinctly for the sake of clarity of thought. But all the divisions of its meaning rest at bottom upon three ideas of which they are the several subdivisions. The first idea is that of being 'remote from experience'; the second idea is that of preferring matter to form; the third idea is that of subordinating the whole to its part. Now I shall have no difficulty in showing that in each of these three basic meanings the word 'romantic' can be used to mean a good thing or a bad thing and, if this is so, it follows that to use the word 'romantic' as in itself conferring praise or blame is either meaningless or unscrupulous. Everybody who uses the word 'romantic' must either explain precisely what he means by it or, if it is used as it is at present, merely as a term of abuse, it should be understood that it has about as much weight when applied to an artist and supplies about as much information about him as the word 'German' applied to Beethoven or 'Englishman' applied to Shakespeare does.

Let us now examine these three main ideas contained in the word 'romantic.' When we say 'remote from experience' do we mean something unusual or something false? It is clear that we might mean either. Wordsworth and Coleridge wrote *Lyrical Ballads* intending to get the same results, namely the achieving of poetry as distinct from prosaic verse, from two approaches. Wordsworth wanted to reveal the uncommon in the common, or the supernatural in the natural; Coleridge wanted to reveal in the supernatural the natural, and both succeeded. What makes the success of their effort is the truth of their work. Hence, when the word 'romantic' is applied to Wordsworth and Coleridge in the first of its three categories it can only mean by 'remote from experience' something uncommon or unusual and not at all something false; in other words it can only be a term of praise. But supposing other and inferior writers in imitating Wordsworth and Coleridge obtained (1) the common without the uncommon, or (2) the supernatural without the natural, we should be entitled to describe their work as either dull or false; but how can we call it 'romantic' when, if we call Coleridge and Wordsworth 'romantic,' these others lack the very essence of the word? The most we can do is to call them pseudo-romantics. Let us now examine the second meaning of the word 'romantic,' that of preferring matter to form. I will define 'matter without form' as unintelligibility, and 'form without matter' as vacuity. In other words, we see that these are negative ideas, definitions of something non-existent, and the notion of preferring matter to form or vice versa is mere illusion, an illusion peculiar to critics and unknown to real human beings. Now let us take the third idea, that of subordinating the whole to the part. The idea of a work of art as a whole is an extremely difficult conception, and I suspect that most minds that express their opinions so glibly on this matter have little philosophical understanding. There is a sense in which no work of art can be a whole, just as no scientific theory can be a whole, and the reason is in both cases the same, namely, that the part cannot contain the whole. Every work of art, every scientific theory is in a sense a 'part.' No artist has ever put the whole of humanity into a work of art, and no scientist has ever put the whole of the physical universe into a theory. And if Spinoza is correct such things are for ever impossible.

On the other hand, the question of degree enters here and also the exact meaning of 'form,' because we know from our experience both of life and of works of art that there is another sense in which a thing can be a 'whole.' We have, for example, some method of judging the degree of perfection of a machine. If I compare a motor car of 1904 with a motor car of 1934 I shall say the later car has the better form and is a more perfect whole; because it is, for example, stream-lined, and what is superfluous to its purpose has been eliminated to a greater extent. People generally will agree with this opinion, and especially motorists. Here we can see that to be more of a 'whole' means, paradoxically, to be more of a 'part.' What is a motor car designed for? It is by continually asking this question that, with the aid of experiment, the designer discovers the superfluous and achieves 'form' and that wholeness which results from the severest restriction of structure to purpose. Speed, comfort, and holding capacity make the triple goal of a motor-car designer—since we can include 'safety' in a machine as the equivalent of 'intelligibility' in a work of art and assume that it is to be taken for granted as the basis from which all effort starts. Now it is clear that the more multifold the purpose the harder the task of achieving form or wholeness. Where the purpose is complex and multifold, the form, even where strictly related to that purpose, rarely achieves that sense of wholeness which produces in us the idea of beauty. This is why most modern ships are less beautiful than most old-time sailing ships. But I believe there is also another factor, and that is the proportions of the relations of the several purposes in the whole. It is clear that in any real motor car (that is to say one that can be driven safely on a good road) something of each of the items of its triple purpose has to be sacrificed—something of speed, something of comfort, something of holding capacity. Now this is a matter of judgment for each individual designer, and his individuality plays a part in his selection. Three good designers may produce three different designs and in each something of the ideal will be sacrificed; but that necessary and inescapable sacrifice will be made in different places by different designers. How are we to judge which is the best design? In the last resort we may have to admit frankly that only our personal preference decides. Some motorists will prefer a little more speed for a little less comfort, and so on. But is there one combination which is nearer the ideal than any other in the sense that it makes more of a self-contained discernible whole in which no one fact *appears* to preponderate at the expense of another? Personally, I think there always is, but I would not admit that it is easily or at all recognizable by everybody. In fact, I think we may leave this case out of consideration in criticizing works of art; it is rare, and as difficult to perceive as to create. I therefore dismiss as either humbugs or self-deluders those critics who are still prepared to condemn on formal grounds many great works of art. For some critics, Shakespeare's *Hamlet*, Marlowe's *Hero and Leander*, Berlioz's *Faust*, Michelangelo's Medici Tomb, Beethoven's Ninth Symphony are imperfect, examples of the sacrifice of form to matter. I suspect them of thinking the form of such works of art as Molière's *Tartufe*, Pope's *Rape of the Lock*, Canova's monument to the Archduchess Maria Christina, Beethoven's Fifth Symphony, and Verdi's *Falstaff* as, respectively, superior. Here, I think, the critic must go very warily so as not to give rise to misapprehension. It is possible to give the description 'romantic' to the first list of works mentioned above and the description 'classic' to the second list on these grounds of an assumed sacrifice of form to matter in the works of the first list, but I would ask the question whether it is possible to conceive of, say, *Hamlet* or the Ninth Symphony or *Faust* (Goethe's or Berlioz's) as other than it is? Can one honestly say that in any one of these great works of art there is any failure of expression of the matter? I would suggest that it is not the form that is lacking but that the lack of symmetry (shall we suppose?) of the form is an element in the expression of the matter which could not truly be conveyed otherwise. I believe that in the greatest works of art there is an *excess*, and this excess always results in a breaking of the general idea of symmetry held by mankind at large.

This is all I have to say about the use of the word 'romantic' at present. I hope I have shown that it is useless as a term of abuse and that therefore to call Berlioz a 'romantic' without further explanation is merely to say that like Wordsworth, Coleridge, Mozart, Beethoven, and Michelangelo he was decidedly and unmistakably out of the ordinary.

CHAPTER III

EARLY MUSICAL EDUCATION

MOST of his biographers say that it was about the same time as the meeting with Estelle just related, namely about the age of twelve, that Berlioz began to learn music, but Berlioz himself says in his *Mémoires* that already at this age he could sing at sight and play two instruments, the flageolet and the flute. He showed sufficient facility to make his father seek to arrange with other families of La Côte to unite to get a master to come from Lyons to give lessons. They chose a professor of Lyons named Imbert, who was second violin at the Théâtre des Célestins and also played the clarinet. An agreement was signed on 20th May 1807 between the Mayor of La Côte and this musician, engaging him to teach a dozen pupils the violin and the clarinet 'for the price of eight francs a month' and to conduct the military band of the Garde Nationale. It appears that Berlioz studied the flute with this teacher, and no mention is made by him or others that he ever had violin or clarinet lessons. Berlioz says that he had two lessons a day and soon learned the flute well enough to play the most difficult concertos of Drouet. This Drouet (1792–1873) was one of the first flautists of the age and was appointed solo flute to Napoleon I in 1811, retaining his post after the Restoration. He appeared at the Royal Philharmonic Society, London, on 25th March 1816, and according to Fétis composed some one hundred and fifty works, greatly esteemed by flautists but of little account musically. Berlioz's master, Imbert, had a son a little older than Berlioz who was a good horn-player. One day he came to see Berlioz, who was going to visit his grandfather at Meylan: 'What!' he said, 'you are going without saying good-bye to me! Embrace me; perhaps you will never see me again. . . .' And that very day in the absence of his parents young Imbert hanged himself in his house. The motive of this suicide, Berlioz says, was never discovered; but it caused Imbert *père* to leave La Côte, and another master, named Dorant, took his place. Dorant came from Colmar and, according to Adolphe Jullien, was a superior musician to Imbert; he played most instruments but specialized in the clarinet, the violoncello, the guitar, and the violin; he was Berlioz's first serious teacher and taught him and his sister the guitar to the point of acknowledging Berlioz as his equal on this instrument. Berlioz, after relating these facts in his *Mémoires*, characteristically adds:

> Thus, I was now master of these three majestic and incomparable instruments, the flageolet, the flute, and the guitar! Who would not recognize in this judicious choice the guiding impulse of nature pushing me towards the more immense effects of the orchestra and music *à la* Michelangelo!
>
> The flute, the guitar, and the flageolet! I have never possessed any other executive talent; but these appear to me to be already very respectable. But, no, I am wrong, I also played the drum.
>
> My father did not wish me to study the piano. Otherwise it is probable I should have become a redoubtable pianist like forty thousand others. Far from wishing me to be an artist he, no doubt, feared that the piano would attract me too violently and draw me further into music than was desirable. I have often felt the want of this instrument; it would have been useful to me in many circumstances; but when I consider the terrifying quantity of platitudes whose daily output it facilitates—shameful platitudes which the majority of their authors, however, would not have been able to write had they been deprived of their musical kaleidoscope and furnished only with pen and paper—I cannot help feeling grateful to chance which has put me under the necessity of composing silently and freely, thus guarding me from the tyranny of finger-habits, so dangerous to thought, and from the seduction which the mere sonority of vulgar things has always, to a greater or less degree, for the composer.

We know little of his early studies of musical theory, but he tells that he had discovered, among a number of old books, Rameau's treatise on harmony, simplified with commentary by d'Alembert, which he read but could not understand because it is a book for those who know already a great deal about the

La Côte St André le 6 Avril 1819
Répondu le 10 Do

Monsieur

Ayant le projet de faire graver plusieurs œuvres de musique de ma Composition je me suis adressé à vous esperant que vous pourriez remplir mon but ; Je désirerois que vous prissiez à votre Compte l'Edition d'un pot-pourri Concertant composé de morceaux choisis, et concertant pour flutte, Cor, deux violons, alto et Basse ; Voyez si vous pouvez le faire et combien d'exemplaires vous me donneriez. Répondez moi au plus-tôt je vous prie si cela peut vous convenir combien de temps il vous faudra pour le graver et s'il est nécessaire affranchir le Paquet ; J'ai l'honneur d'être avec la plus parfaite Considération votre Obeissant Serviteur

Hector Berlioz

Mon adresse est : à Mr Hector Berlioz
à la Côte St André Dept de l'Isère

LETTER FROM BERLIOZ TO THE MUSIC PUBLISHER, PLEYEL

subject. Nevertheless, he tried to compose, and made unsuccessful arrangements of duets into trios and quartets. Later, after hearing Pleyel's quartets played on Sundays by amateurs and having procured a treatise on harmony by Catel, he got, almost suddenly, he says, a grasp of the mystery of the formation and sequence of chords and immediately wrote a sort of six-part potpourri on Italian themes from a collection he possessed. He followed this with a quintet for flute, two violins, alto, and bass, which he and his master, with the help of three amateurs, performed. Berlioz says in his *Mémoires* that these were composed at the age of twelve and a half, and adds: 'The biographers who have written, even lately, that at the age of twenty I did not know my notes have strangely erred.' It might be thought that Berlioz was guilty of a certain exaggeration in claiming to have written these early works of which no trace remains, but there are two letters in existence which prove that at the age of fifteen years and three months he certainly was trying to get some of his compositions published. The first letter was written to the publishers Janet et Cotelle, Paris, and is as follows:

LA CÔTE, 25th *March* 1819.[1]

GENTLEMEN,

Desiring to have several of my musical works engraved, I am addressing you in the hope that you will help me to achieve my aim. I should like you to take on the publication for your own account less a certain number of copies to be sent to me; please let me know as soon as possible whether you wish to undertake it. I therefore send you a *potpourri concertant* for flutte [*sic*], horn, two violins, alto, and bass. While you are engraving this work I can let you have some songs with accompaniments for piano, etc., all on the same conditions.

HECTOR BERLIOZ.

My address is: Côte-Saint-André, department of Isère.

Twelve days later, on 6th April 1819, he wrote a similar letter to the famous house of Pleyel, and the original is on view at Pleyel's in Paris. Both publishers replied refusing his offer. It will be seen that the potpourri mentioned in the letter to

[1] *Les Années romantiques*, correspondence published by Julien Tiersot.

Janet et Cotelle is not for the same combination of instruments as the one on Italian airs mentioned in his *Mémoires*, but includes a part for horn; we may therefore assume that Berlioz did not err in stating his age as twelve and a half when he composed the Italian potpourri. In any case these letters prove finally that the widely spread notion that Berlioz was handicapped as a composer because he began to study music later than most great composers is without foundation.

His father wished Berlioz to follow his own profession of medicine, and at sixteen years of age he began his medical studies with his cousin, Alphonse Robert, who afterwards became a distinguished doctor. Luckily Robert was also musical and played the violin well, and the two boys did rather more music than medicine together, Robert taking part in the performances of Berlioz's first quintets. Berlioz tells us that all the attempts at composition of his adolescence were in a vein of profound melancholy and that nearly all his melodies were in a minor key, a fault of which he was aware but could not avoid. His thoughts were overshadowed by his passion for Estelle of Meylan, and he composed a romance, among other things, in words expressing his despair at leaving the woods and the places 'honoured by her footsteps, lit by her eyes.'[1] In 1848, in London, writing the beginning of his *Mémoires* he says:

> This pale poetry came back to me to-day with a ray of spring sunshine at London where I am a prey to serious preoccupations, to a mortal anxiety, to a concentrated rage at finding here also as elsewhere so many ridiculous obstacles. . . . As for the melody of this romance, burned like the sextet and the quintets before my departure for Paris, it came humbly back into my mind when in 1829 I began to write my *Symphonie fantastique*. It seemed to me to fit the expression of this overwhelming sadness of a young heart beginning to be tortured by a hopeless love and I welcomed it. It is the melody which the first violins sing at the commencement of the *largo* of the first part of this work, entitled *Reveries, Passions;* I have not changed it at all.

---

[1] La Fontaine, *Les Deux Pigeons*—'honorés par les pas, éclairés par les yeux.'

CHAPTER IV

GENERAL EDUCATION

Berlioz was sent to the Catholic seminary of his native town to which the majority of the local families sent their children. This seminary kept no records, but two contemporaries of Berlioz, named Favre and Charles Bert, who were fellow students at this school informed Edmond Hippeau that Berlioz was at least four years there. This supplemented the instruction given by his father, preceding it, as Berlioz himself relates. The seminary was closed for some time by an edict of Napoleon, and Berlioz was probably not there up to the time when he began his first medical studies with his cousin Alphonse Robert in 1819. Latin, French, arithmetic, with a little geometry and astronomy, were the subjects taught at the seminary, and Berlioz certainly acquired a fair knowledge of Latin and an acquaintance with Virgil that he kept throughout his life. His friends Daniel Bernard and Ernest Legouvé have both declared that he was not a very well-informed man, but Edmond Hippeau tells us that in order to judge Berlioz's education more exactly he went to the trouble of making a list of all the classical quotations in Berlioz's correspondence made spontaneously at the point of the pen. Out of the two hundred odd quotations he found more than half were from French or Latin classics and chiefly from Virgil, who alone is responsible for more than forty. La Fontaine, Molière, Boileau, and Racine account for twenty-five, fourteen, ten, and nine respectively; Horace has eight, and the rest come from Livy, Ovid, Lucan, Corneille, and Bossuet. Of the other half the majority are scraps of Shakespeare and English phrases. He found a similar quantity of quotations from contemporary writers, including Lamartine, Hugo, Auguste Barbier, and Lebrun; also a little of Goethe, Moore, Dante, Alfieri, Voltaire, and frequent bits of the Old and New Testament. It is clear that Berlioz had a sound schooling, all the sounder for being rather limited, and since Edmond Hippeau tells us that in 1843 Berlioz still knew enough Latin to be able to talk in that language with the German scholar Schilling at Stuttgart we may conclude that his love of Virgil was based on real knowledge of that author. He himself says in his *Mémoires*:

> The Latin poet, long before the French fabulist [La Fontaine], whose profundity, hidden by naivety, children in general are as incapable of feeling as they are of discerning the perfection of his style, veiled by a naturalness so rare and exquisite—the Latin poet, I repeat . . . was the first who knew how to find the way to my heart and inflame my dawning imagination.

At this point it is interesting to note that in writing the first part of his *Mémoires* in London in 1848 Berlioz quoted two lines from Virgil's *Aeneid* referring to Dido; that it was the episode of Dido and Aeneas that moved him to tears as a child; and that not until 1856 did he begin to write the poem of *Les Troyens*, his last and greatest opera. There were two other significant features of Berlioz's reading as a boy. One was his passion for unexplored countries and adventurous travels; while his second passion was for reading Michaud's *Biographie universelle*, which contained biographical notices on Gluck and Haydn which, he says, moved him profoundly. Now Edmond Hippeau has discovered that this same volume of the *Biographie universelle* also contains an article on Handel (of which Berlioz makes no mention), and he has found in a letter written to A. M. Bennet that Berlioz asks how any artist 'could be taken with the heavy periwigged face of this barrel of pork and beer named Handel.' If, says Edmond Hippeau, you open Michaud at the article on Handel you will find mention of the enormous white wig and also the statement 'that he [Handel] loved good living and never composed better than when he was at his third bottle.' This is significant as an example of Berlioz's natural idealism. This description of Handel was quite enough to make such an impression on the boy that it could never be altogether effaced by his music. And it is important to get this first glimpse at a side of Berlioz's nature quite clear. He was not finical or squeamish in the least, but also he was not gross, and we shall see that he retained the pure and passionate nature of his boyhood to the end of his life. This also is one of the peculiar qualitites of his music, which is never erotic, dubious, or pathological, but always fresh, direct, and impassioned from his earliest to his latest works.

The passion for reading about foreign and distant countries also corresponded to something fundamental in his nature. His father complained that he did not know the number of the departments of France but knew the names of each of the Sandwich Islands, of the Moluccas, of the Philippines, Java, and Borneo. He once declared that he would have been a sailor had he been born in a seaport. Later in Paris he wishes he could go to China, India, Australia, Mexico, even if only as a second flute in an orchestra. About 1846 he is obsessed with the idea of going to some far country on the return of a friend, the virtuous Halma, from Canton, whom he would press to talk about China, Malaya, Cape Horn, Brazil, Chile, and Peru which he had visited. That this was more than the ordinary boyish love of adventure is shown by its persistence throughout his life and by the numerous references in his writings on music to the most out-of-the-way places. Also it is fit to mention here that his only son Louis had a strong inclination to be a sailor before he had ever seen the sea, and that in a letter to Louis in 1846 Berlioz writes:

> You are always talking of becoming a sailor; you wish to leave me then? . . . because once at sea God knows when I shall see you again! . . . If I were free, entirely independent, I would go with you and we would set out to tempt fortune in India or elsewhere. . . .

Seventeen years later, in 1863, this dream recurs and he writes in a letter to Louis that he would like to be on board with him 'under the great eye of the sky and far from our little world.' Although Berlioz never went out of Europe he was nevertheless a much more travelled man than the majority of the composers of his day. We shall see that he was more frequently out of France than any other French composer has been, making numerous journeys to England, to Russia, and throughout Germany, Austria, and Hungary. Here again we may see, if we please, a trait that is not characteristically French. But what was typically French was his passion for Paris. In no other place was he ever really at home. He was a true Frenchman in his delight in intellectual intercourse. Rarely out of Paris did he find the conversation and the friends after his own heart. He knew most of the brilliant minds of his age, and even his adversary the famous musicologist Fétis, in writing to Liszt on 1st April 1855, after Berlioz and his wife had dined with him, cannot help saying of Berlioz, 'He is a man of great intellectual power, not only musically, but in general.'

It was at the end of October 1821 that Berlioz first left his native province. His passport designating him as a medical student is dated Côte-Saint-André, 26th October 1821; it describes him as follows: 'Height 5 feet 5 inches; hair blond; eyebrows blond; beard incipient; forehead average; eyes grey; complexion warm.' The first letter from Paris to have been preserved is addressed to his sister Nanci and is dated Paris, 13th December 1821, when he was eighteen years old.

BOOK II
(1822–30)

CHAPTER I

STUDENT OF MUSIC AND MEDICINE

THERE are numerous inaccuracies in all the biographies of Berlioz. For example, even so careful a writer as Edmond Hippeau states in his *Berlioz intime* that Berlioz was eighteen and a half in October 1821, when he arrived in Paris. Grove's *Dictionary of Music and Musicians* (third edition, 1927) states that Berlioz was sent to Paris in 1822. The facts as we have seen are that Berlioz left his home in October 1821, before his eighteenth birthday, which was on the 11th of the following December; so that actually he was only seventeen years and ten months old when he arrived in Paris with his cousin Alphonse Robert to study medicine, and took lodgings in the Latin Quarter at 104 rue Saint-Jacques.

To be able before you are eighteen to sing well at sight (not by ear, as so many choristers do), play the flute, the flageolet, the guitar, the drum, and to have already composed a quantity of music, of whatever quality, is not a bad beginning for a future musical career, however unconventional an equipment it may seem. But so hidebound are the majority of academic musicians that Berlioz has never ceased to suffer from either ignorant or merely stupid observations about his lack of adequate early musical training. I have not the slightest doubt that just as what is most necessary to a writer of genius is to learn early to read and write in his native tongue rather than to have an intensive scholarship—Shakespeare and Dickens are obvious examples—so the important matter for a composer of genius is an early familiarity with the reading and writing of music. This Berlioz had from the age of twelve. He was only fifteen years and three months old when he wrote to the Paris publishers (25th March 1819) offering them a work for flute, horn, two violins, viola, and violoncello. Wagner was sixteen when he had his first instruction in harmony from a Leipzig musician named G. Müller, which he said filled him with disgust; he was eighteen before he had any serious lessons, and then only for about six months with Theodor Weinlig. This was all the serious musical instruction Wagner ever had, the rest he picked up for himself. Now we shall find that Berlioz, on the contrary, had an exceptionally long and severe academic training. He begins the serious study of music as soon as he reaches Paris, and in the earliest extant letter written by Berlioz from Paris, that to his sister Nanci dated 13th December 1821, two days after his eighteenth birthday, he writes of his distaste for the study of medicine and then describes the overwhelming impression the Paris Opéra has made on him:

Short of fainting, I could not experience a greater impression than when I saw the performance of *Iphigénie en Tauride*, the masterpiece of Gluck. Imagine first an orchestra of eighty musicians who play with such perfection of ensemble that one would say it was a single instrument. The opera begins: one sees afar an immense plain (oh! the illusion is perfect), and still beyond one sees the sea; a storm is announced by the orchestra, one sees black clouds descend slowly and cover the whole plain; the theatre is lit only by the trembling brightness of lightning splitting the clouds, but with a realism and perfection one must see to believe. There is a moment's silence, not an actor appears; the orchestra murmurs indistinctly, it is as though one heard the wind (as you certainly have noticed in winter when one is alone, how one hears the north wind blowing; well, it is just like that); imperceptibly the disturbance increases, the storm bursts and one sees Orestes and Pylades in chains led by the barbarians of Tauris, who sing this frightful chorus: 'We must have blood to avenge our guilt.' One can bear it no longer; I defy the dullest not to be profoundly moved at seeing these two unhappy men disputing over death as the greatest of blessings, and when it is Orestes whom death rejects, well then, finally it his sister Iphigenia, priestess of Diana, who must cut the throat of her brother. It is appalling, I tell you; I could never describe to you, in any way that would approach the reality, the feeling of horror that one has when Orestes, overcome, falls saying: 'Calmness re-enters my heart.' He swoons and one sees the shade of the mother he has murdered moving around him with various ghosts who hold in their hands two infernal torches which they wave around him. And the orchestra! all this is in the orchestra. If you only heard how every situation is painted by it, above all when Orestes appears calm: well, then the violins sustain a holding-note which breathes tranquillity, very *piano*; but below one hears the basses murmuring like the remorse which, despite his apparent calm, makes itself heard deep in the heart of the parricide. But I forget myself; farewell, my dear sister, forgive these digressions and always believe your brother loves you with all his heart.

Embrace everybody warmly for me.

Most of Berlioz's biographers have incorrectly placed his first hearing of Gluck's *Iphigénie en Tauride* much later; Adolphe Jullien, for example, makes it two years later, in 1823, following Edmond Hippeau, who also places in that year Berlioz's first announcement to his family that he is determined to be a musician, not a doctor. It is difficult to follow Berlioz's movements exactly during his first year in Paris, and his *Mémoires* are not reliable; no doubt because his memory deceived him when he was writing more than twenty years after the events related, also because he was not writing a chronological document but a literary work of art.

. . . After three months' [*sic*] sojourn in the capital I had not yet seen on a poster the name of an opera of Gluck. Every morning the hour of posting the advertisements brought me a fresh disappointment, and after having seen placarded *Le Rossignol*, or *Le Devin du village*, or *Les Prétendants*, or the ballet from *Nina* I would go back cursing Lebrun, Rousseau, Persuis, and the director of the Opéra.[1]

How different this tone is from that of the letter to his sister! It is the later Berlioz who is speaking in his *Mémoires*. Now we know that he had heard Gluck's *Iphigénie en Tauride* before 13th December 1821, the date of his letter to his sister Nanci. J. G. Prod'homme states that *Iphigénie en Tauride* was performed at the Paris Opéra on 26th November 1821 and again on 13th March, and on 21st and 26th August 1822. It is obviously one of these later performances Berlioz is referring to in his *Mémoires*; most probably the one on 13th March, as he says it was 'after three months in the capital.' Later in this same

[1] *Nina* was by Dalayrac; the ballet, which appears to have been separately performed, was by Persuis. See the *Mémoires*, chap. v.

passage from his *Mémoires* he says that he has forgotten to mention that before this great day he had already found his way into the library of the Paris Conservatoire, where he read and re-read until he knew by heart the scores of Gluck's great operas, and where he studied the first two symphonies of Beethoven. It was here that he encountered a young student of music named Gerono, a pupil of the famous Lesueur. Lesueur had been since 1818 professor of composition at the Paris Conservatoire and Gerono advised Berlioz to present himself to Lesueur and try to get admitted to his class.

It is difficult to fix exactly the date when Berlioz first saw Lesueur. He states in his *Mémoires* that he took to him a cantata for full orchestra on a poem of Millevoye's, *Le Cheval arabe*, with a three-part canon, and that Lesueur read them attentively and said that there was plenty of warmth and dramatic movement in his work but that he did not yet know how to write and that his harmony was so faulty that it was useless to particularize the mistakes. Lesueur suggested that his pupil Gerono should give Berlioz lessons and acquaint him with his principles of harmony, and that when Berlioz was sufficiently familiar with them to understand him he would take him as a pupil. From the available evidence this event may be placed in the year 1822. Fortune favoured Berlioz in this his first year in Paris. Scarcely was the summer vacation over when the Medical School was closed on account of a political agitation in which some of the students had been involved, and it remained closed from November 1822 to February 1823. It was probably about the middle of this year (1822) that he wrote to his father that he felt an irresistible vocation in music and would be nothing but a musician, begging him not to uselessly oppose him. His father replied affectionately, telling him he would soon see this was folly and return to his preparations for a sensible career; meanwhile Berlioz had all his time free to give to music, and it is not likely that he wasted any.

In a letter to his sister Nanci, dated Paris 20th February 1822, he writes again of the opera, after telling her how little the balls at Paris during Carnival differ from those at home. Of the balls he says:

The costume is uniformly white for the ladies and black for the men. The orchestra! Perhaps you think it superb? Well, it is not comparable to ours; just imagine two violins and a flageolet; if that isn't pitiable—two violins and a flageolet! Oh, I shall not go there any more. Further, these three unfortunates play almost every evening the quadrilles I have heard at the Opéra; you may imagine what a pretty contrast. . . .

We went to the Feydeau to hear Martin;[1] they were playing that evening *Azemia* and *Les Voitures versées*. Ah! what a compensation! I absorbed the music. I thought of you, dear sister, what pleasure it would have given you to hear it. The Opéra would perhaps please you less, it is too learned for you, whereas this touching, enchanting music of Dalayrac,[2] the gaiety of Boieldieu's,[3] the incredible *tours de force* of the actresses, the perfection of Martin and of Ponchard . . . Oh! well, I would have thrown my arms round the neck of Dalayrac if I had found myself by his statue when I heard that air to which one cannot give any epithet: 'Ton amour, ô fille chérie.' It is almost the same sensation that I experienced at the Opéra on hearing in *Stratonice* the air 'Versez tous vos chagrins dans le sein paternel.' But I am not going to describe this music to you also. . . .

Early in 1823 Berlioz had made sufficient progress to be accepted by Lesueur as a private pupil, and he soon began to think of composing an opera and to look for a libretto. As he was regularly attending a course of lectures on literature at the Collège de France by a well-known member of the French Academy, Andrieux, it occurred to Berlioz to write and ask him for a libretto. Berlioz's letter has not come to light, but it was no doubt so extraordinary as to provoke the following reply:

Your letter has interested me extremely; the passion you show for the beautiful art you practise guarantees your success in it; I wish it for you with all my heart and I should like to be able to help you to achieve it. But the task you propose is not for my age; my ideas and my studies are elsewhere; I should appear to you a barbarian if I told you how many years it is since I was either at the Opéra or at the Feydeau.[4] I am sixty-four, and it would not beseem me to write long verses and, as for music, I ought scarcely

---

[1] A well-known singer of the Opéra-Comique.

[2] Dalayrac, French opera composer, 1753–1809.

[3] Boieldieu, French opera composer, 1775–1834.

[4] The Théâtre Feydeau, where comic opera was performed.

think of anything but a Requiem Mass. I regret that you did not come thirty or forty years sooner, or I later. We might have been able to work together. Please accept my excuses, which are only too real, and also my sincere and affectionate regards.

ANDRIEUX.

17th June 1823.

Andrieux was described by Stendhal as 'ingenious, witty, and without power . . . a man of good taste but whose works no longer suit the vigorous and serious age in which we live. The generation of dolls who began the Revolution in 1788 has been replaced by a generation of strong and sombre men who do not know yet with what to amuse themselves. The hard exaggerations of Messrs. Hugo[1] and Delavigne[2] suit us better than the sweet little verses in excellent taste of Messrs. Andrieux and Baour-Lormian.'

Daniel Bernard relates that Andrieux took his letter personally to Berlioz's address, curious no doubt to see his strange correspondent:

He climbed several floors, stopped at a small door through the cracks of which escaped a strong smell of burnt onions; knocked, and it was opened by a young man, thin, angular, with dishevelled, reddish-brown hair; it was Berlioz in the midst of preparing a stewed rabbit for his student's meal and holding in his hand a casserole.

'Ah, Monsieur Andrieux, what an honour! You find me busy . . . but if I had known!' 'That's all right, don't apologize. Your stewed rabbit ought to be very good and I would have been glad to share it with you; but my stomach won't manage it. Go on, my friend, don't let your dinner spoil because you have as a guest an academician who has written some stories.'

Andrieux sat down; they began to talk of many things including music. At this period Berlioz was already a fervid and intolerant Gluckist. 'Ah, yes!' said the old professor, jerking his head, 'I love Gluck, don't you know? I love him to distraction.'

'You love Gluck, sir?' cried Hector, rushing towards his visitor to embrace him and brandishing his casserole without regard for its contents.

'Yes, I love Gluck,' continued Andrieux, not noticing the gesture

---

[1] Victor Hugo (1802–85), French poet; he wrote his first famous drama, *Hernani*, in 1830.

[2] Casimir Delavigne (1793–1843), famous French dramatist and poet.

but leaning forward on his stick and following his thoughts half-aloud, '. . . and I love Piccini also.'[1]

'Ah!' exclaimed Berlioz coldly, replacing his casserole.

This delightful and characteristic story comes through Daniel Bernard from an intimate friend to whom Berlioz had often related it. Oddly enough, Berlioz gives merely an abbreviated account of the incident in his *Mémoires*; which goes to show—if any one ever doubted it—how rich in phantasy Berlioz was. He has such a creative abundance that it is quite spontaneously active; he does not have to gather up the crumbs. But the Berlioz of nineteen was widely receptive. If he had no tolerance for the enemies of Gluck and, later, of Beethoven, he could, as we have seen, appreciate the gifted writers of comic opera, and after the revival at the Opéra on 17th March 1923 of *La Mort d'Abel* by Kreutzer,[2] he wrote to Kreutzer, who was first solo violin at the Opéra, the following letter:

O genius!

I succumb! I die! Oh, tears stifle me! *La Mort d'Abel!* Gods! . . . What a wretched public! It feels nothing! What is there can move it? . . .

O genius! What shall I do if one day my music paints the passions; and I am not understood, since they neither crown, nor carry in triumph, nor prostrate themselves before the author of all that is beautiful!

Sublime, heartrending, pathetic!

Ah! I am finished; I had to write! To whom do I write? to genius. . . . No, I dare not.

It is to the man, it is to Kreutzer . . . he will make fun of me . . . it is all the same to me . . . I would die . . . if I kept silent.

Ah! If I could see him, talk to him, he would understand, he would see what passes in my devastated soul; perhaps he would give back to me the courage I have lost in seeing the insensibility of these scurvy villains who are scarcely worthy of hearing the buffooneries of that puppet Rossini.

If the pen did not fall from my hands I would not finish. AH! GENIUS!!!

Many young men have since imitated Berlioz, and this may be a sign of a certain grace in them; but Berlioz when he wrote this letter was not imitating anybody, and let us remind ourselves

[1] Piccini (1728–1800), Italian opera composer, rival to Gluck.

[2] Kreutzer, Rodolphe, (1766–1831), famous violinist and composer.

that between the genius and the imitation there is an indescribable difference. This letter to Kreutzer has that particular quality of excess which Blake attributes to beauty. For me it is, indeed, a beautiful letter, beautiful and profoundly sad.

Failing to get a libretto from Andrieux, he persuaded Gerono to dramatize Florian's *Estelle.* To this libretto, *Estelle et Némorin*, he wrote a score which he says in his *Mémoires* was, to say the least, as ridiculous as Gerono's verses. This work of 'a tender rose colour' was balanced by a sombre dramatic scene entitled 'Béverley ou le Joueur,' the text taken from a drama by Saurin.[1] Wondering how to get this performed, Berlioz saw an opportunity in a benefit performance for Talma,[2] at the Théâtre-Français, playing *Athalie* with the choruses by Gossec. This is what he says in his *Mémoires*, but as Boschot has pointed out, he has probably confused two things in his memory and the benefit was that for the singer Lays on 1st May 1823, when Talma played in *Athalie* and Lays sang in *Le Rossignol.* Berlioz describes how he went to ask Talma to get his 'Béverley' performed on this occasion:

> Since there are choruses, I said to myself, there will also be an orchestra to accompany them; my scene is easy to play, and if Talma wishes to put it in the programme, certainly Dérivis will not refuse to sing it. Let us go to Talma.—But the mere idea of speaking to the great tragedian, of seeing Nero face to face, overcame me. Approaching his house [rue de la Tour-des-Dames], I felt my heart beating in a way that boded ill. I arrive: at the sight of his door I begin to tremble; I stop on the threshold in an incredible perplexity. Dare I go farther? . . . Shall I give up my project? . . . Twice I lift my arm to seize the bell-pull, twice my arm sinks . . . the blood rushes to my face, my ears hum, I become really dizzy. At length timidity wins and, sacrificing all my hopes, I go away; or rather, I fly for all I am worth.

After the fruitless composition of 'Béverley' Berlioz began an oratorio with Latin words destined to be played on Innocents' Day, 28th December 1823, at the church of Saint-Roch,

[1] Saurin's *Béverley ou le Joueur* is a translation or adaptation of Edward B. Moore's *The Gamester.*

[2] Talma, François Joseph (1763–1826), famous French actor.

where he had got into touch with the musical director Masson. This oratorio, entitled *Le Passage de la mer Rouge*, was, he says, a maladroit imitation of the style of Lesueur, who 'like most masters approved most those passages which most faithfully reproduced his own style.' With the assistance of Lesueur he induced Valentino, who was the head of the orchestra at the Opéra, to conduct his oratorio. When the day of the general rehearsal came, instead of the 'great masses of voices and instruments' Berlioz expected, there were only fifteen tenors, five basses, twelve children, nine violins, an alto, an oboe, a horn, and a bassoon.[1] Berlioz says he was ashamed to offer Valentino, conductor of one of the first orchestras in the world, such a 'musical phalanx,' but Valentino, resigned, gave the signal and they began. In a few instants they had to stop on account of innumerable errors made in copying the parts.

'It is an unrecognizable muddle, I suffer all the torment of hell; and we are obliged to give up absolutely on this occasion my so long-cherished dream of a performance with full orchestra. This lesson was not lost on me. . . .'

With this first attempt at the performance of a big work we come to the end of the year 1823. Berlioz is now twenty years old. His parents—to whom he possibly confided his expectations of the forthcoming performance—no doubt learned of its failure, but they were probably more interested in the fact that he had continued his medical studies sufficiently to be made a bachelor of science (*bachelier ès sciences physiques*) on 12th January 1824.[2]

Berlioz, among other things, was a very unusual combination of adventurousness and solid good sense. During the whole of his first year in Paris (1822), when he was experiencing music with an extraordinary intensity; by night at the Opéra, the Théâtre Feydeau, and elsewhere; by day reading and learning by heart the scores at the library of the Conservatoire, and taking lessons in composition from Gerono; he was also keeping on with his medical studies. Edmond Hippeau consulted the

[1] These figures are given by Berlioz in his *Mémoires*. [2] Boschot.

register of the School of Medicine and found Berlioz's signature for the last quarter of 1821 and for the four quarters of 1822. During 1823, when he began to study with Lesueur and to compose profusely, he had begun more or less to abandon medicine; but during 1822 at least he regularly attended the lectures by Amussat,[1] Thénard,[2] and Gay-Lussac;[3] also the history and literature courses at the Collège de France by Lacretelle and Andrieux respectively.

I will conclude this chapter by quoting Berlioz's own account of his first day in the dissecting room:

I was to undergo a severe test when Robert, having told me one morning that he had bought a subject (a corpse), took me for the first time to the dissecting theatre of the Hospice de la Pitié. The aspect of that horrible human charnel-house, those scattered limbs, those grimacing heads, those split-open skulls, the bleeding sewer into which we walked, the revolting smell, the swarms of sparrows quarrelling over shreds of lungs, the rats nibbling bleeding vertebrae in the corners, filled me with such horror that, leaping out of the window, I took flight as fast as I could and ran panting to my lodgings, as if Death and his frightful train were at my heels. I passed twenty-four hours under the weight of this impression, not wishing to hear about anatomy, dissection, or medicine, and meditating a thousand follies to sustain me in the future that threatened me.

Robert exhausted his eloquence fighting my repugnance and showing me the absurdity of my projects. He succeeded in making me try a second experience. I agreed to follow him again to the hospital, and we entered the funereal chamber together. How strange! in seeing on a plank those objects which at first had inspired me with such profound horror I remained perfectly calm, I experienced nothing but a cold disgust . . .

I followed, if not with interest at least with stoic resignation, the course of anatomy. A secret sympathy attached me to my professor, Amussat, who showed for this science a passion equal to that I felt for music. He was an artist in anatomy. A bold innovator in surgery, his fame is to-day European; his discoveries excite in the world admiration and hate. Day and night hardly suffice for his labour. Although worn down by the fatigue of such an existence, he continues, melancholy dreamer, his bold researches and persists in his perilous path. His traits are those of a man of genius. I see him often; I love him.

---

[1] Amussat, Professor of Anatomy.

[2] Thénard, Professor of Chemistry.

[3] Gay-Lussac, famous French physicist and chemist.

CHAPTER II

MUSIC AND JOURNALISM

DURING 1823, his first year as pupil of Lesueur, when nineteen years old Berlioz composed, as we have seen, a number of pieces, although he did not succeed in getting any one of them performed. But he did appear in print; no word of this is mentioned in his *Mémoires*, where in Chapter XXI he describes his entry into journalism, under the heading of 'Fatality—I become critic,' as occurring much later when one of his friends, Humbert Ferrand, and others, he says, founded the *Revue européenne*. Actually he contributed an article to a daily paper, the *Corsaire*, on 12th August 1823, which was his first appearance in the Paris press as far as is known. The *Corsaire* devoted itself to chronicling literary, artistic, and theatrical events. In spite of its title and the engraved figure of a Barbary corsair in full sail, it was not averse from making fun of the new school of Romantics and their eccentricities. Byron's[1] *The Corsair* was published in 1814, and I do not know whether the founders of the *Corsaire* had him in mind, but certainly even before 1823 his European fame rivalled that of Goethe.[2] At this moment the great musical novelty in Paris was Rossini,[3] and his overwhelming success had eclipsed all the older operatic composers. But Berlioz in his article ridicules the Rossini fanatics: 'Who could deny,' he says, 'that all the operas of Rossini put together would not be able to bear comparison with one line of a Gluck recitative, three bars of a Mozart or Spontini melody, or the least significant chorus of Lesueur.' Five months later, in the *Corsaire* of 11th January 1824, he contributes another article, entitled 'Les Dilettanti,'[4] in the course of which he defines

[1] Byron (1788–1824). [2] Goethe (1749–1832). [3] Rossini (1792–1868).

[4] One of these dilettantes was Stendhal, whose *Life of Rossini* was published in 1823.

dilettantes as 'people of taste who only go to the Théâtre-Italien, never read scores for a good reason which everybody can guess and decide, without appeal, the merit of works, of singers, and of orchestras. Their sensibility is such that they can hardly breathe, hearing a pathetic bit from the *Gazza ladra*,[1] where the servant is led to death, while they have complete sang-froid during the performances of the *Iphigénies*,[2] of *Les Danaïdes*,[3] etc.' If one asks the reason for this attitude, he continues, one will discover that these dilettantes consider that the singing at the Opéra is bad because, he adds sarcastically, there 'one is content with being dramatic and often sublime with the sole idea of rendering faithfully the composer's conception. What could be more ridiculous than Mme Branchu in the role of Clytemnestra; she does not add a single note to her part, above all in the air "Jupiter lance la foudre," which lends itself so well to such treatment since after the first verse a roulade of a dozen notes would admirably paint the lightning which splits the cloud . . . in a word, a dilettante is a man in the fashion and without sense, who ceaselessly talks about music.'

Here, already, a month after his twentieth birthday, we hear the characteristic style of Berlioz the critic. He might well exclaim: 'Fatality—I become critic,' for he was destined to continue to write in the columns of the Paris press for forty years. At first he wrote only occasionally, but later it became, as we shall see, his regular means of livelihood. Writing was in his family. I have already quoted[4] from his father's *livre de raison*, and I shall have occasion presently to quote from his sister Nanci's diary.[5] Berlioz's talent for writing is abundantly proved by the demand that always existed for it during his lifetime; he was one of the most successful journalists in

[1] A popular Italian opera of its day by Rossini (1792–1868).

[2] Two operas by Gluck (1714–87), *Iphigénie en Aulide* (1774) and *Iphigénie en Tauride* (1779).

[3] Opera by Salieri (1750–1825), in which he was helped by Gluck.

[4] Pp. 8–10.

[5] *Journal inédit*, kept by Nanci Berlioz.

Paris, where the competition is fiercer than anywhere else, and the contrast between the demand for his writing and the lack of demand for his music is one of the striking ironies of his life. It is also perfectly natural and understandable. He attempted no creative, only critical work in writing, so his talent and his personality, but not his genius, are present in it. But as it is the personality of a truly extraordinary man, his writing has a flavour all its own which is perceptible from the beginning. Also, as a musician of genius his judgments on music have a quality and a validity that no journalist, however talented, could achieve or pretend to.

His third appearance in print was in the *Corsaire* of 19th December 1825. It arose from one of those impudent articles, so often written when a great work is revived, by a journalist who pretends to know more th[illegible] the artist he is criticizing. The characteristic of this type of [illegible]m—from which we suffer just as much in the London of 1934 as our predecessors did in the Paris of 1825—is that the critic ignores all the beauties of the work to fasten on some petty details which for some reason (generally for no good reason) he finds unsatisfactory. The offender on this occasion was Castil-Blaze, who had written under the signature XXX in the powerful *Journal des Débats* about Gluck's *Armide*, first produced in Paris in 1777. Berlioz, who could not fail to have been profoundly moved by *Armide*, a great work which produces the same effect on all men of genius susceptible to music whenever it is performed, wrote as follows:

If Gluck returned . . . he would smile in pity: 'What,' he would probably say, 'cannot one find in my *Armide* other subjects of discussion than faults of printing, or pretended reminiscences of popular airs? . . . Is there nobody who combines with some literary talent sufficient knowledge of dramatic music to be able to analyse my work, to give an idea of the spirit in which it was composed, to discover the traits of genius which are to be found in it and which escape a public blinded by prejudices!'—I certainly do not possess all the qualities needed to fulfil this task, but without having a great knowledge of literature, I have a knowledge of music which can be useful in such a controversy. I know all Gluck by heart, I have even memorized the greater number of the orchestral parts,

I have copied a good many of his scores for study; indeed, I believe that I know them as well as is possible.

Consequently, it is clear to me that in the dispute that has arisen . . . there are errors and truths and much misunderstanding. 'Ah! Ah!' both sides will cry, 'Here is something new; we are both wrong and we shall be treated by this amateur like the litigants of La Fontaine.'[1]

Don't be scared, gentlemen; first, I am not an amateur but an artist, and as such I can speak of my art with the assurance given by long studies, familiarity with the great masters, and profound reflection. Now then: . . . faults of printing—consecutive fifths, written certainly with intention by Gluck and veiled with an astonishing skill. . . .

But who could help being indignant when reading the account given of *Armide* by several journalists, among them Mr. XXX of the *Débats*? What? The finale of the first act *produces no effect*? The 'Notre général vous rappelle' *causes no emotion*? The airs of Renaud and of Armide *are without any development and always seem cut short*? The whole work is composed on *a false system of declamation which* ONE *has long abandoned*? . . .

Well, fellow, what do you want, then? You have indeed no blood in your veins if the terrible cry of war which recalls the amorous Renaud to glory does not make you tremble! . . . But what signifies this ONE? Mr. XXX. Who has long since abandoned Gluck's system? Mr. XXX. Who finds half the music of *Armide* ridiculous? Mr. XXX. Who thinks the poem bad, the principal role anti-musical, the *décor* shabby, the ballets stale? It is Mr. XXX. But who is this inexorable critic, this finder of faults, this universal corrector? No doubt it is some great composer, some wonderful poet, or, at least, a member of the Academy. . . . No, it is more than all of these: It is Mr. Castil-Blaze.

I have quoted this at length, with various cuts, firstly, because it is clearly the letter of an artist who, although he has only just attained his twenty-second year a few days previous to writing it, knows that he is a man of genius; secondly, because here we have a clear example of the difference between genius and non-genius. Genius always recognizes itself wherever it appears. It is, in a way that is inexplicable, something apart from the man who is possessed by it and yet it is also of his very essence. To the genius of Berlioz the genius of Gluck was as evident as is the heat of the sun to an ordinary man. And just as no

[1] La Fontaine (1621–95). Berlioz is referring to the litigants in La Fontaine's fable of that name, *Les Plaideurs*.

ordinary man thinks of the spots on the sun when he is enjoying its warmth, so no artist is concerned with the paltry blemishes in a work whose genius is blazing within him like a fire.

This contribution to the *Corsaire* by Berlioz is in the form of a letter, and probably he received no payment for it. His first job as a professional journalist seems to have been in the *Correspondant*, a weekly paper founded in 1829 by a Conservative-Royalist group with whom Berlioz got in touch through Humbert Ferrand and other friends. His first article appeared in it on 11th April 1829 and was entitled 'Considérations sur la Musique religieuse.' In a letter to Humbert Ferrand dated Paris, 3rd June, 1829, he says:

> I am charged with the correspondence, almost gratuitous, for the *Gazette musicale* of Berlin; my letters are translated into German; the proprietor of the paper is in Paris now, and he bores me to death. One of my articles appeared in the *Correspondant*, but in my second article, as I attacked the Italian school, I was asked by M. de Carné the day before yesterday to write another on a different subject. I am considered to have been rather hard on the Italian school. Fire and thunder! *La prostituée* finds some lovers then, even among religious folk!
>
> I am preparing a biographical notice on Beethoven.
>
> I am on the free list for the German performances. *Der Freischütz* and *Fidelio* gave me some new sensations in spite of the abominable orchestra at the Théâtre-Italien. . . . I have been offered an introduction to Rossini but I declined it, as you may well imagine. I do not care for that Figaro, or, to speak accurately, I hate him more and more every day. The absurd remarks he made about Weber in the lobby of the German theatre exasperated me; I regretted exceedingly that I did not hear him and had no chance of giving him a bit of my mind on the subject. . . .

It is best to give here a few more particulars about Berlioz's critical activity. He wrote an article in the *Correspondant* on 22nd October 1830, entitled 'De la Musique classique et de la Musique romantique,' after having won the Prix de Rome two months before (21st August 1830). Then, as the prize-winner, he had to spend two years in Italy. He did not resume journalism until after his return to Paris, when he became a contributor to the *Renovateur*, founded on 17th March 1832, for which he wrote until its extinction on 31st December 1835.

His first article in the powerful *Journal des Débats* appeared in October 1834, but he became a regular contributor with an article on Beethoven's Mass in D on 25th January 1835. He remained on the staff of the *Journal des Débats* until 1863, when he wrote his last article, which was on Bizet's opera *Les Pêcheurs de perles*; it appeared in the *Journal des Débats* of 8th October 1863. I shall have occasion to consider Berlioz's critical writings later, but it is convenient for the sake of clarity to put the main points of his journalistic career together in this chapter.

CHAPTER III

STRUGGLING IN PARIS

AFTER the digression in the last chapter, made in order to give a view of the development of Berlioz's secondary activity as a journalist, we must now return to where we left him at the end of Chapter I of this book at the beginning of the year 1824. He is on the side of his master Lesueur, and Cherubini, Berton, and Kreutzer against the popular Rossini, who had paid his first visit to Paris in November 1823. Although Rossini behaved with tactful respect to the heads of the Conservatoire, Cherubini, Lesueur, and Reicha, the French capital was split into two factions, for and against Rossini, whom Berton always called 'Monsieur Crescendo.' Stendhal's *Life of Rossini* was published at this opportune moment, but Rossini did not establish himself in Paris until August 1824, when he was engaged at a salary of £800 a year as musical director of the Théâtre-Italien, against which Berlioz constantly fulminated. Here he produced some operas which had not yet been performed in Paris, *La Donna del lago* (7th September 1824) and *Semiramide* (8th December 1825). The triviality of the great bulk of Rossini's operatic music and its almost complete lack of sublimity and dramatic power could not but alienate the young Berlioz with his passionate admiration for Gluck, who achieves a grandeur that Rossini never attains even in his finest works. We can therefore understand Berlioz's disgust with Stendhal, of whom he writes later with contempt for his opinions on music, if he read in the preface of Stendhal's *Life of Rossini* such extravagances as: 'Since the death of Napoleon one other man has been found of whom every one speaks every day, in Moscow as in Naples, in London as in Vienna. . . . The glory of this man knows no other bounds than those of civilization itself, and he is not yet thirty-two years old.'

Here is another example of the fatuousness of applying vague descriptions such as 'romantic' to a man of genius like Berlioz, for we shall find that although nobody has ever written such dithyrambs of praise as Berlioz, they were directed with a discrimination that the most fastidious might envy. No talent however great, no success however extraordinary, won from him the tributes that he gave from his youth to the highest order of genius. The explanation is simple, it was nothing more nor less than natural affinity that made him prefer Gluck and Beethoven to Rossini, to whom, however, he is just, giving him his due later, as we may see in his *Treatise on Instrumentation*.

The spring of 1824 found Berlioz continuing his musical studies with Lesueur, reading scores in the library of the Conservatoire, and taking one with him to the Opéra to follow attentively during the performance as often as possible. He had now quite given up bothering about the School of Medicine, which, as it happened, was closed again for three months in the spring of 1824 because there had been a political demonstration at the distribution of prizes at the end of 1823. He was now making acquaintance in Paris with young men of about his own age, among whom was Humbert Ferrand, who, in spite of his ardent catholicism and quiet, conservative temperament, became Berlioz's most intimate and lifelong friend. Ferrand came from the same part of France as Berlioz and was a man of noble character but without Berlioz's force. They had musical and literary tastes in common, and Ferrand wrote poems and provided Berlioz with some of his earliest texts. They visited the Opéra together, and one of the events of the spring of 1824 was the revival of Gluck's *Orphée* on 14th May. At the beginning of June Berlioz paid his first visit to his home since his arrival in Paris. Probably rumours of his musical activities had already reached his family, and he may have had letters from home which might have made clear to him the necessity of thrashing the matter out with his father and obtaining his consent (and with it the continuation of his allowance) to his openly abandoning medicine and taking up music as a career.

He arrived at Côte-Saint-André early in June, and in a letter to his friend Ferrand in Paris which sometimes is dated 10th June 1825 but which apparently ought to be dated 10th June 1824, he writes from Côte-Saint-André, saying that although he had himself proposed that Ferrand should not write to him until a fortnight after his departure, he now wants him to write as soon as possible:

. . . because I hope that you will not be so lazy as to write only once to me and then let me languish for two months, like the man of sorrow who, far from the rock of Hope, longed to go to Tortoni's for a vanilla ice. . . .

I had taken a rather wearisome trip to Tarare; then, having alighted to make the ascent on foot, I found myself in spite of myself, as it were, in conversation with two young men who had a dilettante appearance and, as such, were unapproachable as far as I was concerned. They began by telling me that they were on their way to Mont St. Bernard for the purpose of landscape painting, and that they were pupils of Messrs. Guérin and Gros. I, in my turn, told them I was a pupil of Lesueur; they complimented me highly on the talent and character of my master, and while we were talking, one of them began humming a chorus out of the *Danaïdes*.

'What!' I exclaimed, 'the *Danaïdes*! . . . Then, you are not a dilettante?'

'I, a dilettante?' he replied; 'I have seen Dérivis and Mme Branchu thirty-four times in the *Danaïdes*.' 'Oh—!' And we were straightway on the best of terms. . . .

'But, gentlemen,' I said to them, 'how is it that, not being musicians, you have not been infected by the dilettante virus and that Rossini has not made you turn your back on what is natural and accords with common sense?' 'Because,' they replied, 'having become accustomed to seek in painting what is grand, beautiful and, above all, natural, we could not overlook the sublime scenes of Gluck and Salieri.' . . .

That is something like, my dear Ferrand, that is something like! Here we have men who can feel, good judges who are fit to go to the Opéra, capable of hearing and understanding *Iphigénie en Tauride*. We exchanged addresses and shall meet again in Paris on our return.

Have you seen *Orphée* again . . . and have you succeeded in getting hold of it to any extent?

Adieu! All is going well with me; my father is completely on my side, and my mother is already talking calmly of my return to Paris.

It would seem as if Berlioz had no great difficulties with his parents on this occasion. His father was too intelligent and by temperament too reasonable to try to force his son where he had no wish to go; especially as it was quite clear that in any case Berlioz would go his own way and it would only mean, if his father broke with him by stopping supplies, that he would handicap him in his struggles to make his way as a musician without gaining anything by it. Berlioz's elder sister Nanci was now eighteen years old and she had begun to keep a diary in the year 1824. To this diary we owe some interesting observations on her brother, made at this period:

Hector has very little to say this evening. With him everything is spontaneous, he always shows himself openly; never the least effort to hide the caprices of his humour. If he is lively, so much the better; if he is sad, so much the worse. It is just as if he were not there: no matter what one says, he takes no part in it. . . . When I think seriously of his situation I am sad; if my ideas are not entirely black they are at least a deep grey.

Hector was now twenty years and six months old. After his almost three years' absence in Paris it must have been pretty clear to his father and his sister, if not to his more fanatically tempered mother, that he was no ordinary young man, not even a particularly talented ordinary young man like his clever cousin Alphonse, but something quite outside their provincial experience. The idea of his ever settling down as a country doctor must have seemed even to them quite fantastic. It is, therefore, not surprising that Berlioz was soon writing to his teacher Lesueur that he was returning to Paris and that he had been attempting to compose a Mass, but:

I remained so cold, so icy when reading the *Credo* and the *Kyrie* that I have given it up. I started to retouch that oratorio *Le Passage de la Mer Rouge* which I showed you seven or eight months ago and which I find terribly muddled in some places. I hope to get it performed at Saint-Roch on my return.

A little later Nanci writes in her diary: 'How much pain my brother causes me! . . . If he would at least show some feeling, if he would only stay a little longer with us . . . but he is "as inflexible as a rock."'

On the eve of his departure she notes: 'My brother is not to be shaken. . . .' (24th July 1824).

On the following day, the 25th, she enters in her diary: 'He has gone, but not without causing us to shed many tears . . . mother, above all.'

In Berlioz's letter to Lesueur he says that he was welcomed by his family with much affection, and that although he did not have to endure any reproaches from his mother, yet his father recommended him not to speak of music before her. With his father he spoke incessantly of music:

I told him of your interesting discoveries about ancient music which you have been good enough to impart to me. I could not persuade him that the ancients knew harmony; he was full of the ideas of Rousseau and other writers who hold the opposite opinion. When I quoted him the Latin passage from the elder Pliny in which there are details on the method of accompanying the voice and on the facility with which the orchestra can depict the passions by means of different rhythms from that of the vocal part, he was thunderstruck, and admitted that he had no reply to it.

His troubles with his family, however, were not over. At the end of August he received a disturbing communication from his father to which he replied at length in a remarkable letter, dated Paris, 31st August 1824. This new trouble was caused by a letter he had left at Côte-Saint-André for his cousin, Alphonse Robert, in which, no doubt, he had boasted of having overcome the opposition of his parents. In his reply he says, firstly, that there was nothing in his letter to his cousin that he had not told his father a hundred times; secondly, that in speaking of his parents he had never expressed anything but the sentiments of a respectful and affectionate son; then he continues:

I have voluntarily embarked upon a magnificent career (one can give no other epithet to that of the arts) and not upon my destruction; because I believe that I shall succeed, yes, I believe it: it is not an occasion for modesty; to prove to you that I leave nothing to chance, I consider, I am convinced that I shall distinguish myself in music, everything points to it outwardly; and within me the voice of nature is stronger than the strictest objections of reason. I have everything imaginable in my favour, if you will support me: I begin young; I shall not need to give lessons like so many others to support myself; I have certain attainments and possess the foundations of others in a way that leads to a deeper development, and indeed I have experienced passions of sufficient strength not to be mistaken as to their true accents whenever it may be necessary to depict them or make them speak.

If I am mercilessly condemned to die of hunger in the event of failure (and in truth I would not stop sooner), your reasonings and your disquietude would be better founded; but there is no question of that, and, fixing it at the lowest, I shall have one day two thousand francs income; but let us say fifteen hundred, I could live all the same on this sum; even with twelve hundred I should be content, supposing music brought me in nothing. In short, I want to make my name; I want to leave some trace of my existence on the earth; and so strong is this feeling, which indeed in itself is wholly noble, that I would prefer to be Gluck or Méhul, dead, than what I am in the prime of life. . . .

Such is my way of thinking, such I am and nothing in the world can change me; you can withdraw all help from me or force me to leave Paris, but I don't believe it; you would not thus make me lose the best years of my life and break the charmed needle, being unable to prevent it from obeying the attraction of its pole.

Adieu, my dear father, re-read my letter and do not attribute it to a momentary state of exaltation, for I have never been more calm.

I embrace you tenderly, also mother and my sisters,

Your respectful and affectionate son,

H. Berlioz.

PS. Charles is well.

Is it possible to read this hundred-years-old letter of a boy not yet twenty-one without being deeply moved? One can imagine, then, its effect upon his father. It will bring tears to the eyes of those who are sensitive enough and have imagination enough to reflect upon the subsequent career of this great man, whom life was to break utterly. They will also smile at his admonishment to his father to re-read his letter. In this there is the marvellous confidence of youth. Berlioz was young, young as only the few are young in a time of renaissance. And the best sense in which the word 'romantic' may be applied to him is to describe this youthfulness of spirit.

In the midst of what is new the old persists. Louis XVIII, first restored King of France after Napoleon I, died on 16th September 1824. His brother, the Comte d'Artois, was proclaimed King Charles X. The funeral of the one and the coronation of the other were celebrated with the ancient ceremonial of the pre-revolution kings of France. Berlioz was not concerned with these things but was studying with Lesueur and composing a Mass. When the Mass was finished the question was how to get it performed. One of the heroes of the time was Chateaubriand,[1] of whom the young Victor Hugo said that he had been found faithful to the three great necessities of a great people: religion, monarchy, and liberty.[2] What the young Berlioz thought of this we do not know, but whatever the necessities of a great people are, the first necessity of a young artist is money; and so Berlioz wrote to Chateaubriand, whose writings he must have admired, since many years later in a note to Mendelssohn he compares their exchanging of conductors' batons to the exchanging of tomahawks by Red Indian chiefs, and this 'tomahawk' he certainly got from Chateaubriand. There is unfortunately no trace of his letter to Chateaubriand, who could not guess that his young unknown correspondent was destined to be the greatest musician that his country had ever produced. We possess, however, Chateaubriand's reply, which runs as follows:

PARIS, 31*st December*, 1824.

Sir, you ask me for twelve hundred francs; I have not got them; I would send them to you if I had. I have no means of helping you with the ministers of the Government. I take a lively interest in your struggles. I love the arts and artists; but the trials to which talent is subjected sometimes make it triumph, and the day of success compensates for all one has suffered.

Accept, sir, my fullest regrets; they are indeed sincere!

Chateaubriand's statement about the trials of talent is irreproachable. True, it applies more to genius than to talent,

[1] Chateaubriand (1768–1848).
[2] *Muse Française*, May 1824.

for mere talent is quickly successful. That Chateaubriand was himself an artist is shown by his use of the word 'sometimes.' An ordinary rich man would have left out the word 'sometimes.' The rich are nearly always certain that 'talent' triumphs over all obstacles, including themselves. Again this may be true of talent. As for genius, its path is more mysterious.

Nevertheless if everybody behaved on Chateaubriand's principle even the path of talent would cease to be a path and turn into an unscalable precipice. Berlioz had to look elsewhere for help. It is essential to a young composer to hear his works performed; it is part, and a principal part, of the education of his gift. Also, Berlioz needed to give some evidence of his ability to his father. Luckily he found a young friend, Augustin de Pons, from his own part of France, willing to lend him the money. He also needed official permission from the Vicomte Sosthène de la Rochefoucauld—who was the Superintendent of the Royal Department of Fine Arts which controlled the Opéra—before he could obtain the use of the orchestra of the Opéra. He was able to get this through the influence of his master and his young friends Humbert Ferrand, Albert Du Boys, and Augustin de Pons, who were all fervent Royalists and ardently ultramontane. Berlioz and his friends also worked hard to secure all possible publicity, and the performance was announced in two papers, the *Pandore* and the *Corsaire*. Finally the event took place in the church of Saint-Roch on 10th July 1825, with a hundred and fifty musicians from the Théâtre-Italien and the Opéra, conducted by Valentino, with a well-known singer, Prévost, as soloist. In one paper, the *Corsaire*, to which, as the reader will remember, Berlioz had already been a contributor, the following notice appeared:

> The Mass we had announced was performed on Sunday at Saint-Roch by the artists of the Académie Royale de Musique, and this brilliant début produced the strongest effect. We admired his touch, by turns graceful and forceful. The *crescendo* of the *Kyrie* is not the work of a pupil but of a great master. The theme, pure, simple, yet altogether new, of the *Gloria* enchanted the audience, which was numerous. The progression

of chromatic chords in the *Crucifixus*, the colossal and terrible effect of the last chorus of the *Credo*, show extraordinary gifts for great tragic music. It is clear that this young and turbulent composer listens more to his inspirations than to the strict rules of fugal counterpoint, and we can only congratulate him on it. The *Salutaris* is of the most noble and religious cast: the principal theme of this section appears at the end crossed with another theme of entirely different character, which produces a marvellous combination of grandeur and grace. The *Agnus* is much too sad for a solemn Mass; it was nevertheless well sung by M. Trévaux, whose voice was a little weak. There remains the *Domine salvum*, a piece in the grand style, whose end is especially effective. We must also praise MM. Valentino and Prévost, whose talents have contributed not a little to the ensemble of this fine performance.

It has been suggested that this notice was written by Berlioz himself or by one of his friends. This is probably true, for such expressions as 'colossal and terrible' are typical of Berlioz. Also typical of him is the sensible general tone of the article, in spite of its lavish praise. Berlioz himself tells us in a letter to Albert Du Boys, dated Paris, 20th July 1825, that Humbert Ferrand 'lost his head, he showered on me the most extravagant epithets, and, breathing fire and flame, he wrote a grand and fine article for the *Gazette de France* (whose editor he knew) which they promised to publish but which has not appeared. . . .'

The enthusiasm which Berlioz at twenty-two had inspired in a small group of friends, all young men of about his own age and of unusual quality, was one of his greatest assets. It was also one he was destined to keep throughout his life. Few artists have had better, warmer, more whole-hearted believers and more active supporters than Berlioz. His friends always believed in him and were always faithful to him, whether musicians like Liszt or littérateurs like Humbert Ferrand. Also his master. In this same letter to Du Boys he gives a description of this great day in his life, which is already completely Berliozian:

I believe that my Mass has produced a hellish effect (*un effet d'enfer*). . . . When I heard the *crescendo* at the end of the *Kyrie* my breast blew out like the orchestra, the throbbings of my heart followed the blows of the kettle-drummer's stick. I don't know what I was saying, but at the end of this piece Valentino said to me: 'My friend, try to keep quiet, if you don't want me to lose my head.' In the *Iterum venturus*, after having announced by all the world's trumpets and trombones the arrival of the Supreme Judge, the choir of human souls withering with fear gives voice; O God! I floated on this agitated sea; I swallowed these waves of sinister vibrations; I wanted to commit to no one the charge of machine-gunning my auditors, and having announced to the sinners by a last volley of brass that the moment of tears and of the grinding of teeth had arrived, I gave such a blow on the gong that the whole church trembled. It is not my fault if the women, above all, did not believe themselves at the end of the world.

The public of amateurs has declared for the *Gloria in excelsis*, a brilliant piece, light in style; it could not fail.

Nothing more curious than the moment it was all over. In two minutes I was surrounded, crushed, overwhelmed by the artists, the executants, and auditors who filled the church. One took me by the hand, another by my coat: 'There 's no holding you in!' 'Sir, you must be more moderate, you will kill yourself.' 'My flesh still creeps.' 'Young man, you will go far, you have ideas.' 'You have got to the bottom of this business; there are people I can see from here for whom it is no laughing matter.' . . . Compliments have fallen like hail. . . . The curé wanted to tell me that my ideas came from the heart not from the head. '*Ex pectore*, sir, *ex pectore*, as the great St. Augustine has said.' Finally I escape , go to my master. . . . 'Come, let me embrace you; you will be neither a doctor nor an apothecary, but a great composer; you have genius, I tell you so because it is true; there are too many notes in your Mass, you have let yourself be carried away, but through this bubbling of ideas no intention has failed to hit its mark, all the scenes are true; the effect is inconceivable. And I should like you to know that the public has felt this effect because I placed myself alone in a corner especially to observe. . . .'

In a letter to his mother, dated 14th July 1825, Berlioz wrote in a more restrained style; in the course of it he says:

. . . in spite of the desire you might have, and papa also, to see me turn my studies in another direction, your affection for me is too great for what has given me such joy to be able to give you pain. Know then, my dear mother, it is only the desire I have had to see my success confirmed by the journals that has delayed me. There are six which give me encouragement and praise; unfortunately none of them is read at La Côte; they are the *Aristarque*, the *Drapeau blanc*, the *Moniteur*, the *Corsaire*, and the *Journal de Paris*. I buy them as they appear; I want to come to you armed with my documentary proofs. . . .

So here the first step has been successfully made; but I have none the less perceived how much I need to work; numerous faults which have escaped the multitude carried away by the fire of the ideas have been noted by me; I have discovered them and shall try to avoid them another time. . . .

In the spring of 1826 Berlioz was occupied with another composition, *La Révolution grecque*, a *scène héroïque*, with choruses, the words by Humbert Ferrand. He vainly tried to get Kreutzer, musical director of the Opéra, to perform this at one of the Concerts Spirituels, and obtained the support of the Vicomte de la Rochefoucauld and of his master Lesueur; but Kreutzer was not like the generous Lesueur, and Berlioz tells in his *Mémoires* how, pushed by Lesueur, he at last replied without disguise: 'Well, indeed, what will become of us if we help youngsters like this?'

This work, retouched later, is the only one of Berlioz's early compositions that has survived; the rest he either destroyed completely or made use of parts of them in later works. The words of *La Révolution grecque* are an exhortation to the Greeks to regain their lost liberty, written in the spirit of Shelley and of Byron, who had died at Missolonghi on 19th April 1824. The work lasts about ten minutes, is simple, and shows the influence of Gluck, Spontini, and Lesueur. If it is poor in purely musical interest, it is nevertheless dramatic and expressive. The poem was published in March 1826 and some songs by Berlioz, *Le Dépit de la bergère* (poetry by Mlle ***, music by M. Hector Berlioz), *Toi qui m'aimes, verse des pleurs*, *Le Montagnard exilé* (words by Albert Du Boys), *Le Maure jaloux*, *Pleure, pauvre Colette*, were published at Berlioz's expense somewhere about the same time.

Berlioz was living on as little as possible in order to pay back to Augustin de Pons the 1,200 francs borrowed for the performance of the Mass. He also owed his cousin Alphonse Robert 84 francs. Robert asked Berlioz's father for the money, and this caused more disturbance, judging from a letter, dated Paris, 12th December 1825, to his sister Nanci, in which Berlioz explains that he owes one friend 300 francs. As he was paying it back bit by bit, he probably felt justified in understating the amount. In any case, it was essential not to frighten his father. In this same letter there is an interesting account of himself:

I feel . . . that I am capable of producing what is great, vital, passionate, true—beautiful, in short. . . . I am on my guard as much as anybody against the delusions of self-love, and when I want to find out whether something I have done is good, after having completed it, I let it rest, I give myself time enough to recover thoroughly from the effervescence which composition always produces in me, and when I am quite calm I read my work as if it were not mine; then if it arouses my admiration I am convinced that it deserves the admiration of all who have the sensibility and knowledge necessary to understand it.

Pressed by his family, Berlioz saw before him only one way of ensuring his future as a musician, and that was to win the Prix de Rome, an annual prize awarded by the Academy under the Ministry of Fine Arts for composition, which gave the recipient a gold medal and a pension for five years. To win the Prix de Rome was the greatest distinction a young musician in France could attain, and it was coveted by all pupils of the Paris Conservatoire who were composers. But Berlioz was not a pupil of the Conservatoire, only a private pupil of Lesueur, one of the professors there. However, Berlioz in June competed and was set aside at the preliminary trial at which the weakest are excluded. This was only to be expected, for although his master, Lesueur, could perceive the genius of his inspired pupil, the formidable purist and conservative head of the Conservatoire, Cherubini,[1] was not likely to be lenient to the irregularities of the young Berlioz. The first result of this disaster was a warning from his father that his allowance would be stopped. Berlioz rushed home and arrived at La Côte in the summer of 1826. Lesueur wrote to Berlioz's father a vigorous letter, saying that he had no doubt about his musical

[1] Cherubini (1760–1842).

future and that music 'streamed out of his pores'; being a religious man, Lesueur also added some arguments about the need to respect gifts which came from Heaven, which only drew from Dr. Berlioz an uncompromising letter beginning: 'Sir, I am an unbeliever.'

What happened after his arrival home we know only from Berlioz's own account. After a chilly reception and a few days' respite, his parents asked him to choose some other activity if he refused to be a doctor, to which he replied that his bias towards music was so absolute that he could not imagine he would not go back to Paris to study music. 'Nevertheless, you must get used to this idea,' replied his father, 'for you will never go back there.'

> From this moment [says Berlioz], I fell into complete silence, hardly replying to questions put to me, eating nothing, spending a part of the day wandering in the fields and woods and the rest shut up in my room. To tell the truth, I had no plans: the heavy ferment of my thoughts and the constraint I was undergoing seemed to have entirely deadened my mind. Even my rages were extinguished; I was perishing for want of air.
>
> Early one morning, my father came to wake me. 'Get up,' he said, 'and when you are dressed come to my study, I want to speak to you.' I obeyed without any idea of what it was about. My father's manner was grave and sad rather than severe. Nevertheless I expected a fresh attack when these unexpected words overwhelmed me: 'After several sleepless nights I have made my decision. . . . I consent to let you study music in Paris . . . but only for a while; and if after new trials the results are still unfavourable you will do me the justice to admit that I have done all I reasonably can and you will decide, I hope, to choose another path. You know what I think of mediocre poets; mediocre artists of all kinds are not worth any more; and it would be a great grief and a profound humiliation to me to see you sunk in the crowd of those useless men.'
>
> My father, without being aware of it, had shown more indulgence towards mediocre doctors who, while just as numerous as bad artists, are not only useless but highly dangerous! But it is always thus even with the best minds; they fight the opinions of others with reasons of a perfect propriety without noticing that their arguments are double-edged and can be equally fatal to their most cherished ideas.

Berlioz had a difficult scene with his mother before his re-departure to Paris, but it appears that his account of it in his

Mémoires is exaggerated. He leaves La Côte with his father's permission to become a regular student at the Conservatoire, and on 26th August 1826 he is entered by Lesueur as a pupil in the composition class at the Royal School of Music, the Paris Conservatoire. A rule was relaxed in his favour by the director, Cherubini; this compelled students to study counterpoint and fugue in Reicha's class before going into Lesueur's class, but Berlioz was allowed to follow both classes contemporaneously from 2nd October 1826.

CHAPTER IV

INFLUENCES ON THE YOUNG STUDENT

BERLIOZ remained a diligent student under Lesueur and Reicha at the Paris Conservatoire for the next two years, from 1826 to 1828. When we consider that this followed on a period of about three years' private study with Lesueur, during which he had composed several works on a large scale, and that, in addition, he was going constantly with the scores to performances at the Opéra and the Théâtre-Italien in Paris, at each of which there was a repertory of opera performed almost all the year round, it is clear that to talk in the loose way many ill-informed writers have done about Berlioz's lack of early musical training is sheer nonsense and quite the reverse of the truth.

Berlioz had two years of the best academic training in the finest school of music in Europe under exceptionally talented masters, Reicha and Lesueur; of whom it is now necessary to give some particulars. Reicha (1770–1836) was born in Prague and at the age of eighteen, on the appointment of his uncle (J. Reicha) as musical director to the Elector of Cologne, went to Bonn, where he played the flute in the same band with Beethoven, who played the viola. He studied the theoretical works of the famous Kirnberger and Marpurg, and wrote many compositions which his uncle's orchestra performed. In 1794 Reicha went to Hamburg and composed several operas. In 1799 he went to Paris, where he succeeded in getting two of his symphonies and other music performed. From 1802 to 1808 he was in Vienna and in close association with Haydn, Beethoven, Salieri, and Beethoven's teacher, Albrechtsberger. He finally settled in Paris in 1808, where he had three operas performed; but it was his chamber music, of which he wrote an immense quantity (there are, for example, no fewer than twenty quartets for strings and twenty-four quintets for wind instruments), and his theoretical works which gave him his reputation. This reputation was of quite a special character, for his music was 'more remarkable for striking harmonies and novelty of combination than for abundance and charm of ideas.'[1] Also he was famous among contemporary musicians for his gift for solving problems in music. These qualities, and his remarkable theoretical works, *Cours de Composition musicale ou traité complet et raisonné d'harmonie pratique* (Paris, Gambaro, 1818), *La fugue et le contrepoint en* 34 *études* (Paris, Schonenberger), and the vast treatise on musical composition which was translated into German by Carl Czerny and published in four volumes in Vienna by Diabelli and Co. in 1833, gave him a unique position. He was appointed professor of counterpoint and fugue at the Paris Conservatoire in 1818 and had thus been in this position for eight years when Berlioz became his pupil.

A great theorist, a master of the craftsmanship and science of his art such as Reicha is not necessarily a great teacher, but Berlioz, who was not inclined to be over-indulgent towards professors, himself declares in his *Mémoires*:

> Reicha taught counterpoint with remarkable clarity; he made me learn a great deal in a short time and with few words. As a rule he did not omit, as the majority of teachers do, to give to his students, as far as possible, the reasons for the rules whose observance he recommended.

Considering that Reicha was one of the greatest theoreticians of a great period in the history of music and that Berlioz was for a long time his pupil—coming to him before he was twenty-four years of age, keen to learn all he could and to develop his innate musical gifts to their utmost with a passion far more intense than students normally bring to their work—how is it possible that the legend that Berlioz had an inadequate training was ever started? The answer is simple, and it rests almost entirely on the fact that Berlioz never studied and could not

[1] Gustave Chouquet.

play the pianoforte, so that from the beginning he thought in vocal and orchestral tone. From the theoretical standpoint Berlioz had as fine and thorough a training as any musician who has ever lived. Many of the greatest musicians have had a far more haphazard and empiric training; and what is even odder, considering the nonsense written about Berlioz's inability to write fugues, is that Berlioz's training was especially strong on the contrapuntal side.

It is true that Berlioz did not like composing, and made fun of, mere scholastic fugues; but that was because his creative powers were so strong that for him music was a form of expression, an act of creation, not an exercise. He says: 'I once asked Reicha what he thought of fugues vocalized on the word *Amen* or on *Kyrie eleison*. . . . "Oh!" he exclaimed warmly, "it is barbarism!" . . .'

Still more barbarous are the barbarians who, because they cannot feel the unique quality of Berlioz's music—that incomparable style, so pure, so masterly, so devoid of the hackneyed finger-work of the mind—try to justify their bewilderment by accusing him of deficiencies which are their own. As if Berlioz, by the time he had won the Prix de Rome in 1830, did not possess more intellectual knowledge of the art of music (quite apart from his genius as a composer) than any but a few of the greatest masters of all time have done!

If we want evidence of this even apart from his music, *and* his academic studies, *and* his success, in spite of his originality and wildness, in winning the second *grand prix* in 1828 and the first *grand prix* in 1830 in face of all the competing young musicians of the Paris Conservatoire—at that time, as I have said above, the first in the world; if, I repeat, we need further evidence, we shall find it in his criticism and in his great theoretical work, the *Traité de l'instrumentation*, which is the classic on the subject. Berlioz stands out conspicuously even among the greatest musicians in general intellectual power; he had the Latin lucidity and strength of reasoning, and he never showed himself more French than in his remark that

Chopin could not play in strict time.[1] Is it not worse than ludicrous, disgusting indeed, that even to-day musicians and critics are to be found who, when Berlioz's works are performed, will speak of defects of training and inadequate knowledge? In this country much of this sort of inept comment (one cannot call it criticism) has been due to lack of musical instinct, or to ignorance of the facts of Berlioz's early life and training. But in future, now that all this material has been made easily available in English, we shall only be able to ascribe it to dullness of hearing, deficiency in musical instinct, and wilful disregard of the facts.

Here is the place to quote Berlioz's criticism of Reicha, who, when Berlioz became his pupil, was in the prime of his life:

Reicha, before coming to France, had been at Bonn the colleague of Beethoven. I don't believe that there was ever a very lively sympathy between them. Reicha attached great importance to his mathematical knowledge. 'It is to mathematics,' he told us during one of his lessons, 'that I owe the achievement of a complete mastery of my ideas; it has tamed and cooled my imagination which formerly led me wildly, and in submitting it to reason and reflection it has doubled its power.' I am not sure that this idea of Reicha's is as correct as he believed or that his musical faculties gained much by the study of the exact sciences. Perhaps the taste for abstract combinations and *jeux d'esprit* in music, the real charm he found in resolving certain thorny propositions which serve only to turn art from its true path in making it lose sight of the goal towards which it should ceaselessly tend—were the results of this; perhaps this love of calculation was even very harmful on the other hand to the success and worth of his works, making them lose in melodic or harmonic expression, in purely musical effect, what they gained in difficult combinations, obstacles overcome, out-of-the-way elaborations made rather for the eye than for the ear.

However, Reicha appeared as indifferent to praise as to criticism; he seemed to care only for the success of the young artists whose education in harmony was confided to the Conservatoire, and he gave them lessons with all imaginable care and attention. He ended by giving me his affection; but at the beginning of my studies I perceived that I bothered

[1] This is bound to give rise to more misunderstanding, but I may say that it is compatible with an appreciation of *tempo rubato* and of Chopin's genius, of which Berlioz wrote one of the earliest appreciations.

him by always asking for the reason of every rule; reason which in some cases he could not give me since . . . there is none. His quintets for wind instruments have enjoyed a certain vogue for years in Paris. They are interesting compositions, but a little cold. I recall, however, on the other hand, having heard a magnificent duet, full of fire and passion, in his opera *Sapho*, which had several performances.

Berlioz's master for composition, Lesueur, was ten years older than Reicha, having been born in 1760. He was thus sixty-six, the same age as the director Cherubini, when Berlioz entered the Conservatoire. I mention these ages to show that none of Berlioz's masters, not even the head of the Conservatoire, were old men when Berlioz became a student. All three men were finer artists and more learned musicians than any that followed them at the Conservatoire during the whole of the nineteenth century. Academic musicians live to a great age, and during the nineteenth century the Paris Conservatoire only had three directors after Cherubini, namely, Auber from 1842 to 1871, Ambroise Thomas from 1871 to 1896, and Théodore Dubois from 1896 to 1905. Cherubini, whom Beethoven in his later life considered to be the greatest of his contemporaries, is probably the most eminent musician who has ever held such an academic post, and he had an exceptionally distinguished staff of forty-five professors, including many famous virtuosos. It was through him that the library of the Conservatoire obtained the right to one copy of every piece of music or book upon music published in France. Many well-known musicians, including Berlioz, have held the official post of librarian, and some idea of the quality of this library may be had from the fact that the collection of Bottée de Toulmon, Berlioz's predecessor as librarian, contained eighty-five volumes of MS. copies of the musical masterpieces of the fourteenth, fifteenth, and sixteenth centuries, from Munich, Vienna, and Rome, including all Palestrina's masses.

Lesueur has been described almost as a Berlioz *manqué*, but this is rather unjust. He was a profound scholar and an original composer. In 1786, at about the age of twenty-six, he was appointed musical director of Notre-Dame, Paris; there he had under him about one hundred orchestral musicians and singers and gave magnificent performances of motets, masses, and sacred oratorios which were attended by the queen, Marie Antoinette, who had been a patron of Gluck. Many of these were his own compositions, and he had a very definite conception of how devotional or liturgical music should be composed. In spite of his scholarship, he did not aim at writing abstract music but always strove for dramatic and picturesque effect. He was ambitious to compose operas for the stage, and he was so far ahead of most musicians of his time that the arbitrary division between sacred and profane music did not exist for him. His masses (one of them was preceded by an overture) and his oratorios were dramatically conceived, just as if they had been operas. But it must be remembered that in opera he belonged to the grand and serious school of Gluck, the later Sacchini,[1] and Méhul[2] in which dramatic truthfulness, depth of feeling, and a sublimity of expression were aimed at, so that between music for the stage and the church there were only technical differences. This was a return to an older attitude or perhaps, rather, a rediscovered inheritance. Later in the nineteenth century, church and stage music were again divorced in the general mind but not without a second marriage in triviality and sentimentality, which infected and dominated both spheres. Historically, in music, the dominating spirit of the age has always shown itself in both places, stage and church. Operatic and church music are always essentially of the same quality. When the one is trivial so is the other. The fact that they are set to different words makes no difference to the spirit of the music.

Lesueur's dramatic church music drew such crowds to Notre-Dame that his opponents called it *L'Opéra des gueux* (The Beggars' Opera). He was attacked and wrote pamphlets defending and explaining his attitude. He published in 1787

[1] Sacchini (1734–86), famous Italian composer.
[2] Méhul (1763–1817).

his *Essai de musique sacrée, ou musique motivée et méthodique pour la fête de Noël*, which was an explanation of a sort of 'mass-oratorio' composed by him for Christmas; and in reply to his opponents he wrote his *Exposé d'une musique, une imitative et particulière à chaque solennité*, published by Herissant, Paris, 1787. In this he defended his methods of composing dramatic and descriptive music—'programme-masses,' they have been called—for the festivals of the Church. In fact, Lesueur was a religious man of upright, straightforward character, who believed in the events which the festivals of the Catholic Church celebrate and treated them as realities. In his *Exposé* he writes:

> Music by the magic of its effects can depict everything to some degree; for example, the gloom of a silent night, the brightness of a calm day, the fretful tumult of a tempest, the joyful serenity which follows it, the horror of an underground prison, the freshness of a shady wood; it can introduce without difficulty in the flow of its themes, the heights, the depressions, the violences, the reserves, and even the silences of declamation; it can give an idea of every situation; but what, above all, is in its power are the feelings which are most intimately connected with the human heart . . . it can supply what words cannot say.

In the same *Exposé* he writes a panegyric on Gluck: 'In most of his masterpieces he knows how to make us feel the most delicate movements of the human heart.'

There is something like fatality in Berlioz's becoming the pupil of a musician of this character. In art, as in science, there seem to be two polar types of mind, corresponding to the Platonists and the Aristotelians. The parallel is perhaps not exact because in creative art a point may be reached where the two fuse or achieve some temporary synthesis. Whether this happens in science or not I do not know. But it happens in poetry and in music; and in both arts it happens when in some rare genius there is a successful combination of what we may describe as the lyrical and the dramatic elements. Shakespeare is the best example in poetry; for although he can write the poetry of pure lyrical singing or pure metaphysical thinking, he can paint dramatically and truthfully the more physical world of nature—of sensations, of feelings, and of dramatic events. In his case it would be hard to say where the natural bias lay, or if a bias exists in either direction. In music we find that this Shakespearian blend is a characteristic of the great masters. Bach, Handel, Haydn, Mozart, Beethoven, Schubert (I do not go earlier, because I am not sufficiently acquainted with the music of earlier composers) were both lyrical and dramatic, abstract and concrete. All of them—including Bach and Beethoven, who might be reckoned by a superficial observation to be the most abstract—loved to write downright descriptive and dramatic music. How far they go in any one direction depends upon their musical genius, not upon their bias towards one pole or the other. The composer of *Auf dem Wasser zu singen* is also the composer of *Erlkönig*; the composer of the prisoners' choruses in *Fidelio*, of the *Leonore* overtures, and of the 'Pastoral' Symphony is also the composer of the C sharp minor Quartet. The composer of the last movement of the C major ('Jupiter') Symphony—one of the finest pieces of abstract contrapuntal musical thinking in existence—is also the composer of *Don Giovanni*. But *Don Giovanni*, although a dramatic work, itself exhibits the abstract and the concrete, what we may call 'pure' thought and 'pure' description; also the lyrical and the dramatic. The same may be said of Gluck's best works, although Gluck, who has written some of the purest music, does not often, to my knowledge, write 'pure' music—in the sense that we are apt to call some of Bach's and Mozart's instrumental work 'pure' music.

Here, I think, there is often some confusion of thought. By pure music most people seem to mean (*a*) instrumental music, (*b*) non-descriptive music. All opera is thus ruled out. All choral music is apt to be excluded also, because most choral music, from Bach's B minor Mass and Handel's oratorios, is dramatic. The average critic or amateur of music, when he thinks of pure music, thinks of Bach's preludes and fugues and Mozart's quartets. But I think the word 'pure' is misleading. I would suggest that the right description of Bach's famous

Forty-eight Preludes and Fugues, for example, is not 'pure' but 'lyrical,' but some are more lyrical than others. This applies also to the quartets of Haydn, Mozart, and Beethoven. All this instrumental music ranges from the lyrical to the dramatic. The same is true of purely choral and of mixed choral and instrumental music. Masses, motets, cantatas, oratorios, *and* operas are made up of music ranging from the lyrical to the dramatic. I call the lyrical the Platonic pole and the dramatic the Aristotelian pole; or, if you like, the subjective and the objective.

Let us next consider the word 'descriptive,' used nowadays by the best musicians as a term of reproach. I would say that all music, whether lyrical or dramatic (all art, in fact, not only music!) is made up of the descriptive and the non-descriptive, that is to say, the exterior and the interior. Now just as the psychologist Jung, after making this separation, then declared that introvert and extrovert are not hard and fast divisions, but that most human beings partake of both characters; so in works of art, I maintain that you cannot make a hard and fast division between the descriptive and the non-descriptive. Sometimes the interior is expressed by the exterior, sometimes the exterior is described by the interior. Let us take *Hamlet*, for example: does Shakespeare describe Hamlet by his appearance and his conduct, or does he describe his conduct and his appearance by his thinking? In other words, what is the relation between the outward Hamlet, visible in appearance and behaviour to the outside world, and the inner Hamlet expressed in his monologues? Would the monologues alone or the plot of the play alone be enough to describe Hamlet? The monologues, the pure thinking of Hamlet, would be a Platonic description; the action of the play, the pure plot, would be an Aristotelian description. Does it not appear, then, that an adequate and complete description in art of any event requires both—the interior and the exterior, the subjective and the objective, the Platonic *and* Aristotelian approach.

Now, I suggest that when the word 'descriptive' is used by

modern musicians as a term of reproach—as it might be applied, for example, to Richard Strauss's 'Alpine' Symphony—they mean by it that the work suffers from too much exterior and too little interior description. Description *per se* is not a defect; on the contrary, in the fullest sense of the word, art is all description and nothing else.

If the word 'descriptive' is applied to Gluck or Berlioz it cannot be applied in the derogatory sense that it may be applied to Strauss's 'Alpine' Symphony. Gluck and Berlioz, in the greater bulk, and certainly in the best, of their work, range from the lyrical to the dramatic, from the internal to the external. The human heart in its tenderest, most delicate emotions participates in all the tempests and dramatic storms of their music. What Berlioz found congenial in Lesueur was the absence of that dryness, that empty intellectualism, which produces nothing but mere note-spinning.

What Lesueur objected to in opera was 'making a serious character sing on words such as "glory" and "victory" thirty bars of roulades vulgarly called *gargouillades*!' To do this was, in his opinion, to turn a hero into a warbling canary, and was just nonsense. And here he makes one of those profound, simple remarks that only an honest man can make: '*The greatest nonsense is want of expression.*'

How often have I thought of this when hearing the symphonies of my fellow-countrymen in the Queen's Hall! Why are so many modern compositions dead and empty in spite of an apparent plenitude of craftsmanship? Why is so much cleverness in art absolutely worthless and sterile? The answer is, because it is nonsense through want of expression. We need seek no further for a reason; this is adequate and goes to the bottom of the matter. Now whatever criticism can be brought against the music of Berlioz there is one that can not, namely, want of expression. All Berlioz's music is expressive. In other words, Berlioz's music is sense, not nonsense; always it is significant, it has meaning, it is music.

Lesueur was an indefatigable student of ancient music and

of ancient classical literature; he considered that the abundance of rhythms in the ancient poets proved that the Greek musicians had a greater mastery of rhythm than the moderns; and so we may trace the extraordinary development of Berlioz's mastery of rhythm—one of the conspicuous features of his music, in which he has no rival among his contemporaries or successors—as owing something to Lesueur's instruction. The use of the ancient modes was another of Lesueur's predilections, and Berlioz's music is full of this influence.

Finally, Lesueur was a true artist, with the character of an artist in the highest sense of the word. Adolphe Boschot had access to an unedited manuscript by Lesueur that was in the collection of Charles Malherbe (1853–1911), who was for many years archivist to the Paris Opéra. This manuscript is entitled, *Réflexions philosophiques; Immortalité de l'âme; Conseils aux jeunes compositeurs.* It would make an ordinary printed volume of our time, says Adolphe Boschot, and it is full of Lesueur's philosophic, religious, and artistic ideas. For Boschot these ideas are rather out of the mode. Boschat, excellent writer and intelligent critic though he is, belongs to the latter half of the nineteenth century in its enslavement to rationalistic propriety, a period which to-day seems to us of the third decade of the twentieth century more remote and less sympathetic even than the eighteenth century. We, I think, will read the following words of Lesueur's with a new sympathy:

> When men of letters, scientists, artists, composers, painters, sculptors, architects, etc., make their works, they all need the Ability, the Health, the POWER to make them; but this does not suffice; they need, in addition, the desire, the WILL, or the love of their work in order to have the courage to achieve it. This also is not enough: *each* of these men needs, further, the UNDERSTANDING to complete his work. And this exists in all the productions of human intelligence. And these three necessary things are nevertheless not three things, three men, but one thing, ONE MAN. . . . Thus, the POWER, the MERCY, and the supreme UNDERSTANDING of God are essentially ONE . . . and this TRIPLE direction was THE CAUSE OF THE CREATION OF THE WORLD.

In 1804 Lesueur succeeded Paisiello as Maître de Chapelle to the First Consul. This became the Chapelle Impériale after the coronation of Napoleon and the Chapelle Royale on the restoration of the monarchy (Louis XVIII); but Lesueur, to whom Napoleon had presented a gold snuff-box inscribed: 'The Emperor of the French to the Author of *The Bards*,' in admiration of his opera *Ossian ou les Bardes*, produced in 1804, retained his position. He became a member of the Institut (Académie des Beaux-Arts) in 1813 and professor of composition at the Conservatoire in 1818, a position he retained until his death in 1837. Twelve of his pupils, including Berlioz, Ambroise Thomas, and Gounod, won the Prix de Rome, but Berlioz was his favourite pupil. As early as 1824 Berlioz was constantly at his house and at the musical performances at the Chapelle Royale, where Lesueur explained to him the principles on which he composed the masses, oratorios, etc., which were given there under his direction. That there was a strong affinity between Lesueur and Berlioz is abundantly clear. Lesueur seems to have believed in him from the beginning, and it was Lesueur who paid the fees for his entrance to the competition for the Prix de Rome in 1828[1] and, probably, in 1827. In some respects Berlioz's relation to Lesueur was like that of Weber to Vogler. 'There is in me,' said Vogler, 'a something which I have never been able to call forth, but these two will do it'—a reference to Weber and Meyerbeer.

[1] Information given by Berlioz in a letter to Humbert Ferrand, 15th July 1828.

CHAPTER V

BEFORE THE 'THUNDERBOLTS'

AT the beginning of 1826 Weber came to Paris on his way to London. His opera *Der Freischütz* had been produced for the first time in Paris on 7th December 1824 in an inadequate French arrangement by Castil-Blaze under the title of *Robin des Bois*. It was soon a considerable success, but it does not seem to have made a deep impression on Berlioz. On 14th January 1826 Weber's *Euryanthe*, in a still more mutilated form under the title of *La Forêt de Sénart*, was given in Paris. It was less of a success than the version of *Freischütz*, but Berlioz became an enthusiastic admirer of Weber, though he never met him. Weber left Paris on 2nd March 1826 and died in London on 24th June of the same year. Berlioz relates in his *Mémoires* how he just missed meeting Weber at Lesueur's house and, palpitating with excitement, rushed all over Paris trying to find him, but in vain:

> Oh! [he adds] if these inspired men could divine the sublime passions their works arouse in us! If it were given to them to learn of the enthusiasms of a hundred thousand souls concentrated and intensified in one alone, how precious it would be to receive and thus to be consoled for the envious hate of some, the unintelligent frivolity of others, and the lukewarmness of all!

Berlioz had now gathered around him a group of kindred spirits who went constantly to the Opéra. 'The fanaticism we professed for our favourite authors,' he says, 'was only comparable to our profound hatred of others. The Jupiter of our Olympus was Gluck, and the devotion we rendered him is not to be likened to anything that the most frenzied dilettantism could imagine nowadays.' Berlioz was the pontiff of this sect of believers. However ardent they were, he inflamed them to a greater passion. He bought tickets himself and drove them willy nilly to the Opéra, where he placed his adherents in the best positions for hearing.

For he says that in one place the horns were too near, in another they could not be heard; on the right trombones predominated; to the left, through an echo, their effect was bad. Also he made his adherents change positions in different acts, according as to whether an out-door or interior scene diminished or increased the power of the choruses. Having given these instructions he would see if the followers knew the piece well enough. If they had not read the words he would take the book from his pocket and read it, with comments, before the curtain rose; they always came very early and enjoyed every moment of preparation, including the arrival in their places of the orchestra, on whose members, as they appeared, Berlioz would make aloud favourable or unfavourable remarks, such, for example, as the following:

> The conductor will have to pay attention to Monsieur Guillou, the first flute who is now coming in; he takes singular liberties with Gluck. In the religious march in *Alceste*, for example, the composer has written for flutes in the lower register so as to obtain the special effect of the low tones of this instrument; such a disposition of his part does not please M. Guillou; he wants to dominate and be heard, and so he transposes his part an octave higher, thus destroying the effect the composer desired and turning an ingenious idea into something trivial and vulgar.

As Berlioz already knew by heart every one of these operas it was, as he says, extremely imprudent of the performers to make any changes. He and his followers, all young men in the early twenties, would stand no nonsense. If a member of the audience talked during the overture near any one of them he would cry aloud this pre-arranged phrase: 'Heaven blast these musicians who prevent me from hearing this gentleman!' They were on the look-out for any wilful alterations, and Berlioz did not wait to protest in writing, but would accuse the offenders in a loud and indignant voice in face of the public. He relates how, having noticed that in a performance of *Iphigénie en Tauride* cymbals had been added to the first Scythian Dance in B minor, where Gluck only uses strings, and that in the great recitative of Orestes in the third act the parts written so effectively for trombones by Gluck had been omitted, he determined not to allow these mutilations to pass unremarked a second time. Sure enough, however, the cymbals were used. Boiling with rage, he contained himself until the end of the dance and then, making use of the short pause before the next piece began, he cried out with all the power of his lungs:

'There are no cymbals there; who has dared to improve Gluck?'

You can imagine, he says, the astonishment of the public, but it was even worse when, in the third act, the trombones, as he feared, being suppressed, the audience heard the same voice cry aloud:

'The trombones did not play! This is unendurable!'

The astonishment of the public was nothing, however, to the rage of the orchestra and its conductor Valentino; nevertheless, after this, in the following performances everything was put right, and Berlioz characteristically remarks that he contented himself then with growling between his teeth: 'Ah! that 's a good thing!'

He learned a great deal from Lesueur and Reicha, but he did not learn from them instrumentation; this he acquired for himself, having an extreme natural sensitiveness to combinations of tone and timbre, which he developed by the incessant practice of hearing actual performances at the Opéra, which he followed with a concentration of attention to every detail beyond the capacity of the ordinary musician. One of the most amusing of these youthful adventures happened one night at a performance of Sacchini's *Œdipe*. Berlioz and his friends did not rank Sacchini with Gluck, but they admired him sincerely. On this occasion Berlioz had brought a friend, Léon de Boissieux, whom he was trying to proselytize; but after the first act, seeing that he remained unmoved by the music, Berlioz took up a position in front of him so as not to be annoyed by his obvious indifference. During the then famous recitative 'Mon fils! tu ne l'es plus!' although absorbed by this scene ('so beautiful both for its simplicity and its feeling for antiquity'), he could not help hearing a dialogue between his young friend, who was calmly skinning an orange, and an adjacent stranger who was greatly moved by the music:

'Good heavens! sir, calm yourself!'

'Impossible! It 's irresistible! It 's overwhelming!'

'My dear sir, it 's not right to carry on in this way. You will make yourself ill.'

'No, leave me alone. . . . Oh!'

'For goodness' sake pull yourself together! After all, it 's only a show . . . will you have a piece of this orange?'

'Ah, it 's sublime!'

'It 's from Jaffa.'[1]

'How heavenly!'

'You 'll have some, then?'

'Ah, sir, what music!'

'Yes, it 's very pretty.'

Berlioz goes on to say that during this conversation the opera had arrived at the beautiful trio: 'O doux moments!'; he was so affected that he began to weep with his head between his hands; but hardly was the trio ended when he was lifted off his seat by two strong arms and passionately embraced by the stranger, who exclaimed in a convulsive voice:

'Sacrrrrredieu! how beautiful!'

Not at all astonished, and with tears in my eyes, I replied by asking him:

'Are you a musician?'

'No, but I am moved by music as much as any one.'

'That 's all right, give me your hand. By God, sir, you are a fine fellow.'

Thereupon, quite indifferent to the tittering of the people about us—and to the astonishment of my friend the orange-eater—we exchanged a few words in low tones. I gave him my name, he his and his profession.

---

[1] 'Malta' in the original; I have taken the liberty to contemporize it in order that some orange merchant reading this book in the distant future may be amused by these two bits of information.

He was an engineer! a mathematician!!![1] In what devilish odd places sensibility takes refuge!

Thus inimitably drawn by Berlioz in 1848, we have a picture of the young artist as he was more than twenty years before. There are people who will call this picture 'romantic' and this sensibility 'romanticism,' using the words with double meaning, each of which is intended to be depreciatory. They intend to infer firstly that such sensibility is childish, and secondly, that it is consciously exaggerated. It *may* be true that it will never happen to young men again to behave quite in this way, but I have already dealt with the significance of the word 'romantic,'[2] and I need only add here that in my opinion, although the forms of expression may change with time, place, and social conditions, yet in essence there is nothing false or exaggerated in Berlioz's description of this episode. Certainly we all know that every external expression of genuine feeling and of thought may be copied by those incapable either of the thought or the feeling. But the imitators are never convincing to those who are themselves capable of the real thing. To those who are not they may be not only convincing but more pleasing, because they reduce the experience to a more ordinary level.

Is this not the secret of the success of most imitators? Novelists, poets, painters, composers—are they not all successful with their contemporaries according as they lack genuineness and originality, but *copy* adroitly the works of the past, adding a dash of topical spice to make them seem novel. These, generally, have a success with their contemporary public that the artist of true genius rarely, if ever, has. For how should he be recognized? The popular artists are recognized because they *seem* like their predecessors, but the new creative artist *seems* unlike and so he cannot be recognized for what he is except by the few who are, for one reason or another, more perceptive.

Berlioz was now, at the end of 1826 and the beginning of

[1] Berlioz tells us that his name was Le Tessier, and that he never saw him again.

[2] Pp. 13–15.

1827, receiving an allowance of 120 francs a month from his father. However, he still owed Augustin de Pons 600 francs and was economizing as much as possible to pay him back.

He shared a lodging in the rue la Harpe in the Latin Quarter with a young student named Charbonnel, who was the son of the Charbonnel who succeeded Berlioz's father as Mayor of La Côte-Saint-André. Daniel Bernard received a note-book from Mme Damcke, a friend of Berlioz's, in which he kept an account of his expenses from 6th September 1826 to 22nd May 1827. It shows that he lived on next to nothing. Some days the students fed on raisins, other days on bread and salt. Nevertheless such economies did not suffice to pay back Augustin de Pons, who, perhaps in order to save his friend from excessive privations, apparently wrote to Berlioz's father asking for payment. Dr. Berlioz had already paid 300 francs and now learnt that there were still 600 francs to pay for the performance of his son's Mass; he paid, but suppressed his son's allowance. Berlioz was now reduced to thinking of emigrating and indulging his inclination for distant countries by obtaining a post, as he says in his *Mémoires*, of first or second flute in an orchestra in New York, Mexico, Sydney, or Calcutta. But this was mere fancy; his real passion for composition made him find a way out of his difficulty. He obtained a job in the chorus of the Théâtre des Nouveautés, in which vaudeville and light opera was played. The theatre opened its season on 1st March 1827 and, according to his friend d'Ortigue, he stayed in the chorus for about three months, earning fifty francs a month, on which he could just live. He attended his classes under Reicha and Lesueur by day and sang in the chorus of the theatre at night.

On 26th March 1827 Beethoven died in Vienna; his music was then very little known in Paris. His name is never mentioned by Lesueur in his theoretical works. Berlioz knows only his first two symphonies, but the hour of revelation, of several revelations, is near. In the meantime he has to compete in June for the Prix de Rome. He is also busy composing an opera, *Les Francs-Juges*, the book being written by his friend

Humbert Ferrand. This was a subject that Weber might have treated. The scene is laid in the Black Forest at the time, presumably, of the secret tribunals prevailing in the fourteenth and fifteenth centuries, especially in Westphalia, called by the Germans *Vehmgericht*, hence *Die Vehmrichter*, the Secret or Free Judges. Berlioz composed a good deal of the music during 1827 and the following year, but never completed it. There is a manuscript score in the Paris Bibliothèque Nationale among Berlioz's papers; but there is not much music, according to Boschot, who had examined it and found that some pages of the music in the second act, still bearing the title *Francs-Juges*, are contained in a manuscript of the *Symphonie fantastique*, being utilized for the *andante* of that work, the *Scène aux champs*. Also, a *Marche des gardes* from the same work became the *Marche au supplice* in the *Symphonie fantastique*. Out of other music from this unfinished opera Berlioz, some time after 1830, made, together with some new music, a sort of ballet in one act entitled *Le Cri de guerre de Brisgaw*. This has disappeared. There remains of the opera the magnificent overture, *Les Francs-Juges*, which was first performed a year later, on 28th May 1828, at Berlioz's first concert in Paris. This sombre and powerful work holds its own among the finest concert overtures in the repertory of modern orchestras, it was composed in Berlioz's twenty-third or twenty-fourth year. It is rarely played in England (I have only heard it once in London), where it may be said to be, like most of Berlioz's music, unknown to the majority of conductors.

At this period Berlioz and the young French intelligentsia were influenced by the poetry of Thomas Moore and Byron and by the prose of Walter Scott. Shakespeare and the later Goethe were unknown to them, and the opera *Les Francs-Juges* had something of the Gothic atmosphere of certain of Scott's novels.

For the Prix de Rome Berlioz composed a cantata, *Orphée déchiré par les Bacchantes* ('Orpheus torn to pieces by the Bacchantes'). The jury of musicians who judged the competition for the Prix de Rome was composed of members of the Institut: Cherubini, Paër, Berton, Lesueur, Catel, and Boieldieu. There was no orchestra to play Berlioz's work but only a pianist, and it was declared unplayable. The first prize was given to Guiraud and two second prizes were awarded, but nothing to Berlioz. This work has disappeared, but the fourth number[1] of *Lélio; ou le Retour à la vie*, the beautiful *Chant de bonheur*, was taken from it; also the fifth number, *La Harpe éolienne*.[2] In his letter of 1831 to Ferrand from Rome, mentioned in the footnote to this page, he writes:

Send me the *adagio* which follows the *Bacchanale* at the point where the violins take the mutes and make the *tremolandi* accompanying the distant air given to the clarinet with a few chords on the harp; I cannot recall it well enough to write it from memory and I wish to change nothing. As you will see from this, I have sacrificed the *Mort d'Orphée*; I have taken from it all I liked and I should never be able to get the *Bacchanale* performed. Consequently, on my return to Paris, I shall destroy my copy, and the one you have will be the sole and only one, if indeed you keep it.[3]

Writing to Ferrand from Paris on 29th November 1827, Berlioz refers to his failure to win the Prix de Rome with his *Orphée*. He is describing a new performance of his Mass at the church of Saint-Eustache on 22nd November, St. Cecilia's Day:

My Mass was performed on St. Cecilia's Day, with twice the success which attended the first representation; the small corrections I made in it have improved it considerably; the passage *Et iterum venturus*, which was ruined on the first occasion, was interpreted in a terrifying manner this time by six trumpets, four French horns, three trombones, and two ophicleides. The chorus which follows . . . produced a tremendous

---

[1] Not No. 3, as incorrectly given by Adolphe Boschot in *La Jeunesse d'un Romantique*.

[2] Stated in a letter from Berlioz to Humbert Ferrand dated Rome, 3rd July 1831.

[3] This copy, consisting of 82 pages, turned up at a sale (*vente* Martin) in 1885 and was bought by a Marseilles music-lover. Under the title were the words: 'Work declared *unplayable* by the music section of the Institut and *played* at the Royal School of Music—the author to his friend Ferrand.' This piece ought to be included, if discoverable, in the projected supplementary volume of Breitkopf & Härtel's unfinished edition.

impression upon everybody. . . . I had up to this point maintained my self-possession . . . but when I saw this picture of the Last Judgment, the announcement sung by six bass voices in unison, the awful *clangor tubarum*, the shouts of fear from the multitude represented by the drums . . . rendered precisely as I had conceived it, I was seized with a convulsive trembling which I had just sufficient strength to subdue up to the end of the passage, but which then compelled me to sit down and to allow my orchestra to rest for some moments. I could no longer stand, and feared lest my baton should fall from my hand. Ah! if you had only been there! . . .

I sent invitations to all the members of the Institut, and I was delighted that they should hear the performance of what they call impracticable music, for my Mass is thirty times more difficult than the cantata I sent in for the competition, and you know that I was compelled to withdraw that because M. Rifaut was unable to play it on the piano, and M. Berton was emphatic in declaring that it was incapable of being performed even by an orchestra. My great crime (at all events at present) in the eyes of this cold and old classic, is my seeking to produce something new.

'That is a chimera, my dear fellow,' he said to me a month ago; 'there is nothing new in music; the great masters adhered to certain musical forms which you will not adopt. Why seek to do better than the great masters? And, as I know that you have a great admiration for a man who, certainly, is not devoid of talent and genius—I mean Spontini——'

'Oh, yes, I have a great admiration for him, and always shall have.'

'Well, my dear fellow, Spontini, in the eyes of veritable connoisseurs, is not very highly esteemed.'

Upon that, as you may well imagine, I lost all respect for him. The old imbecile! . . .

Must I demean myself so far as to compete once more? I must, for my father wishes it, and attaches much importance to the prize. For his sake I will be represented and will write them a homely composition which will be quite as effective when played on the piano as by the richest orchestra; I will be lavish in redundancies, *because they are the forms to which the great masters adhered, and one must not do better than the great masters*, and if I gain the prize, I swear to you that I will tear up my *Scène* before the very eyes of these gentlemen as soon as the prize has been awarded to me.

This last paragraph reveals what Berlioz's attitude was as early as 1827, before his twenty-fourth birthday. He has now been one year an official student of the Conservatoire; he has had one year's hard study of fugue and counterpoint under one of the best teachers of the time, Reicha, and it is clear that he has taken the measure of the Conservatoire and its professors.

It would be stupid to interpret this straightforward statement of Berlioz to his friend Ferrand as idle boasting. The mixture of hard-headed common sense and imaginative genius in Berlioz is not to be mistaken. Although he knows already (and he is not wrong) that he has genius and his professors have only talent in various degrees, he will compete again for academic honours. He will win the second Prix de Rome in 1828; no prize will be given at all in 1829—no doubt, because his *scène lyrique*, *Cléopâtre*, is still too much of a good thing for the academicians and yet they dare not give the prize to another; and, finally, he will win the great prize in 1830 with his *scène lyrique*, *Sardanapale*. I do not know of another case in the whole history of music, or any other art, where a creative genius of such power and originality as Berlioz has shown such patience and persistence in compelling academic professors and scholars to recognize officially his prowess and excellence *on their own ground*. And yet, in spite of this unique exhibition, there are musicologists and professors still extant to-day who suggest that the qualities of Berlioz's music are due to imperfect training. The explanation is simple. Berlioz's music is still as incomprehensible to these fatheads as it was to the fattest of academic heads during his youth.[1]

[1] One of the worst offenders in this country was Edward Dannreuther (1844–1905), who has written some incredible nonsense about Berlioz in the *Oxford History of Music*, Vol. VI. This volume ought to be scrapped and rewritten. See p. 131.

CHAPTER VI

THE 'THUNDERBOLTS' BEGIN

In the letter to Ferrand dated Paris, 29th November 1827, from which I have already quoted in my last chapter, there occurs the following paragraph:

> I write warmly of all this to you, my dear friend; but you do not know how little importance I attach to it. For three months I have been a prey to grief from which nothing can distract me, and my disgust with life has gone as far as possible; even the success I have just obtained has only momentarily been able to lift the grievous weight which oppresses me, and it has fallen back on me heavier than before. I cannot give you now the key to this enigma; it would take too long; I don't think I could form the letters to speak of this subject. When I see you again you will know everything. I finish with this sentence, addressed by the ghost of the King of Denmark to his son Hamlet:
>
> Farewell, farewell, remember me.

The year 1827 was the year of the revelation of the genius of Shakespeare to the young artists of France. Five years earlier an English company had come to Paris and experienced a dismal failure. At the performance of *Othello* the curtain had to be lowered in the midst of a frenzied tumult and to the cries of 'Down with Shakespeare! He is a lieutenant of Wellington's!' Finally, cavalry had to be used to disperse the rioters.

But it was not only a political antagonism. The Parisians made fun of *Othello*, and some of their jokes were in extremely bad taste. However, five years can, as we know, work a great change in the spirit of a people, and when William Abbott brought Charles Kemble and an English company to the Odéon in 1827 the atmosphere had completely altered. On 11th September *Hamlet* was produced with Kemble as Hamlet and

Harriet Smithson as Ophelia. At this time most of those who were to become the great figures in French literature and art during the first half of the nineteenth century were young men under thirty. Practically the cream of the young French intelligentsia were in the theatre on this first night of *Hamlet*, 11th September 1827. We know from various sources the names of some of these young men who witnessed this performance—Alexandre Dumas, Victor Hugo, Sainte-Beuve, Alfred de Vigny, Gérard de Nerval, Delacroix. And Berlioz was there also. All these young French romantics were delirious with excitement and enthusiasm, and we are told that the auditorium of the theatre was in a frenzy impossible to describe. Three years later (in 1830) Victor Hugo wrote *Hernani*, which was the foundation of the French romantic movement in dramatic literature.

As for Berlioz—the youngest of all except Gérard de Nerval, not having yet reached his twenty-fourth birthday—Shakespeare coming thus on him unawares, he says, 'struck him like a thunderbolt.' More than twenty years later, writing the first part of his *Mémoires*, he gives the following account of this experience:

> His lightning in opening the heaven of art with a sublime crash illuminated the most profound distances. I recognized the true grandeur, the true beauty, the living dramatic truth. At the same time I took the measure of the immense absurdity of the ideas spread in France about Shakespeare by Voltaire—
>
> . . . ce singe de génie
> Chez l'homme, en mission, par le diable envoyé [1]—
>
> and the pitiful shabbiness of our old Art of Poetry according to pedagogues and ignoramuses. I saw . . . I understood . . . I felt . . . that I was alive, and had only to rise and walk.

On the next day, he says, *Romeo and Juliet* was announced, and although he had free entry to the orchestra of the Odéon,

[1] . . . that genius-monkey
The devil sent to man to be his flunkey.
VICTOR HUGO (*Chants du crépuscule*).

he was so fearful of missing the performance that he rushed and bought a seat so as to be doubly sure.

After the melancholy, the heart-rending griefs, the weeping love, the cruel irony, the black meditations, the heart-breaks, the madness, the tears, the mourning, the catastrophes, the sinister accidents of *Hamlet*, after the black clouds, the icy winds of Denmark, to expose myself to the burning sun, the balmy nights of Italy, to see this spectacle of love prompt as thought, burning as lava, imperious, irresistible, immense, and pure and beautiful as the smile of angels, to see these scenes of furious vengeance, these fatal embraces, these despairing combats of love and death, was too much. Therefore after the third act, hardly breathing, and suffering as if an iron hand gripped my heart, I said to myself with complete conviction: 'Ah, I am lost!'—I must add that I did not know a word of English, that I understood Shakespeare only through the fog of the translation of Letourneur, and that in consequence I was not aware of the poetic web which envelops like a golden net his marvellous creations. It is my misfortune to be almost in the same case to-day. It is indeed more difficult for a Frenchman to plumb the depths of Shakespeare's style than for an Englishman to feel the finesse and originality of that of La Fontaine or of Molière. Our two poets are rich continents. Shakespeare is a world. But the play by the actors, that of the actress above all, the succession of scenes, the pantomime, and the accent of the voices, meant more to me and impregnated me with the Shakespearian ideas and passions a thousand times more than the words of my pale and inaccurate translation.

As I translate these words I wonder what effect they will have on those who read them. I cherish the hope that outside narrow, sophisticated, intellectual circles there remain many more modest and more sensitive human beings who have felt a sympathetic glow in reading them. Reflect a moment on Berlioz's words, 'I did not know a word of English,' and you will realize by what profound intuition genius recognizes genius. Only a like genius (and by 'genius' I do not ever mean extraordinary cleverness but the creative spirit of life in man) recognizes genius in the absolute certainty with which Berlioz recognized Shakespeare. I am certain that there is not the slightest exaggeration or hysteria in Berlioz's description of his experience, but a simple, straightforward, and truthful account of it.

Mixed with this revelation of Shakespeare was the impression made upon him by the tall, graceful Irish actress, Harriet Smithson. The Paris press raved about her, for not only was she beautiful, with lovely arms and a dazzling complexion, but her acting had a rare sweetness and charm, and her voice, like that of so many Irish men and women, was music in itself. The shock of this double experience had a serious effect on Berlioz:

'To an intense, profound, insurmountable sadness was added,' says Berlioz, 'a state of nerves bordering on illness of which only a great psychological writer could give even an approximate idea.'

Losing for the time his vivacity of spirit, the desire and even the possibility of working, Berlioz would wander aimlessly about the streets and outskirts of Paris:

By dint of fatiguing my body, I remember having obtained during this long period of suffering a deep sleep like death on four occasions; a night on some sheaves in a field near Ville-Juif; one day in a meadow near Sceaux; another time in the snow on the edge of the frozen Seine near Neuilly; and last, on a table of the Café du Cardinal at the corner of the boulevard des Italiens and the rue Richelieu, when I slept five hours to the great fright of the waiters, who were afraid of finding me dead.

It was coming home after one of these excursions in which I had the air of being in search of my soul, that finding open on the table the volume of *Irish Melodies* [1] by Thomas Moore, my eyes fell on the one beginning with the words: 'When he who adores thee.' I took my pen and, all at one stretch, I wrote the music of this heart-rending farewell that is to be found under the title of *Élégie*, at the end of my collection entitled *Irlande*.[2] This is the sole occasion on which I was able to express such a feeling while still under its immediate influence. But I believe I have rarely attained to such a poignant truthfulness of melodic accent set in such a storm of sinister harmonies.

[1] This would be in the translation by his friend Th. Gounet.

[2] This song *Élégie*, for tenor with pianoforte accompaniment, is No. 15 on p. 95 of the *Collection de 33 Mélodies pour une ou plusieurs Voix et Chœur* by Berlioz, published by Richault et Cie., Paris. It is No. 9 of the *Mélodies irlandaises*, Op. 2 (1830), and is No. 26, Series VII C, *Songs with Pianofòrte Accompaniment for a Single Voice* in Breitkopf & Härtel's complete edition of Berlioz.

This piece is immensely difficult to sing and to accompany; it needs, to reproduce it in its true sense—that is to say to bring again to birth, more or less weakened, the despair, sombre, proud, and tender, which Moore must have felt in writing these verses and which I experienced in flooding them with my music—it needs two practised artists and, above all, a singer gifted with a sympathetic voice and an exquisite sensibility. To hear it interpreted in a mediocre fashion would be, for me, an inexpressible pain.

So as not to expose myself to this, never, during the twenty years of its existence, have I proposed that any one shall sing it. Once Alizard, having seen it at my house, tried it without accompaniment, transposing it (to B) for his bass voice, and so upset me that in the middle I begged him to stop. He understood; I saw that he would sing it thoroughly well; that gave me the idea of scoring for orchestra the pianoforte accompaniment. Then, reflecting that such compositions are not for the big concert-going public and that it would be a kind of sacrilege to expose it to their indifference, I ceased to go on with it and burned what was already instrumented. By good fortune the French prose translation was so faithful that later I was able to adapt my music to the original English verses of Moore.[1]

If ever this *Élégie* is known in England or Germany it may find there perhaps some sympathetic response; lacerated hearts will recognize themselves in it. Such a piece is incomprehensible to the greater part of the French, and absurd and mad to Italians.[2]

Harriett Smithson was born at Ennis, Ireland, on 18th March 1800; she was thus, in September 1827, about three years older than Berlioz, who was not yet twenty-four. She had played in the principal towns of Ireland and made her first appearance in London at Drury Lane on 20th January 1818. In Paris she

[1] Berlioz tells us in an introductory note to this song printed in Richault's edition that when he was in England he sought to discover the historical occasion of Moore's verses, and was informed by the 'celebrated English poet Leigh Hunt' that the person who speaks in Moore's poem is meant to be the famous Irish patriot Robert Emmett, executed after the Irish insurrection of 1803. Berlioz prints the end of Emmet's address to his judges at the beginning of the song.

[2] This song, like all Berlioz's songs (not even excepting *La Captive*, of which only the name is familiar to a few musicians), is still virtually unknown in England, Ireland, Germany, and the rest of the civilized musical world. Busoni said, 'The first thing about music is it should be more difficult of access.' Well, Berlioz's beautiful and original songs—only to be compared with Schubert's—fulfil this proud condition. But they should be accessible to the few who are capable of appreciating them. It is, however, better that they should never be sung than sung as most singers would sing them.

played in *The School for Scandal*, *Romeo and Juliet*, *Hamlet*, Rowe's *Jane Shore*, and also the part of Belvidera in Otway's *Venice Preserved.*

The state of mind described by Berlioz in the passage I have quoted above from his *Mémoires* is confirmed by the extract I quoted from the contemporary letter to Ferrand. It lasted for some months and was not relieved by the performance of his Mass at the church of Saint-Eustache on 22nd November 1827, which he describes in the same letter to Ferrand already quoted.[1] Not only was he, to use his own word, *foudroyé* (i.e. struck by lightning), by Shakespeare but also by Miss Smithson, and the contrast between her fame and his obscurity was an additional but depressing factor. But the elasticity of extreme youth was bound to come to his aid, and he determined to give a concert of his own works. Some time in this year (1827) he had composed the overture to *Les Francs-Juges* and the cantata for the competition in June–July 1827 for the Prix de Rome, *Orphée déchiré par les Bacchantes.* He proposed to give at his concert this overture, the cantata, the *Scène héroïque grecque* composed in 1826, and a new overture, *Waverley.* We do not know exactly when the idea of giving a concert of his own works came into his head, but we know that on 27th April 1828 he wrote to the Vicomte Sosthène de la Rochefoucauld[2] who was Surintendant des Beaux-Arts and the official superior of Cherubini, the director of the Conservatoire, asking for permission to see him. He needed to obtain the free use of the hall of the Conservatoire for his concert. He first asked Cherubini who, possibly in order to get rid of him, referred him to the Vicomte de la Rochefoucauld, but Berlioz, who was extremely skilful in these matters, used the influence of his friends the Comte de Chabrillant and Chenavez, who was the deputy of Berlioz's province, Isère. Having failed to get a

[1] Dated Paris, 29th November 1827, see p. 79.

[2] Letter in the Archives Nationales. Berlioz puts under his signature, 'Élève de l'école royale de musique (composition),' i.e. student of the Royal School of Music (composition).

definite promise from Rochefoucauld, Berlioz wrote again on 3rd May 1828, pressing for a favourable response and a definite date, so that he could make the necessary arrangements with the musicians required. From this letter I take the following:

This concert, being solely for the purpose of making me known, is of the utmost importance to me; it concerns my whole musical existence. . . . The career of composers becomes daily more thorny and, in spite of my steadfast persistence, if a strong hand does not come to my aid, I fear I shall waste myself in sterile efforts and never attain the goal which I pursue so ardently.

The Vicomte de la Rochefoucauld forwarded Berlioz's request to Cherubini, asking if there was any reason why Berlioz should not be given the use of the hall at the end of the month; at the same time he added:

'This artist having been recommended to me in the most urgent manner by several persons whom I very much desire to oblige, I have thought it necessary to commit myself to some extent.'

This did not please Cherubini at all, and he attempted to dissuade Berlioz from his project, one of his reasons perhaps being his fear that Berlioz would perform his cantata *La Mort d'Orphée*, which the judges for the Prix de Rome the previous year had declared 'unplayable,' and thus ridicule the academic musicians. Berlioz has given an amusing account of this interview in his *Mémoires* which, except in some minor details, is corroborated by the letter, now in the Archives Nationales, from Berlioz to the Surintendant des Beaux-Arts, dated Paris, 12th May 1828, which I reproduce with certain cuts:

M. Cherubini having this morning informed me that he had written to you to dissuade you from granting me the hall of the Royal School of Music for my concert, I have to acquit myself in your eyes of any lie in this matter. Indeed, having asked you for the hall, declaring that M. Cherubini had referred me to you, it may seem strange to you that he should oppose it now. Nevertheless it is a fact that had not he said positively to me, 'You must ask M. le Vicomte de la Rochefoucauld,' I would never have importuned you with my letter.

The objections he has made this morning are extremely feeble . . .

[expense, loss of time to students, etc., which Berlioz shows are imaginary]. I left him painfully affected and forced to recognize that, far from finding a protector in the director of the Royal School of Music, I, doubly a pupil of this institution since I attend the classes of both M. Lesueur and M. Reicha, have on the contrary in M. Cherubini a man disposed only to impede my progress and put obstacles in the way of my achieving my purpose.

If this letter arrives too late and you have already made your decision, it will be *the second time that your benevolent intentions with regard to me have been frustrated by a subordinate official.*

You may remember still the letter that you generously wrote to M. Kreutzer three years ago, asking him to look at a score which I wanted performed at one of the Concerts Spirituels. In spite of your recommendation, and before having read the work, he refused, saying that the Opéra was not made for the young and that there was no time to learn new works. He resisted the requests made to him by MM. Lesueur, Gardel, Prévost, Valentino, Du Boys, etc. etc.

To-day, having vainly attempted every way of making myself known as a dramatic composer, I want to attempt to give a concert. I have already overcome the principal obstacles; everything is ready, singers, chorus, and orchestra, but the only place suitable is the one I ask for. Must I lose from M. Cherubini's ill-will a month and a half's time, peace of mind, and four hundred francs' expense of copying merely to be discouraged and disgusted? . . .

The italics in the above letter are mine; they serve to draw attention to the adroit way in which Berlioz handled this situation. He completely out-manoeuvred Cherubini, who received from his superior a brief note, saying that he could not go back on his promise to Berlioz. The concert took place on Monday, 26th May 1828, and consisted entirely of music by Berlioz; but Berlioz was sensible enough not to affront the academicians, who would be his judges again in the coming June–July competition for the Prix de Rome, by performing his 'unplayable' cantata *La Mort d'Orphée.* His programme was in two parts; the first consisted of the *Waverley* overture, the *Mélodie pastorale* for solo voices and choir from the second act of his opera *Les Francs-Juges*, the *Marche religieuse des Mages*, the *Resurrexit* from his Mass, already performed at Saint-Roch and Saint-Eustache. The second part was made up of the *Francs-Juges* overture and the *Révolution grecque.*

All these works, with the exception of the *Mélodie pastorale*, which I have not been able to trace, still exist and are available in the Breitkopf & Härtel edition of Berlioz edited by Felix Weingartner and Charles Malherbe, if not elsewhere. Apart from some vocal works for one or more voices these are the earliest compositions by Berlioz to have survived. They were all written before his twenty-fourth year and deserve a few words of comment.

The *Waverley* overture, written after reading Scott's novel, is hardly known to-day outside of Germany, where during the nineteenth century Berlioz's music was always appreciated more than anywhere else. Schumann wrote of this overture in 1839 that in spite of its unusual and—for German ears—shocking effects, it had for him an irresistible charm. Why this brilliant and delightful overture is never performed in England is a mystery; it only shows what a rut musicians move in, with their ceaseless repetitions of the vogue of the day in their concert programmes. The *Francs-Juges* overture is in a grander and more dramatic style, worthy at least to rank with the best overtures of Weber and of Wagner, and yet I have only once heard this work performed in a concert hall in London, and that was at a B.B.C.[1] symphony concert under Dr. Adrian Boult. As for the *Resurrexit*, the *Marche des Mages*, and the *Révolution grecque*, they are all completely unknown to music-lovers, while the vast majority of professional musicians, conductors, and musicologists have never even seen them in the score. Seven out of Berlioz's eight overtures[2] are, however, available in Eulenburg's miniature scores, so there is no excuse either for the almost total neglect of five of them or the idea that might occur to concert-goers that the popular *Benvenuto Cellini* and *Carneval romain* are the best of them. Brilliant and superb as these two latter overtures are, they can no more be compared to the *Francs-Juges* and *Roi Lear*

[1] British Broadcasting Corporation.

[2] *Waverley*, *Francs-Juges*, *Roi Lear*, *Carneval romain*, *Le Corsaire*, *Benvenuto Cellini*, *Béatrice et Bénédict*.

overtures than Shakespeare's comedies can be compared to his tragedies.

Before his concert Berlioz wrote a letter to the Paris press explaining that for four years (he was now twenty-four years and five months old!) he had knocked in vain at every door and none had opened, that he had neither been able to get an opera libretto allotted to him nor to get a performance of one that he had worked on, so that now there was only one thing he could do, give a concert of his own works. This, he says, has been treated as great presumption on his part:

Because concerts have been given composed entirely of the works of Mozart and Beethoven, does it follow that in doing likewise I have the absurd pretensions attributed to me? I repeat, in doing this, I am only using the easiest means to make known my essay in dramatic music. . . . I think I am not doing ill in taking for my motto this verse of Virgil's:

Una salus victis nullam sperare salutem.[1]

This letter was published in the *Revue musicale* of 16th May, the *Corsaire* of 22nd May, and the *Figaro* of 27th May 1828. The concert made a vivid impression and Berlioz got several very favourable notices. The following extract is taken from the *Figaro*:

M. Berlioz had taken as his motto:

Una salus victis nullam sperare salutem.

Now he can substitute for it:

Audaces fortuna juvat.[2]

. . . There is in the works of this young composer a superabundant verve which at first excites enthusiasm and then exhausts the attention; his style is full of energy and originality; but it is sometimes savage, if I may use this expression; success, as one knows, justifies the strangeness of ideas. The most striking piece, in our estimation, is the *Waverley* overture . . . and the second part of the *Cantate héroïque.*

Courage, Monsieur Berlioz! you have everything necessary for success. Always remain yourself and imitate nature only. . . .

In the light of after events this advice has, for us, an ironic flavour. It is the nature of genius to remain, under all cir-

[1] 'The only safety for the vanquished is not to hope for it.'
[2] 'Fortune favours the brave.'

cumstances and influences, itself, and Berlioz's relative lack of success all his life, compared with contemporary composers far inferior to himself, was due precisely to this fact that always until the end he remained Berlioz.

But Fortune generally begins by smiling on young men, and her first greeting is especially sweet to those for whom she is reserving her worst treatment.

In the *Revue musicale*, founded in 1827 by Fétis, the famous musicologist, there appeared a favourable notice on Berlioz's concert by Fétis himself, from which I take the following:

> How many judges there are who have been guilty, perhaps involuntarily, of this erroneous syllogism: 'The music of a young composer without experience cannot be good; now M. Berlioz is a very young composer, therefore M. Berlioz's music is bad.' . . . But let the beneficiary (if I may use this word, seeing that the hall was almost empty) . . . let M. Berlioz, say I, take heart; his precocious talent inspires in us a lively interest. M. Berlioz has the happiest of gifts . . . he has genius. His style is forceful and lively. His inspirations often have charm. But, oftener still, the composer carried along by his young and ardent imagination exhausts himself in combinations of an original and passionate intention . . . often his originality touches the bizarre . . . he sows with profusion great musical effects, and his exaggeration makes him overshoot his goal. . . .

We may place this perspicacious review among the few examples in the history of criticism where genius has been recognized at its first appearance; but as is often the case, Fétis became less appreciative as the genius of Berlioz matured and took its own natural course.

CHAPTER VII

SHAKESPEARE, BEETHOVEN, AND GOETHE

Several months before his concert another thunderbolt had descended upon Berlioz's head. On the principle of taking a hair of the dog that bit you, it may be that it was this second thunderbolt that restored Berlioz to activity from the stupefying double effect of Shakespeare and Miss Smithson. In his *Mémoires* he says that after the two apparitions, Shakespeare and Weber, there came Beethoven, and the shock that he received was 'almost comparable to that given him by Shakespeare. He opened to me a new world in music as the poet had unveiled a new universe in poetry.'

This statement, ranking the revelation of Beethoven *after* that of Shakespeare in its effect on him, seems to me richly significant; especially when we remember that as Gluck was his first inspiration Beethoven was his second, and that all his life Gluck and Beethoven remained Berlioz's musical gods. Before I explain the significance I see in this statement I shall continue the account of Berlioz's first real acquaintance with the music of Beethoven, whose first two symphonies alone were known to him at this date.

At the beginning of 1828 the conductor Habeneck[1] founded the famous Société des Concerts du Conservatoire, which has existed in Paris ever since. The first concert of the Société took place at 2 p.m. on Sunday, 9th March 1828, in the hall of the Conservatoire (the same hall which Berlioz borrowed for his concert two months later), and the programme included the first performance in Paris of Beethoven's third ('Eroica')

[1] Habeneck (b. 1781, d. 1849), one of the most celebrated of French conductors, of German extraction. He was conductor of the Société des Concerts du Conservatoire from 1828 to 1848.

symphony. Some time later Beethoven's fifth (C minor) symphony was performed and the whole of musical Paris was in an uproar.

In his *Mémoires* Berlioz describes in his usual vivid manner the attitude of his professors to this new music. Beethoven had been dead one year (d. 26th March 1827) and it was only through the persistent efforts of Habeneck, continued over many years after this first concert, that Beethoven's music gradually made its way in Paris. But in 1828 nearly all the official musicians were hostile. Berlioz says that Berton 'regarded with pity the whole modern German school'; that Boieldieu 'did not know what to think'; that Cherubini (to whom Beethoven had sent a copy of his *Missa Solennis*) was full of bile and irritated; that Paër, who professed to have known Beethoven, 'related anecdotes more or less unfavourable to this great man and flattering to himself'; that Catel 'cared only for his garden and his roses'; that Kreutzer 'shared Berton's disdain for everything that came across the Rhine.'

Lesueur had stayed away from the first concert, but Berlioz persuaded him to go to hear the C minor symphony:

> When the symphony was over I came down from the upper circle . . . to find out what he had felt and what he thought of this extraordinary production. I found him in a corridor; he was very red and pacing along with large strides. 'Well, dear master?' I said. . . . 'Ouf! I must go out; I must have air. It 's unheard of! It 's marvellous! I have been so moved, so disturbed, so overcome, that in leaving my seat and wanting to put on my hat I thought that I couldn't *find my head again*. Leave me now, until to-morrow. . . .
>
> I was triumphant. The next day I went to see him. The conversation began about the masterpiece which had so strongly affected us. Lesueur let me speak for some time, endorsing with an air of constraint my enthusiastic expressions. But it was easy to perceive the change from the previous evening, and that the subject was painful. I continued, however, until Lesueur, from whom I wished to get a fresh acknowledgment of his profound emotion on hearing Beethoven's symphony, said, shaking his head and with a strange smile: 'Nevertheless, one should not make such music'; to which I replied, 'Don't worry, dear master, there won't be much of it.'

Poor human nature! . . . poor master! . . . There is in this remark, expressed in terms more or less the same by many others in similar circumstances, obstinacy, regret, terror of the unknown, envy, and an implicit admission of impotence. . . .

Berlioz says that Lesueur considered instrumental music as being of an inferior kind and, for him, Haydn and Mozart had set its limits which could not be passed.[1] All artists will, I think, understand Lesueur's attitude, for it is perennial and brings us to the everlasting conflict which is expressed in the words 'romanticism' and 'classicism.' The polar character of art, the fact that, like every other human activity—political, social, or individual—it is and must ever remain dual and oscillate between two opposite poles, has not yet been adequately understood by critics, who are for ever dividing themselves into the two parties and maintaining, each camp, that its camp is the correct place for an artist.

The correct place for an artist is where he naturally finds himself, and the greatest artists are those whose best works are built like a bridge, uniting both poles and grounded firmly on them at each end. Even this statement is too rigid to be satisfactory, for there is something static and dead in the idea of a bridge. It would be truer to say that the two poles are those of life and death and that life grows out of death as a 'living' flower grows out of 'dead' earth. This simile will enable us to realize that the words 'living' and 'dead' are only relative. A collection of standardized blooms can be more 'dead' than a heap of earth. What happens historically to works of art is that they tend to become standardized blooms, and so Haydn and Mozart are used to set limits from which Beethoven can be described as 'excessive' or 'romantic.' When Beethoven in his turn becomes familiar and standardized, he is used to set limits to Berlioz. It is, I think, evidence of the unique position of Berlioz in the history of music that he has not even yet—more than a hundred and thirty years after his birth—become standardized. In this respect he resembles Shakespeare. And

[1] *Mémoires*, chap. xx, p. 74.

this brings me to the point to which I promised to return, namely, the significance of Berlioz's own admission (the nature of which he was perhaps far from being consciously aware of at the time) that the lightning blast of Beethoven was less powerful on him than the lightning blast of Shakespeare. *Foudroyé* (thunderstruck) is Berlioz's own word for these experiences, and is figuratively correct.

As it is the purpose of this book to set Berlioz in full view as the greatest creative force in music that has so far appeared since the death of Beethoven, I wish to draw attention also to the significance of the opposing phrases used by him when he says that Beethoven revealed 'a new world' and Shakespeare 'a new universe.'[1]

None of Berlioz's biographers or critics have dealt adequately with Berlioz's passion for Shakespeare, yet surely there must be something deeply revealing in this life-long enthusiasm of Berlioz for Shakespeare. It is by what is within ourselves that we discover what is outside, and nothing can be revealed to him who, in some sense, 'knew it not before.' Now Berlioz not only introduces his *Mémoires* with a quotation from *Macbeth* and makes frequent reference to Shakespeare throughout his writings, but, as the list[2] of his compositions shows, was inspired to composition by Shakespeare right up to the end of his career. Some of his greatest works—of which I shall have occasion to speak in more detail as we meet with them chronologically—are on Shakespearean subjects; for example, his great dramatic symphony *Roméo et Juliette*, his tragic overture *Roi Lear*, the remarkable lyrical monodrama *Lélio*, those two superb and quite unknown works *La Mort d'Ophélie* and *Marche funèbre pour la dernière scène de Hamlet*, and, finally, the last work he wrote, the exquisite opera *Béatrice et Bénédict*, based on *Much Ado about Nothing*.

Berlioz's affinity with Shakespeare is not only to be felt intuitively and to be shown by the felicity and frequency with

[1] Berlioz's original French reads: 'un monde nouveau,' and 'un nouvel univers.'

[2] See Appendix.

which he treats Shakespearean subjects, but it is also to be demonstrated by other facts. Firstly, his unusual combination of the lyrical and dramatic gifts. Beethoven—and I, at least, shall never be thought guilty of any blindness to Beethoven's genius—was not remarkable as a song-writer nor as an operatic composer. *Fidelio*, his one opera, is a masterpiece that bears witness to his lack both of dramatic instinct and of lyrical gift. It is not so much that Beethoven's songs and arias have a conventional Italianate character with none of the lyrical spontaneity and inventive ecstasy of either a Schubert or a Mozart, but essentially one feels they are not lyrical. Beethoven's music is so passionate in its presentation of emotional conflict that it has this element of the dramatic, but this element is best expressed in his purely instrumental works. As for that prime dramatic quality, the power of uttering himself impersonally, of expressing objectively human personality, that protean sympathy with human beings of every type and character, Beethoven had none of it and understood it so little that he blamed Mozart for composing operas on such subjects as Don Juan and Figaro.

Here Berlioz resembles Mozart and Shakespeare. He had their universality of dramatic sympathy, and he also had the lyrical gift which distinguishes Shakespeare from many other dramatists. Berlioz's songs can be compared only with Schubert's for freshness, sensitiveness, originality, spontaneity, beauty, and something that I can only describe as an out-of-door quality that is not to be found in the songs of Schumann and Brahms. Such an early song as *La Belle Voyageuse*, from the group entitled *Irlande*, Opus 2 (1829), would be a revelation to those who think of Berlioz as the great master of orchestration, the demoniacal wielder of vast instrumental masses, the *Jupiter tonans* of music. But this is only one of many exquisite songs by Berlioz, whose operas are also full of lyrical beauties of a quality rarely to be found outside Gluck, Mozart, Purcell, and the finest of the old Italian masters.

But Berlioz's affinity with Shakespeare is finally revealed in connection with Goethe, the last 'thunderbolt' of his youth.

The translation of Goethe's *Faust* made by Gérard de Nerval was published in November 1827, and Berlioz must have made its acquaintance some time in 1828, after he was 'thunderstruck' by Beethoven Of the three thunderbolts—Shakespeare, Beethoven, and Goethe—which fell on his head between September 1827 and September 1828, Goethe seems to have been the least violent and consequently the most immediately productive. Berlioz does not once use his favourite word *foudroyé* in describing the effect on him of Goethe. In his *Mémoires* he is as restrained as a physician making a diagnosis, and writes:

I ought to notify as one of the remarkable incidents of my life the strange and profound impression I had in first reading the *Faust* of Goethe, translated into French by Gérard de Nerval. This wonderful book fascinated me straight away; I never left it; I read it constantly at table, at the theatre, in the streets, everywhere.

This prose translation contained some versified fragments, songs, hymns, etc. I yielded to the temptation to set them to music; and this difficult task was hardly finished before I had the idiocy—without having heard a note of my score—to get it printed at my expense.

In a letter to his friend Ferrand dated Grenoble, 16th September 1828, he is more expansive. He had left Paris on 30th August to visit his home for the first time since the summer of 1826. On 16th September he writes from Grenoble:

I start to-morrow for La Côte, from which place I have been absent since the day your letter arrived. It is impossible for me to pay you a visit. I must leave [for Paris] on the 27th inst., and I cannot even mention any further absence to my people. I have already spoken of you to my family; they fully expected to see you, and your letter redoubled their impatience to meet you. This desire, on the part of my sisters and our young ladies, is somewhat interested: it is a question of balls and picnics in the country. Amiable cavaliers are in request, the species not being a common one here, and though perhaps all this fuss is being made on my account, I am not in the least adapted to contribute either animation or gaiety. . . . Come as soon as possible, I beseech you; your music awaits you.

We will read *Hamlet* and *Faust* together. Shakespeare and Goethe! the dumb confidants of my life. Come, oh, come! Nobody here understands the rage of genius. The sun blinds them. It is thought merely eccentric. The day before yesterday I have written, driving in the carriage, the ballad of the *Roi de Thulé* in Gothic style; I will give it to you to put in your *Faust* if you have one. . . . 'Horatio, you are the man whose society has suited me best! I suffer much. It would be cruel of you not to come. . . .'

The *Huit Scènes de Faust*, as Berlioz entitled his work, which he concluded on his return to Paris at the end of September, was published in the following March. On 3rd March 1829 he wrote the following letter to the Vicomte de la Rochefoucauld:

I am just publishing the score of the *Huit Scènes de Faust* by Goethe for which I have composed the music; this is the first work I have delivered to the press;[1] please do me the honour, Monsieur le Vicomte, to accept its dedication.

I owe you much and I shall be happy indeed if you accept. . . .

On 10th April 1829 Berlioz sent two copies of his score to Goethe with the following letter:

Faust having been for several years past[2] my habitual reading, by dint of meditating on this astonishing work (although I could only see it through the mist of a translation), it has finally put a spell on my mind; musical ideas have grouped themselves in my head around your poetic ideas, and, although firmly resolved never to unite my feeble tones to your sublime ones, little by little the temptation has grown so strong, the attraction so powerful, that the music for several scenes was completed almost without my being aware of it.

I have just published my score, and however unworthy it may be to be presented to you, I to-day take the liberty of paying you this homage. I am well convinced that you have already received a very large number of compositions of all kinds inspired by this prodigious poem; I fear, then, that in following so many others I am only being a nuisance. But if, in the atmosphere of glory in which you live, obscure tributes cannot reach you, at least you will pardon, I hope, a young composer who, his heart filled and his imagination inflamed by your genius, has not been able to keep back a cry of admiration.

It was Goethe's habit, when he received musical compositions,

[1] He had already published various songs, but he made the *Huit Scènes de Faust* his Opus 1.

[2] A pardonable exaggeration. As we know, Nerval's translation was first published in November 1827.

to send them to his friend Zelter,[1] the teacher of Mendelssohn; accordingly he sent Berlioz's score to Zelter, asking him to return some friendly acknowledgment. Zelter, however, wrote back:

Certain people only let their presence be known by their coughing, snoring, croaking, and spitting. M. Hector Berlioz seems to me to be of their number. The odour of sulphur which Mephistopheles spreads penetrates to him and forces him to sneeze and to explode, so that he makes all the instruments of the orchestra rain and spit without even disturbing a hair of Faust's head. Nevertheless I thank you for your parcel; there will be an occasion in a review to speak of this miscarriage, the result of an abominable incest.

The result was that Berlioz never heard from Goethe.[2] It is worth remarking that Zelter, though an excellent musician and a worthy man, showed his limitations not only with respect to Berlioz (which, indeed, was pardonable considering the extreme originality of Berlioz's work) but also in his much more discreditable attempt to simplify and rewrite parts of the score of Bach's *St. Matthew Passion*, which he bought and brought to the attention of Mendelssohn. It is also an amusing example of how misleading even an apparently correct criticism can be to reflect that Zelter's description of Berlioz's work is not inaccurate so far as it goes. That is to say, it is a fair description of the effect Berlioz's setting would have made on the average elderly musician of the time, but what it says is merely that Zelter found the music unintelligible. He was more concerned, however, to try to be witty about it than to find out the truth; otherwise he would have said to himself: 'Is it possible that this young composer, so ardently admiring *Faust*, has gone to all this trouble of setting eight scenes to music and publishing them at his own expense merely to cough, snore, croak, and sneeze over them?' But no doubt of their

[1] Zelter, Carl Friedrich (1758–1832), director of the Berlin Singakademie which first performed Bach's *St. Matthew Passion* on 11th March 1829 under Mendelssohn.

[2] It is worth noting that Eckermann told Hiller (*Goethe Jahrbuch*, 1890) that Goethe found Berlioz's letter 'well-written and elevated in tone.' All Berlioz's official letters were beautifully written in a clear hand on specially fine paper.

own infallibility ever crosses the minds of these bumptious pundits.

The *Revue musicale* of Fétis was more cordial and said: 'This score, original to the point of the bizarre, is the work of a man full of talent and facility.'

These *Huit Scènes de Faust* were used by Berlioz about eighteen years later (1846) as the basis of one of his finest works, the *Damnation de Faust*. Berlioz destroyed all the copies he could find of his earlier work, but some are still extant though they are exceedingly rare. A copy came up for auction at the Adolphe Jullien sale in Paris in 1933, but I could not afford to buy it, although I bought a good deal of other Berlioziana at this sale. However, its contents are known and have been analysed.[1]

Mr. Ernest Newman once remarked to me that the *Huit Scènes de Faust* was the most marvellous Opus 1 that any composer had ever produced, and I entirely concur. As it is not generally known to what extent the *Damnation de Faust* is already present in this early work, published in 1829 when Berlioz was twenty-five years and three months old, I will give some particulars. Each of the eight scenes is preceded by a quotation from Goethe and, in English more or less correct, from Shakespeare. On the cover are two inscriptions, the first from Goethe's *Faust*, the second from Thomas Moore's *Irish Melodies*:

(*a*) I consecrate myself to unquiet, to the most painful pleasures,
To Love which feels hatred, to Peace which feels despair.

(*b*) One fatal remembrance, one sorrow that throws
Its bleak shade alike o'er our joys and our woes.

(1) The first scene, *Chant de la fête de Pâques* (Easter-song), has for inscription these words of Ophelia from Shakespeare's *Hamlet*: 'Heavenly powers restore him' and, as a direction, the words: *Caractère religieux et solennel* (solemn and religious character).

[1] It is also reproduced in the Breitkopf & Härtel edition of Berlioz.

The first part of this piece is identical with that in the *Damnation de Faust*. There are small changes in the second part: the substitution of women's voices for tenors after the the second call of the sopranos, 'Christ vient de ressusciter,' and the addition of a coda.

(2) The second scene, *Paysans sous les tilleuls* (Peasants under lime-trees), has at the head Capulet's words from *Romeo and Juliet*: 'Who 'll now deny to dance? she that makes dainty, she I 'll swear hath corns.' The musical direction is: *Gaieté franche et naïve*. This is the same as in the first scene of the *Damnation de Faust*, except that there it is raised a tone and has the addition of a final *presto* in two-four time.

(3) *Concert des Sylphes*. This is in essence the same as the wonderful scene by the banks of the Elbe in the *Damnation de Faust*, but Berlioz made various alterations and additions.[1] He prefaced it with Mercutio's words: 'I talk of dreams, Which are the children of an idle brain, Begot of nothing but vain fantasy, Which is as thin of substance as the air, And more inconstant than the wind.' Berlioz adds the musical direction: *Caractère doux et voluptueux*.

(4) *Écot de joyeux compagnon*. This is the tale of a rat, sung by Brander, and is absolutely identical with that sung in the cellar-scene of the *Damnation de Faust*. It is inscribed with the words of Hamlet: 'How now? a rat? dead, for a ducat, dead,' and has the direction: *Joie grossière et désordonnée*.

(5) *La Chanson de Mephistophélès*, the tale of a flea. This also is unchanged in the *Damnation de Faust*. It bears the inscription from *Hamlet*: 'Miching mallecho: it means mischief,' and the direction: *Raillerie amère*.

(6) *Le Roi de Thulé* (*chanson gothique*). This is very slightly altered in the *Damnation de Faust*. The original inscription was Ophelia's words: 'He is dead and gone; at his head a grass-green turf, at his heels a stone,' and the direction: *Caractère simple et ingénu*. One has only to compare this extraordinary

[1] For example, he added the extremely effective vocal part of the demon, which is heard above the long holding-notes of the choir.

conception with the charming but superficial setting by Gounod of this ballad of the King of Thule to realize the Shakespearian character of Berlioz's genius.

(7) Consists of the *Romance de Marguerite*, with Romeo's words: 'Ah me! sad hours seem long,' and the direction: *Sentiment mélancolique et passionné* (this is unchanged in the *Damnation de Faust*), followed by the 'Chœur des soldats' with Mercutio's: 'Come, let 's be gone, the sport is over,' and the direction: *Joyeuse insouciance*. This is only very slightly altered in the *Damnation de Faust*.

(8) *Sérénade de Méphistophélès*, with Hamlet's words: 'It is a damned ghost,' and the direction: *Effronterie*. This remains unchanged except for the guitar accompaniment; in the *Damnation de Faust* the guitar is replaced by strings *divisés pizzicato*.

Such is the *Huit Scènes de Faust*, the bulk of it composed before Berlioz's twenty-fifth birthday and containing already half of that wonderful masterpiece, the *Damnation de Faust*. It will be noticed, too, that it includes many of the finest things in the later score. Every one of these eight scenes is the work of a master, and Nos. 3, 4, 5, 6, and 8 are unlike anything that had ever been conceived in music before. As for No. 7, I don't know of anything even by Schubert that is more poignant or more beautiful than this *Romance de Marguerite*.

The next thing I have to say about the *Huit Scènes de Faust* is to draw attention to the Shakespearian quotations. Is it not remarkable that in setting scenes from Goethe's *Faust* to music Berlioz should have prefaced every one of them with a passage from Shakespeare? What is still more remarkable is the fact that every one of these quotations is absolutely in accord with the spirit of the music. One of the most puzzling pieces, even to the most sensitive musicians of to-day, in the *Damnation de Faust* is the King of Thule ballad. It has an extraordinary and sombre character not at all characteristic of Goethe's words. But if we remember that in the original *Huit Scènes de Faust* it bore Ophelia's words: 'He is dead and gone; at his head a grass-green turf, at his heels a stone,' then we have at once the key to it.

The spirit of Shakespeare breathed in Berlioz even when he was occupied with Goethe, and I venture to declare that the *Damnation de Faust* is saturated with Shakespearian feeling and has very little connection with Goethe.

CHAPTER VIII

A WONDERFUL YEAR

We have now to retrace our steps a little. After his first concert on 26th May, 1828, he writes to Ferrand on 6th June about the effect of the overture to their opera, *Les Francs-Juges*:

I must relate what happened at the first rehearsal of this piece. Hardly had the orchestra heard that terrible solo for trombones and ophicleide[1] for which you wrote the words for Olmerick in the third act, when one of the violins exclaimed: 'Ah! ah! the rainbow is the bow of your violin, the winds play the organ and the elements beat time!' Whereupon the whole orchestra applauded an idea whose extent they in no way understood The day of the concert . . . I was seated by the side of the drummer, who, holding my arm, which he gripped with all his might, could not help crying convulsively at intervals: 'It 's superb! It 's sublime, my friend! . . . It 's terrifying! It 's enough to turn one's brain! . . .' With my other arm I tore at my hair: I longed to be able to cry out, forgetting that it was my own work: 'How *monstrous*, colossal, horrible!' . . .

Ah! my dear friend, send me an opera! Robin Hood! How can you expect me to do anything without a poem! . . .

Again, on 28th June, he wrote to Ferrand:

Yes, we understand each other fully, we feel alike; life is not altogether destitute of charm. Although I have, during the last nine months, led a poisoned, disillusioned existence which my music alone has rendered me capable of supporting, your friendship is a connecting chain whose links grow closer and closer day by day, while others break. (Do not indulge in conjectures; you would be mistaken.) I will do my utmost to spend a few days at La Côte in about six weeks' time; as soon as my departure is settled I will let you know and appoint a meeting at my father's house. . . .

28th June, eight hours later.

I have returned . . . from Villeneuve-Saint-Georges, four leagues from Paris, where I went for a walk. It has not killed me, in proof of which I am writing to you. How lonely I am! All my muscles are trembling, as if I were on the point of death. Oh! my friend, send me some work

[1] This word is derived from two Greek words meaning snake and key; it was given to the invention of a French musician named Frichot, an improvement on the serpent and bass horn. It has been superseded now by the tuba.

or other—throw me a bone to gnaw. How lovely the country is; how all-pervading the light! Every living thing I met on my way back seemed to be happy. The trees sighed sweetly, and I was alone in that vast plain. Space, remoteness, the sense of being forgotten, grief and rage surrounded me. In spite of all my efforts, life escapes me; I am holding on to it by a single thread.

At my age and with my temperament, to possess nothing but distracting sensations—and with all this the persecutions of my family are beginning again. My father sends me nothing now, and my sister writes to say that he will persist in his resolution. Money—always money—yes, money brings happiness. If I had enough I might be happy, and death is not happiness, so much is there wanting in it.

Neither during life—nor afterwards—nor before? What then? Never! Inflexible necessity!

And still the blood courses through my veins, and my heart beats as if it were jumping for joy.

In fact, I am in wild spirits—joy, by Heaven, joy!

Sunday morning.

Do not distress yourself about these wretched aberrations of my heart; the crisis is past; I do not care about explaining the cause of them in a letter because it might go astray. I insist upon your not saying a word about my state to anybody; a word even is so easily repeated, and if one reached the ears of my father he would not know a moment's peace. No one can do anything for me, and all that I can do is to suffer patiently until time, which changes so many things, shall change my destiny too.

Be prudent, I beseech you; be careful not to say a word to Du Boys, because he might repeat it to Casimir Faure, and from him my father will hear it.

That frightful walk yesterday has undone me; I cannot move, all my joints are paining me, and yet I must walk the whole day long.

Need I point out the toughness and soundness of character of the young man who wrote these letters? Chekhov in a letter gave his younger brother an admirable description of the things a disciplined, civilized man should not say or do, and Berlioz is one of those rare men who do not do them. His nature is as pure and sound as that of a sea-gull or a cat, in spite of the fact that not only is he that much more complex thing, a human being, but also has to bear the additional burden of the sensibility and the power of genius.

What had happened was that the English players with Harriett Smithson were again in Paris and Berlioz had seen her in the tragedy *Virginius*, for in a paragraph I omitted from the first part of the letter to Ferrand dated 28th June, he writes:

> Two operas are in preparation for the Feydeau, one for the Opéra, and I am now going to call upon M. Laurent, director of the English and Italian theatres. It is a question of arranging the English tragedy *Virginius* for the Italian opera. As soon as I know anything definite I will write to you.

Nothing more is heard of this, and probably Berlioz realized the futility of going—a young unknown man—to the director, for he begins the second part of his letter: 'I have returned, not from M. Laurent,[1] but from Villeneuve-Saint-Georges. . . .' Conscious of the hopelessness of his situation, a penniless, unknown young musician, in love with the famous English actress, he could only turn to the one hope visible, namely, the Prix de Rome. He entered (for the third time) the competition on 10th July and completed the prescribed *scène lyrique* for voice and small orchestra on the subject of *Herminie*,[2] signing his completed manuscript 22nd July.

On 23rd July the English players with Harriet Smithson performed *The Merchant of Venice* and, two days later, Rowe's drama *Jane Shore*. There is no doubt that Berlioz saw these performances, and they must have added fuel to his fire.

It appears that Lesueur lent him the money necessary for entering for the Prix de Rome. On 2nd August the judges announced their final decision, and this time Berlioz was awarded the second prize.[3] Before leaving Paris for La Côte on 30th August 1828, he made an appeal for financial help to the minister, the Comte de Martignac, Secrétaire d'État à l'Intérieur. The second Prix de Rome brought with it a gold

[1] I purposely omitted these words between commas when quoting this letter on p. 102.

[2] Written by a French poet, Vieillard. This cantata is published in Series VI B of the Breitkopf & Härtel edition, and is a charming work.

[3] The first prize went to a musician now unknown.

medal, the right of free entrance to all the opera-houses, but no money, whereas the first Prix de Rome meant an annual pension of three thousand francs for five years. In his petition to the minister, dated Paris, 20th August 1828, he begins: 'I am twenty-four years of age, I belong to an honourable but numerous family of the Côte-Saint-André (Isère) . . .'; and he goes on to say that his father can no longer support him in Paris and begs for a small annual grant to help him complete his studies and try for the first Grand Prix. To his request his master Lesueur adds a testimonial that is a striking proof of Lesueur's perspicacity and faith in his pupil. He says:

I have the honour of attesting to His Excellency that the petition of M. Berlioz is based on the most brilliant hopes that he gives by virtue of his talent, amounting to genius, which only requires developing to achieve its full power. This young man, well-informed in all the other branches of learning, will become—I will answer for it—a great composer who will be an honour to France. . . . M. Berlioz is born for music. . . .

LESUEUR.

Membre de l'Institut, surintendant de la musique de la chapelle du Roi, chevalier des ordres royaux de Saint-Michel et de la Légion d'honneur, professeur de composition a l'École royale de Musique.

The petition was refused. Berlioz left for La Côte on 30th August, and it was on 16th September, as we have already seen in the previous chapter, that he wrote to Ferrand from Grenoble, saying that two days before he had composed the ballad of the *Roi de Thulé* from *Faust* while travelling in a carriage.

While he was at home the English actors were at Rouen, but they returned to Paris and opened their season at the Théâtre-Italien on 24th September. Berlioz returned to Paris at the beginning of October, but at the end of this month the English company went to Bordeaux. In a letter to Ferrand dated Paris, 11th November, Berlioz writes: '. . . La Fontaine was quite right when he said, "Absence is the greatest of all evils." She has gone! She has been at Bordeaux for the last fortnight. I live no more, or rather, I live too much. . . .'

In the midst of the torments of his apparently hopeless passion for Miss Smithson, which he confides to Ferrand, his letters to his family show no sign of his state of mind. There is a charming letter to his elder sister Nanci, dated Paris, 1st November, which I should like to quote in full, but it is much too long. He begins with a list of commissions that he has had to fulfil for his mother and a friend, also for his Uncle Victor—chains, ear-rings, lamps, music, books; he enumerates every item and its price, the cost of packing and postage, accounting in true French fashion for every *sou*. He then tells Nanci that he had been invited to a banquet given by the musicians of the Odéon theatre to their conductor, M. Bloc,[1] and that after the usual toasts Bloc had got up and said 'I drink to the success of an artist who is not connected with the Odéon but whom we should be proud to possess—M. Berlioz'; whereupon Berlioz proposed a toast to the memory of Weber and Beethoven, which was drunk with enthusiasm. He adds that he is sending her a *Walze* [*sic*] *au Chalet* by Weber that is ravishing in its grace and freshness, but very difficult. He explains that she must

> learn it by heart bar by bar and, above all, not be surprised at the oddities it contains; the G sharp in the key of D and the C sharp in the key of G are only there to give the melody local colour; for you know that the instruments the Swiss shepherds use have the fourth note of the key too high, which Weber has rendered by a sharp and which one accustoms oneself to very quickly. The pace is very quick and the expression that of frank and natural gaiety. Imagine a Swiss mountain, a setting sun, a country dance, the smell of thyme and *serpolet*, a beautiful calm evening. O Weber, Weber! . . . to die at thirty-five, alone in London, far from his wife and his two children, he who asked nothing more than to live!

He then goes on to say that he has met a young German[2] who knew Weber and that they pass hours together, he playing and Berlioz singing extracts from *Freischütz*, *Oberon*, and

[1] Bloc had conducted Berlioz's first concert in May that year at the Conservatoire.

[2] Schlösser, Louis (b. Darmstadt 1800, d. 1886); he became a well-known musician and composer.

Euryanthe to M. Lesueur, all from memory. He adds that the attraction of this young German is that he knows English, admires Shakespeare, has seen Goethe at Weimar, detests the absurdities of the Italian school, and hates the commonplace in music and literature. And in this letter we have the sole indication existing of Berlioz's knowledge of English, for he says that nothing makes him more impatient than to hear strangers speak his language well when he cannot speak a word of theirs:

I bitterly regret not to be able to learn English quicker; it is so little to attend three times a week a public class where one takes an hour to learn what one would learn in fifteen minutes in a private lesson; but I cannot, for want of cash, have a master to myself.

In the meantime he goes on with, and completes, his *Huit Scènes de Faust*. At the end of January, about a month after his twenty-fifth birthday, he seems to have heard indirectly from Miss Smithson, to whom evidently he has been sending letters, for he writes to Ferrand on 2nd February 1829:

I have been waiting all this time, my dear and excellent friend, in order to send you with this letter the complete score of my *Faust*, but as the work has assumed greater dimensions than I foresaw, the printing is not yet finished and I cannot go any longer without writing to you.

Three days ago I was for twelve hours in a fearful delirium of joy. Ophelia is not so far away from me as I imagined; there exists some reason or other about which I am not to be told for some time to come, and it is consequently impossible at present to speak openly of it.

'But,' she has said, '*if he loves me truly*, if his love is unlike the love of those whom I have a right to despise, a few months' waiting will not exhaust his constancy.' . . .

Listen to what I say, Ferrand: if ever I succeed, I feel beyond a doubt that I shall become a colossus in music; for some time past I have had a descriptive symphony of *Faust* in my brain; when I set it at liberty, I want to astound the whole musical world with it.[1]

The love of Ophelia has increased my abilities a hundredfold. Send me the *Francs-Juges* [2] as soon as you can, in order that I may profit by a moment's sun and quiet, and ensure their reception; darkness and storm

[1] The first mention of what was to become the *Symphonie fantastique*.

[2] Berlioz means the completed text for the opera.

come to prevent my onward progress only too often; it is absolutely necessary that I should work now. . . .

I am going to send her my score to Amsterdam.[1] I have only just put my initials on it. What if I should attain to being loved by Ophelia, or at least, if my love should flatter her and be pleasing to her? My heart swells high and my imagination in vain makes terrible efforts to comprehend the immensity of such happiness. What if I should live? Should write? Should expand my wings? Oh, my dear friend! Oh, my heart! Oh, love, love! All! All!

There are devitalized people alive to-day who call themselves critics and even poets (poets, mark you!), who have the habit of sneering at men of genius such as Shelley and Berlioz. They look upon such outpourings as I have quoted as 'romanticism'—seeming incapable of ever losing themselves in anything outside themselves. And from what they suppose is the immense height of their indifference they see everything as it really is. What is notable, however, is that what they see and describe gives other people as little cause for satisfaction as it does themselves. But, leaving aside those who merely follow the fashion, are not the leaders of this contemporary anti-romantic movement just as full of illusions as any of the romantics? Is not that their sole merit? But what is not a merit is the cunning way in which they pretend to have no illusion, to be completely clear-sighted and realistic. Art is an inferior substitute for religion, argues one of them.[2] What is he doing but substituting the 'illusion' of religion for the 'illusion' of art? Is it not possible to be as 'romantic' about religion as about art or love? What is deciding is the intrinsic value of the passion for religion or for art—'by their fruits ye shall judge them.' By 'art' Berlioz would mean the poetry of Shakespeare, the music of Gluck and Beethoven. What does Mr. Eliot mean by 'religion'? Not the ideas of Spinoza, Lao Tse, Jesus, Buddha, but presumably, as he is only an

[1] The English company and Miss Smithson left Paris to play in Holland in February or March 1829.

[2] Mr. T. S. Eliot, the most dogmatic and yet the most ambiguous of our contemporary poets.

Anglo-Catholic and not a Catholic, the Thirty-nine Articles. Now, we have only to put Mr. Eliot's belief in a plain, unambiguous form to see how much it means, for it amounts to this: *Beethoven's Nine Symphonies are an inferior substitute for Cranmer's Thirty-nine Articles.*

To return to Berlioz: he adds immediately after his rhapsody about Ophelia (Harriet Smithson) in his letter to Ferrand the following sentence:

> Do not let my ecstasy alarm you; it is not so blind as you may fear; misfortune has made me defiant; I look straight before me, and I see nothing certain; I tremble as much with fear as with hope.
>
> We must wait for time; nothing stops that, so we may rely upon it.
>
> Good-bye; send me the *Francs-Juges* quickly, I beseech you.
>
> Have you read *Les Orientales* of Victor Hugo? There are countless sublime thoughts in it. I have set his *Chanson des Pirates* to music, with a tempest accompaniment. If I write it out fairly and have time to make a copy, I will send it to you with *Faust.* It is the music of the sea-rover, the corsair, the brigand, the rough and savage-voiced filibuster; but I need not explain it to you, because you understand poetic music as well as I do.

We shall best be able to follow Berlioz's life during the next few months through his letters, especially those to Ferrand. I propose to quote freely from these, because they have an extraordinary charm and bring Berlioz before one better than any description. The letters are addressed to Ferrand except where otherwise stated.

To Albert Du Boys

Paris, *Monday evening, 2nd March* (1829).

My dear Albert,

. . . I thank you from the bottom of my heart for your affectionate letter. All is finished. On leaving you I wrote in English to Ophelia; I begged her again to give me one word in reply. The servants have never given her my letters. She had expressly forbidden them to receive any message from me. Finally, the performance took place; [1] exasperated

[1] This refers to a benefit performance for *La Maison de Refuge* at which Bériot and his young pupil Henri Vieuxtemps, aged eight years, played the violin and the English players, with Abbott and Harriet Smithson, performed two acts of *Romeo and Juliet* prior to their departure from Paris. Berlioz in his *Mémoires*, and in this letter to Du Boys, speaks of an overture of his which was performed on this occasion, but no mention of it is made in the press notices of the benefit performance.

with grief I heard my overture, which, better played than I anticipated, made a mediocre impression on the small audience in the hall. I felt that it was beyond my strength to see Juliet and renew the so painfully lacerating sensations that I have not experienced since two years ago.[1] I fled immediately after the last note. . . .

She leaves to-morrow. . . .

I do not weep, I hardly suffer; excess of grief has made me insensible. Perhaps I shall accustom myself to life. However, it seems as if I am at the centre whose circumference is always enlarging; the physical and intellectual world seems placed on this circumference, which ceaselessly moves away, and I live alone with my memory in ever greater isolation. In the morning when I emerge from the oblivion of sleep I wake gaily, the idea of happiness being natural to me; this fleeting illusion soon gives place to the fearful conception of the reality which overwhelms me with its weight and freezes my whole being. . . .

Yesterday I went to the Conservatoire concert. Beethoven's Symphony in A made a sensation. . . . This inconceivable product of the most sombre and reflective genius is placed exactly among all that the most intoxicating, the most tender and naïvest joy, can offer. It has only two ideas: 'I think, therefore I suffer,' and 'I remember, therefore I suffer more.' Oh, unhappy Beethoven! he too had in his heart an ideal world of happiness into which it was not given to him to enter. . . .

She has just put out her light [2] . . . I will go out early in the morning; she leaves at midday. Hiller [3] expects me at ten o'clock. He will play for me an *adagio* by Beethoven, my eyes will not remain dry as this evening, that is all I hope for.

Adieu—what silence!

Don't be uneasy, the blow has fallen; I am pulverized, but I am not dead. . . .

To his Sister Nanci

Paris, *29th March*, 1829.

I came in at 8.30; I intended to go to bed at once, my evening being free, so as to escape by sleep from this persistent scourge of boredom and disgust; I find three letters, from my two sisters and from Charles Bert. . . .

---

[1] Berlioz refers to the first performance of *Hamlet* on 11th September 1827, with Harriet Smithson as Ophelia.

[2] By a coincidence Harriet Smithson at this time lodged opposite No. 96 rue Richelieu, where Berlioz lived, in an apartment at the corner of the rue Neuve-Saint-Marc.

[3] Hiller, Ferdinand (1811–85), German pianist and composer, pupil of Hummel, studied in Paris 1828–35. He was the first to play Beethoven's E flat Concerto in Paris.

That from Charles made me smile with pleasure, Adèle's gave me pleasure without smiling, and yours has made me weep without pleasure. Instead of sleeping I want to reply to you, to speak to you, not of what concerns me only but of what concerns me because it concerns you. I believe that with friendship as with love, absence increases it; every time I get a letter from you it seems that you become dearer to me. How I should like to see you happy! Yet the more affinities I find in our characters, the more disquieted I am about your future. It is certain that the more intelligence and sensibility you develop, the more openings you give to suffering. And you haven't, like me, the resource of a strong distraction; you haven't in truth a task, a so pressing necessity; however, I believe that a stay in Paris with its new sensations would be invaluable . . . only this delicious liberty which I enjoy would not fall to your lot. It is truly an existence of which you can have no idea. Sometimes alone for two or three hours in this beautiful sunshine which tortures me, I find myself without any pressing occupation on the boulevards or in the Tuileries garden. . . . In what direction shall I go? Southwards?—nothing. East, or west?—nothing. And north? . . . North lies the country of fogs, ice, winds, and tempests. . . . Nothing. . . .

I confess, my dear sister, that inwardly I am hurt by the silence maintained with me about your future . . . several times I have had news from outside sources. . . . I have been treated as if I were a stranger. However, we won't speak of that, for the language of reproach is shabby and contemptible.

Well, I have no more ideas. . . .

Ah! you speak to me of the *beautiful*, the *grand*, the *sublime* . . . but the sublime is not sublime for everybody. What transports some is unintelligible to others, sometimes even ridiculous. . . . As genius rises in its flight it puts itself further out of reach of those who pretend it is made for them. . . . The other day I heard one of the late quartets of Beethoven at one of M. Baillot's[1] evenings . . . there were nearly three hundred persons present, of whom six found ourselves half-dead through the truth of the emotion we had experienced, but we six were the only ones who did not find this composition absurd, incomprehensible, barbarous. He rose to such heights that our breath began to fail us. He was deaf when he wrote this quartet; and for him as for Homer, 'the universe was enclosed in his own soul.' This is music for him or for those who have followed the incalculable flight of his genius. . . .

---

[1] Baillot (1771–1842), famous violinist, and leader of one of the finest string quartets of the time.

To Ferrand

Paris, *9th April*, 1829.

I have not written to you, my poor dear friend, because I was incapable of writing. All my hopes were so many frightful illusions . . . she merely left this message to be conveyed to me: 'There is nothing more impossible.' . . .

She has been absent for thirty-six days, each one twenty-four hours long, and *there is nothing more impossible*. . . .

Paris, *3rd June*, 1829.

My dear Friend,

It will soon be three months since I heard from you . . . something extraordinary must, therefore, necessarily have happened.

I sent you *Faust* with the copies of the *Stabat* without any title-page; you have not acknowledged their receipt, and I am at a loss to understand it. Is there some fresh anonymous quarrel? Does your father intercept our correspondence? Or are you perchance attaching credence to the absurd calumnies which are current about me among your family? . . .

Faust has had an immense success among the artists; Onslow [1] called on me one morning and made me feel quite uncomfortable, so warmly did he praise it. Meyerbeer has just written to Schlesinger from Baden for a copy. Urhan, Chélard, and many of the most prominent artists of the Opéra have procured copies and I receive fresh congratulations every night. But nothing has made such an impression on me as the enthusiasm of M. Onslow. . . .

Spontini has just produced his opera, the *Colporteur*, at Berlin . . . he is extremely difficult to please on the score of originality, and has assured me that he knows nothing more original than *Faust*.

'I am very fond of my own music,' he added, 'but I conscientiously believe that I am incapable of producing such a work.' [2] To all this I could only answer trivialities, so upset was I by this unexpected visit. On the following day Onslow sent me a copy of his two grand *quintetti*. Up to the present this compliment has touched me more closely than any other.

I have paid the printer what I owed him, a pupil having come to my rescue.

I am still very happy, my life is as charming as ever; no sorrow, no

---

[1] Onslow, George (1784–1853), French composer of English descent.

[2] This is one of those superb remarks that only a real character such as Spontini could have made. See Wagner's description of Spontini in his *Mein Leben*. It is one of the most entertaining passages in his autobiography and shows Wagner in an exceptionally attractive light.

despair, plenty of illusions, and to put the finishing stroke to my enchantment, *Les Francs-Juges*[1] has been rejected by the jury of the Opéra. . . .

I am going to have it translated into German. I will finish the music and make an opera of it like *Der Freischütz*. . . .

I am told that Spohr[2] is not jealous, but on the contrary is anxious to help young composers. Consequently, if I gain the prize at the Institut I will start at once for Cassel. . . .

I am preparing a grand concert for December, in which I shall produce *Faust* together with two grand overtures and some Irish melodies which are not printed. I have only completed one up to now; Gounet is keeping me waiting for a long time for the rest. . . .

I cannot undertake any important composition. When I am strong enough to work I copy out the parts for the future concert, and I have not much time to devote to that, owing to being constantly worried by newspaper articles. I am charged with the correspondence, nearly gratuitous, for the *Gazette musicale* of Berlin.[3] . . .

My poor Ferrand, I write you interminable digressions which have no interest whatever for you, and I am inclined to fear that my letters no longer possess the interest in your eyes that they formerly had. . . .

You have not even sent me a friendly word since I told you that I was losing all the hopes with which I had been deluding myself. I am no farther advanced than I was on the first day; this passion will kill me; it has been so often said that hope alone can sustain love! I am a convincing proof to the contrary. Ordinary fire has need of air, but electricity burns in a vacuum. All the English newspapers are loud in praise of her genius.[4] I remain obscure. When I have written an immense instrumental composition, such as I am meditating,[5] I want, above all things, to have it performed in London, so that I may gain a brilliant success under her very eyes!

My dear friend, I can write no more; my pen is falling from my fingers through sheer weakness.

15th June 1829.

Yes, my dear friend, it is quite true that I did not hear from you until the 11th inst. . . .

I shall be delighted to have a notice in the *Journal de Genève* if you can

---

[1] This refers to the libretto written by Ferrand.

[2] Spohr, Louis (1784–1859), famous violinist and composer; conductor at Cassel from 1822.

[3] See p. 41 for the part of this letter about his writings, Beethoven, and Rossini.

[4] Harriet Smithson.

[5] The *Symphonie fantastique*.

manage it. In writing about my *Faust* do not, I beseech you, be led away by your feelings of friendship for me; nothing appears so strange to the calm reader as enthusiasm which is unintelligible to him.[1] I do not know what to say to you about the summary of articles you mention. Look at the one in the *Revue musicale* and allude to each subject in detail; or, if that is beyond the compass of the paper, lay more stress on the *Premier Chœur*, the *Concert des Sylphes*, the *Roi de Thulé*, and the *Sérénade*, specially on the double orchestra of the *Concert* which has not been mentioned by the *Revue*, and wind up with a few considerations on the melodic style and the innovations you consider the best.

I am not having any announcement put in the other papers, because I am momentarily expecting a reply from Goethe, who sent word that he was going to write to me but does not do so. Heaven! how impatient I am to receive that letter! I have been somewhat better the last two days. Last week I was seized with a nervous depression so severe that I could hardly move or dress myself in the morning. I was recommended to take baths, but they did me no good; I remained quite quiet, and youth regained the upper hand. I cannot get used to the impossible, and it is precisely because it is impossible that I have so little life in me.

Nevertheless, constant occupation is an absolute necessity in my case; I am writing a life of Beethoven for the *Correspondant*. I cannot find a moment for composition; during the rest of the time I have to copy out parts. What a life!

PARIS, *29th June* 1829.

The contest [for the Prix de Rome] begins the day after to-morrow. . . .

I reckon on the prize to pay what I owe you; the copies of *Faust* Schlesinger has sold already cover a part of the costs. . . .

To-morrow there is an examination at the Conservatoire; I am going to show them the *Concert des Sylphes*; I am curious to hear what they will say to me. . . .

TO HIS FATHER

PARIS, *2nd August* 1829.

MY DEAR PAPA,

I have been waiting till all was finished before replying to mamma's last letter, which I received with its enclosure at the Institut. The decision was made yesterday: there is no first prize, either for me or for any one else. The Institut having declared that there is no good cause to give one, it has been reserved for next year when two will be awarded if fitting. M. Lesueur, being ill, has not been concerned in it, which has harmed me terribly. Nevertheless, Cherubini and Auber

---

[1] An example of Berlioz's level-headedness.

supported me; MM. Pradier and Ingres,[1] great admirers of the German school, delivered at the end of the meeting a long disquisition, in which they gave vent to their indignation, saying it was inconceivable that such an assembly should judge me so superficially, knowing my antecedents and how impossible it was to judge my composition from such a performance.

Indeed, Madame Dabadie, who was to have sung for me, was compelled to break faith on account of the dress rehearsal of *William Tell*,[2] which was at the same hour as the competition. She sent her sister, a pupil of the Conservatoire, who is totally inexperienced and had only a few hours in which to prepare herself.

But the principal cause of all this is that in the general opinion the prize was mine. I believed myself to be sufficiently solidly backed to allow myself to compose as I felt, instead of restraining myself like last year. The subject was the *Death of Cleopatra*; it inspired in me many things which appear to me to be both great and new, which I have not hesitated to write. All these gentlemen were well disposed towards me, but they simply haven't understood anything in my work, and as for the musicians, it was a sort of criticism of their manner which has wounded their self-respect.

I have just run across Boieldieu[3] on the boulevard. He came immediately up to me and talked to me for an hour; this is the gist of it:

'Oh, my friend! what have you done? We reckoned on giving you the prize. We thought you would be more sensible than last year, and, on the contrary, you were a hundred times worse. I can only judge what I can understand: but then, I am far from saying that your work is not good; I have already heard so many things that I have only understood and admired by dint of hearing them! But what can you expect? I have not yet been able to grasp half of Beethoven's works, and you go further than Beethoven. You have a volcanic constitution on whose level we cannot put ourselves. On the other hand, I could not prevent myself saying to my colleagues:

'"This young man, with such ideas, and such a way of writing, must despise us from the bottom of his heart; he will not write a note like anybody else. He must even have new rhythms; he would invent new

---

[1] The practice in awarding the Grand Prix de Rome was to add to the musician judges two members of other sections of the Institut; thus it was that the painter Ingres was concerned. See chap. XXII of Berlioz's *Mémoires*.

[2] Rossini's opera; the first performance took place in Paris on 3rd August 1829.

[3] See p. 31; a member of the jury.

modulations if it were possible. All that we do must seem to him commonplace and platitudinous." '[1]

There is the clue to the enigma as far as Catel and Boieldieu are concerned. Auber and Cherubini were in my favour on personal grounds, but they felt the same about my work; Cherubini, however, much less than the others.[2]

As for the non-musicians among the members of the jury, they understood nothing at all; for them it was as if one were to read *Faust* to Prosper.[3] . . .

I shall write to you again soon. This evening I must go to Boieldieu's. He has made me promise, so as to continue our conversation. He says he wants to study me.

Adieu, dear papa, I embrace you tenderly.

To Ferrand

21st August 1829.

My dear Friend,

At last I am sending you the music for which you have been waiting so long; the fault rests with me and the printer. As for me, the competition at the Institut is some excuse, and all my new sources of agitation, *the new pangs of my despised love*, are unfortunately only too sufficient a justification for my thinking of nothing else.

Yes, my poor dear friend, my heart is the centre of a horrible conflagration; it is a virgin forest encircled by lightning; every now and then the fire appears burnt out, but there comes a puff of wind, it blazes up again, and the moaning of the trees as they succumb to the flames reveals the dread power of the devastating scourge. . . .

This absurd and shameful competition at the Institut has done me a severe injury as regards my parents. The judges, who are not the *Francs-Juges*, do not wish, so they say, to encourage me in my mistaken course. Boieldieu said to me[4] . . .

On the other hand, Auber took me aside at the Opéra, and, after having told me almost the same thing, with the additional information that one ought to write *cantatas as one writes symphonies*,[5] added:

---

[1] It is worth noting that this conversation is also given in a letter to Ferrand of 21st August 1829, and in the *Mémoires*, written twenty years later.

[2] This is an interesting fact for students of musical history.

[3] Berlioz's brother, aged nine years.

[4] Here follows a report of the conversation, which is much the same as in Berlioz's letter to his father, already quoted.

[5] An interesting remark for musicians. It reveals how formal a thing the writing of symphonies was to most musicians of that period—one might say, to all musicians who were then living, Beethoven and Schubert being dead.

'You avoid the beaten track, but you need never fear writing platitudes. Consequently the best advice I can give you is to endeavour to write flatly, and when you have achieved something which appears to be horribly flat to you, it will be exactly what it ought to be. And do not forget that if you were to write music in accordance with your own conceptions, the public mind would not understand you, and the music-sellers would not buy your works.'[1] . . .

Oh, my dear Ferrand, I wish I could make you hear the scene where Cleopatra reflects upon *the greeting her shade will receive from those of the Pharaohs entombed in the Pyramids.* It is terrible, frightful! . . .

In the midst of all this my father stops my indispensable allowance. I am going back to La Côte, where I foresee no end of worry. And yet, I live only for music; it alone supports me in this abyss of ills of every description. . . .

William Tell? I think all the journalists have gone mad. It is a work possessing a few good numbers, which is not absurdly written, in which there is no *crescendo* and rather less big drum—that is all. Beyond that there is no real feeling, but everywhere art, habit, *savoir-faire*, and the knowledge how to manage the public.[2] . . .

I am composing some Irish melodies to Moore's words which Gounet is translating for me. . . .

La Mort de Cléopâtre, the cantata with which Berlioz failed to obtain the Grand Prix in 1829, is now published in Series VI B of the Breitkopf & Härtel edition of Berlioz's works. It has no opus number, for it was never published in Berlioz's lifetime. It is still to-day practically unknown to musicians. It has never, to my knowledge, been performed since it was first, most inadequately, performed before Cherubini, Auber, etc. One French critic says:

For us who, a century later, *read* [my italics] this *Cléopâtre* with a sensibility helped by the whole of Berlioz's work, for us, clearly, this lyrical scene in spite of its conventional forms is full of genius and ingenuity: to go over this almost unknown score is for the Berliozian to give himself one of the very choicest experiences.

If our schools, our Royal Colleges, Royal Academies, Guildhalls of Music and their like throughout the country, were real

---

[1] Profound and eternal truth!

[2] Speaking from the highest standpoint, this is not an incorrect appraisement of an opera far above the general level.

centres of musical learning instead of the conventional, moribund, effete little pettifogging phalansteries they are, then the students would be given opportunities for performing such neglected and historically interesting works as Berlioz's *Cléopâtre*; also many others equally neglected and equally interesting from the historical point of view. As for the intrinsic aesthetic interest of such a work as Berlioz's *Cléopâtre*, we shall never know it until it is properly and understandingly performed. In the meantime our musical students repeat interminably the symphonies of Brahms, and perhaps they hear the 'Ring' once every year at Covent Garden. I should like to know how many students at the principal schools of music in London visit the opera at Sadler's Wells or the 'Old Vic.' One might think—if one did not know our English musical student and his professors better—that this was because it is only recently that the Vic-Wells Opera gave tolerable performances of Mozart and only this year (1934) that an opera by Gluck has ever been performed there. I am certain, however, that most of our music professors and consequently (perhaps 'similarly' is fairer) their students *prefer* bad performances to good, just as they prefer bad operas to good. Is there a single professor or teacher at any school of music throughout the British Empire who does not prefer, for example, Wagner to Gluck? If there is one I should—if he ever happens to read this book—be glad if he will send me his name and I will see that it is honourably inserted in a second edition, should there be a sufficient number of readers eccentric enough to send it into a second edition.

After his failure to win the Grand Prix, Berlioz published his biography of Beethoven in three articles in the *Correspondant*, in the course of which he says of the Ninth Symphony, which had not yet been played in Paris:

> For us, having read attentively this symphony, we do not hesitate to consider it as the culminating point of the genius of its author. Nevertheless one cannot conclude that this is one of his works which will produce most effect in Paris—in two centuries' time, perhaps! . . .

Berlioz was also teaching the guitar in a school, the Institut Orthopédique, and preparing a second concert of his own works. Some extracts from his letters will give us the best idea of these events:

To Ferrand

3rd October 1829.

I send you a few lines in great haste. Hostilities have commenced. I give a concert on 1st November, All Saints' Day. I have already secured the Menus-Plaisirs concert-room; Cherubini, instead of opposing me, this time is ill. I shall give two grand overtures, the *Concert des Sylphes* and the *Grand Air de Conrad*, to which I have added an accompanied recitative, and have improved the instrumentation. . . . Hiller is to play a pianoforte concerto of Beethoven which has never been performed in Paris. Sublime! Immense![1]

Habeneck is to conduct my orchestra, which, as you may well imagine, will be astounding. . . .

Friday evening, 30th October, 1829.

O Ferrand, Ferrand my friend, where are you? This morning we had the first rehearsal of *Les Francs-Juges*. Forty-two violins and a total of a hundred and ten players. I am writing to you from the Lemardelay restaurant while I am waiting for my dessert. Nothing, I swear to you, nothing is so terrifically fearful as my overture to the *Francs-Juges*. O Ferrand, my dear friend, you would understand me. Where are you? It is a hymn to despair, the most deplorable, horrible, tender despair that can be imagined. . . .

Yesterday I was too ill to walk; to-day the demons of the infernal regions who dictated *Les Francs-Juges* have given me incredible strength. This evening I must run all over Paris. The concerto of Beethoven is a prodigious, astounding, sublime conception! I do not know how to express my admiration.

Oh, the sylphs!

I have composed a *pianissimo* solo for the big drum in *Les Francs-Juges*.

Intonuere cavae gemitumque dedere cavernae.[2]

In a word, it is terrible. All the fury and tenderness that my heart contains are in this overture.

O Ferrand!

---

[1] Beethoven's pianoforte concerto, No. 5 in E flat.

[2] Virgil (*Aen.* ii. 53) wrote *Insonuere* (sounded); the misquotation, if it is one, is characteristic. 'The hollow cavities thundered and gave forth a groan' suits the big drum, if not the Trojan horse. But as Berlioz wrote *pianissimo* it is probably a printer's error.

To his Father

Paris, 3rd November 1829.

My dear Papa,

First, to appease your anxiety, you must know that I have had an enthusiastic success with the artists and the public, that I have covered the costs of my concert and gained one hundred and fifty francs.[1] . . .

My orchestra of a hundred musicians was conducted by Habeneck. Apart from some faults, due to insufficient rehearsals, my big pieces were played in a splendid manner. Only the sextet from *Faust* I hadn't time to teach properly to the performers.

I have been put to a terrible test, which I had not foreseen. Hiller, the young German of whom I have spoken to you, played at my concert a pianoforte concerto of Beethoven which is a truly marvellous composition. Immediately after came my *Francs-Juges*. Seeing the effect of this sublime concerto, all my friends believed me lost, crushed, annihilated, and I admit that I experienced a moment of mortal fear. But immediately the overture began I realized the impression it made, and I was completely reassured. The effect has been terrific, frightful, volcanic: the applause lasted almost five minutes. . . .

The *Figaro* to-day has a notice of my concert; I will send it to you with other papers.

Since yesterday I have been in a state of overpowering sadness; the desire to weep has been incessant; I should like to die. . . . I must, I think, have a great deal of sleep.

I cannot connect my ideas.

Adieu, my dear papa. I embrace mamma, and you, and my sisters and brother.

To his Mother

Paris, 20th November 1829.

I send you, my dear mamma, the papers you ask for; I don't include the *Gazette de France* nor the *Débats*, because I think you have them at La Côte. It is very difficult to get the directors of these great journals to come to concerts; there is only one theatre privileged to obtain from them long and frequent articles, the Théâtre-Italien . . . they will write two columns on the reappearance of a singer, but not a word that really concerns the art of music. . . .

Since my success gave you pleasure, I will tell you, my dear mamma, that it continues to be talked of. . . .

---

[1] Of this sum, he says in a letter to Ferrand dated Paris, 6th November 1829, he is going to hand over two-thirds to Gounet, 'who has been kind enough to lend me money and who is, I fancy, more pressed for it than you are.'

I am very glad you have had a little distraction at Grenoble, but I would almost wager that you have had more worry than pleasure. . . . You have not told me if the vintage is good or bad. The box of books ought to have reached you long ago, it left here on the 6th. . . .

PARIS, 27*th December* 1829.

MY DEAR FERRAND,

Business first. I saw M. Rocher on the evening of the day I received your letter . . . he told me that there had been a judge-auditorship vacant at Lyons, but that it had been filled up. There is consequently no hope.

Congratulations next. I congratulate you a thousand times on the brilliant success you have had. I am not at all at a loss to imagine the impression you must have made, animated as you were by indignation and the interest with which your client inspires you. . . .

Reproaches now. You are beyond all forgiveness for having left me so long in anxiety. I wrote to you three times, and you reply six weeks after my third letter. . . .

Now for promises. You will receive between now and three weeks hence our collection of *Mélodies irlandaises*, together with the *Ballet des Ombres*. . . . I have attempted to set one of the couplets of your satanic song to music. It is passable, but it will not stand by the others. It is a horribly difficult thing to do. You are too much a poet to suit a musician. . . .

Finally, a confession. I am weary. I am weary! The same thing over and over again. But I grow weary now with astonishing rapidity and I get through as much weariness now in an hour as I used to do in a day, and I drink time as ducks do water for the purpose of finding something to live upon, and, like them, I only find a few uncouth insects. What am I to do? What am I to do?

Thus the year 1829 ended. At its beginning Berlioz had published his *Huit Scènes de Faust* and at the end he published, at the joint expense of himself and his friend Gounet, who translated the words of Thomas Moore, his nine *Mélodies irlandaises*. Another composition, *Ballet des Ombres*, for chorus with pianoforte accompaniment, the words by his friend Albert Du Boys, was also printed. Both were designated Opus 2, but finally, the *Ballet des Ombres* is given the Opus 2 and the *Mélodies irlandaises* becomes Opus 2 *bis*, as the *Waverley* overture is Opus 1 *bis*, *Faust* being Opus 1.

According to Boschot, Berlioz was soon dissatisfied with the *Ballet des Ombres* and destroyed all the copies he could lay his hands on. It contains, however, the first germ of the later 'Queen Mab' Scherzo in *Roméo et Juliette*. When Boschot wrote, this work was completely inaccessible, and he says that the manuscript belonged to M. Raoul Pugno.[1] Since then, however, the *Ballet des Ombres* has been included in the Breitkopf & Härtel edition.

The *Mélodies irlandaises* have been mentioned several times. A few words more are necessary. The first number, the *Coucher du soleil*, is a reverie of an extraordinary, tranquil, luminous beauty that reminds one of a Giorgione landscape. No. 2, *Hélène*, is a romantic ballad for two voices; the pianoforte part with its sixths and thirds suggests horns playing in the open air. The melody is simple but with a characteristic Berlioz flavour due to his peculiar chromaticism; it was orchestrated later (about 1848), but as compositions for two voices have completely gone out of fashion, we are not likely ever to hear this charming piece in a concert hall. No. 3, *Chant guerrier*, No. 5, *Chanson à boire*, and No. 6, *Chant sacré* are really operatic choruses. They are full of merit, combining spontaneity, verve, and effectiveness; but, alas, they have no place in the modern concert hall. Of No. 4, *La Belle Voyageuse*, I have already written. It is an exquisite song of unstainable freshness. Only in Schubert can one find anything to compare with it; and Schubert's songs were absolutely unknown to Berlioz at the time this was written, one year after Schubert's death.[2] No. 7, *L'Origine de la Harpe*, is for single voice and pianoforte. It is a simple but expressive melody with an arpeggio accompaniment. No. 8, *Adieu, Bessy*, is for two tenor voices with pianoforte accompaniment, but there are two versions and it appears in Breitkopf & Härtel's edition under 'Songs for single voice and pianoforte.'[3]

[1] Pugno, Raoul (1852–1914), a famous French pianist.

[2] *La Belle Voyageuse* was also arranged for voice and orchestra by Berlioz in 1834.

[3] Rearranged in 1850.

This beautiful and poignant song is thoroughly Berliozian in character and somewhat resembles in colour the *Romance de Marguerite* in the *Huit Scènes de Faust*. It is quite undeservedly neglected. No. 9 is an *Élégie* for tenor, with pianoforte accompaniment. It originally bore the dedication 'F. H. S.' (for Harriet Smithson), but later was dedicated by Berlioz 'to the memory of the unhappy Emmet.'[1] This is the song which he says he composed on the spot, after reading Moore's poem on returning from a walk.[2] It has that broken, unrhetorical expressiveness so characteristic of much of Berlioz's lyrical writing. This is the sort of music which never appealed to the later nineteenth century; it is too direct and simple.

Berlioz's last occupation at the end of 1829 was correcting the proofs of the score of Rossini's opera *William Tell*, for which he received two hundred francs. On 11th December 1829 he reached his twenty-sixth birthday. Since 26th August 1826 he had been a student at the Paris Conservatoire under Lesueur and Reicha. In August 1828 he had won the second Grand Prix. He had learnt all that the most renowned musicians and professors of his age had to teach him, and he had already composed works which can be compared only to the achievements of Mozart, Beethoven, and Schubert. At twenty-six Beethoven had only written a few trios and sonatas, and Wagner at the same age had written nothing in the least comparable to the *Francs-Juges* or *Waverley* overtures, to say nothing of the *Huit Scènes de Faust*; even the early *Rienzi* overture was still to come. I emphasize these facts in order to kill for ever the false idea (put forth by some writers ignorant of the facts) that Berlioz was a composer of genius but inadequately trained; or the stupid notion that any of his characteristics are to be put down to his having started the serious study of music too late.

[1] Robert Emmet, Irish patriot, see p. 83.

[2] See p. 82.

CHAPTER IX

'EPISODE IN THE LIFE OF AN ARTIST'

A FEW extracts from Berlioz's letters will provide the best picture of his life at the beginning of the year 1830, his last year of nominal apprenticeship at the Conservatoire.

PARIS, 30*th January* 1830.

MY DEAR NANCI,

I ought to have replied sooner to your last letter; I had a thousand things to say which have gone out of my head, for which I ask pardon. I lead an excessively active life this winter; I am constantly occupied. . . .

I have just settled to give a big concert at the Théâtre des Nouveautés in three and a half months. . . . To accomplish my purpose I prepare a great deal of new music; among other things, an immense instrumental composition of a new kind [1] . . . unfortunately it is very long, and I fear not being able to have it ready for 23rd May, Ascension Day . . . this fiery labour greatly fatigues me; although I have had the skeleton of my work in my head for a long time, it needs much patience to connect the parts and properly organize it. . . .

Ah! my sister, you cannot imagine the pleasure a composer has in writing *freely* under the direct influence of his will. When I have sketched out the first plan of my score when my instruments of different sorts are ranged for battle, when I think of the field of tones which scholastic prejudices have kept virgin up till now, and which, since my emancipation [2] I regard as my domain, I rush forth with a sort of fury to forage these. Sometimes I address my soldiers: 'You, rough fellows, who up till now have only known how to utter stupidities, come and let me teach you to speak; you gracious musical spirits whom routine had relegated to the dusty pigeon-holes of theoretical savants, come dance before me and show that you are good for something better than acoustical experiments'; and above all I say to my army, 'Forget the songs of the watch and the habits of the barracks.' . . .

---

[1] The *Symphonie fantastique*.

[2] It was clear from his works that by now, although only twenty-six, Berlioz had left the Paris Conservatoire and its professors of composition and counterpoint behind him for good, but it is interesting to find him conscious of the fact.

To Ferrand

Paris, *6th February* 1830.

. . . After a period of calm . . . I have just been plunged once more into all the anguish of an interminable and inextinguishable passion, devoid of both motive and subject. She[1] is still in London, and yet I seem to feel her near me; all my former feelings for her are aroused, and combine to tear me to pieces; I hear my heart beat, and its pulsations shake me as though they were the strokes of the piston-rod of a steam-engine.[2] Every nerve in my body trembles with pain. In vain! Frightful!

Unhappy woman! If she could realize for an instant all the poetry, all the infinity of such love, she would fly into my arms, even if death lurked in the embrace.

I was on the point of commencing my great symphony wherein the development of my passion is to be portrayed; I have it all in my head, but I cannot write a line. Patience!

. . . My dear friend, write to me often and at length, I beseech you; I am separated from you; let your thoughts, at all events, reach me. I cannot bear not being able to see you. Is it a stern necessity that through the thunder-clouds which mutter over my head no single ray of peaceful light should console me? I expect a letter from you in nine days if your health will permit of your writing.

To Ferdinand Hiller

Paris, *probably 5th March* 1830.

My dear Ferdinand,

I must write to you this evening; this letter will not, perhaps, be any happier than the others . . . but no matter. Can you explain to me this power of emotion, this faculty for suffering that is killing me? Ask your good angel . . . that seraph who has opened for you the gates of paradise.[3] An end to groaning! My fire is dying out. . . . Oh, my friend, I am indeed unhappy beyond expression.

I have spent many an hour drying the tears that fall from my eyes. . . . Meanwhile I think I see Beethoven, who eyes me severely; Spontini, cured of my ills, gazing at me with an indulgent air; and Weber, who seems to whisper in my ear like some familiar spirit, dwelling in a happy place, where he is waiting to console me.

All this is mad . . . quite mad, for a man who plays dominoes at the

---

[1] Harriet Smithson.

[2] It was only in 1829 that Stephenson's 'Rocket,' the first locomotive, made its first successful trials. Our fiery 'romantic' had a very up-to-date heart.

[3] Camille Moke, see p. 137.

Café de la Régence or a member of the Institut. No, I want to live . . . still . . .; music is a heavenly art, nothing is above it except true love; the one will, perhaps, make me as miserable as the other,[1] but at least I shall have lived—in suffering, it is true, in rage, in lamentation, in tears, but I shall have—nothing.

My dear Ferdinand, I have found in you all the symptoms of genuine friendship, and mine for you is also very real; but I fear that it will never give you that calm happiness which is to be found far from volcanoes—far from me, all incapable as I am of saying something—reasonable. It is a year to-day since I saw *her*[2] for the first time.—O unfortunate one! how I loved you! I write murmuring how I love you!

If there be a new world, shall we meet each other once more? Shall I ever see Shakespeare?

Will she be able to recognize me? Will she understand the poetry of my love?

Oh! Juliet, Ophelia, Belvidera, Jane Shore—names that hell itself repeats incessantly.

To the point!

I am a right miserable man, a being well-nigh isolated in the world, an animal weighted with an imagination he cannot support, consumed by a boundless love which is repaid only by indifference and scorn; yes, but I have known certain musical geniuses, I have laughed at the faint gleams of their lightnings and at the mere recollection of them I gnash my teeth!

O sublime, infinite ones! exterminate me! Summon me within your golden clouds, that I may be set free!

Reason speaks: Be tranquil, fool; in a few years there will be no more question of your sufferings than of what you call the genius of Beethoven, the impassioned sensibility of Spontini, the dreamy imagination of Weber, the colossal power of Shakespeare!

Trust me, Henriette Smithson[3]
and Hector Berlioz
will be reunited in the oblivion of the tomb, which will not prevent other unhappy ones from suffering and dying!

PARIS, *16th April* 1830.

MY DEAR FRIEND,

. . . Since my last I have encountered some terrible storms, but the vessel that was almost shipwrecked has recovered herself at last and now sails calmly on.

---

[1] An accurate prediction, as we shall see. [2] Harriet Smithson.
[3] It will be noticed that Berlioz always writes Henriette, not Harriet.

The discovery of frightful but indisputable truths has aided my recovery,[1] and I think it will be as complete as my tenacious nature will allow. I have just strengthened my resolution by a work with which I am perfectly satisfied, and of which this is the subject, to be set forth in a programme and distributed in the concert-room on the night of the performance —*Épisode de la Vie d'un Artiste*,[2] a grand fantastic symphony in five parts.

First part, in two sections, composed of a short *adagio* followed immediately by an *allegro* developed—flood of passion, aimless reveries, delirious passion, with all the accessories of tenderness, jealousy, fury, fear, etc.

Second part: Scene in the fields, *adagio*, thoughts of love and hope troubled by dark presentiments.

Third part: A ball—music brilliant and inspiriting.

Fourth part: March to the scene of execution—music pompous and wild.

Fifth part: Vision of a night of revelry.

That is the present plan of my romance or my history, the hero of which you will easily recognize.

For my subject I take an artist gifted with a lively imagination, finding himself in that state of mind which Chateaubriand has depicted so admirably in his *René*, beholding for the first time a woman who realizes the ideal of beauty and charm for which his heart has long yearned, and falling violently in love with her.

By an odd singularity, the image of her he loves never presents itself to his mind unless accompanied by a musical thought in which he discovers qualities of grace and nobility similar to those with which he has endowed his beloved. This double and fixed idea haunts him incessantly, and it is the reason of the constant appearance, in all the parts of the symphony, of the principal melody in the first *allegro* [3] (No. 1).

After almost interminable agitation, he discovers some grounds for hope, he believes himself beloved. One day when he is in the country, he hears from afar two herdsmen singing a *ranz des vaches*; their pastoral duet plunges him into a delicious reverie (No. 2). The melody reappears for an instant through the themes of the *adagio*.

---

1 What this 'discovery' was and how it was made is a mystery. But about this time Harriet Smithson was engaged in the dumb role of Caecilia in *L'Auberge d'Auray*, a play with music by Hérold and Carafa, at the Opéra-Comique, Paris.

2 This analysis or 'programme' of the *Symphonie fantastique* (*Épisode de la Vie d'un Artiste*) is Berlioz's own, and therefore worth giving.

3 This recurrence of the same theme, the *idée fixe*, in all five movements of the symphony is a technical novelty preceding Wagner's use of the leading theme, or leit-motiv. Most critics exaggerate, in my opinion, the importance of these technical devices, whether as novelties or not.

He is present at a ball, but the tumult of the fête is powerless to distract him; his fixed idea still comes to trouble him, and the cherished melody makes his heart beat in the midst of a brilliant waltz (No. 3).

In a fit of despair he poisons himself with opium,[1] but the narcotic, instead of killing him, produces a horrible dream, during which he imagines that he has killed her he loves, and that he is condemned to death and to witness his own execution. March to the scene of execution; immense procession of executioners, soldiers, and people. At the end the melody appears once more, like a last thought of love, interrupted by the fatal blow (No. 4).

He then beholds himself surrounded by a disgusting crowd of sorcerers and devils, assembled to celebrate the night of revelry. They call him from afar. The melody, which up to this time has seemed full of grace, now appears under the guise of a trivial, ignoble, drunkard's song; it is his beloved coming to the revels, to assist at the funeral *cortège* of her victim. She is no longer anything but a courtesan—worthy of figuring in such an orgy. The ceremony then commences. The bells toll, the infernal elements prostrate themselves, a choir chants the *Dies Irae*, which is taken up by two other choirs who parody it in a burlesque manner; finally there is a whirl of revelry, and when it is at its height it mingles with the *Dies Irae*, and the vision comes to an end (No. 5).

There you have the plan, already carried out, of this stupendous symphony. I have just written the last note. If I can contrive to be ready by Whit-Sunday, 30th May, I will give a concert at the Nouveautés with an orchestra of two hundred and twenty performers. I fear I shall not have the copies of the parts ready. At present I am quite stupid. The fearful strain of thought to which my work is due has fired my imagination and I am continually wanting to sleep and rest myself. But if my brain slumbers my heart is awake, and I feel the want of you keenly. Oh, my friend, shall I not see you again?

To his Sisters (Nanci and Adèle)

Paris, *about 18th April* 1830.

My dear Sisters,

Édouard will hand you a letter which ought to be long and detailed but which will be short and dry; that 's bad, but there it is. I am in one of my fits of general hatred. Yesterday I was quite different: the joy of having finished my symphony had made me forget the fatigue this enormous composition has brought upon me. At present I reflect seriously, and besides, it is weather that makes me suffer as if someone had skinned me from head to foot; superb weather.

---

[1] De Quincey's *Opium-Eater* had just been published in a French translation by Alfred de Musset.

I ought to write separately to you, Nanci, and to you Adèle, but how am I to find anything pleasant to say? Adèle conjugates the verb *to laugh*, Nanci the verb *to be bored*, and I several others less gay and less tranquil, for example, *to gnash the teeth*.

Apropos of the gnashing of teeth, I recall Firmin in *Hernani*; you have asked me, Nanci, what I thought of *Hernani*;[1] well, then! I find sublime things, and above all, sublime thoughts in it, also ridiculous things and ideas, very little novelty in all that; but as for verse, since I detest it in the theatre, this enjambment of lines, these broken hemistichs which send the classics to the devil, are to me a matter of complete indifference, because when spoken they sound just like prose . . . however, since *Hernani* has been written in verse, and since Hugo knows how to write verse when he wishes, it would have been simpler to make verses according to the customary rules and taste, that would have saved from much fatigue the lungs of the villains of the pit; it is an innovation which leads nowhere. But Hugo has destroyed the unity of time and place; for this reason alone I am interested in him as a brave fellow who has crossed fire to put a light to the mine which will blow up an old bulwark. . . .

To Ferrand

Paris, 13*th May* 1830.

. . . Your letter affected me excessively; your anxiety about the danger you imagined I was running in connection with Henriette Smithson, the outpourings of your heart, your advice! Ah, my dear Humbert, it is indeed a rare thing to find a complete man who has a soul, a heart, and imagination. . . .

I think you will be satisfied with the plan of my *Symphonie fantastique* which I sent you. . . . The vengeance is not too severe. Moreover, I did not write the vision of a night of revelry in that spirit. I have no desire for vengeance. I pity and despise her. She is but an ordinary type of woman, endowed with an instinctive power of expressing those pangs of the human soul which she has never felt, and incapable of entertaining a grand and noble sentiment such as that with which I have honoured her.[2]

---

[1] Victor Hugo's drama *Hernani*, performed for the first time, in Paris, on 25th February 1830. Berlioz was present on this famous occasion, which heralded the French Romantic Movement in literature.

[2] There is no authentic explanation of this change of attitude on the part of Berlioz towards Harriet Smithson. Whether it was due partly to gossip defamatory of her character, of which an actress is always liable to be the target, whether partly to the fact that in May she had descended from Shakespeare to a dumb role in a musical piece by a musician Berlioz despised, or whether a new attachment had chiefly to do with it, cannot now be determined.

To-day I am concluding my final arrangements for my concert on the 30th of this month . . . we shall begin the rehearsal of the *Symphonie gigantesque* [*sic*] in three days; all the parts have been copied out with scrupulous care; there are two thousand three hundred pages of music, nearly four hundred francs' worth of copying. . . . That wonderful singer Haitzinger[1] is to take part, and I hope to secure Mme Schroeder-Devrient,[2] who with her rival is enchanting the Salle Favart on alternate nights in *Der Freischütz* and *Fidelio*. . . .

I may tell you that you are almost at one with Onslow . . . about my *Mélodies*. He prefers . . . the *Chanson à boire*, the *Élégie*, the *Reverie*, and the *Chant sacré*. My dear fellow, it is not as difficult as you imagine, but it needs a pianist. When I write for the piano I write for people who know how to play, and not for amateurs who do not know even how to read music. The Mlles Lesueur, who certainly are not virtuosi, accompany the *Élégie en prose* very well, and it, with the *Chant guerrier*, is the least easy.

. . . But my symphony? I hope that unhappy woman will be present . . . if she reads the programme she cannot help recognizing herself. . . .

The projected concert did not take place on account of difficulties in getting singers and orchestra, but the *Figaro* printed the 'programme' of the *Symphonie fantastique*.

I do not propose to say much about the *Symphonie fantastique*, having given Berlioz's own analysis of it.[3] It is the best known of all his compositions and is one of the most original and astonishing works in the history of music. As the work of a young man of twenty-six it must be considered unique. It was composed in the three months from January to April 1830, but Berlioz made use of a certain amount of earlier music. For example the fourth movement, *Marche au supplice* (March to the Scaffold), was taken from the *Marche des gardes* in his opera *Les Francs-Juges*.[4] The third movement, *Scène aux champs* (Scene in the Fields), *adagio*, resembles in character a scene at the beginning of the second act of *Les Francs-Juges*

[1] A fine German tenor.

[2] The famous German opera singer. See Wagner's *Mein Leben*.

[3] It will be noticed that Berlioz originally placed the Ball Scene after the Scene in the Fields.

[4] This opera was never published or performed, although it was almost, if not quite, completed by Berlioz.

and, according to Adolphe Boschot who examined it in the Bibliothèque Nationale in Paris, the manuscript of the *Symphonie fantastique* contains pages taken straight out of *Les Francs-Juges* and still bearing that name.

Berlioz polished this score from time to time in later years, as was his general practice. As with Beethoven, we feel in most of his works a tremendous pressure of inspiration, and under this pressure there is no time at moments for detail. The thought must be caught as it flies and the work of exact adjustment and combination left for later. It is interesting to learn, however, from the same authority, Adolphe Boschot, that the original manuscript of the *Marche au supplice*[1] does not differ at all from the final printed version and is the same, apart from an interpolation of the *idée fixe*, as the earlier *Marche des gardes*. In this case it is an even more remarkable testimony to the extraordinary mastery of instrumentation which Berlioz had acquired before he was twenty-six. There was nobody living who could have taught him this.

One point, however, remains to be discussed, namely, whether the *Symphonie fantastique* is, or is not, music. Boschot states: 'This *Symphonie fantastique* (like almost all the work of Berlioz) is, and is not, music.' Edward Dannreuther,[2] a learned and conscientious musician, a friend and champion of Wagner, writes in the sixth volume of the *Oxford History of Music*: 'In a large part of the *Symphonie fantastique*, notably the finale, the music is sheer nonsense unless the hearer has knowledge of the programme; yet even if he has full knowledge, the heterogeneous factors interfere with one another, and leave an annoying sense of incoherence and incongruity.'

Almost everywhere Dannreuther's criticism of Berlioz (from which almost all English musicians and critics have taken their

[1] Sergei Rachmaninoff, the famous Russian musician, relates in his *Recollections* that he once heard Gustave Mahler in New York in 1909 rehearsing Berlioz's *La Vie d'un Artiste*, and that in the fourth movement (*Marche au supplice*) he obtained a *crescendo* of the brass instruments 'such as I have never before heard. . . . The very windows shook, the very walls seemed to vibrate.'

[2] See p. 78.

opinions of Berlioz) reveals, firstly, the fact that Berlioz's music is much more difficult of access than Wagner's, and secondly, that Dannreuther was incapable of understanding most of it. On the first point I would say that Berlioz's musical genius was of a much rarer type than that of Wagner, Brahms, Liszt, or any other of his contemporaries. In the work of every artist there is a stratum of convention, of cliché, of dead matter. It is this which helps the public to understand it. Some artists, however, have next to nothing of it. This does not necessarily make their work better—or so I will assume—but it does make it more individual and harder to understand. It is a very queer thing about Berlioz that still to-day, in spite of all the developments of the twentieth century in atonality and the like, his music every time we hear it strikes us by its originality. Now I think one reason for this (apart from his unique personality) is that there is practically no padding in Berlioz's music.[1] Even the most fanatical admirers of Wagner must admit that his music is full of padding; in fact one might say that his was the art of padding, the art of going on, page after page, saying nothing more, but seeming to say more by saying nothing.

Berlioz, on the contrary, is concise, epigrammatic, more personally expressive, and has a *far quicker pace*. Also, his musical cataclysms have more lightning in their thunder than Wagner's and are more strange and terrifying. I am not just now drawing a full comparison between Berlioz and his contemporaries or other great musicians, so I will not say any more in this direction. This comparison with Wagner is merely to give some reasons for the greater difficulty of Berlioz's music.

To come now to the point of the programme and the comprehensibility of the *Symphonie fantastique* without its literary programme. Now here the issue is narrowed down to one assertion against another. Dannreuther and those musicians who still think as he did are faced with an opposite assertion by those who think, as I do, that the literary programme of the *Symphonie fantastique* is wholly superfluous.

[1] The fact that he did not compose at the pianoforte is also contributory.

I ask any musician who reads these pages to consider the following facts. I would not venture to assert that my instinct for music was secondary to my instinct for words, yet what talent I have is entirely literary. But I do not need any programme—and never did need a programme—to understand Berlioz's *Symphonie fantastique*, my pleasure in hearing it being purely musical and precisely of the same nature as my pleasure in hearing any one of Beethoven's quartets. Further, I find the greatest difficulty in even reading the 'programmes' or literary explanations of pieces of music, and am never helped or in any way enlightened as to the music by them.[1]

I carry this so far that I have never even read and rarely understood the texts of the majority of operas I have heard. For me music always speaks adequately without any words, and I judge it (rightly or wrongly) without reference to words. Even in the case of a modern opera like *Wozzeck* [2] I have never read Büchner's play, and on the sole occasion on which I heard *Wozzeck* I did not understand one word in a hundred of the German text. But this did not prevent me from enjoying Berg's music or from having very definite opinions about it. In short, I am of the opinion that the whole ancient controversy about programme music was the result of a misconception and is a controversy about an illusion. The text of an opera, the words of a song, the programme of a symphony or tone poem or whatever name in the future may be given to any musical composition is of *no importance or significance whatever*. I know this will be going too far for the majority of musicians, nevertheless I am convinced that it is true, literally and strictly true.

In order, however, to help make my meaning clearer, I will offer an analogy. If a painter like Cézanne were to make two pictures, two 'still-lifes,' one a picture of an apple and one a picture of a pear; and suppose in the catalogue by a mistake 'The Pear' was numbered as 'The Apple,' and vice versa.

[1] One reason for this may be my literary sense, for all these texts and 'programmes' bore or irritate me by their (for me) unreadableness.

[2] *Wozzeck*, an opera by Alban Berg.

Now the fact that one picture had as its subject an apple and the other a pear would have no bearing on the pictorial or artistic merit of the paintings. In fact, when looking at them you wouldn't bother about the subjects 'apple' or 'pear' at all. But if you looked at the catalogue and saw the apple picture labelled as 'The Pear,' you would be worried at once. Why 'The Pear'? you would ask. And unless you noticed that the pear picture was labelled 'The Apple' and so surmised immediately that it was a simple mistake in cataloguing, you would be so fretted by this incongruity that you would no longer be able to look at the picture as a picture, a work of pictorial art, at all.

Now this is what happens with programme music and opera. Those whose innate sense of music is weak fasten on the label and cannot hear the music for seeing the label. Take the label off, bury it, and let them forget it utterly (if they can); and only then will they be able to listen to the music and hear what it is. But even then they may hear nothing at all, just as any one whose pictorial sense is weak is incapable of seeing a picture but sees only a likeness to something. If the likeness to the label is for him invisible he declares it to be a bad picture, but he really doesn't know what a picture *is*, good or bad. So those who say Berlioz's music is not music are simply saying they can't see its likeness to the label. To them I say, tear off the label, forget all about it and listen again. If they have ears they will find it is music, pure music. Indeed, what else can it be, being merely a succession of sounds? The merit of this sucession of sounds, its virtue, must be judged, can only be judged by listening to it and ignoring all words, labels, descriptions, analyses, and explanations.

Now, I am perfectly aware that a deeper question is involved here, namely, the relation of the artist to his nominal subject. But people in general are not discussing this problem when they are discussing 'programme' music, abstract or representative art, or 'pure' poetry; and I do not propose to discuss it either, for this is not the place for it. I will only say that in any case what is primarily important is the *relationship* between the artist and his subject. One can no more estimate the value of the *subject in itself* in a work of art than one can estimate the relative value of a sparrow or an eagle, a vegetable or a man, in the love of God. It is the love that gives value, and I do not propose, I repeat, to attempt to explain why God loves a sparrow or why Berlioz loves Harriet Smithson and composes a *Symphonie fantastique* rather than a string quartet. The value of the *Symphonie fantastique*—as of the C sharp minor Quartet (Beethoven's Opus 131)—depends equally upon what Berlioz and Beethoven respectively *give* in their work. If Van Gogh chooses to paint a sunflower and Rembrandt an old woman, the virtue of their pictures depends entirely upon Van Gogh and on Rembrandt, and not upon the sunflower or the woman —which have both been the subjects of many lifeless and valueless but recognizable paintings. And if any humanist says there is more life in an old woman than in a sunflower, I reply, 'How do you know?' It may be so, but to choose an old woman rather than a sunflower as a subject of a picture does not ensure a better picture.

I therefore dismiss all this loose talk of 'pure' music in the abstract as leading nowhere. We can only judge music as music, and its value is entirely independent of its programme or label. If any one says to me that Beethoven's Pastoral Symphony is inferior to his Second Symphony because the former has a 'programme' and the latter has none, I simply do not understand him; his words seem to me to have no more meaning than if he were to say that the Sixth Symphony was inferior to the second because six is an inferior number to two, or vice versa.

This *Episode in the Life of an Artist* (*Symphonie fantastique*) is as genuine a musical creation, wholly musical and nothing else, as any quartet by Mozart or symphony by Beethoven. It is completely convincing and *lives* from the first bar to the last. It is in the strictest meaning of the term a masterpiece, and is completely intelligible to any musician without a word of explanation or programme. And we may truthfully add, that no composer has ever written anything like it either before or since, nor will anything like it ever be written in the future. For this *is* Berlioz just as the Ninth Symphony or the Hammerklavier Sonata *is* Beethoven. And neither Berlioz nor Beethoven will ever come again.[1]

The best criticism of the *Symphonie fantastique* is still that by Schumann in 1835. Schumann said that the prospectus (programme) of the symphony could be ignored, but that you couldn't change a note of the music without harming it. Many other things are said in his long analysis, but when he had said that he had said everything. It is noteworthy that when Schumann wrote this famous article[2] he had only Liszt's pianoforte arrangement before him (Berlioz's score was not then published) and he had never heard the work performed.

[1] Note the selection of the pieces. There are works by Berlioz and Beethoven of a less personal character.

[2] Schumann's *Gesammelte Schriften*, vol. I, pp. 118 onwards.

CHAPTER X

A 'DISTRACTION' AND THE PRIZE

SOME time in the spring of 1830 Berlioz had become acquainted with a young girl, Marie (Camille) Moke, who taught the pianoforte at the same school where he taught the guitar. She was a very talented pianist, extremely attractive, nineteen years old, and a friend of Berlioz's friend Hiller, his seraph or good angel.[1] Berlioz seems to have replaced Hiller in her affections or interest about the time the *Symphonie fantastique* was concluded, for we find him writing to Ferrand as follows:

PARIS, *24th July* 1830.

. . . How lazy you are! for I hope you are not ill. I am still awaiting your letter. Fortunately, my dear friend, everything is going well.

All the tenderness and delicacy that love can hold, I possess. My ravishing sylph, my Ariel, my life, appears to love me more than ever. As for me, her mother is incessantly repeating that if she were to read in a novel the description of a love like mine she would not believe it.[2]

We have been separated for a few days, as I have been shut up in the Institut *for the last time.* I must win the prize, for upon it depends our happiness in a great measure; like Don Carlos in *Hernani*, I say '*je l'aurai.*' She torments herself by thinking of it continually. To give me some comfort in my imprisonment, Mme Moke sends her maidservant to me every other day with a message telling me how they are going on and asking for news of me. What ecstasy when I see her again in some ten or twelve days hence! We shall in all probability have many obstacles to overcome, but we shall conquer them. What do you think of all that? Can you imagine anything like it—such an angel, and the *most striking talent in Europe*! It has recently come to my knowledge that M. de Noailles, in whom the mother has great confidence, actually pleaded my cause and was strongly of the opinion that, as her daughter loved me, she should be given to me without so much importance being attached to the monetary side of the question. My dear fellow, if you only heard her *thinking about* the sublime conceptions of Weber and Beethoven you would lose your head. I have so strongly advised her not to play any *adagio* movements that I hope she will not often do so. Such engrossing music kills her.[3] Of late she has been in such suffering that she thought she was

[1] See p. 125. [2] A sidelight on the character of the mother.
[3] She outlived Berlioz.

going to die; she urged that I should be sent for, but her mother refused. On the following day I saw her, pale and lying on a sofa. How we wept! She was under the impression that she had something the matter with her chest. I thought I should die with her, and I told her so; she made no reply, but the idea was a source of infinite pleasure to me. When she got well she reproached me for having entertained it.

'Do you think God has given you musical organization for nothing? You have no right to abandon the task confided to you; I forbid you to follow me if I die.'

But she will not die. No, those eyes so full of genius, that slender figure, all that delicious being is more fit to wing its flight towards the skies than to lie withered beneath the humid ground. . . .

PARIS, *23rd August* 1830.

You have left me for a very long time without any news of you. Something altogether out of the common is evidently necessary to induce you to take hold of a pen—but I will not reproach you.

The prize [1] was awarded to me unanimously, the first time such a thing has been known. So the Institut is conquered. The noise of the salute and the *feu de joie* [2] had a favourable effect upon my last piece which I was at that time finishing.

Oh, my friend, what happiness it is to have achieved a victory which is a source of enchantment to a being beloved! My idolized Camille was almost dead with anxiety when I brought her, last Thursday, the news so ardently longed for. Oh, my *delicate Ariel*, my sweet angel, your wings were all ruffled, but joy has given them back their lustre; even her mother, who looks upon our love with a certain amount of disfavour,[3] could not help shedding tears of tenderness.[4]

I never suspected it, but in order not to alarm me she had persistently concealed the immense importance she attached to the prize. . . .

My scene will be performed in public with full orchestra on 2nd October; my sweet Camille will be there with her mother. . . . This ceremony, which without her would be childish in my eyes, will become an intoxicating fête. . . .

---

[1] Grand Prix de Rome. It gave Berlioz a pension of 3,000 francs a year for five years, the free entry to all the subsidized theatres, and obliged him to stay for two years in Italy and a year in Germany.

[2] There was a revolution in Paris while Berlioz was shut up in the Institut competing for his prize. King Charles X lost his throne and fled, to be succeeded by Louis Philippe.

[3] She heartily disliked Berlioz; it infuriated her that this young man should talk so wildly about love and not about money.

[4] It is even possible. Berlioz's fury of happiness must have been overwhelming.

I am going to write [for the director of the Théâtre-Italien] an overture to *The Tempest* of Shakespeare, for pianoforte, chorus, and orchestra. It will be a new style of piece. On 14th November I shall give my monster concert, for the production of my *Symphonie fantastique*. . . . In the course of the winter the Concert Society will perform my overture to *Les Francs-Juges*. . . . But I must achieve a success at the theatre; my happiness depends upon it. Camille's parents cannot give their consent to our marriage until that has been accomplished.[1] . . . I do not want to go to Italy and I shall ask the king to dispense with that ridiculous journey in my case. . . .

I have just relinquished the hand of my adored Camille and that is the reason why mine shakes so and I am writing so badly. She has, however, played neither Weber nor Beethoven to me to-day.

That wretched girl Smithson is still here. I have never set eyes upon her since my return.

Berlioz's treatment of his passion for Camille Moke in his *Mémoires* is wholly inadequate. Since it was written many years later, after the fatal disillusionment which he was soon to experience, he was at pains to minimize the extent of his interest in her and he heads the chapter (XXVIII) devoted to her: 'Distraction violente.—F. H ***. Mlle M ***.'[2] One must remember that Berlioz expressly asserts more than once in his *Mémoires* that he is not writing his confessions but composing a book. This book, like every work of art, must have truth as a basis, but the author has the right when it comes to intimate personal matters to throw dust in his readers' eyes. This Berlioz does plentifully.

This experience with Camille Moke was in reality a profound humiliation, but Berlioz hides the fact, pretending that Camille Moke's 'irritating beauty' merely set his senses aflame and that this passion had no resemblance to the complete, grand, and profound passion which he had felt and continued to feel for Harriet Smithson. That there was a difference is possible, but the contemporary letters I have already quoted show that

[1] Berlioz's illusion as to the character of his new beloved and her mother was complete; but it must be remembered that he was only twenty-six and that Camille was very attractive and a highly gifted musician.

[2] The initials 'F. H.' stand for Ferdinand Hiller, Berlioz's predecessor in the 'affections' of Miss Moke.

Berlioz was in love to a far greater degree than he admits later. And he does not even mention the fact that he and Camille Moke became, as we shall see, regularly engaged to be married.

The following letter to Ferrand, dated October 1830, gives a vivid picture of Berlioz's state of mind:

Oh, my dear, my inexpressibly dear friend! I am writing to you from the Champs-Élysées, in the corner of an arbour exposed to the setting sun. I see its golden rays glistening upon the dead or dying leaves of the young trees which surround my retreat. I have been talking about you all day to one who understands, or rather divines, your soul. I am irresistibly compelled to write to you. What are you doing? You are eating away your heart, I would wager, by reason of misfortunes which only affect you in imagination; there are so many which touch us nearly, that it grieves me to see you succumb under the weight of sorrow to which you are a stranger, or from which you are removed. Why? Why? I understand it better than you imagine; it is your existence, your poetry, your *Chateaubriandisme*.

I suffer strangely from not seeing you; chained down as I am, I am powerless to annihilate the space which divides us. And yet I have so much to say to you. If any good fortune which falls to my lot can serve to lighten your sombre thoughts, I can tell you that my music is to be performed at the Opéra in the course of this month. To my adored Camille once more I owe this honour. And this is how it came about.

In her slender form, her capricious flight, her distracting grace, and her musical genius I recognized the Ariel of Shakespeare.[1] My poetic ideas, attracted by the drama of *The Tempest*, have inspired me with a gigantic overture, in an entirely novel style for orchestra, chorus, two pianos (each four hands), and *harmonica*.[2] I proposed it to the director of the Opéra and he has undertaken to produce it. . . .

My dear fellow, it is far grander than the overture to *Les Francs-Juges*. It is entirely new. With what profound adoration did I thank my idolized Camille for having inspired me with this composition! I told her a short time ago that my work was going to be performed and she literally trembled with joy.[3] I told her confidentially, whispered it in

---

[1] Harriet Smithson becomes Ophelia, and Camille Moke Ariel. Is it not curious, this persistent Shakespearizing of Berlioz?

[2] A musical instrument made of glasses. Gluck gave a concert in London on 23rd April 1746, at which he played violin and harpsichord music on a harmonica.

[3] Prosaic minds will feel very superior when they read such expressions and will think of Berlioz as an undisciplined, over-excitable fellow. If you think this, dear reader, I can only envy your calmness!' But, of course, Camille did not tremble, it was only Berlioz.

her ear, after two devouring kisses and a mad embrace, love, grand and poetic, as *we* understand it. . . .

My dear Ferrand, if I die, do not turn monk, as you have threatened you will, I beseech you; live as prosaically as you can; it is the best mode of being—prosaic. . . . I hear people singing that wretched *Parisienne.*[1] Some half-intoxicated National Guards are bellowing it in all its platitude.

Good-bye; the marble slab on which I am writing is freezing my arm. I think of unhappy Ophelia; ice, cold, the damp ground, Polonius dead, Hamlet living. She is very unfortunate! By the failure of the Opéra-Comique she has lost more than six thousand francs. She is still here; I met her recently. She recognized me with the greatest calmness. I suffered throughout the whole evening and then I went and told the graceful Ariel all about it.

'Well,' said she, with a smile; 'you were not upset, were you? You did not faint?'

'No, no, no, my angel, my genius, my art, my every thought, my heart, my poetic life! I suffered without a groan, for I thought of thee; I adored thy power: I blessed my cure; I braved, in my isle of delight, the bitter waves which broke against it; I saw the vessel shipwrecked,[2] and casting a glance at my leafy bower, I blessed the bed of roses whereon I could lie. And Ariel, Camille, I adore you, I bless you, in a word, I *love you*, more than the weak French tongue can say; give me an orchestra of a hundred performers and a chorus of a hundred and fifty voices and I will tell you.'

Ferrand, my friend, adieu; the sun has set, I see it no longer, adieu; more ideas, adieu; far more sentiment, adieu. It is six o'clock, I need an hour to reach Camille. Adieu.

In a letter to his younger sister Adèle, dated Thursday, 21st October 1830, Berlioz refers to Camille, for he has now told his family of his desired marriage, and is treated indulgently;[3] his official success as crowned laureate of the Institut naturally having completely justified his choice of a career. Adèle was his favourite sister; he adds:

What are your winter prospects? Always the same monotony, the same boredom? Your sister was not so constructed as to be enlivening

---

[1] This song by Casimir Delavigne nearly became the French national anthem, the *Marseillaise* being neglected during the Restoration.

[2] *The Tempest.*

[3] Berlioz's father writes to Lesueur: 'If my son already finds himself on the threshold of the Temple of Glory and Fortune; it is to your affectionate advice, to your scholarly lessons, it is to you, his master and his friend, that he owes all this.'

. . . nor your brother (the elder, I mean); perhaps Prosper's teasings will make you lose patience and distract you a little. . . .

M. Amédée will give you a crystal-glass which I want you to keep always out of affection for me. I should have liked to find something more interesting to send you, but I thought that an object which you would be using twice a day would recall me oftener to your mind and that is why I chose it.

Adieu, my dear Adèle. I embrace you tenderly.

The crowned cantata with which Berlioz gained the Grand Prix was *Sardanapale*.[1] Before the official performance on 30th October 1830 he added ('fearing the academicians no more,' as he writes to his father) a piece descriptive of the burning of the palace of Sardanapalus, in which he let himself go.

On 7th November, at a benefit performance for pensions at the Opéra (rue Lepelletier), Berlioz's *Grande Ouverture pour La Tempête* (*Drame de William Shakespeare*) [2] for orchestra, choir, two pianos (four hands), and harmonica, was performed, and Ferdinand Hiller was one of the pianists. Berlioz thought this was an entirely new combination, Beethoven's Fantasia for choir, pianoforte, and orchestra, Opus 80, being probably unknown to him.[3]

On 19th November 1830 he writes to Ferrand:

At two o'clock on 5th December I am to give a concert at the Conservatoire in which will be performed the overture to *Les Francs-Juges*, the *Chant sacré* and the *Chant guerrier* out of the *Mélodies*, the scene from *Sardanapale* with a hundred performers for the conflagration, and lastly the *Symphonie fantastique*.

Come, come; it will be awful! Habeneck will conduct the gigantic orchestra. I count upon you.

The overture to *La Tempête* will be performed for the second time, next week at the Opéra. Oh, my dear, new, fresh, strange, great, sweet, tender, brilliant—that is what it is. The Storm . . . has had an extraordinary success. Fétis has devoted two superb articles to me in the *Revue musicale*.

[1] *Sardanapale* has never been published and the manuscript seems to be missing, although it ought to be in the possession of the Institut or the library of the Conservatoire.

[2] This work was included in the following year (1831) in a new composition, *Lélio; ou le Retour à la Vie*, of which it forms the final movement.

[3] This work of Beethoven's has only once been performed in my time in London, through the suggestion of Artur Schnabel who played the pianoforte part.

He said the other day to somebody who remarked that I had the devil in my body, 'If he has the devil in his body, he has a god in his head.'

Come, come—the 5th of December—Sunday; an orchestra of a hundred and ten performers—Conflagration—*Symphonie fantastique*[1]—Come, come!

Two brief letters to Ferrand will bring to a conclusion this year of triumph for Berlioz:

7th December 1830.

MY DEAR FRIEND,

This time you absolutely must come. I have had an unheard-of success. The *Symphonie fantastique* was received with shouts of applause; the *Marche au supplice* was encored; the satanic effect of the *Sabbat* was overwhelming. I have been so pressed to do it that I shall repeat my concert on the 27th of this month. You will be there, will you not? I expect you.

Good-bye. I am thoroughly over-wrought. Spontini has read your poem of the *Francs-Juges*; he told me this evening that he would much like to see you; he leaves six days hence.

On 11th December 1830 Berlioz celebrated his twenty-seventh birthday. On the next day he wrote to Ferrand:

I cannot give my second concert for several reasons. I shall leave Paris at the beginning of January. My marriage is put off till Easter 1832, on condition that I do not lose my pension and that I go to Italy for a year. My music has compelled the consent of Camille's mother. My dear *Symphonie*, to it I shall owe her.

I shall be at La Côte towards the 15th of January. I must absolutely see you; arrange so that we may not miss each other. . . .

Spontini sent me a superb present yesterday; it is the score of his *Olympie*, worth a hundred and twenty francs, and on the title-page he has written with his own hand, 'My dear Berlioz, when you look at this score, think sometimes of your affectionate Spontini.'

I am in a state of intoxication! Camille, ever since she heard my *Sabbat*, calls me nothing but 'her dear Lucifer, her handsome Satan.'

Good-bye, my dear fellow, write me a long letter immediately, I conjure you. Your devoted friend for all time.

At Berlioz's concert on 5th December 1830, when the *Symphonie fantastique* was performed for the first time, Liszt[2]

[1] The first performance of this work.

[2] Liszt, Franz (1811–86), one of the greatest pianists of all time, a remarkable composer, and the most enlightened Mecaenas of music in the nineteenth century.

was among the auditors; he was then only nineteen years of age, but already a famous, much-travelled virtuoso. In a letter written by Berlioz to his father, dated 6th December, the day after the concert, he says: 'Liszt, the celebrated pianist, carried me off, as it were by force, to dine with him, overwhelming me with the most vigorous enthusiasm.'

This, the first meeting between Berlioz and Liszt, was the most important external event in Berlioz's musical career. Liszt never forgot the impression made on him by Berlioz's music; a little later he made the brilliant pianoforte version of the *Symphonie fantastique* which first made this work known to German musicians and on which—as we have seen—Schumann wrote his famous criticism. In after years, when Berlioz was neglected by his own countrymen, Liszt, as we shall see, fought for Berlioz's music by his pen, his personal influence, and, best of all, by constantly performing his works. In this same letter to his father about his concert on 5th December, Berlioz writes:

'Pixis,[1] Spontini, Meyerbeer, Fétis applauded like furies and Spontini declared on hearing my *Marche au supplice*, "There has never been but one man capable of a similar piece, and that is Beethoven; it is prodigious."'

Berlioz's last letter of the year 1830 is dated 29th December and is addressed to Rouget de Lisle, the then almost forgotten author of the words and music of the *Marseillaise*. Berlioz had orchestrated this famous song and received a letter from the composer dated Choisy-le-Roi, 20th December 1830,[2] asking for a meeting. The story is told in full in the *Mémoires*, but I cannot help quoting the characteristic Berliozian substitution on his score of the *Marseillaise* for the words, 'tenors, basses,' the words: 'All who have a voice, a heart, and blood in their veins.'

[1] Pixis, Johann-Peter, a German composer.

[2] Printed in Berlioz's *Mémoires*, chap. XXIX, p. 103. It is worth mentioning as an example of the civilization of this epoch, about 1830 onwards, that King Louis Philippe gave Rouget de Lisle a pension.

BOOK III
(1831–1843)

CHAPTER I

SHATTERED ILLUSIONS

BERLIOZ arrived at La Côte-Saint-André on 3rd January 1831 for a short stay with his family before proceeding to Rome, as the regulations of the Institut prescribed. His despair at leaving Camille Moke, to whom he was now regularly engaged, seems to have been accentuated either by the absence of letters from her or by the tone of her letters. A few extracts from his letters will best depict his state of mind:

TO FERRAND

CÔTE-SAINT-ANDRÉ, *6th January* 1831.

I have been staying with my father since Monday last; and I am now on the eve of beginning my fatal journey to Italy. I cannot bear the idea of this harrowing separation; the tender affection of my parents and the caresses of my sisters can scarcely distract me. I must absolutely see you before my departure. . . . So many storms threaten both of us that it seems to me to be necessary that we shall be near each other to resist them. We understand each other, and that is so rare a thing. . . .

TO FERDINAND HILLER

CÔTE-SAINT-ANDRÉ, *9th January* 1831.

I have been with my father now for eight days, surrounded by a tender and affectionate family and friends, overwhelmed with every kind of compliment and felicitation; but my heart beats with such difficulty and I am so oppressed that I do not speak ten words in an hour . . . Will you please put this letter in the post for me.

TO THE SAME

CÔTE-SAINT-ANDRÉ, *23rd January* 1831.

I have just been making a stupid stay at Grenoble. . . . I arrived here yesterday, after having spent a wearisome day without saying a word. My father, who had just been informed of my state by my mother, embraced me silently and told me that there was a letter from Paris for me. I gathered from his manner that it was from Madame; in fact it was a double letter and I became calm; I was as delighted as I could be in such detestable exile. To-day your letter must needs arrive to upset my tranquillity. The devil take you! What need had you to tell me that I delight in a despair for which nobody thanks me, 'nobody so little as the people for whom I give way to despair.'

First, let me tell you I do not lapse into despair for the sake of *people*; next, I say, if you have your reasons for judging severely the person for whom I give way to despair I have mine also for assuring you that at present I know her character *better than any one else.* I know very well that *she* does not despair; the proof of that is my being here, and the fact that had she persisted in begging me not to go away, as she has done on several occasions, I should have stayed. Why should she despair? She knows very well what to believe as far as I am concerned; she knows now all the devotion of my heart for her (not all, however; there is still a sacrifice, the greatest of all, which she does not know and which I will make for her). You do not know what torments me, nobody *but she* knows it and not long ago even she did not know it.

Do not give me any of your epicurean advice, it does not suit me in the least. It is the means to the attainment of a slight happiness and I will have none of that. Supreme happiness or death, a life of poetry or annihilation. So, do not talk to me of a superb woman with a magnificent figure, and of the part *shared or not shared* in my griefs by those who are dear to me; because you know nothing about it, who has told you?

You do not know what she feels or thinks. Because you have seen her gay and content at a concert is no ground for drawing a conclusion adverse to me. If it were, what would you not be able to conclude from my behaviour at Grenoble; if you had seen me one day at a large family dinner, having on my right and left charming young women (cousins), seventeen and eighteen years old, with whom I joked and laughed in rare fashion?[1]

My letter is brusque, my friend, but you have ruffled me horribly. . . .

To the Same

31st January 1831.

Although my consuming agitation has not ceased for a moment since I arrived here, to-day, however, I am able to write to you more calmly. Seeing that you have already at your age hit upon a vein of gold in this paltry mine in which we are all digging, hasten to follow it up to the end; but remember that you are in a tunnel which you hollow out as you advance and which may subside behind you.

The blunder you have made in asking Cherubini for the hall of the Conservatoire before the Concert Society had finished is unpardonable. You ought to have known very well that it would never be allowed, and it is

[1] A very good example of Berlioz's solid common sense.

very unpleasant to find oneself thwarted by a will against which one's own is powerless. I cannot help telling you that you occasionally act too hastily. Reflection, and plenty of it, is absolutely necessary before undertaking anything, and when once your mind is made up you should strike to such purpose that all obstacles fall to pieces before you. . . .

Although I am compelled to be mysterious about a frightful annoyance which I shall have to suffer from perhaps for some time yet; it refers to circumstances in my life which are known to nobody (except C——); I have at least the consolation of having told her without . . . but enough.

Although forced to be mysterious with you on this point, I do not see that you have any reason to be so with me on others. I beg of you, therefore, to let me know what you mean by this sentence in your last letter: 'You want to make a sacrifice; I have long been afraid of one which, unfortunately, I have every reason to believe you will make one day.'

To what do you allude? I entreat you never to use in your letters ambiguous phrases, above all, where she is concerned. They only torture me. Do not forget to give me a frank explanation of this. Write to me *poste restante*, Rome, and prepay your letter as far as the frontier, otherwise it will not reach me.

To Ferrand

Lyons, *Thursday, 9th February* 1831.

Instead of this letter you ought to have received me, my very self in person. . . . I even engaged a seat in the *diligence* and paid the full price down. Finally, after changing my mind, I do not know how many times I decided upon not going to see you. In spite of the state of torture in which I am; despite the overpowering desire I have to reach Italy, so that I may be able to come back again as soon as possible, notwithstanding the weather and the distance I should have gone . . . But a few random words which I heard yesterday made me afraid that I should have a cool reception at the hands of your parents, and that your mother, especially, would be anything but charmed to see me. . . .

I start for Marseilles in four hours' time. I shall return, hissing like a red-hot cannon-ball. Meet me at Lyons; I shall only call at La Côte. My address at Rome will be: Hector Berlioz, student of the Académie de Rome, Villa Medici, Rome.

Good-bye; a thousand maledictions on you, myself, and all nature. Suffering is driving me mad.

To reach Rome Berlioz took first a boat from Marseilles to Leghorn, then proceeded overland by way of Florence. From Marseilles he wrote a letter to his sister Adèle on 12th February, expressing his delight with the sea; on 2nd March he wrote to his father from Florence, describing the fearful storm the boat had encountered in the Gulf of Genoa.[1] He also tells him that he has had no letter from Camille and that in Florence he has seen a new opera by Bellini, *Roméo et Juliette*, which he describes as 'ignoble, ridiculous, impotent, null.'

On Berlioz's arrival in Rome at the Villa Medici, whose director was the well-known painter Horace Vernet, the other pensioners—sculptors, painters, musicians—nicknamed him straightway 'Père la Joie' (Father Joy). He must have presented an indescribable appearance, oppressed as he was by fearful forebodings.[2] There is a portrait of him made later in this year (1831) by Signol, one of the young painters at the Villa Medici; it still hangs, I understand, on the walls of the Villa Medici, but even the reproductions of it are sufficiently striking to give one an idea of the extraordinary appearance of this young man with his hooked nose, grey-blue eyes, well-cut mouth and chin, and enormous mop of chestnut hair. An appropriate nickname is often of profound significance, and 'Father Joy' is, as a brief description of Berlioz, one of the most fitting imaginable.

Among the young musicians in Rome was Mendelssohn,[3] aged twenty-two, and thus about five years younger than Berlioz. They met almost immediately, and Mendelssohn wrote to his mother on 29th March a letter which I will quote presently. But Berlioz, a prey to agitation, could not conceal his growing anxiety and impatience; he had not been quite three weeks in Rome when on 1st April, having received no letter from Camille, he left for France via Florence, at the risk of losing his pension if he passed the Italian frontier.

On reaching Florence he was taken ill with a bad throat.

[1] I will not transcribe this letter, as Berlioz has given a superb description of this storm in chap. xxxii of his *Mémoires*.

[2] No letter for him at Rome. Only those who know what it is to have suffered in their youth in this way, awaiting a letter, can understand Berlioz's situation in those days of slow communications.

[3] Mendelssohn-Bartholdy, Felix (1809–47), the famous composer.

He sends a letter to his friend Pixis, asking for information about Camille and her mother, and then sends the following remarkable letter to Ferrand:

FLORENCE, *12th April* 1831.

Oh, my sublime friend! You are the first Frenchman who has given me any sign that he is alive since my arrival in this garden, peopled by monkeys, which is called *La Belle Italie* ! I have this moment received your letter; it has been sent on to me from Rome, and has taken seven days, instead of two, to come here. It is all right—curse it! Yes, everything is right because everything is wrong! What am I to say to you? I left Rome with the full intention of returning to France, letting my pension go to the winds because I had no letter from Camille.[1] An infernal sore throat kept me prisoner here; I wrote to Rome to ask that my letters might be forwarded, and but for that yours would have been lost, which would have been a pity. How do I know whether I shall receive any others?

Do not write to me any more, because I cannot tell you where to address your letters. I am like a lost balloon, destined to burst in mid-air, or to be engulfed in the sea, or to be brought to a standstill like Noah's ark; if I reach the top of Mount Ararat safe and sound I will write to you at once. . . .

I quite appreciate your disgust and anger in regard to what is going on in Europe. Even I, although I do not take the least interest in it, find myself giving way to an oath! Liberty, forsooth—where is it? Where was it? Where can it be in this half-hearted world? No, my dear fellow, the human race is too grovelling and too stupid for the sweet goddess to bestow upon it one divine ray from her eyes.

You talk to me about music—about love! What do you mean? I do not understand you. Are there such things on earth as those we call music and love? I fancy I have heard, as in a dream, these two words of sinister augury.[2] Unhappy mortal that you are to believe in them; as for me, I believe in nothing at all.[3]

I should like to go to Calabria or Sicily, to enlist under the command of some *bravo* chief or other, even as a simple brigand. At all events I should witness magnificent crimes, robbery, assassination, abduction,

---

[1] Berlioz's solid sense intervened, once he had partly satisfied his restlessness by leaving Rome, and made him wait at Florence a little in the hope of news.

[2] Correct, as we shall see.

[3] In 1853 Berlioz, at the request of Professor Lobe, wrote a confession of faith for Lobe's paper, *Fliegende Blätter für Musik*. This remarkable and almost unknown document the reader will find reproduced on p. 351 of this volume.

incendiarism, instead of all these petty wickednesses and dastardly outrages which turn me sick. Yes, this is the world for me—a volcano, rocks, stolen treasure heaped up in cases, a concert of shouts of horror to the accompaniment of an orchestra of pistols and guns, blood and lachryma Christi, a bed of lava rocked by earthquakes—that would be life indeed! But there are not even any brigands near.[1] O Napoleon, Napoleon, genius, power, strength, will! Why did you not crush in your iron grasp one more handful of this human vermin. Colossus with feet of brass, how would your slightest movement overthrow all their patriotic, philanthropic, philosophic edifices! Absurd rabble!

And they speak of thought, imagination, disinterestedness, even poetry, as if it all existed for them.

Such pygmies to talk of Shakespeare, Beethoven, and Weber! But what a fool I am to concern myself about them. What is the whole world to me, except three or four individuals in it? They may extol themselves as much as they please; it is not for me to pick them up out of the mire. Besides, it may all be nothing but a tissue of illusions. There is nothing true except life and death. I met the old sorceress out at sea. Our ship, after a sublime storm which lasted for two days, nearly foundered in the Gulf of Genoa; a squall laid us on our beam-ends. In a moment I was enveloped, legs and arms, in my cloak so that I might not be able to swim; everything was giving way, everything was sinking, within and without. I laughed as I saw the white valleys coming to cradle me in my last sleep; the sorceress came on with a grin, thinking to frighten me, and as I was preparing to spit in her face the vessel righted—she disappeared. . . .

When in Rome I wanted to buy a piece by Weber. I went to a music shop, and asked the proprietor for it.

'Weber, che cosa è? Non conosco. Maestro italiano, francese, ossia tedesco?'

'Tedesco,' I replied gravely.

The man searched for a long time, and then said with a self-satisfied air:

'Niente da Weber, niente di questa musica, caro signore.'

Idiot!

'Ma ecco *El Pirata*, *La Straniera*, *I Montecchi e Capuletti*, dal celeberrimo maestro Signor Vincenzo Bellini; ecco *La Vestale*, *I Arabi* del Maestro Paccini.'

---

[1] This is no mere momentary fancy of Berlioz's. We shall see that these things he described are what most genuinely appealed to him in Italy. He actually spent most of his time there wandering alone over the country around Rome and Naples like a solitary brigand with a gun and a guitar, fraternizing with the peasants. He was not attracted much by Rome's aesthetic treasures.

BERLIOZ IN 1831
Signol

'Basta, basta, non avete dunque vergogna, corpo di Dio?'

What was to be done? Sigh? That is childish. Gnash one's teeth? That has become idiotic. Have patience? That is still worse. One must concentrate a dose of poison, letting a portion of it evaporate so that the rest may have all the more strength, and then shut it up in one's heart until the end comes. . . .

Two days after sending Ferrand the above letter, on 14th April 1831, Berlioz at last received a letter from Paris, not from Camille but from her mother, announcing the marriage of her daughter to M. Pleyel, the maker of pianofortes.[1] In his *Mémoires* [2] Berlioz has described this epistle as 'of an impudence so extraordinary and so wounding for a man of my age and character at that time that it had a frightful effect on me. Tears of rage rushed to my eyes and my decision was made instantly. It was to go to Paris, where I must kill without mercy two guilty women and one innocent man.' In order to get into their presence unsuspected he bought in Florence as a disguise the clothes of a lady's maid, also two pistols, some laudanum and strychnine. He then set forth via Genoa. When he arrived at Genoa the disguise was missing from his luggage, so he bought another there and proceeded.

No doubt the time travelling took in those days helped him to digest his experience, and on the way from Genoa to Nice the first sign of his restoration to comparative equilibrium was the fact that he sent a letter to Horace Vernet at Rome, asking him to retain him on the list of pensioners of the Academy of France, if he had not already been crossed off, and promising on his honour not to cross the frontier out of Italy until he had received Vernet's reply at Nice,[3] where he would await it.

[1] Pleyel, Camille, was the eldest son of Ignaz Pleyel, the Austrian founder of the famous French firm of pianoforte makers. His wife (Berlioz's Camille) continued her career after her marriage and, as Madame Pleyel, became one of the most famous pianists of the age.

[2] The story told in the *Mémoires* is purposely vague and gives no idea of the real situation. Reading only the *Mémoires*, one would not even know what this letter was about or why Berlioz would dream of killing 'two guilty women and one innocent man.'

[3] Nice or, in Italian, Nizza, belonged then to Italy.

While waiting in Florence he had begun to compose a coda to the Ball Scene of the *Symphonie fantastique* and had read Shakespeare's *King Lear* and begun an overture on this subject. At Nice he received a most benevolent reply from Horace Vernet, informing him that he was still on the list of pensioners and that the Ministry would not be informed of his escapade, and assuring him of a hearty welcome on his return to Rome. Immensely relieved, he stayed at Nice and began slowly to recover from the fearful shock he had received. After all, it was final and better than the intolerable suspense and uncertainty which he had been suffering for months. He then wrote a letter to his friends in Paris:

To MM. Gounet, Girard, Hiller, Desmarest, Richard, and Sichel

Come, Gounet, read us your letter. Nice, *6th May* 1831.

In the first place, I embrace you all; I am delighted to see you once more, to find myself again near friends whose affection is so dear to me and to chat with you about music, enthusiasm, genius—in a word, *poetry*. I am saved, I begin to see that I am reborn better than I was and I have no longer any rage in my soul. As I have not written to you since my departure from France, I must tell you about my voyage. . . .

I experienced a very kindly reception from M. Horace and his family; but when old Carle Vernet found that I admired Gluck he would hardly leave me, 'Because, you see,' he said, 'M. Despréaux would have it that all that was rococo and that Gluck was out of date.'[1]

I have met Mendelssohn; Montfort[2] had already made his acquaintance, and we speedily fraternized. He is an admirable fellow, his executive talent is on a par with his musical genius, which is saying a great deal. All that I have heard of his music has charmed me, and I firmly believe that he is one of the greatest musical talents of the period. He has been my cicerone. I called on him every morning; he played me a sonata of Beethoven's, we sang Gluck's *Armide*, then he took me to see all the famous ruins which, I admit, impressed me very little. Mendelssohn is one of those candid souls one meets so rarely; he believes firmly in his Lutheran religion and I much scandalized him more than once by laughing at the Bible. I owe him the only tolerable moments I had during my stay in Rome. I was a prey to anxiety; I never had a single letter from

[1] How little the world changes in some respects!

[2] Montfort was the other winner of the Grand Prix for music.

my *faithful fiancée*, and but for M. Horace I would have left at the end of three days. . . . As I was no better off at the end of the month I left on Good Friday. . . . Mendelssohn would not believe that I really meant to go; he bet me a dinner for three that I would not start, and we ate it with Montfort on Good Friday, when he saw that M. Vernet had paid my fare and that I had ordered my carriage.

At Florence I got a bad throat. . . . There I read for the first time *King Lear*, and exclaimed aloud in admiration of this work of genius. I thought I should burst with enthusiasm and I rolled in the grass, it 's a fact, rolled convulsively to give expression to my feelings of rapture. . . .

Here I am restored; I eat as usual, although for some time I have only been able to swallow oranges. In short, I am saved and they are saved. I return again to life with delight; I throw myself into the arms of music and feel more vividly than ever the happiness of having friends. I beg all of you, Richard, Gounet, Girard, Desmarest, Hiller, to write to me, each separately, a letter. . . .

Gounet, Mlle Vernet has sung your melodies [1] and finds the verses full of grace and freshness.

Is the German theatre open? And Paganini? And *Euryanthe* [2] . . . that wretch Castil-Blaze has again mutilated this score by making incongruous additions to it. And the Choral Symphony of Beethoven—tell me about all this.

Girard, are you going to produce *Iphigénie en Aulide*? . . . Hiller, has your concert taken place? Desmarest, what is going on at the Opéra? And you, Richard, how is it I see your name mentioned in the Loëve-Weimar papers as translator of Beethoven's symphony? That puzzles me. Tell me, Gounet, is the newly married Auguste happy in his home? My dear Sichel, have you plenty of patients?

I have a delightful room, looking on to the sea. I am quite accustomed to the continual murmur of the waves; in the morning when I open my window it is glorious to see their crests come rolling in like the curling manes of a herd of white horses. I fall asleep to the artillery of the breakers battering the rock on which my house is built. . . .

PS. Remember me to Pixis, Sina, Schlesinger, Seghers, M. Habeneck, Turbri, and Urhan.

I have nearly finished the overture to *King Lear*; I have only the instrumentation to complete. I am going to do a lot of work.

A few days later he wrote to Ferrand:

NICE, 10*th or* 11*th May* 1831.

Well, Ferrand, we are moving at last; more rage, more vengeance, more tremor, more gnashing of teeth; in a word, more hell!

---

[1] *Mélodies irlandaises.*

[2] Opera by Weber.

You have not answered me; no matter, I am writing to you again. You have made me accustomed to write three or four letters to your one. . . .

Nevertheless, I can scarcely understand how it comes to pass that you have not answered me. I so sorely needed a friend's heart, and I almost thought that you would have come in search of me. My sisters write to me every day. . . . Hear me—if it is from sheer indolence, from laziness or neglect, it is bad, very bad. I gave you my address—Maison Clerici, aux Ponchettes, Nice. If you only knew, when one enters into life again, or perhaps falls into it once more, how ardently one longs to find the arms of friendship open! When the heart, torn and wounded, begins to beat again, with what ardour it seeks another heart, noble and strong, which can help to reconcile itself to existence.

I have so often begged you to answer me by return of post! I never doubted your eagerness to add consolation to that which I received from all sides, and yet it has failed me. Yes, Camille is married to Pleyel. I am now glad of it. From it I have just learnt the danger I have escaped. What baseness, what insensibility, what villainy! It is the immensity, almost the sublimity of wickedness, if sublimity can ally itself with ignobility (a new word and a perfect one, which I have stolen from you).

I shall return to Rome in five or six days; my *pension* is not lost. . . .

My repertoire has just been increased by a new overture. Yesterday I finished the one to Shakespeare's *King Lear*.

Berlioz's *King Lear* is one of the finest of his overtures, it is a powerful and sombre work, comparable only with Beethoven's *Coriolan* overture.[1]

One would hardly believe (as Richard Pohl pointed out long ago) that the composer of the brilliant *Carnaval romain* overture and the tragic *King Lear* overture were one and the same man. Why this grand work should be so neglected to-day is incomprehensible; it can only be due to ignorance.

Berlioz left Nice about 19th May, passed through Genoa, where he heard Paër's opera *Agnese*, passed Lucca and Pisa, found his luggage and some manuscripts at Florence, stayed a day at Bolsena and arrived in Rome at the beginning of June 1831.

[1] Richard Pohl relates that in 1863, during the interval of Berlioz's concert in the palace of Prince Friedrich Wilhelm von Hohenzollern-Hechingen at Löwenberg, the prince asked him which overture he thought the greatest and Berlioz replied immediately, '*Coriolan.*' Pohl adds: 'Who could have heard, as we did, *King Lear* performed at Löwenberg under Berlioz without thinking of Beethoven!'

CHAPTER II

ITALY

We have read Berlioz's description of Mendelssohn; it was enthusiastic and sympathetic. But it is a philosophical truth, as well as a physical fact, that the lesser cannot comprehend the greater; in other words, you cannot get a quart into a pint pot. So this is Mendelssohn's description of Berlioz, written to his mother:

> During Holy Week . . . the two Frenchmen have again lured me into idleness. When one sees these two men together, it is tragic or comic —as you wish. Berlioz, a caricature without a shadow of talent, groping in the darkness, believes himself to be the creator of a new world—he writes the most detestable things, and dreams and thinks only of Beethoven, Schiller, and Goethe; with that he has a boundless conceit,[1] throws a superior glance at Mozart and Haydn, so that to me all his enthusiasm is suspect. . . . With me they [Berlioz and Montfort] make the most comic contrast. I promenade willingly with them because they are the only musicians here, and are very agreeable and amiable.—You say, dear mother, that . . . [Berlioz] must have some aim as an artist; I don't agree with you; I believe he only wants to get married and is really worse than the others because he is the most affected., I cannot bear this wholly external enthusiasm, these affected despairs before women,[2] and this genius in gothic letters, black on white, and were they not Frenchmen, with whom one always has agreeable relations and who always know how to converse and be interesting, it would be unbearable.

In fairness to Mendelssohn, one must remember that when he wrote this in March 1831 Berlioz was in a state of extreme agitation; but Mendelssohn, unlike Schumann, seems never to have felt much sympathy with Berlioz's music.[3] In Rome

[1] Berlioz, as any reader of this book will discover, was quite devoid of vanity; as for conceit, a great man knows precisely what he is, and therefore cannot be conceited.

[2] Mme Vernet and her daughter, probably, who, as we shall see, had a high opinion of Berlioz.

[3] See pp. 233 et seq.

Berlioz also met Glinka,[1] whose music he warmly praised in 1845 in the *Journal des Débats*. The enforced stay in Rome was in those days a mere waste of time for musicians and, as a sightseer of the monuments and architectural features of Rome, only St. Peter's seems to have impressed Berlioz. After his return to Rome in June, however, he was busy finishing a new overture, *Rob Roy*,[2] which he had sketched at Nice and composing his sequel to the *Symphonie fantastique*, a melologue entitled *Le Retour à la Vie* (the Return to Life). In a letter to Ferrand he gives some account of this:

ROME, *3rd July* 1831.

At last I have news of you. . . . From Florence to Rome I travelled with some good monks who spoke French very well and were extremely polite. . . . I journeyed . . . during the whole of the day along the lovely Lake of Bolzena and among the mountains of Viterbo, composing the while a work which I have just committed to paper. It is a melologue, the continuation and conclusion of the *Symphonie fantastique*. For the first time I have written both words and music. . . . There are six monologues and six musical movements.

(1) A ballad with pianoforte accompaniment.

(2) A meditation for chorus and orchestra.

(3) A scene from brigand life for chorus, single voice, and orchestra.

(4) A song of happiness for a single voice with orchestral accompaniment at the beginning and end, and in the middle the right hand of a harp accompanying the air.

(5) The last sighs of the harp for orchestra alone.

(6) The overture to *The Tempest*, already performed at the Paris Opéra, as you know.

For the song of happiness I have made use of a phrase out of the *Mort d'Orphée*, which you have with you, and for the last sighs of the harp, the small orchestral movement concluding the scene which comes directly after the *Bacchanale*. Will you therefore kindly send me that page. . . .

I shall await it in the mountains of Subiaco, where I intend staying for a short time; but address it to Rome. I am going to try, by climbing rocks and crossing torrents, to get rid of that leprosy of triviality which covers me from head to foot in our infernal barracks. The atmosphere which I share with my fellow-*manufacturers* of the Académie does not

[1] Glinka, Michael Ivanovitch (1803–57), a famous Russian composer.

[2] *Rob Roy*, the least known of all Berlioz's overtures.

suit my lungs; I am going to breathe a purer air. I am taking with me a bad guitar, a gun, some quires of ruled paper, a few books, and the germ of a grand work which I shall try to hatch in the woods. . . .

The full title of the melologue became later *Lélio ; ou le Retour à la Vie*, and although it was performed in Paris on Berlioz's return from Italy, in the hall of the Conservatoire, on 9th December 1832, after the *Symphonie fantastique* as intended by Berlioz, the first edition was published by Richault et Cie of Paris and bears the sub-title: *Monodrame lyrique avec orchestre, chœurs, and soli invisibles*, followed by the words, 'performed for the first time at the Court Theatre at Weimar, 21st February 1855.'

In spite of the fact that Berlioz made use of fragments of earlier works in constructing this melologue, or lyrical monodrama, it has a real unity and is as original a composition as the *Symphonie fantastique*. The pianoforte and vocal score, which was published by Richault in 1855, was arranged by Camille Saint-Saëns,[1] who was then only twenty years old. I possess a copy of this delightful edition and, besides being a brilliant piece of transcription by Saint-Saëns, it is among those of Berlioz's scores that lose least in a pianoforte arrangement. Before giving my own opinion, I should like to quote Mr. Ernest Newman on this extraordinary work. He says: 'Some of the music of *Lélio* is among the finest Berlioz ever wrote; but the scheme as a whole, with its extraordinary prose tirades, is surely the maddest thing ever projected by a musician.'

It may be mad, but it is the madness of genius, and I think if this work were properly performed as Berlioz prescribed,[2] it would be a revelation of dramatic power and musical beauty and completely justify Berlioz's constructive scheme. But this proper production needs special conditions. First of all it needs a theatre, and secondly an exceptional actor in the part of Lélio—which is the name given by Berlioz to the artist who

[1] Saint-Saëns, Charles Camille (1835–1921), a phenomenal musician and one of the most famous of French composers.

[2] It has never been performed in England in my lifetime and I have never heard it on any stage.

returns to life and is, of course, Berlioz himself. The six musical numbers are introduced by six monologues spoken by Lélio, and there is a short monologue in conclusion after the sixth number (fantasia on Shakespeare's *Tempest*). Now to the insensitive ears of many semi-sophisticated and semi-literate people of the present age these monologues may, if read in cold blood without understanding, appear ridiculous; but they are not essentially ridiculous at all; it is merely that our mode of expression has changed. It only needs an actor with imagination and a fine technique to make all this live for us again as it did for Berlioz. I am certain, for example, that Chaliapin [1] could produce a marvellous effect in the role of Lélio, and it is one of my great regrets that this is very unlikely to happen now. Nevertheless I commend the role of Lélio to any artistically ambitious English actor (such, for example, as John Gielgud) as a part to be played on some future occasion in the Shakespeare Memorial Theatre at Stratford-upon-Avon.

For it is at Stratford-upon-Avon as part of the annual Shakespeare festival that this remarkable work by Berlioz, which is Shakespearian through and through (Shakespeare's name actually appears in three out of the six monologues), should be performed.[2] The six musical numbers are as follows:

(1) A ballad for tenor, *Le Pêcheur* (The Fisherman), words by Goethe, translated into French by Berlioz's friend A. Du Boys. This is a charming barcarolle which makes one think of Schubert. It has his open-air freshness and spontaneity.

(2) *Chœur d'Ombres* (Chorus of the Shades), for choir and full orchestra. The words for this piece were originally in an unknown language of the dead invented by Berlioz,[3] such as:

Muk lomeror, muk lunda merinunda
Irmensul forgas menera.

But later on he translated this language into French, and it is

[1] Chaliapin, Fedor Ivanovitch (b. Kazan, 1873), a famous Russian opera-singer and one of the finest actors of the age.

[2] Perhaps Sir Thomas Beecham will be able to induce the governors of the Shakespeare Memorial Theatre to make this experiment one year.

[3] He did the same later for his chorus in the 'Pandemonium' of *Faust*.

only the latter which appears in the 1855 edition. This is a quite original and impressive piece.

(3) *Chanson des Brigands* (Brigands' Song), for baritone, male chorus, and full orchestra, full of verve and colour.

(4) *Chant de Bonheur* (Song of Happiness), for tenor voice, harp, and orchestra. The orchestra has no brass parts, all the strings are *divisi* (the 'cellos into four), and there are no double-basses; the woodwind consists of two flutes, two clarinets in A, and one cor anglais. This is a gem of exquisite lyrical expressiveness and perfect instrumentation.

(5) *La Harpe éolienne—Souvenirs* (Aeolian Harp—Recollections). This is a short but miraculous orchestral piece, written for clarinet in A (Berlioz adds a footnote to say that to get the *con sordino* effect the instrument should be enveloped in a cloth bag), harp, first and second violins, viola, violoncello, two double-basses (*soli*), and double-basses.

(6) *Fantaisie sur la 'Tempête' de Shakespeare.* This is the piece for chorus, orchestra, and piano for four hands already performed in Paris before Berlioz's departure for Italy, but with certain not very important alterations. At the end of this movement Lélio speaks again, and then the theme which is the *idée fixe* of the *Symphonie fantastique* is heard. Lélio starts up and murmurs: 'Once more, once more—and for ever.' This is the end of the piece.

I hope to hear this truly Berliozian masterpiece, so original, so utterly unlike anything else in music, at least once in my lifetime. But it must be approached in complete sympathy and understanding before it will reveal its many beauties and its unique character in a performance.

In the same letter to Ferrand, dated Rome, 3rd July 1831, Berlioz refers to another new work:

I had a general plan in my head which I wanted to carry out with your assistance; it related to a colossal oratorio, to be produced at a musical fête to take place in Paris, either at the Opéra or at the Panthéon, or in the courtyard of the Louvre. It was to have been called *Le Dernier Jour du Monde* (The Last Day of the World).

I sketched out the plan and wrote a portion of the words at Florence three months ago. It would have required three or four soloists, choruses, an orchestra of sixty performers in the front of the theatre and another of two or three hundred instruments ranged in amphitheatre fashion at the back of the stage.

This is the idea. Mankind arrive at the last degree of corruption, give themselves up to all kinds of infamy, and are governed despotically by a species of antichrist.[1] A small number of upright men, led by a prophet, appear in the very midst of the general depravity. The despot oppresses them, carries off their young women, insults their faith, and destroys their holy books amid a scene of orgy. The prophet appears, reproaching him for his crimes and proclaiming the end of the world and the Last Judgment. The enraged despot throws him into prison and giving himself up once more to impious voluptuousness, is surprised in the middle of a fête by the terrible trumpets of the Resurrection; the dead coming out of their graves, the distracted living uttering cries of horror, the world in course of destruction, and the angels thundering in the clouds compose the end of this musical drama. As you may well imagine, we should have to make use of some entirely novel means. In addition to the two orchestras, there would have to be four groups of brass instruments placed at the four cardinal points of the place of execution. The combinations will be quite new, and a thousand effects impracticable with ordinary means would sparkle out of the mass of harmony.

See if you can find time to write this poem, which would suit you admirably, and in which I feel sure you would be magnificent. Very few recitatives—very few solos. Avoid noisy scenes [2] and those which would require brass, as I do not want that to be heard until the end. Opposite effects, such as religious choirs mingled with dance choruses; pastoral, nuptial, and bacchanalian scenes, but out of the beaten track—you understand.

We need not flatter ourselves that we should be able to secure a performance of this work just when we liked, especially in France; but, sooner or later, the opportunity would present itself. On the other hand, it would be a source of tremendous expense and an extraordinary loss of time. Think well if you would care about writing such a poem with the possibility of its never being heard. And, whatever you do, write to me as soon as you can.

---

[1] Note the date of this, 1831!

[2] It is one of the stock phrases of ignorant musicians and critics that Berlioz was too fond of noise. It is the opposite of the truth, and we shall see that one of Berlioz's criticisms of Wagner was that his orchestration was noisy.

This oratorio or opera,[1] *Le Dernier Jour du Monde*, never materialized, unfortunately; but the idea served to enrich the *Requiem* (*Messe des morts*) composed in 1837–8.

Berlioz admired to the full the beautiful country around Rome, and he was only happy when he could leave the Villa Medici on some excursion. On 17th September 1831 he writes to Hiller:

> . . . Nothing pleases me so much as this vagabond life amid the woods and the rocks, among these good-natured peasants, by day sleeping on the banks of a torrent, in the evening dancing the *saltarelle* with the men and women who frequent our inn. I make them happy with my guitar; before I came they danced only to the *tambour de basque* [tambourine], and they are in ecstasies over my more melodious instrument. I am going back there [Subiaco] to escape the weariness which kills me here [in Rome]. . . .
>
> The scenery of Rome is so stern and majestic, especially at night. All the ruins of palaces and temples lit up by the setting sun on the ground bare as one's hand, treeless, intersected by deep ravines, form a most picturesque and sombre scene. In the morning I breakfast on an old reservoir or Etruscan tomb; at noon I slept in a temple of Bacchus, but I had only water to pour out my libations. I hope the *conqueror of the Ganges* will forgive such an unworthy offering.
>
> So you have been kind enough to take possession of my medal and a few gold tomfooleries. So, as they are in all worth about two hundred francs, if I die of cholera before I get back to France, my small debt will be paid. Is Paris frightened of this famous cholera?
>
> Has Mendelssohn arrived? His talent is enormous, extraordinary, masterly, prodigious. I am not open to a charge of *camaraderie* in saying this, because he told me frankly that he did not understand my music. Remember me very kindly to him; he has quite a virginal character and still has some beliefs; he is a little cold in his relationships, but although he does not suspect it, I have a sincere affection for him.

In letters to his family about this time Berlioz complains of the boredom he suffers in Rome, where 'everything is fifty

[1] In a letter to Ferrand dated Rome, 8th January 1832, he repeats his scenario as, not hearing from Ferrand, he thinks he has not received his letter of 3rd July. In the later letter he says: 'I send you the same plan for an opera in three acts. Here is the carcass, you must supply the sinews.' The ingenious alterations Berlioz makes in this plan show his rare dramatic instinct and his power of invention.

years behind civilization'; and he adds: 'Oh! if this beautiful country were peopled by the English, what a change there would be.'[1] In a letter to Mme Lesueur he talks of possible political troubles in France, and says: 'Heaven confound all these ambitious manikins devoid of genius who upset the social order to no purpose but loss . . . these cross-road heroes [stump orators] . . . who, in my opinion, serve only to discredit the cause of glory and liberty . . . as for me, the aversion I have always had for politics grows stronger'; and he adds one of those concrete images characteristic of his prose style: 'This great squint-eyed cuttle-fish [politics],[2] pale in colour and hard of heart, seems to me more and more detestable; unhappily one can hardly move a step without meeting it.' He then continues that he has to remain isolated because his companions think him 'mannered,' merely because he does not affect *their* manners and habits, and, as he cannot remake himself, he prefers to leave the field to them and go out into the country with his guitar, a gun, and a few books. Characteristic is his courtesy and good manners as a civilized Frenchman, he tells Mme Lesueur that he is grateful to her for not communicating to an Italian friend, Mlle Corinaldi, his remarks about her fellow-countrymen: 'I should not like to have vexed her and, besides, one can find *men* everywhere, even in Italy.'

But he adds: 'This country is an unjust and partial mother who has given everything to her eldest sons: Dante, Ariosto, Tasso would seem to have devoured all the inheritance of genius, except perhaps a little portion that may have escaped to the agreeable and intelligent author of *Les Fiancés*.'[3]

To his family he describes his wanderings among the mountains with immense relish; he would be away for weeks at a time, and he tells an amusing story of a climb near Subiaco:

I climbed this morning a majestic elevation which the landscape painters

[1] In a letter to his parents dated Rome, 24th June 1831.

[2] Need I remind the reader that the cuttle-fish ejects a poisonous obscurity to conceal its actions, which we may describe by the word *propaganda*?

[3] Manzoni, Alessandro (1784–1873), author of *I Promessi Sposi*.

call 'The Whale,' because it resembles an immense whale rising out of the sea to breathe. An hour after midday I arrived at the very summit; there I built with pieces of rock a little pyramid, completed with a flat stone like a Druid altar. Oh! how I have breathed, how gazed, how lived! not a cloud. . . .[1] Before arriving at these sublime heights I had found a little house, inhabited, and passed through a garden full of vines and maize; then, jumping the thicket fence, I found myself in a charming meadow, like a platform, planted with olives. . . . Immediately I thought I heard *Maman*, fifteen years ago, singing this verse:

Que je voudrais avoir une chaumière
Dont un verger ombrage l'alentour,
Pour y passer la saison printanière
Avec ma mie et ma muse et l'amour.[2]

Higher, where the vegetation finished, I found some peasants mowing . . . they seemed disturbed at seeing me climbing alone and without apparent purpose (I had left my gun at Subiaco). There is a superstition here about people who can cast a spell. I believe they took me for one of them; they asked me none too good-humouredly where I was going and what I wanted up so high; luckily I had a good idea. I replied to them that I had made a vow to the Madonna and was climbing to fulfil it. Then they went on mowing without troubling about me. . . .

Yesterday evening the children danced the *saltarelle* to the Basque tambour. . . . I was looking on when the eldest girl, who is twelve, said with a coaxing air: 'Signore, O Signore; pigliate la chitarra francese' (Sir, O sir; play the French guitar). I took the *chitarra francese* . . . and improvised *saltarelles* until my fingers burned.

Berlioz constantly refers to the boredom he suffers, from which he can only escape in excursions into the mountains. The many long letters to his family (his parents and his sisters) are full of interesting descriptions of these excursions and of the triviality and monotony of Roman society. 'It is always

[1] Elsewhere, referring to a quadruple intoxication of *eau-de-vie*, recollections, poetry, and music ('I chanted the death of Pallas, the despair of Evander in a strange recitation on a still stranger harmony'), he adds: 'Reasonable people do not know to what degree of intensity the feeling of existence may attain; the heart dilates, the imagination takes an immense flight, one lives with fury.'

[2] A cottage I should like to have
Round about with an orchard shaded,
To pass the springtime with my love
By Venus and the muses guarded.

the same song,' he writes to Adèle, 'one looks at engravings, reads old newspapers, drinks insipid tea . . . then in the moonlight utters some ancient reflections—very platitudinous, very trite, very academic, very silly . . .'[1] To Hiller he writes: '. . . Must I remain shut up here, in this gloomy, anti-musical country, while in Paris they are performing the Choral Symphony, *Euryanthe*, and *Robert* . . .'[2] and from another letter to Hiller dated Rome, 1st January 1832, I take the following:

. . . At present I am copying out parts and writing a long article on the existing state of music in Italy . . . for the *Revue européenne*. . . .[3] I have been to Naples; it is superb. I returned on foot . . . across the mountains of the frontier as far as Subiaco, sleeping in the haunts or strongholds of the *banditti*, devoured by fleas, eating grapes, either stolen or bought, all along the road in the daytime, and eggs, bread, and grapes at night. After resting two days at Subiaco, where I found one of my Académie comrades who lent me a shirt, not before I wanted one, I set out, still on foot, for Tivoli, and thence to Rome. . . .

Remember me to Mendelssohn. . . . Madame Foult recently gave me an opportunity of hearing at her house the symphony, *deranged* for violin, violoncello, and piano (four hands), which he has had performed in London.[4] The first part is superb, the *adagio* has not made a very clear impression on me, the *intermezzo* is fresh and taking; the *finale*, in which a fugue appears, I detest. I cannot understand how so great a talent as his can stoop to merely stringing notes together. . . .

You have done well, in my opinion . . . in preserving your *adagio* and putting it in the key of C; it is full of delicacy. You have not, it seems, written a *minuet*; we have had enough of that kind of thing; it is played out. . . .

In Rome Berlioz suffered greatly from not being able to get books to read and had only after much difficulty procured a copy of Victor Hugo's recently published *Notre Dame de Paris*.

[1] Letter to Adèle dated Rome, 7th August 1831.

[2] Letter to Hiller dated Rome, 8th December 1831. *Robert* is Meyerbeer's opera *Robert le Diable* first produced in 1831.

[3] This article was entitled *Lettre d'un enthousiaste sur l'état de la musique en Italie*. It was reprinted, with alterations, in his book *Le Voyage musical* in 1844, and passages were again made use of in his *Mémoires*.

[4] Symphony No. 1 in C minor (?).

In a letter to his grandfather Marmion, dated Rome, 15th September 1831, he makes an interesting criticism on Lamartine,[1] whose last work (*Épître à Barthélemy*) he has just read. Berlioz was a warm admirer of Lamartine, and he says of this work: 'It is, in my opinion, all that one could wish for in suavity, delicacy, and heavenly charm. Oh! he is a great poet! What a pity he is so incomplete! He never leaves the skies; nevertheless a poet should be a mirror in which all objects, gracious and horrible, brilliant and sombre, calm and agitated, are reflected. . . .'[2]

I must extract one or two other remarks of interest to artists from his letters about this time and quote them here. In a letter to Ferrand dated Rome, 8th January 1832, he first of all refers to Ferrand's comments on the political troubles at Lyons:

> You waste your breath in trying to prove to me things which are quite clear; assuredly there is neither absolute good nor absolute evil in politics. Equally certain is it that the heroes of to-day are the traitors of to-morrow. I have known for a very long time that two and two make four; I regret the whole of the space you have allotted in your letter to Lyons; it would have been quite enough to have told me that Auguste and Germain were safe and sound. . . .

After a few more words on this subject Berlioz then makes the following extraordinarily interesting remark:

> Your *Noce des Fées* is charming in its gracefulness, freshness, and brilliancy. I shall keep it until later on, as this is not the moment for composing music on such a theme. Instrumentation is not sufficiently far advanced and we must wait until I have *immaterialized* it to some extent. Then the world shall hear of the followers of Oberon. . . .[3]

---

[1] Lamartine (1790–1869), famous French poet, died in the same year as Berlioz.

[2] Compare Beethoven's criticism of Klopstock—'always in the key of D flat major *maestoso*. Nevertheless he is great and uplifts the soul.'

[3] No advance has been made in this respect since Berlioz; he has gone further in the immaterialization of music than any other composer before or since, excepting perhaps occasionally Beethoven in his last quartets. It is not right, however, to compare quartet writing with orchestral instrumentation.

To Ferrand

Rome, *26th March* 1832.

. . . You have read me a nice homily, but I assure you that you are on the wrong scent . . . my remarks about rhyme were only intended to put you at your ease, for it annoys me to see you employing your time and your talents in a useless conquest over such unprofitable difficulties.

You know as well as I do that a thousand instances exist where verses set to music are so arranged that the rhyme, and even the hemistich, completely disappears; what, then, is the use of the versification? Well-balanced and rhyming verses are in their proper place in pieces of music which do not admit, or scarcely admit, of any repetition of the words; then, and then only, is versification apparent and sensible; under no other circumstances can it be said to exist.

There is a great difference between verses *spoken* and verses *sung*. . . .[1]

In the matter of music I am going to clear a Brazilian forest, where I promise myself untold wealth; we shall advance like bold pioneers as long as our material forces will let us. . . .

I am going to make another excursion to Albano, Frascati, Castel-Gandolfo, etc. etc.—lakes, plains, mountains, old sepulchres, chapels, convents, smiling villages, clusters of houses perched on rocks, the sea as my horizon, silence, sunshine, perfumed air, the birth of spring—it is a dream of fairyland!

I took another splendid trip a month ago among the lofty mountains on the frontier; one evening while sitting by the fireside, I wrote in pencil the little air I now send you.[2] On my return to Rome it was so successful that it is sung everywhere, from the *salons* of the Embassy to the studios of the sculptors. . . .

Although Berlioz was supposed to stay two years in Italy, he contrived to leave Rome on 1st May 1832. In an interesting letter to Mme Lesueur dated Rome, 12th January 1832, he says that it is well known that the most dissimilar characters are the ones which sympathize most strongly with one another, and that two people exactly the same can only bore each other

[1] Every poet knows this, and knows also that poetry is an art by itself; when verse is used in combination with music it has a quite different function.

[2] The famous song, *La Captive*, the words by Victor Hugo. Afterwards Berlioz arranged it for orchestra. Even such an anti-Berliozian as Dannreuther goes into ecstasies over this song and calls it a 'marvel,' which it is.

—which is why Rome bores him since, he adds, 'there are in me so many ravaged plains, deserted palaces, desolate ruins.'[1]

There is no doubt that Horace Vernet and his family had become much attached to Berlioz, and no difficulties were put in his way on leaving Rome six months before his due date. He passed through Florence, Milan, and Turin on his way home to La Côte, where he had to remain until it was safe to put in an appearance at Paris. Two extracts from his letters *en route* are worth quoting:

To Hiller

Florence, 13*th May* 1832.

. . . I left Rome without regret; the confined life of the Académie was becoming more and more insupportable. I spent all my evenings with M. Horace, whose family I like very much. On my departure they all showed me many signs of their attachment and affection, for which I was all the more grateful as I did not in the least expect them. . . .

I beheld Florence once more with emotion. It is a town that I really love. Everything there pleases me: its name, its sky, its river, its surroundings—everything—I love it, I love it. . . .[2]

[M. de Sauer] is bent upon making me intimate with Bellini, but I sternly refuse; *La Sonnambula*, which I saw yesterday, redoubles my distaste for such an acquaintance.[3] What a score! How pitiful! . . . Ah! my dear fellow, you ought to see Italy to have an idea of what they have the audacity to call music in this country. . . .

PS. What a cold and stupid letter; but I am very sad. Every time I see Florence I experience an inward trouble, a confused agitation which I can hardly explain. I do not know a soul in the place—I have never had any adventures in it—I am as much alone in it as I was at Nice. Perhaps it is that which affects me so strangely. It is most peculiar. It seems to

---

[1] It is worth noting as an example of his lifelong attachment to Virgil that in this same letter he rhapsodizes over Vesuvius, and the Gulf of Baia 'filled with Virgilian souvenirs.' His description of his arrival on foot at midnight at Vesuvius with the stars sparkling over his head and the sea scintillating at his feet is remarkably impressive.

[2] Berlioz's feeling for Florence found expression later in the opera *Benvenuto Cellini*.

[3] Berlioz, in his detestation of the most popular kinds of Italian opera which had seduced the French public from the far superior operas of Gluck, was sometimes a little unfair to the merits of Rossini, Bellini, and Donizetti, who *at their best* are by no means so devoid of merit as he suggests.

me that when I am in Florence I am no longer myself but some stranger, a Russian or an Englishman, who strolls along the lovely quay of the Arno. Berlioz is elsewhere and I am one of his acquaintances. I act the dandy, spend my money, and swagger like a fop. I do not understand it in the least. *What is it?*[1]

To Ferrand

Turin, 25*th May* 1832.

My dear Humbert,

Here I am, quite close to you, and on Thursday next I shall be at Grenoble. . . .

At Milan I heard, for the first time, a vigorous orchestra; there was the beginning of something like music, in execution at least. But the score of my friend Donizetti may go with those of my friend Paccini and my friend Vaccai. The public is worthy of such productions. They talk as loudly during the performance as they do at the Bourse, and their sticks keep up an accompaniment on the floor, almost as loud as that of the big drums. If ever I write for such blockheads I shall merit my fate; there is nothing more degrading for an artist. What humiliation!

As I came out, the divine lines of Lamartine occurred to me (he is speaking of his poetical muse):

Non, non, je l'ai conduite au fond des solitudes,
  Comme un amant jaloux d'une chaste beauté,
J'ai gardé ses beaux pieds des atteintes trop rudes
  Dont la terre eût blessé leur tendre nudité.
J'ai couronné sa front d'étoiles immortelles,
  J'ai parfumé mon cœur pour lui faire un séjour,
Et je n'ai rien laissé s'abriter sous les ailes
  Que la prière et que l'amour.[2]

That comprehends all poetry and is worthy of it.

---

[1] In English, in the original.

[2] No, no, I have led her deep into solitude,
  Like a lover jealous of his mistress chaste,
Her lovely feet from roughness I have guarded
  Lest the earth in its sharpness their tenderness pierced.
Her brow I have crowned with stars everlasting,
  My heart I have perfumed for her long abode,
And near her and around her I have allowed nothing
  But love and a prayer to God.

On Thursday, 31st May 1832, Berlioz arrived at Grenoble, having been in Italy fifteen months. During his stay he had retouched his *Symphonie fantastique* and composed the pendant work *Lélio; ou le Retour à la Vie*, the song to Victor Hugo's words *La Captive*, the two overtures *King Lear* and *Rob Roy*, and a meditation for six voices with orchestra entitled *Le Monde entier n'est qu'une ombre fugitive*,[1] the words in prose translated from Thomas Moore.

[1] This is published in the Breitkopf & Härtel edition as *Méditation religieuse*, No. 1 of *Tristia* (Op. 18, 1831), in Series VI, *Chants avec Orchestre*.

CHAPTER III

MARRIAGE

ARRIVED in his native province Berlioz quickly began to feel as bored and restless there as in Italy. He much enjoyed seeing his family and especially, no doubt, his two sisters. At Grenoble he stayed with his brother-in-law M. Pal, a judge to whom his elder sister, Nanci, was now married.[1] On 11th June 1832 he writes to Gounet, arranging to pay him some money he owes him and telling him not to speak too freely of his return to France as it might compromise Horace Vernet as he is still supposed to be in Italy; he also asks for information about his friends in Paris—Desmarest, Prévost, Casimir, Turbri, and Girard.

In another letter to Gounet dated Grenoble, 10th July 1832, he says:

> . . . Here I have done nothing but play my ordinary role of vagabond; from place to place, so many uncles and cousins, married and marrying friends, weddings, festivities, bowling-green parties, bathing parties, idiotic reflections, drums of soldiers which, like a child, I love following — There now!
>
> You see it is not my fault. I have become, truly, as stupid as a conspirator.

On 25th July 1832 he writes a long letter to Mme Horace Vernet, from which I take the following:

> I was afraid when I got back to France that I should have to alter that line of Voltaire's and confess that 'the more I saw of other countries the *less* I should love my own'; but nothing of the kind has happened, and my memories of the Kingdom of Naples have remained powerless against the aspect of our lovely valley of the Isère, so smiling, varied, fresh, rich, picturesque, lovely as a whole as well as in detail. . . .

---

[1] This family was royalist and ultra-conservative, but Berlioz all through his life had friends of all political colours. Adolphe Boschot, who had access to Nanci's diary, quotes a remark of hers about provincial life: 'To live here one must be a machine; here the genius of Hector lacks air.'

This does not hold good with regard to the . . . society I saw habitually at Rome and that which I resumed after my long absence. This time the advantage is altogether with the distant, if not foreign beauties, and the proverb, 'Les absents ont tort,' appears to me to be absolutely false.

In spite of my efforts to divert the conversation from such subjects, the people will persist in talking to me about art, music, and poetry—and God knows what sort of talk that is in the provinces—giving vent, with perfectly horrible coolness, to the strangest ideas, and judgments calculated to congeal the blood of any artist. To hear them talking about Byron, Goethe, and Beethoven would lead you to suppose that they were alluding to some more than ordinarily talented tailor or bootmaker; nothing is good enough for them; they are destitute of both respect and enthusiasm and would literally smother their heroes with rose leaves. . . .

I am really in a most profound and cruel state of isolation. Besides, I am choking for want of music; I can no longer look forward to seeing Mlle Louise[1] seated at the piano in the evening nor to hearing the sublime *adagios* she was ever ready to play to me, without allowing my obstinacy in making her repeat them over and over again, either to exhaust her patience or detract from . . . her playing.

I think I can see you laughing; you are, no doubt, saying that I do not know what I want or where I should like to be and that I am half a lunatic. To that I reply that I know perfectly well what I want; so far as my *mezza pazzia* is concerned, I play my part very easily, more especially as there is a general disposition to assign it to me and also because there is, under very many circumstances, a positive advantage in being taken for an idiot.

Quite lately my father hit on a novel method of making me sensible. Presuming, rightly or wrongly, from information received, that my addresses would be very favourably received by a certain extremely wealthy person, he urged me strongly to become a candidate for her hand, alleging as a peremptory reason that a young man whose inheritance would be . . . a hundred thousand francs had no right to throw away an opportunity of marrying three hundred thousand down and as much more *in prospectu*. I . . . treated it as a joke for a time, but as my father's entreaties became more and more pressing, I was at last compelled to declare categorically that I felt myself quite incapable of loving the young lady in question and that I was not on sale at any price. . . .

I was disagreeably impressed by the whole affair, as I thought my father knew me better. . . . After Marie Louise had recovered from an illness, the emperor said to M. Dubois, who had attended her:

'What do you want, Dubois—money or honours?' 'Sir,' was his reply, 'money *and* honours.' If anybody were to ask me, 'Will you have

[1] Daughter of Horace Vernet.

money, love, or liberty?' I should say, 'Liberty, love, and money.' But as I shall never be in a position to make such an answer to a Napoleon, I renounce the money for ever in order to retain or secure one of the other two. . . .

At Belley in August Berlioz met his old friend Ferrand, whom he had not seen for years, and from there writes to Gounet in Paris, telling him how he spends his time copying, reading 'M. de Balzac, Saintine, Michel Raimond', playing bowls, and going excursions. In October he makes another effort to see Ferrand, to whom he writes: 'I dare not hope that you have any portion of your grand dramatic machine,[1] notwithstanding your promise. After all, it does not matter; only come and write to me beforehand.' But this meeting did not take place, and on his way to Paris he writes again to Ferrand from Lyons, under date of 3rd November 1832:

After all, we have not met. I leave this evening for Paris. I have been wandering about in the mud of Lyons since yesterday, and during the whole of the time I have not had a single idea which has not been oppressive and melancholy. . . .

Last night I went to the Grand Théâtre, where I was deeply but painfully affected by hearing a worthless orchestra, during a worthless ballet play a fragment of Beethoven's Pastoral Symphony. . . . It seemed to me as if I had discovered in some disreputable haunt the portrait of an angel, and that angel the subject of my dreams of love and enthusiasm. Ah, this comes of being away for two years!

I verily believe that I shall go mad when I listen to real music once more. . . .

I am suffering cruelly to-day. I am all alone in this huge town. . . .

Oh, how lonely I am! How I suffer inwardly! What a wretched organization is mine! A regular barometer; now up, now down. . . . I feel convinced that you are doing nothing in connection with our great work, and yet my life is ebbing away, and I shall have accomplished nothing great ere it closes. . . .

Arriving in Paris on 7th November, he sent a note to Gounet: 'I am lodging in rue Neuve-Saint-Marc No. 1, in the old lodging of H. Sm——. It 's very odd! I am dying to see you; this evening at 8 o'clock at the Café Feydeau.'

After getting in touch with his friends and the musical life

[1] *Le Dernier Jour du Monde.*

of Paris, Berlioz's first plan was to arrange a concert to give the first performance of *Lélio*, his sequel to the *Symphonie fantastique*. In the meantime the English actress Harriet Smithson had returned to Paris at the head of a new English company and announced a season at the Théâtre-Italien of Otway, Rowe, Sheridan, and Shakespeare. She opened with *Jane Shore* on 21st November, and got a bad press. One paper, the *Courrier des Théâtres*, said that the company was detestable, 'including Miss Smithson, whose previous success was due to other qualities than her talent.'

The novelty of the English actors for Paris had now gone and also, very likely, Miss Smithson's company was inferior to that in which she first appeared. On 5th December Miss Smithson's company gave *Isabella, or the Fatal Marriage*, and the *Courrier des Théâtres* which had already written: 'The English actors are judged: to the packet-boat!' now wrote: 'The best fortune of the English company is that it is only seven leagues from Calais to Dover. A good wind!' Other papers, including the *Figaro*, were less virulent but unfavourable.

On 9th December Berlioz gave his concert at the hall of the Conservatoire at half-past one o'clock. It had been well prepared by advance notices. Berlioz's friends were as usual active on his behalf, his admirers and supporters were the cream of the young intellectuals of Paris, including d'Ortigue, a journalist who supported him all through his career, Gounet, the famous critic Jules Janin, Alexandre Dumas, Eugène Sue, Legouvé, and Hiller. A ticket had been sent through the publisher Schlesinger to Miss Smithson, who came to the concert. The famous actor Bocage played the title role of Lélio and the success of the concert was great.

In a letter written the next day to his sister Adèle, Berlioz says the performance of his works was good, that he had a huge success and the warmest congratulations from friends and acquaintances present, among whom were Paganini, Victor Hugo, Alexandre Dumas, Pixis, and Nourrit. In this letter occurs the following sentence: 'I have also obtained quite another approval, more unexpected, which everybody is talking about; I will tell you more about it another time.'

This refers to Harriet Smithson, to whom he apparently was presented shortly after this concert. Berlioz repeated his concert at the same hall on 30th December; the programme consisted of the *Symphonie fantastique*, the melologue *Lélio*, the *Francs-Juges* overture, and 'une orientale de V. Hugo' (*La Captive*). The year 1832 having now come to an end, Berlioz should have set out in 1833 in accordance with the terms of the Grand Prix to spend a year in Germany; instead, he spent nearly the whole of 1833 in persuading Harriet Smithson (who by the end of March 1833 was financially ruined and heavily in debt owing to the failure of her theatrical season) to marry him. In a fervent letter to Liszt, dated 19th December 1832, he declares his love for Harriet Smithson: 'She will beautify the last days of my life, which, I hope,' he says, 'will not be long. One could not endure such emotions for long.'

Naturally Berlioz's family did not approve of his marrying a penniless actress burdened with debts, and Miss Smithson was by no means willing either, being more frightened than anything else by the ardour of her admirer—especially as some kind friend had told her he was an epileptic. The progress of the affair may best be shown by a few extracts from Berlioz's letters. To Ferrand he writes on 2nd March 1833:

Thank you, my dear friend, for your affectionate letter. . . . I am completely absorbed by the anxieties and annoyances of my position. My father has refused his consent and has compelled me to make my request in legal form.

Henriette, throughout this business, is displaying an amount of dignity and force of character beyond reproach. She is persecuted by her family and friends even more than I am by mine in their efforts to withdraw her from me. . . . Her affairs have taken a most unfortunate turn; a performance was arranged for her benefit . . . and everything was going well when at four o'clock yesterday, as she was returning from the office of the Minister of Commerce in a carriage, she attempted to get out before her maid could assist her; her dress caught, her foot slipped on the step, and she broke her leg above the ankle-joint. . . .

What sort of destiny is awaiting us? Fate evidently intends us for each other, and I will never leave her so long as I have life. The more unfortunate she is, the more I will cling to her. If to the loss of her fortune and talent that of her beauty were to be added, I feel I should love her just the same. It is an inexplicable feeling. . . . Do not say a word against this love, my friend, for it is too deep and too full of poetry to be treated by you with aught but respect. . . .

During the early months of 1833 Berlioz contemplated composing an opera on the subject of Shakespeare's comedy *Much Ado about Nothing*. He mentions it in letters to his sister Adèle and to his friend Joseph d'Ortigue, and says he is hoping to get a contract for it from the Théâtre-Italien. He did not get it, however, but, as we shall see, he composed this opera for Baden-Baden nearly thirty years later. The only other musical event of this period was the first performance of his *Rob Roy* overture at the Société des Concerts on 14th April 1833. It did not meet with success, and as Berlioz was in an exceptionally sensitive state he destroyed it. A copy, however, had been sent from Rome to the Académie des Beaux-Arts, and this was found in the library of the Conservatoire and has been published in the Breitkopf & Härtel edition. It is, however, still unknown and I have never heard a performance of it.

Harriet Smithson's sister was violently opposed to her marrying Berlioz, and it required much patience and persistence on his part to overcome all the difficulties, especially on account of his future wife's character. On 1st August he writes to his friend Ferrand:

I shall see Henriette this evening, perhaps for the last time; she is so unhappy that my heart bleeds for her, and her irresolute and timid character prevent her from being able to make any resolution. This, however, must finish; I cannot live like this. The whole of this story is sad and tearful. . . . I have done all that the most devoted heart could do; if she is not happier and in a more settled state, the fault is hers. . . .

On 30th August he writes to Ferrand:

You are right in not despairing about my future! These cowards do not know that *in spite of everything* I observe and improve; that I grow even when bending before the violence of the storm; the wind but strips me of my leaves; the unripe fruit I bear clings too firmly to the branches to fall. Your confidence encourages and supports me.

I forget what I said to you in reference to my separation from poor Henriette, but it has not taken place; she did not wish it. Since then the scenes have become more and more violent; there was the beginning of a marriage, a civil contract which her detestable sister tore up; despair on her part and reproaches that I loved her no longer; tired of the struggle, I replied to that by taking poison before her eyes. Fearful shrieks from Henriette—sublime despair—mocking laughter from me—desire to live once more on hearing her frantic avowals of love—emetic—ipecacuanha [1] —results which lasted for ten hours—only two grains of opium remained! I was ill for three days, but got over it.

Henriette in despair, and wishing to repair the evil she had done me, asked what I wished her to do and what line of conduct she ought to pursue in order to put an end to our uncertain position. I told her—she began very well; but for the last three days she has relapsed into a vacillating mood, overcome by the instigations of her sister and the fear caused by our very unsatisfactory pecuniary position. She has nothing, and I love her, and she dare not trust herself to me. She wants me to wait a few months—months! Damnation! I do not want to wait; I have suffered too much already.

Yesterday I wrote to tell her that if she could not let me fetch her to-morrow and take her to the Mairie I should leave for Berlin next Thursday. She does not believe that I am in earnest and she sent word that she would answer me to-day. There will be more words, entreaties that I will go and see her, protestations that she is ill, etc. But I shall stand my ground and she will see that although I have been as weak as water at her feet for so long, I still have strength to get up, to flee from her, and to live for those who love and understand me. I have done everything for her; I can do no more. I sacrifice everything for her, and she dare not run any risk for me. There is too much weakness and too much *reasoning* in this. Consequently, I shall go away. . . .

My passport is made out; I have only a few things to attend to and then I am off. . . . I am leaving my poor Henriette very unhappy and in a deplorable position, but I have no reason to reproach myself and I can do no more for her. . . .

She will weep and be in despair, but it will be too late. She will reap the consequences of her unfortunate character, which is feeble and incapable alike of deep sentiment or strong resolution. Then she will console herself and discover any number of faults in me. It is always so. As for me I must be off betimes, without listening to the qualms of my

---

[1] All this undoubtedly happened. It was fortunate an emetic was available, but it would not be in the least unlike Berlioz to have taken the emetic as well as the poison with him so as to be prepared for *all* eventualities.

conscience, which is ever telling me that I am too wretched and that life is an atrocity. . . .

Liszt has just arranged my symphony for the piano.[1] It is an astonishing piece of work. I will write to you from Berlin.

But this was the end. Harriet Smithson gave way. On 3rd September Berlioz writes to Ferrand: 'Our banns are published'; and on 3rd October 1833 they were married at the British Embassy in Paris, Liszt being one of the witnesses. Berlioz was twenty-nine years old and Harriet Smithson about thirty-three.

[1] *Symphonie fantastique.*

CHAPTER IV

THE STRUGGLE FOR LIFE

It is worth remarking that his five years' pension as a winner of the Grand Prix de Rome was Berlioz's salvation as a young man. It alone gave him fallow time, time to idle in Italy and his native province and on his return to Paris to occupy himself solely with music and Harriet Smithson. But it was a pension that merely secured his existence; it left no room for luxuries—not even the luxurious necessity of marriage! In fact he had to borrow money (300 francs) from his staunch friend Gounet[1] to set up his home after his marriage. Nor was he able to take his wife farther than Vincennes for a change of scene for the first few days after their marriage, returning with her to his old apartments in Paris in the rue Neuve-Saint-Marc. In April 1834 they moved to 10 rue Saint-Denis (later 22 rue du Mont Cenis), where they stayed for the summer and where their young friends Liszt, de Vigny, Gounet, d'Ortigue, Chopin, etc., were entertained by them.

His marriage alienated him from his parents and his elder sister. In a letter to Adèle from Vincennes dated 7th October 1833, he writes full of happiness about his wife who, he says, is 'deliciously pure and good,' and tells Adèle how right he has been in 'listening to the voice of his heart,' which, though it had often deceived him, had 'on this occasion spoken nothing but the truth.'

In a letter to Liszt dated the same day he confesses the success of his marriage,[2] and asks him if he is going to Victor Hugo that evening to hear Hugo read his new work,[3] for he

[1] Berlioz once wrote to Gounet: 'You are as rare as good music.'

[2] Berlioz, young, ardent, and naïve, was naturally concerned about the reputation of his wife. In those days of strict categories of virtue and vice to marry an actress was, in France especially, to offer a target to stereotyped pleasantries; so in his letter to Liszt Berlioz writes of Harriet, 'tout ce qu'il y a de plus vierge.'

[3] *Marie Tudor.*

will find him (Berlioz) there. To Ferrand on 11th October he writes: 'I am married! At last! After a thousand thousand difficulties and terrible opposition from both sides I have achieved this masterpiece of love and perseverance. . . .' In a letter dated 25th October, acknowledging Ferrand's reply, he says: '. . . Thank you, thank you for your letter, so frank, so touching, so tender. . . . Yes, my dear Humbert, I *believed* in spite of you all, and my faith has saved me. Henriette is a delicious being. She is Ophelia herself; not Juliet, for she has not her passionate ardour; she is tender and sweet and timid. . . .'

In order to raise some money Berlioz arranged a benefit performance at the Théâtre-Italien on 21st November 1833 for his wife, Harriet Smithson, in which she played the fourth act of *Hamlet* and a well-known French actress of the day, Mme Dorval, played an act from Alexandre Dumas's *Antony*. As always, Berlioz's friends rallied to his support. Alexandre Dumas asked no fee for the performance of his work and Liszt played Weber's *Concertstück*.[1] The rest of the music by Berlioz consisted of the *Francs-Juges* overture, the *Symphonie fantastique*, and the cantata *Sardanapale*. Owing to the performance starting at eight, instead of seven as announced, it was after twelve by the time Berlioz, conducting for the first time in public, had concluded his cantata, and numbers of the musicians left in face of the public,[2] so that it was impossible to perform the *Symphonie fantastique*. What was left of the audience, however, wanted to hear it, or at least part of it, namely the *Marche au supplice*. The row was so great that Berlioz had to apologize to the audience: 'Messieurs, ayez pitié de moi.' The success of the evening was Mme Dorval, not Harriet Smithson, and Berlioz's music (what was heard of it) seems to have failed to make its effect, owing to his inexperience as a conductor. However, the receipts were five thousand francs and the costs two thousand,

[1] This brilliant and delightful piece is neglected by pianists to-day. It has, however, been played in recent years in London and Manchester by Artur Schnabel with great success.

[2] Berlioz gives these particulars in a letter to Adèle dated 28th November.

so that Berlioz made three thousand francs.[1] Feeling that this concert was a fiasco, Berlioz immediately prepared another, which took place on 22nd December 1833, conducted by Girard. This was completely successful and covered expenses. The programme included the *Roi Lear* overture and the *Symphonie fantastique*; also two new pieces, a *Romance de Marie Tudor*[2] and *Le Paysan breton*,[3] a song for voice and pianoforte. He writes to Adèle on 26th December that all the poets of Paris were there, naming Alfred de Vigny, Hugo, Émile Deschamps, Legouvé, and Eugène Sue.

In his *Mémoires* Berlioz states that Paganini was present and congratulated him. It is very odd, however, that he did not mention his name in writing to Adèle. He also says that several weeks after this concert Paganini came to see him and told him that he had a splendid Stradivarius viola for which he wanted a piece. Berlioz states that having got an idea, he had written the first part of a composition when Paganini wished to see it; on reading it he objected to the long sections in which the viola had nothing to do and said: 'I must be playing all through'; whereupon Berlioz said: 'What you want is a concerto for the viola, in which case you alone are the man to write it.' This, however, was the genesis of Berlioz's next big work, the symphony *Harold en Italie*, which was composed in the first six months of 1834.

In the meantime he was earning a little money by writing about music in the *Rénovateur*, and in an article of 15th December 1833 he writes the following interesting account of Liszt and Chopin:

> The enthusiasm aroused by Liszt at the Théâtre-Italien several weeks ago has not yet cooled down; wherever the conversation is about music, Liszt is cited as a miracle of verve, audacity, and inspiration. His qualities are so overwhelming, his climaxes so terrifying in their force and precision,

---

[1] He states seven thousand francs in his *Mémoires*. Whatever the precise sum, it went towards paying his wife's debts, which took him several years to settle.

[2] I can find no trace of this.

[3] No. 4 of the *Fleurs des Landes*, Opus 13, included in *Collection de 33 Mélodies* published by Richault, also in Breitkopf & Härtel's edition.

his ornamentation so delicate and so novel in style that truly sometimes one is incapable of applause, he so petrifies you.

Chopin[1] has quite a different talent. To appreciate it thoroughly I believe it is necessary to hear him at no great distance, rather in a *salon* than in a theatre, and to set aside every customary idea, because one cannot apply them either to him or to his music. Chopin as executant and as composer is an artist apart; he has no point of resemblance with any other musician of my acquaintance. His melodies, impregnated with Polish forms, have something naïvely wild which charms and captivates even by its strangeness; in his *Études* one finds harmonic combinations of astounding profundity; he has imagined a sort of chromatic embroidery, reproduced in several of his compositions, whose effect is indescribable; it is so piquant and bizarre. Unfortunately it is almost only Chopin himself who can play his music and give it this original turn, this unexpectedness which is one of its principal charms; his playing is marbled (*marbrée*) with a thousand nuances of which he alone has the secret and which could not be indicated. . . .

There are incredible touches in his mazurkas; further, he has made them doubly interesting by playing them with the last degree of delicacy, a superlative *piano*, the hammers skimming the strings so that one is tempted to go close to the instrument and to bend an ear as one would to a concert of sylphs and will-o'-the-wisps.

Chopin is the Trilby of pianists.[2]

I am glad to quote this fine appreciation of Chopin,[3] more especially as a remark that Berlioz made after the death of Chopin, 'he was dying all his life' (*il se mourait toute sa vie*), is often quoted as 'a famous sneer.' I fail to see that such an exact comment must necessarily be a sneer rather than a simple observation of fact.

A new musical paper, the *Gazette musicale*, founded by the publisher Schlesinger, appeared in January 1834, and Berlioz

[1] Chopin (1810–49). He first came to Paris in 1832, giving his first concert on 26th February. In the winter of 1832–3 he played with Liszt and Hiller Bach's Concerto for three harpsichords (played on pianofortes) at a benefit for Harriet Smithson. Berlioz was one of his earliest friends in Paris.

[2] The reference is evidently to Charles Nodier's *nouvelle*, *Trilby* (1822). Trilby is a spirit, who falls in love with a mortal woman and performs all kinds of menial services for her.

[3] Not even Chopin, Liszt, and Hiller playing together could win Berlioz to an appreciation of Bach. Of their performance of the Concerto for three pianofortes he writes: 'It was heartrending, I assure you, to see three such admirable talents, full of fire, brilliant in youthful vitality, united in a bundle to reproduce this ridiculous and stupid psalmody.'

immediately became a contributor. Schlesinger as a German (a brother was a publisher in Berlin) was not particularly partial to the Italian school, and Berlioz's antipathy to the popular Rossini and the Italianism of Paris at that time found a welcome expression in the *Gazette musicale*, where he wrote in praise of Beethoven (quartets and symphonies), Gluck, and Weber. He also contributed articles to *Europe littéraire*, and some of these, such as the 'Journal d'un Enthousiaste' and the 'Concours de Composition musical de l'Institut,' were included later in his published writings on music.

In March 1834 Mozart's *Don Juan* was performed at the Paris Opéra and, a year later, when Berlioz had become a contributor to the *Journal des Débats*, he wrote an interesting article on this opera,[1] in which he praises particularly the statue scene and speaks of the everlasting freshness of this 'astonishing work.' It is worth noting, in view of Berlioz's incessant abuse of the imbecility of the public and the musicians in the second half of his life, that he declares in this article: 'When Mozart wrote it he was quite aware that the success of such a work could only be slow and that perhaps it would not even be granted to the author to witness it. He often said, speaking of *Don Juan*, "I have written it for myself and a few friends."'

In April 1834 Berlioz and his wife moved out to Montmartre, which was then a village, and found a house with a pretty garden in the rue Saint-Denis. Here he wrote the greater part of *Harold en Italie*.

In May (15th or 16th) 1834 Berlioz writes as follows to Ferrand:

> I am almost dead with worry and work, compelled by my present circumstances to scribble at so much a column for these rascally papers. . . . You want to know what the *Chasse de Lutzow*[2] is; here it is, as it was sung at the Théâtre-Italien by those beasts of chorus-singers who destroyed its effect. [He quotes twenty-two bars of the music.] The prosody of your lines is not the same in each couplet and does not go with the music; but rather than alter the musical rhythm it would be better to effect a change in the metre of the poetry. . . .

---

[1] It appears in his *Les Musiciens et la Musique* (p. 3).

[2] A piece by Weber.

If the music publisher of Lyons stereotypes the piece with your words, remember above all things that on no account do I want to appear as if I had corrected or amended Weber, and that he must consequently stereotype the music in exact conformity to the copy I had sent to you by Schlesinger, in that there is no harmony except at the commencement of the chorus. [He quotes two bars of harmony.] The whole of the remainder is for the voice alone. . . .

I do not know why I am so wretchedly melancholy to-day and incapable of answering your letter as I should like. I thank you sincerely for your affectionate inquiries about Henriette. She is frequently ailing, being in an advanced stage of pregnancy. . . .

My affairs at the Opéra are in the hands of the Bertin family. . . . The question at issue is the production by me of Shakespeare's *Hamlet*, arranged in a superior manner as an opera. We hope that the influence of the *Journal des Débats* will be potent enough. . . .

In the meantime I have made choice, for a comic opera in two acts, of *Benvenuto Cellini*, whose curious memoirs you doubtless have read. . . .

I have finished the first three parts of my new symphony with principal viola part; I am going to set to work to finish the fourth. I think it will be good, and above all, curiously picturesque. I intend to dedicate it to one of my friends whom you know, M. Humbert Ferrand, if he will kindly permit me. There is in it a 'Marche des Pélerins chantant la prière du soir' which I hope will acquire a reputation in December. . . .

In a letter to Liszt about the beginning of May he writes:

My heaven is the world of poetry, but there is a caterpillar on each of its flowers. . . . Now M. Lamennais has written a sublime book in favour of an idea which seems to me absurd . . . is he honest? Equality! Is there such a thing? Is Shakespeare born the equal of M. Scribe? Beethoven the equal of Rossini?

Living happily with his wife at Montmartre and working at his new symphony, Berlioz was in the habit of entertaining his friends to tea in the evening; sometimes they made a party for the greater part of the day. The following letter, dated May 1834, to Chopin, refers to one of these and shows on what intimate terms they were:

---

[1] Unfortunately the influence of the Bertin family, proprietors of the *Journal des Débats*—the most influential paper of its time—did not succeed in getting Berlioz this commission.

My dear Chopinetto,

We propose to make an excursion out of town to Montmartre, rue Saint-Denis No. 10.[1] I hope that Hiller, Liszt, and de Vigny will be accompanied by Chopin.

Terrific nonsense! Never mind! H. B.

Writing on 12th May to Adèle, he says:

Last Monday we had a sort of little country party. My friends came and spent half a day with us. They were musical or poetical celebrities. Alfred de Vigny, Antony Deschamps, Liszt, Hiller, and Chopin. We talked, discussing art, poetry, thought, music, drama, in fact all that constitutes life in the presence of this lovely weather and Italian sunshine we have had lately. . . .

On Friday, 15th August 1834, Harriet gave birth to a son who was named Louis after Berlioz's father, who on learning of this event wrote cordially and a reconciliation was made. In a letter to Ferrand dated 31st August, he mentions this fact and announces that he is arranging for a concert in November at the Conservatoire to perform his new symphony. He also mentions that two friends of his, Léon de Wailly, 'a young poet of great talent,' and Auguste Barbier, had written a libretto for him on the subject of *Benvenuto Cellini* and that all three submitted the text to M. Crosnier of the Opéra-Comique, who declined it.[2]

We think, notwithstanding the protestation of M. Crosnier to the contrary, that I am the cause of the refusal. I am looked upon at the Opéra-Comique as a *pioneer*, an overthrower of the national style, and they will have none of me . . . the words were declined so that they might not be placed in a position to accept the music of an idiot.

I have, however, written the first scene, the *Chant des Ciseleurs de Florence*, with which they are all completely infatuated. . . . Have you read Barbier's last work on Italy. . . . Send me your *Grutli*. I will not fail to introduce it to him, as well as to Brizeux, Wailly, Antony Deschamps, and Alfred de Vigny, whom I see more regularly than the rest. I seldom meet Hugo; he is too domineering. Dumas is a harebrained creature. . . .

Léon de Wailly is not in the least disheartened; he is going . . . to

---

[1] His own address.

[2] Later on, in order to influence the director of the Opéra to accept this libretto, Alfred de Vigny looked over it for Berlioz and gave his name to it temporarily.

complete the plan of a grand opera in three acts for me . . . we shall see if a more propitious fate is in store for it. . . . If I had only enough to live upon I would undertake works far above operas. Music has huge wings, which she can never unfold to their utmost extent within the walls of a theatre.[1] 'Patience and length of time do more than force or rage.' I could write to you all night long, but as I have to be at my oar in my galley during the daytime, I must needs go to sleep. Henriette sends you any number of messages thanking you for your good friendship. . . .

In a charming letter to his sister Adèle, dated 23rd September 1834, Berlioz describes his domestic life. His son, he says,

is very strong, has superb blue eyes, an almost imperceptible dimple in his chin, blond hair, rather fiery, as I had when a child, a little pointed lobe to his ears like mine, and the lower part of his face rather short. Those are all the points of resemblance with his father; unfortunately he has nothing at all of his mother. Henriette dotes wildly on him. She is completely recovered; when I go to Paris she comes with her boy and the nurse, and they wait for me half-way down the descent from Montmartre under an alley of trees. . . .

In eight days we shall be in Paris, rue de Londres, No. 34. We have taken an unfurnished apartment, which at the end of the year is much more economical; but it is bare at the present moment. We must buy furniture, wine, wood, and a thousand other stupid necessities of which one does not dream in furnished apartments.[2]

During the period between 9th November and 28th December 1834, Berlioz gave four concerts for which he obtained the use of the hall of the Conservatoire free.[3] At the first concert on 9th November his programme consisted of the *Symphonie fantastique*, the *Roi Lear* overture, *La Captive* out of Victor Hugo's *Les Orientales*, *Sara la baigneuse*, ballad for double choir and orchestra, words by Victor Hugo, and *La Belle Voyageuse* from *Mélodies irlandaises*. At his second concert on 23rd November his new symphony *Harold en Italie* was given

[1] This is an interesting remark, coming from Berlioz.

[2] A description of this lodging made by Léon Gastinel who saw it in 1840 is as follows: 'Berlioz lived in the rue de Londres and had installed his working-room in a garret under the roof. A chair, a table on which lay the guitar which served him in the composition of his first works, were the only furniture. . . .'

[3] He applied for this permission to the Intendant Général de la Liste Civile. The concerts took place on Sundays at two o'clock in the afternoon.

its first performance with Chrétien Urhan[1] as the solo viola and Girard as conductor. The movement *Marche des pélerins* was encored but was muddled the second time. *Harold* was repeated at the concert on 14th December[2] and again on 28th December, at which Liszt played his pianoforte arrangement of the *Bal* and the *Marche au supplice* from the *Symphonie fantastique* which had recently been published. At the second concert Berlioz's romance *Paysan breton*, words by Barbier, was sung by Mlle Falcon. In his *Mémoires* Berlioz states that it was after the faulty conducting by Girard at these concerts that he made up his mind that in future he must conduct his own works himself. Nevertheless these concerts were a success, and his new symphony, *Harold en Italie*, made a favourable impression. He made very little money, in spite of the gratuitous assistance of most of the musicians and the free use of the hall. The public for serious music was not large and his successes were with the artists and the few genuine music-lovers. So we find him writing to Ferrand on 30th November, saying that he would like to send him the score of Liszt's arrangement of the *Symphonie fantastique*, but:

You know that for some time to come we shall be in somewhat straitened circumstances. However, to judge from the receipts at my last concert, which were 2,400 francs (double the amount taken at the preceding one), I may hope to get something out of the third. All the copying is now paid for, and a heavy outlay it has been. . . . My wife and I are as united and happy as possible in spite of our material annoyances.

And on 10th January 1835 he adds:

If I had time I should be hard at work upon another composition I

---

[1] Urhan (1790–1845) played the viola in Baillot's famous quartet, which first made Beethoven's quartets known to Paris, and succeeded Baillot as leader. Berlioz described in his *Première Voyage en Allemagne* how Urhan played in these quartets: 'Urhan worshipped in silence and lowered his eyes as if before the sun; he seemed to be saying: "God has willed there should be a man as great as Beethoven and that we should be permitted to contemplate him; God has willed it!!!" '

[2] At this concert Chopin played the *andante* of his Concerto in E minor. Berlioz wrote enthusiastically of it in the *Rénovateur*.

am meditating for next year, but I am compelled to scribble wretched articles which pay very badly. . . . However, it comes to the same thing in the end—time will have to be found for everything.

Some comment is due here on Berlioz's second symphony *Harold en Italie*. Most writers waste, in my opinion, many words in discussing the material of this symphony, its composite character, its romantic 'programme.' To me it has no more programme than Beethoven's 'Pastoral' Symphony, and, like Beethoven's 'Pastoral,' it is one of its creator's most genial and delightful works. What is the subject of Beethoven's 'Pastoral' Symphony? Merely the impressions and feelings of Beethoven in the beautiful country around Vienna. 'Mehr Ausdruck der Empfindung als Malerei,'[1] wrote Beethoven of the 'Pastoral' Symphony, and Berlioz might have said the same of *Harold en Italie*, which is the expression of Berlioz's own impressions and feelings in Italy, Harold being merely a convenient dramatic objectification of Berlioz himself. But with Berlioz, as with Shakespeare, it was as natural to express himself dramatically as lyrically; so we find that he writes movements such as the *Marche des pélerins* (No. 2) and the serenade of a mountaineer of the Abruzzi to his sweetheart (No. 3), in which he gives not his impressions of the march or the serenade or a description of the march or the serenade but creates the march and the serenade themselves. The first movement, which is entitled 'Harold in the Mountains—scenes of melancholy, happiness, and joy,' is a masterpiece of musical construction in which the solo viola is used in an extraordinarily vivid and creative way. The remarkable expressiveness of Berlioz's melodic invention, its fluidity and significance of line, always makes me think of the greatest masters of draughtsmanship; it is usual to extol Berlioz as a colourist, but truly he is just as great and even rarer in his greatness as a melodic draughtsman so that, for example, it requires a fine artist to play the viola part in this symphony adequately. When this is done and the work is in the hands of a good conductor with the necessary sensitiveness and subtlety to do justice to Berlioz's unfailing lack of that

[1] 'More the expression of feeling than description.'

crudity and obviousness which is the standby of so many composers, then the first movement of *Harold en Italie* is revealed in all its originality and beauty.

As for the second and third movements, it is no more necessary to explain their merits than that of a song like *The Last Rose of Summer* which, incidentally, when I heard Flotow's *Martha* some years ago at Covent Garden, struck me as far the best thing in the opera,[1] to which of course it does not belong. Indeed, even to call it the best thing in the opera is almost sacrilege, because it has the perfume of one real flower in an artificial bouquet. To create such a melody as *The Last Rose of Summer* or the theme of the Pilgrims' March in *Harold* is not given to every famous composer. A stroke of genius in this movement is the recurring *sforzando* on C natural of horns and harp against the tied F sharp held by the violins in the ninth bar of the canto. Another feature of this movement is the Canto Religioso with solo viola arpeggios *sul ponticello*, which has an exquisite effect. This is, no doubt, the passage referred to by Berlioz in a letter to Ferrand dated 10th January 1835, in which he says:

> You have doubtless seen the last article in the *Temps*; it is by d'Ortigue. I think he has taken a wrong view of the subject, though much of his criticism of detail is just. For instance, he asserts that there is not the shadow of a prayer in the *Marche des pélerins*, and merely notices in the middle of it some harmonies overlaid after the manner of Palestrina. They are precisely the prayer, seeing that all religious music is so sung in the churches in Italy. Moreover, that particular passage made an impression, as I anticipated it would, upon everybody, and d'Ortigue stands alone in his opinion.

The third movement is equally clear and speaks directly for itself. The solo viola is skilfully used in such a way as to unite this movement to the others. The last movement, *Orgie*

[1] I was delighted to find that Berlioz had exactly the same opinion. He remarks, in a letter to Ferrand dated 23rd December 1864, about *Martha*: 'This dull opera is performed in every language and in every theatre in the world. I went the other day to hear the charming little Patti, who played Martha; when I came out I seemed to be covered from head to foot with fleas. . . . Fortunately, it contains the delicious Irish melody *The Last Rose of Summer* . . . whose sweet perfume almost succeeds in disinfecting the remainder of the score.'

des Brigands, is constructed much on the principle of the last movement of Beethoven's Ninth Symphony. There is an introduction with reminiscences of the previous movements (scenes) until at length the orgy of brigands breaks out, whereupon the solo viola remains silent until near the conclusion of the movement when it has a brief reappearance.

Berlioz's wife made a brief return to the stage in a piece entitled *La Dernière Heure d'un Condamné* at the Théâtre-Nautique, Salle Ventadour, in November and December 1834. Berlioz was responsible for this engagement, having influence now as a journalist. This influence was soon to be greatly increased. On 10th October 1834 the most powerful newspaper, the *Journal des Débats*, owned by the Bertin family, reprinted an amusing article by Berlioz on an adventure of the famous tenor Rubini. His friend Jules Janin was a regular contributor, and other friends of Berlioz's, Léon de Wailly for example, were connected with the Bertin family. Aided by these and his own obvious talent as a writer, Berlioz became the regular musical feuilletonist or critic of the *Journal des Débats*.

All Berlioz's friends in the press, supported now by the Bertin family, began to agitate on Berlioz's behalf that the Paris Opéra should accept an opera by him. The text of *Benvenuto Cellini* by his friends de Wailly and Barbier was completed, and the only thing necessary was to induce Véron, the director of the subsidized Opéra, to accept it. The press campaign was incessant. This only annoyed Véron, who arranged for Adolphe Adam to compose a parody of Berlioz to be performed as an interlude at a masked ball at the Opéra on 10th January 1835.

The Duc d'Orléans, who was present at the performance of *Harold*, the Bertin family for whose *Journal des Débats* Berlioz began to write regularly on 25th January 1835, Jules Janin, Liszt, and others were sufficiently powerful to get Berlioz his last year's pension paid without his having to go to Germany, and to prepare the way for his entry to the Opéra. But in spite of all their efforts and intrigues it was not until after the retirement of Véron that the director Duponchel acceded to the pressure put upon him and at the beginning of

1837 agreed to produce *Benvenuto Cellini* after two operas, one by Niedermeyer and one by Halévy, had been produced.

D'Ortigue in the *Gazette musicale* wrote an article in which he declared of Berlioz: 'Besides genius he possesses virtue; and I understand by this word that force of character, that energetic and calm confidence which does not exclude modesty and which in the end will overcome all obstacles. . . . He will lay down the law . . . and you will submit to it. . . .'

Except in the sense that Berlioz remained true to himself and his genius all through his life, this prophecy did not come true. Berlioz, as we shall see, never won the support of the Paris public, and it required all his genius, his energy, and the devoted and active support of his distinguished friends, the powerful Bertin family, *and* the fear inspired by his position as critic in the *Journal des Débats*, to win for him a few opportunities to exercise his talents.

A few extracts from his letters will give the best picture of his life about this time.

April or May 1835.

MY DEAR HUMBERT,

. . . You ask me for details about our home life. Here you have them in a few words—our little Louis has just been weaned and has come satisfactorily through the ordeal, notwithstanding the dismal forebodings of his mother. He can almost walk alone. Henriette grows more and more passionately fond of him, but I am the only member of the household who possesses all his good graces; I cannot go out but he cries for an hour.

I work like a nigger for four newspapers, which gives me my daily bread. They are the *Rénovateur*, which pays irregularly, the *Monde dramatique* and the *Gazette musicale*, which pay but little; and the *Débats*, which pays well. Added to this I have to make head against the horror of my musical position, and I cannot find time to compose. I have commenced an immense work, entitled *Fête Musicale Funèbre à la Mémoire des Hommes Illustres de la France.*[1] I have already written two parts out of the seven of which the work will consist. It would have been all finished long ago if I had only been able to work at it and nothing else for a month, but I cannot get a single day to myself at present lest I should be in want of the needful in time to come. And yet, only the other day, some idiots amused themselves at the Barrière du Combat by

[1] First mention of the *Symphonie funèbre et triomphale.*

spending fifteen hundred francs to see a bull and a donkey eaten alive by dogs. . . .

I do not know what concert you allude to; I have given seven this year. I shall begin again in November, but I shall not have anything new to produce; my *Fête musicale* will not be finished; besides, it is written for seven hundred performers. . . .

In Paris we are now witnessing the triumph of Mussard,[1] who on the strength of his success and the assurance given him by his public-house associates, thinks himself equal to Mozart. I can quite believe it! Did Mozart ever write a quadrille like the *Brise du matin*, or the *Coup de pistolet*, or the *Chaise cassée*? Mozart died in poverty, which of course is only right and proper; Mussard is making at the present time at least twenty thousand francs a year, which is still more right and proper! . . .

Good-bye, love me always as I love you. Write to me as often as you can; in spite of my perpetual bondage, I will find time to answer you. My wife, who grows dearer and dearer to me, thanks you for your message; do not forget to remember me to yours. Oblige me by reading *Chatterton*,[2] by Alfred de Vigny.

To Adèle

Paris, 17*th April* 1835.

You are right, my dear sister, to be astonished at my long silence. . . . You do not know to what degree I am the slave of unavoidable work. . . . Very often in the evening I must go out to visit the theatres which belong to my province and be a party to the depravities they commit, so as to be able to write an account of them the next day. You see that I have hardly time to breathe. This condition of constant working is not the worst; it prevents me from feeling the thousand sharp points with which reflection on many things would torture me; but Henriette despairs at seeing me work all alone and at being unable to help, used as she has been all her life, on the contrary, to be the support of her family. Sometimes she is quite beside herself with vexation; I try to console her, but it is not much use; the facts cannot be gainsaid. I took her to Hugo recently, to get from him a role fitting for her talent and in which her inability to speak French well would not matter. Hugo is trying to do this. . . . He offered me an opera last month. Scribe also; but these offers are useless because of the opposition of the directors of the Opéra and the Opéra-Comique.

In the meantime my life as regards my art is indeed cruel and painful. To be obliged to see the best years of my life lost for dramatic music simply because three villains happen also to be imbeciles! Véron, for example,

[1] Now completely forgotten; his name is not even in Grove's *Dictionary*.

[2] This play was first performed at the Théâtre-Français on 12th February 1835.

whom Meyerbeer has been obliged to compel by legal means to produce *Robert le Diable* and to make his fortune by it. . . . Patience! Everything comes in time.

Let us speak of other things. Louis grows more and more beautiful. [Here follow a number of domestic details.] You tell me that you have talked of us a great deal with my grandfather and *others*; that *we are not forgotten*, etc. I don't know what you mean by this, but I do know that it would be more honourable for certain people to have forgotten me completely and that you should not have thus to defend them by their memory. You have many illusions, my dear little sister, and God grant that you are never put in the position to see them disappear. For me, I believe what I see. I believe in your goodness, because you prove it to me; others I believe to be egoists, fools, ridiculous, and absurd because they also prove to be thus. I judge them by comparing how I am certain I should behave, were I in their place and they in mine, with their behaviour to me.

In letters to his father and to Adèle in May and August 1835 there are much the same expressions, mingled with inquiries about his mother and his brother Prosper; he tells Adèle that his pension is now at an end and he has only his pen to support him. He and Henriette, he says, have even thought of going to North America, but the general uncertainty of what they could do there and the tender age of Louis have prevented them. 'Are you working?' 'When will you give us a new symphony?' These are the questions he meets with constantly, but he has no time to compose. In the letter of 2nd August to Adèle he tells her not to use certain expressions about 'prejudices which time will cure' and 'irritations that will pass away'; these expressions of course refer to the criticism by the family and others of Berlioz for marrying a woman with debts and no money, without having any money himself; he says they only make Henriette weep for two days, and he himself cannot endure these expressions, which are absurd: 'I married because I loved my wife. I knew she had nothing and that I had nothing; I would not find it ill in others to follow my example, and I know exactly what the ideas of the world are worth. . . . I prefer to work as I do and still more.' He then adds:

You ask for details of my situation as regards the Opéra (I don't speak of the Opéra-Comique, which is a theatre for grocers); this is it: I shall have no entry so long as M. Véron is there; now if he goes he gives his place to his associate, M. Duponchel, the designer of costumes, who imagines that he loves my music, although he understands it absolutely no more than M. Véron; Duponchel, six months ago, gave his word of honour to Meyerbeer and M. Bertin in my presence and before Barbier that if, as was probable, he became director of the Opéra, his first act would be to engage me to compose a work for it. . . . However, I know well what these animals of directors are, and I would sell M. Duponchel's word for a hundred crowns. I never forget that Meyerbeer was only able to get *Robert le Diable* produced (to which the theatre owes its entire prosperity for the last four years) by paying sixty thousand francs of his own money to the administration of the Opéra, which would not risk the expense. In order to obtain the sympathy of these villains one absolutely has to be a man as mediocre as they are. That is the most positive fact I can tell you on this subject. . . .

Adieu, my good sister, the model for all sisters, I embrace you tenderly.

In a letter to his mother dated Paris, 11th October 1835, we learn that Berlioz has been ill with throat trouble, to which he was susceptible, and that Louis had been very ill for a month. On 22nd November 1835 he gave a concert at which *Harold* was again performed; also *Le Cinq mai*,[1] a cantata on the death of Napoleon for chorus and orchestra, with words by Béranger composed in 1832; and two songs sung by Mlle Falcon of the Opéra, *La Captive* and *Le Jeune Pâtre breton*. He gave another concert on 13th December, to which he invited Victor Hugo when writing to him on 9th December, congratulating him on *Les Chants du Crépuscule* which the author had sent him. The letter is worth quoting as showing Berlioz's 'professional' style of writing, so unlike the style of his letters to his family and his more intimate friends:

I have received your marvellous poems. You are indescribably good to think of me, and even more to tell me that I must count you among

[1] This work, which does not deserve its neglect, although dated 1832 by Weingartner and Malherbe in their Breitkopf & Härtel edition, seems only to have been sketched as an idea in Berlioz's note-book in 1832; for he says in a letter to Adèle dated 24th December 1835: 'I have composed nothing this year except the song on the death of Napoleon,' and to Ferrand (23rd January 1836) he says: '*Le Cinq mai* is written on some bad verse by Béranger because the sentiment of this quasi-poetry seemed musical. I think the music would please you in spite of the words, it is indeed grand and melancholy.'

my truest friends. These are words which electrify and give to the fatigued soldier the force to take arms again and rush like a lion into the mêlée. Thank you! If I were a great poet like you, perhaps I should find some words to express what I have felt in reading your new work, but in my powerlessness I can only cry like savages at the rising sun: 'Oh!!!'

PS. Will you have the time free next Sunday to come and hear me?

At this concert on 13th December the programme included the *Symphonie fantastique*, the *Marche des pélerins* from *Harold*, and the overture *Roi Lear*. It is notable as the first concert which Berlioz conducted himself; but after this he almost invariably conducted all his concerts. About this time Berlioz had an opportunity to become director of the Gymnase Musicale, which would have brought him in a regular income and allowed him the opportunity to produce his own works, but it came to nothing and the place was given over to dancing instead. However, his name was now becoming known in Germany, thanks to Liszt's pianoforte arrangement of the *Symphonie fantastique* and to Schumann's famous article on that work. Berlioz felt most keenly the fact that he had composed practically nothing during the year 1835, and in a letter to Adèle dated 24th December 1835, he says: 'This necessity of sacrificing not only my art but also a certain financial return through the impossibility of being able to write and the need to have something to live on while composing is one of the most abominable swindles (*mystifications*) that a man can endure.'

In a letter to Liszt dated January 1836 he says:[1]

You are in the best position to write great things, profit by it. Go to Switzerland and to Italy on foot. It is thus that one sees and understands the beauties of nature. . . . Richault[2] asked me a month ago to arrange for four hands my overture to *Les Francs-Juges*. I have done this with the help of Chopin; it is being engraved now, also the full score. . . . I conduct my concerts myself now, with a great gain to the performances, which have always been imperfect. I do not know how to send you the two scores you ask for; I have a ridiculous fear of their being lost on the way. . . .

During 1836 Berlioz began to compose the music to *Ben-*

[1] In writing to Liszt, Berlioz uses the intimate 'tu.'

[2] A well-known French publisher who published many of Berlioz's works.

venuto Cellini; he was kept very busy not only with writing the articles which provided his living but also with assisting Mlle Bertin, the daughter of the proprietor of the *Journal des Débats*, who was a composer; she had already written a three-act opera on *Faust* for the Théâtre-Italien, and now Victor Hugo, partly in order to keep in with the Bertin family, had written her a libretto on the subject of *Notre Dame de Paris* and she had composed an opera on this subject which was entitled *Esmeralda*. Owing to the influence of her father, this work was accepted by the Opéra and Berlioz was asked to assist her at the rehearsals and to supervise the work. This caused much comment at the time. The gossip current may be judged from a letter of Mme de Girardin dated 29th September 1836,[1] in which she writes of *Esmeralda*:

> Some say: 'Truly it is very beautiful!' and one replies: 'I believe it, it is by Berlioz.' Others say: 'The music is admirable'; to which is replied: 'Doubtless, it is by Rossini!' To which our answer is: 'If the music is bad it is by M. Berlioz; if it is good it is by Rossini. If it is admirable, as is said, it is by Mlle Bertin.'

To Ferrand, in a letter dated 11th April 1837, Berlioz writes: 'I have had nothing to do with the composition by Mlle Bertin, absolutely nothing, except giving advice and hints on the musical form; nevertheless the public will have it that I am the author of Quasimodo's air. The judgments of the crowd are fearfully rash.' In the same letter he says that his opera (*Benvenuto Cellini*) is finished.

On 29th February 1836 Meyerbeer's new opera *Les Huguenots* (also known as *La Nuit de Saint-Barthélemy*) was produced at the Opéra and made an enormous success. Berlioz, although he described it as *une encyclopédie musicale*, praised it warmly and vigorously supported Meyerbeer in the *Gazette musicale* and the *Journal des Débats*. Meyerbeer was influential, and without influence nothing could be done at the Opéra. Money also was needed, and Berlioz completed his own opera with the

[1] *Lettres parisiennes*.

help of a loan of two thousand francs made to him by his friend Legouvé. Berlioz also had to praise Mlle Bertin's *Esmeralda*, which was produced at the Opéra on 14th November 1836 and was hissed. From the pit there were cries of 'Down with the Bertins. Down with the *Journal des Débats*!' and it is said that Alexandre Dumas, hostile to this paper which had accused him of plagiarism, cried aloud: 'It is by Berlioz! It is by Berlioz!'

CHAPTER V

ATTACK AND DISASTER

Berlioz fought out of sheer instinct and creative vitality for his livelihood and his music, and nobody has ever fought harder or more adroitly. His tough practical sense made it impossible for him to retire into a tower of refuge and wait there until he was rescued and taken out in triumph as a precious possession for which others, not himself, would fight. Where it was necessary for him to show discretion and tact he did so. When he praised Mlle Bertin's opera *Esmeralda*[1] he was not guilty of deception; he was merely influenced by good solid reasons. She was a cripple, she had talent and was the daughter of his employer, proprietor of the Government organ and a member of the Commission de Surveillance auprès de l'Opéra (Committee of Supervision for the Opéra). He could not ignore her work, and he praised it and criticized it with benevolence and with tact, in such a way as to make neither himself nor Mlle Bertin blush. That is the utmost that can be done by a man in his situation. He probably won the respect and support of the Bertin family more by the decency and decorum of his behaviour than by the mere fact that he eulogized *Esmeralda*, for all his journalist colleagues who wanted to be well in with the *Journal des Débats* did that, but most were merely fulsome where Berlioz was discriminating.

He now found a fresh supporter in the new Minister of the Interior (who had control of the Académie des Beaux-Arts), M. le Comte de Gasparin, who was appointed towards the end of 1836. Gasparin had been prefect of Isère, and at Grenoble he would have contact with Berlioz's friends and relations.

[1] In a letter to Adèle, dated 22nd December 1836, Berlioz praises the air of Quasimodo and says: 'If I contributed to the effect of this air it was only very slightly, it is really by Mlle Bertin but (between ourselves) it finished badly . . . my collaboration was confined to indicating a more effective end; that is all and I have told nobody.'

This was to bear fruit presently, after Berlioz had set in motion every influence that he could bring to bear upon the minister, including that of Bertin.

In addition to his struggle for a living and as an artist, Berlioz began now to suffer from the distortions and mutilations of his work—a form of torture to which musicians and dramatists who depend on public performances are liable. In answer to inquiries from Germany, he steadfastly refused to allow copies of his scores to leave his possession, because he wanted to introduce them there himself when he could be certain they would not be misrepresented. In a letter to Liszt dated 28th April 1836, he complains of receiving from Germany an arrangement for four hands of his *Francs-Juges* overture in which he has hardly recognized his work, and on 8th May 1836, he writes to Hofmeister, music publisher of Leipzig, who was responsible for this abortion, a stinging letter which deserves quotation:

> You have recently published an abridged overture, a duet for the piano, under the title *Ouverture des Francs-Juges*, the arrangement as well as the composition of which you attribute to me. It is painful for me to be obliged to protest that I am a complete stranger to this work . . . the arrangement . . . is *not mine*, neither can I recognize my work in what remains of the overture. Your arranger has cut, taken to pieces and sewn together again my score so that I can see in it nothing but a ridiculous monstrosity the honour of which I beg he will retain for himself. If such a liberty had been taken with me by a Beethoven or a Weber I should have submitted without a murmur to what nevertheless I would have felt as a cruel humiliation; but neither Weber nor Beethoven would have ever made me undergo this: if the work had been bad they would never have taken the trouble to touch it up; if it seemed to them good they would have respected its form, the idea, the details, and even the faults.
>
> Moreover, since men of their stamp are no more common in Germany than elsewhere, I have every reason to believe that my overture has not fallen into the hands of any very extraordinary musician. A mere cursory glance furnishes evident proof of that. [Here follow a number of technical details.] I pray that God may pardon the adapters as I pardon them.

On 19th February 1837 Berlioz wrote a long letter to Robert Schumann thanking him for the interest he had shown in his work, and for the well-prepared performance of his *Francs-Juges* overture at Leipzig, which he contrasts with a performance by the

Philharmonic Society of London at the Argyle Rooms. He says that he regrets having thoughtlessly published this overture and thus delivered it to the mercy of everybody, and that he will not expose his symphonies, 'which are too young to travel without me,' to cruel mutilation through premature publication; therefore he will wait until he will be able in person and as a pilgrim to lay his humble offering at the feet of Germany.

The whole letter to Schumann is a sort of artistic manifesto. In one place he remarks ironically: 'A very special genius is necessary for the creation of such works as the artists and the public alike comprehend at first sight and whose simplicity brings them home to the masses like the Pyramids of Ghizeh. Unfortunately I am not 'one of those geniuses.' He concludes:

> I cannot bring my letter to a close without telling you of the many pleasant hours I have lately spent in the perusal of your admirable pianoforte works; there appears to me no exaggeration whatever in their having been described to me as the logical continuation of those by Weber, Beethoven, and Schubert. Liszt, who thus described them to me, will be giving me a more complete idea of them and will make me know them more intimately by his incomparable execution of them. . . .

In March 1837 Berlioz managed to get out of Gasparin, the Minister of the Interior, a signed commission to write a requiem for the funeral anniversary of the victims of the attempt on King Louis Philippe's life by Fieschi on 28th July 1835, with a guaranteed payment of four thousand francs. Constant intriguing and obstinacy of purpose were needed to achieve this result. Without a definite commission and some guarantee of money to meet the immense cost of copying the parts of a big score and the rehearsing of it, Berlioz could not have started on such a work with any confidence. Also, Berlioz wanted the society in which he lived and his fellow artists and countrymen to participate in his work as far as possible; he was never a man of cliques or groups, but, writing for himself, he believed he was writing for mankind. He was not a democrat; all through his life he fulminates against popular governments and the public at large; but he also has no belief in academies, in the culture or tradition of the few, in any self-appointed *élite*.

Berlioz's frequent attempts to get work commissioned for public occasions or for the Opéra are due to the large scale which his natural genius demanded. He was, in his thirties, simply bursting with music. He had no particular theories or principles but was to a very rare degree instinctively creative, and in spite of a general intelligence far superior to that of most composers, he was not an intellectual or a theorist. He simply wanted an occasion for the exercise of his gift, and he knew that, once started, music would pour out of him like a flood. This explains to some extent the extraordinary character of works like the *Requiem* and the later *Te Deum*. Even to-day the conventionally minded person says, 'But this is not a requiem or a Te Deum as the world understands such things,' and he is right. Like the *Symphonie fantastique*, these works are episodes in the life of an artist.

In a letter to Ferrand dated 11th April 1837, he writes:

My opera is finished. It is now waiting until Messrs. Halévy and Auber shall each of them be kind enough to write an opera in five acts, the production of which . . . must precede mine. In the meantime I am at work on a requiem. . . . The Minister of the Interior commissioned it. For this immense work he offered me four thousand francs. I accepted without making any remark beyond that I should require five hundred performers. After a certain amount of alarm the contract was drawn up, my army of musicians however being reduced by fifty. I shall consequently have four hundred and fifty at least. I am finishing the *Prose des morts* to-day, beginning with the *Dies Irae* and ending with the *Lacrymosa*; it is sublimely gigantic poetry. I was intoxicated with it at first, but afterwards I managed to get it under; I have mastered my subject, and I now think that my score will be passably grand. . . .

To Adèle on 17th April he writes similarly:

. . . In two months I shall have finished, I hope. I have had difficulty in dominating my subject; at first the poetry of the *Prose des morts* had intoxicated and exalted me to such a pitch that nothing clear presented itself to my mind, my head boiled and I was giddy. To-day the eruption is regulated, the lava has furrowed its channel and, God helping, all will go well. It is a great affair! I shall no doubt incur the reproach of innovating because I have wished to bring this field of art to a *truthfulness* from which Mozart and Cherubini appear to me to have often departed. Then there will be formidable combinations that have not been successfully attempted, the idea of which I am, I think, the first to have.

In a letter to Liszt dated 22nd May 1837, he tells him that the *Requiem*[1] is finished, speaks of an arrangement by Liszt of the *Roi Lear* overture and asks him to write an article for the *Gazette musicale* on the works of Schumann that he had sent to Liszt. Berlioz recurs to this in two later letters to Liszt, dated 15th June and 20th July, and ultimately got the article, which appeared on 12th November 1837. It appears from this letter to Liszt that Harriet Berlioz made a temporary reappearance in the theatre about this time in *Jane Shore*, and Berlioz praises her performance for its dramatic poetry and truth.

In spite of the promise of the ministry, the *Requiem* was not performed at the Invalides; Berlioz announces the fact with a terrific outburst of spleen to most of his friends.[2] In a letter to the librarian of the Conservatoire, Bottée de Toulmon, he says that accustomed as he was to let huge waves pass over his head without fear of drowning, he believed this time for an instant that he would not breathe again; nevertheless, he adds, the work exists and it will be heard later. To Liszt he says: '. . . Luckily I have a hard head; it would be a famous tomahawk that could break it.'

To his father he writes: 'Never mind! The *Requiem* exists, and I swear to you, father, that it is a milestone in the history of art.'

However, he did not have to wait long. The din he and his friends and, above all, Bertin, made, had such an effect that, another excuse presenting itself,[3] the authorities were only too glad to order his *Requiem* to be performed at the Invalides. The final rehearsal (*répétition générale*) took place on 4th December and the public performance the next day at a quarter-past twelve. Berlioz had an orchestra of three hundred

[1] The autograph score is dated Paris, 29th June 1837, and belongs to the library of the Paris Conservatoire.

[2] It must not be forgotten how important performance of work is for a composer, especially when he is still young. It is the only way he can check his conceptions by their materialization.

[3] General Damrémont and a number of soldiers having been killed in an attack on Constantine on 14th October 1837.

musicians placed to the right and left of the sanctuary, Habeneck conducted, and the success was considerable, with a good press, on the whole. His friends among the journalists praised it enthusiastically; his enemies attacked it violently, the *Constitutionnel*, for example, saying that from Beethoven to Berlioz was as far as from creation to chaos.[1]

When it was over Berlioz had a certain difficulty in getting the money from the ministry; his letters are full of complaints at the delay, but he was probably paid quicker than anybody else would have been, as his capacity for making a fuss and his physical endurance in making it were alike more than normal.

I shall now say a few words about the *Requiem*, sometimes known as the *Messe des morts*. I have only heard this great work once, when Sir Hamilton Harty, then conductor of the Hallé Orchestra, performed it at Manchester. Many musicians and amateurs from London paid a special visit to hear it, and the excitement was great both before and after the event. It was still living in the train returning the next morning to London. The performance was good without being adequate; for one thing the four small brass bands which Berlioz asks for were reduced to two, and they were not placed at the four angles of the central choral and instrumental mass as prescribed by Berlioz, owing partly no doubt to the difficulty of arranging this in the Manchester hall. But this is not exceptional. Berlioz's great works are rarely performed, and still more rarely are they played as Berlioz demanded, in spite of the emphasis which he laid on following his instructions. Yet it must be plainly said that until we have heard Berlioz's works played exactly as he demanded, we cannot say that we have really heard them. One day a new Gustav Mahler will arrive in the world of music, and he will give us Berlioz's music as Berlioz conceived it, and the world of musicians will be astonished.

Requiem or *Messe des morts*. The first movement (*Requiem et Kyrie*) is a magnificent piece of symphonic construction that

[1] What the *Constitutionnel* knew about Beethoven was next to nothing. Beethoven did not begin to be popular in Paris until about 1880.

every musician must admire and will have no difficulty in admiring. It has not aged or dated, it remains a permanently satisfying piece on a grand scale.

The second movement (*Dies Irae*) offers more difficulties to the normal musician; it has the special Berliozian flavour (like the *Tibi omnes* and the *Dignare* of the later *Te Deum*) which seems to prove too much altogether for many musicians. One cannot define this quality; one can only say that just as some people like and others dislike the very particular taste of quince, so you either like or you dislike that very special nervous, sinuous melody which one can find nowhere but in Berlioz.

Then the thunders of the Last Judgment begin and the four brass bands are used with terrifying effect. There is nothing even in Verdi's magnificent *Requiem* to compare with this *Tuba mirum*. It is an apocalyptic vision unparalleled, unimagined before or since in music.

The third part (*Quid sum miser*) is a short chorus accompanied by wood-wind and strings (two cors anglais, eight bassoons, 'cello, and double-bass). This is one of those broken, piteous, desolating fragments of which Berlioz was a master and which musicians who are not susceptible to suggestion, but only to blatant expression, can never understand.

The fourth part (*Rex tremendae*) cannot fail to make its effect on all; here again the four brass bands are used.

Next, *Quaerens me*, an unaccompanied chorus of beautiful simplicity yet by no means simple.

In the *Lacrymosa* the four brass bands are again used in a much-elaborated movement.

The *Offertoire* is exceedingly original and beautiful. This is the movement about which Schumann exclaimed: 'This Offertory surpasses all!'

In the *Hostias* we have an example of one of Berlioz's entirely novel effects of instrumentation, where he uses three flutes against eight trombones with strings, accompanying the choir. This is a remarkable piece.

The *Sanctus* is a piece of sustained elevation and beauty, containing a fugue on the words 'Hosanna in excelsis.'

The last section (*Agnus Dei*) contains some previous matter and concludes with a serene and peaceful Amen.

What strikes one vividly on reflection after having undergone the unusual experiences which this great work provides is its utter lack of the slightest vulgarity anywhere, in spite of the unusually large means Berlioz employs. Just as Berlioz's instrumentation is never coarse (unlike Wagner's), so his expression is never vulgar.

The publicity made for the *Requiem* was favourable to the production of *Benvenuto Cellini* at the Opéra. Berlioz took up his score again and began to compose an overture, snatching what leisure he could between his articles for the newspapers. When Schlesinger worried him for copy for his *Gazette musicale* Berlioz replied (7th January 1838):

> I am in absolute need of repose and protection against albums. For a whole fortnight I have been seeking in vain for a couple of hours wherein to dream at leisure about the overture to my opera . . . if I have to live on bread and water until my score is finished I don't want to hear a word about criticism. Meyerbeer, Liszt, Chopin, and Kalkbrenner have no need of my praises . . . in short, I want to be an artist; I will be a galley slave again afterwards. . . .

On 18th February 1838 his mother died; his last letter to her was dated 18th January 1838. A few months later his younger and favourite sister Adèle was married to Marc Suat, an old friend of Berlioz's who was an amateur of music and believed in Berlioz as a composer. In fact much later, in 1856, Berlioz writing to Adèle says that he has always suffered much in silence at seeing 'you all (*your husband excepted*) consider only the material results of my efforts and my dreams.'

The production of *Benvenuto Cellini* took place at the Opéra on Monday 10th September, and the second and third performances followed on the 12th and 14th. Prior to this Berlioz had received two setbacks. Rifaut, a professor of harmony at the Conservatoire, died and Berlioz applied for the post; he failed to get it because Cherubini was against him and stated that it was a tradition for the professor of harmony to be able to play the pianoforte, which Berlioz could not do.

The second rebuff was more serious. On the night of the 14th January 1838 the Théâtre-Italien (place Favart, where the Opéra-Comique is now) was burnt down. Bertin and other powerful friends of Berlioz's, the Duc d'Orléans, the Président du Conseil, M. de Montalivet, succeeded in getting the ministry to put a project before the Chamber for rebuilding and subsidizing the theatre and giving the direction of it to Berlioz. At once a furious attack broke out in the anti-ministerial press; the journalists spoke of Berlioz and Co., and no law of libel such as we know in England restrained the violence of the expressions used. It was stated that the whole thing was a 'job' for the Bertin family so that more operas by Mlle. Bertin might be produced. Berlioz was mocked as 'M. Berlioz writer, M. Berlioz composer, M. Berlioz director, belonging to the literary, commercial, and political press,' and surprise was expressed that Berlioz, this hater of Italian music, should accept the position of director of the Italian theatre. The enemies of Berlioz and the Bertin family, and the friends of Rossini and of composers jealous of Berlioz, carried the day. The Commission reported against the project and the Chamber voted against it.

This created a bad atmosphere for the production of Berlioz's opera. The fact is that Berlioz's determined and persistent attack on Paris, while it brought him certain perhaps necessary advantages, such as the commissioning of the *Requiem* and the acceptance of *Benvenuto Cellini* at the Opéra, defeated in the long run his own purpose and destroyed his career. It could not destroy his genius but it maimed the expression of it, and the failure of *Benvenuto Cellini* closed the doors of the Opéra to him for the rest of his life. Further, I believe that the state of spleen which this fighting activity (with the complementary hostility, denigration, and misrepresentation it aroused) produced in Berlioz was harmful to his development. In a letter to Liszt dated 8th February 1838 he says that if he had not put himself into one of his blue fits of rage at the ministry he would still be waiting for his money for the *Requiem*; he adds that he has been trying to write a song to words written for him by Brizeux which he wanted to dedicate to Liszt's friend the Comtesse d'Agoult, but he has been unable to find anything worthy of her: 'My Pegasus is stubborn for these small compositions'; but I believe that Berlioz had merely lost the right mood.

The rehearsals of *Benvenuto Cellini* were not likely to produce a better mood. The agony which a composer or dramatist goes through witnessing the inconceivable stupidity, incompetence, and lack of artistry in the majority of the performers in his work is not to be described. In a letter, dated 31st July 1838, to Legouvé, who had lent him the money to enable him to finish his opera, he says:

> Schoelcher found me in bed the other day. I have been really ill . . . getting up only for rehearsals. We begin to put the orchestra straight in spite of the complaints of all the old fossils who declared they had never seen anything like it for difficulty of execution. The millions of wrong notes, of muddled conceptions, above all of incorrect rhythms, have so cruelly tortured and irritated my nerves that this suffering is the sole cause of my illness.

To his rivals and to the public generally the position of Berlioz in 1838, only thirty-four years of age, seemed unusually brilliant. He was musical critic and chronicler on the most influential paper in Paris; he had been commissioned by the Government to compose a *Requiem*, which had been performed at the public expense, and he had got his first opera, *Benvenuto Cellini*, accepted at the Paris Opéra. All this on top of having been the winner of the Grand Prix de Rome and having, as such, enjoyed a pension for five years. It is no wonder that the attacks on him grew more violent, especially as he was always grumbling and full of spleen. One of his supporters, Mainzer, now wrote in the *Chronique musicale de Paris* of 8th August an article in which he stated that he had once thought that Berlioz was a martyr in the cause of art by reason of his originality, but that now he could only consider him as exploiting his position to turn art into an industry, and he quoted Schiller's saying: 'For some artists art is a celestial divinity; for others it is a cow to be milked.'

In the *Charivari*[1] there was much caustic wit at Berlioz's expense: 'In this century every one tries to get talked of . . . soon it will be impossible to walk down the boulevards without saluting a celebrity in each passer-by. Happy the man who will have enough modesty not to salute himself!'

All Berlioz's friends wrote articles praising *Benvenuto Cellini.* Théophile Gautier wrote in the *Presse* after hearing several rehearsals that it showed 'a great science of harmony, rich orchestration of extreme complexity and concision, but full of daring and originality.' In fact everything conspired to bring about the complete failure of a work that in any case was too unusual to please the public.

At the first public performance on 10th September the verdict was that the libretto was bad and the production poor. At the second performance the receipts were bad; nevertheless the general criticism was favourable to the music and the genuine admirers of Berlioz were more than satisfied and many extremely eulogistic reviews appeared. But *Benvenuto Cellini* did not make money at once, and that was fatal.[2] In a letter dated 20th September Berlioz tells his father that owing to Duprez not wishing to sing the role, the second tenor Dupont has had to be taught to replace him, which means an interruption of eight or ten days in the performances; he adds that he cannot describe what a mass of intrigues and quarrels his opera has given rise to:

> It is a mêlée in which my defenders utter almost as much folly as my detractors . . . this will disappear in time. The French have a passion for arguing about music without the least understanding or feeling for it. The important thing is that one hears me often, *very often*, and I count on my score to win the battle for me more than all that is said in its favour.

But the public did not have the chance to come; also the

[1] The famous French satirical paper.

[2] It was performed three times; then, owing to the change of tenor and for one reason or another, the fourth performance did not take place until 11th January 1839, four months later. After this it was abandoned, and all chance of its making its public was lost.

work was too original, above all, too *fine* for current taste. It was dropped from the repertory of the Opéra and was never revived there during Berlioz's lifetime.

Benvenuto Cellini was originally in two acts, but when in 1851 Liszt proposed to produce it in Weimar Berlioz revised it.[1] A pianoforte edition was published by Litolff of Brunswick in 1855; this edition represents the opera in three acts as it was frequently performed at Weimar under Liszt, and it is from this edition, a copy of which is in my possession, that I make the following brief analysis. This pianoforte edition is by Hans von Bülow and is preceded by his arrangement of the well-known overture for four hands. The German text is by Peter Cornelius, the composer of the comic opera *Der Barbier von Bagdad*.

Benvenuto Cellini. Of the overture it is not necessary to speak, it is in the repertory of every orchestra in the world and is constantly being played. It and its fellow piece, the *Carnaval romain*[2] overture, are composed out of themes in the opera, and these two overtures are the best known and most frequently performed of all Berlioz's compositions, although they only represent one aspect of his genius.

The first act takes place at Rome in the palace of Balducci, treasurer of the Pope, on Shrove Monday. The first scene is between him and his young daughter Térésa, and he goes out grumbling at the favour shown by the Pope to Cellini. Left alone, Térésa hears a chorus (tenors and basses) of the approaching carnival-makers and looks out from her window. Cellini arrives in the crowd below and sends her a bouquet of flowers and a letter, which she draws up on a string. So far the music has been gay and lively; now follows a beautiful cavatina (*larghetto espressivo*), sung by Térésa, which is full of warmth; this is followed by an *allegro con fuoco*, an elaborate, lively aria

[1] It was produced at Weimar on 20th March 1852, and again under Liszt during the Berlioz week at Weimar, 17th November 1852, with great success. After the March production Berlioz made some alterations for the November production. (See bk. IV, chap. ii and iv.)

[2] Composed later, in 1844 and played, Pohl says, as an introduction to the second act of *Benvenuto Cellini*.

in Mozart's style for Térésa, which gives the singer a fine opportunity. Cellini now enters the room and a fine duet is followed by a trio, with the arrival of Fieramosca, a rival sculptor. Cellini and Térésa make a rendezvous in the Piazza Colonna for the next day. Her father Balducci returns, but Cellini escapes and Fieramosca is caught. Balducci calls the servants and the first act finishes with a lively ensemble.

The whole of this act is vital and expressive; there is in it nothing banal, mechanical, or flat, but it goes with unfailing verve and conciseness.

The second act is the carnival in the Piazza Colonna. I do not intend to describe it in detail; there is nothing to equal it for brilliance, variety, gaiety, and electrifying vivacity in the whole history of opera. But in addition to this sparkling magnificence it has a freshness, a spontaneity, a Schubert-like grace and expressiveness which put it in a far higher class than the most brilliant pages of Rossini, while the instrumentation is, of course, incomparably richer and stronger. It is also the longest act.

The third act takes place in the studio of Cellini. The famous statue of Perseus by Cellini is about to be cast. There is a short introduction, then the workmen arrive and there follows a wonderful, sombre chorus, very characteristic of Berlioz. Ascanio, Cellini's friend, arrives with Térésa, who is sad at having left her father. The workmen in the foundry behind the studio are now heard singing a plaintive melody, 'Bienheureux les matelots!' (Happy the sailors!), and two of them make ready the studio; all this music is of an enchanting melancholy. A delightful barcarolle sung by Ascanio, in which he tells of the three of them (Cellini, Térésa, and himself) leaving for Florence that evening, leads to a chorus sung by a religious procession which Térésa watches from the window, 'Maria sancta mater ora pro nobis.' Térésa kneels, and with Ascanio sings a prayer for Cellini, full of bold modulations and most expressive. Cellini arrives, and after some fine recitatives Cellini and Térésa sing a wonderful duet, full of subtlety of expression and beauty of line. Suddenly Balducci appears with Fieramosca and there is a powerful dramatic scene; the

Cardinal arrives, a sextet follows and there are pages of masterly ensemble music, full of variety and colour; then there is a beautiful air for Cellini, *andante* in six-eight time, leading to the finale. Cellini is pardoned, and allowed to marry Térésa; the last scene is in the foundry, where the statue is cast with fiery gusto by Cellini and his workmen. The opera ends in a blaze of sonority with unfailing *élan*.

The fate of *Benvenuto Cellini* is a good example of what can befall artistic creations when they belong to no school or movement and cannot be made into a tool of aesthetic or sociological propaganda. In a letter to Carl Czerny dated Weimar, 19th April 1852, Liszt writes: 'The remarkable and extraordinary works to which our theatre owes its new renown—*Tannhäuser*, *Lohengrin*, *Benvenuto Cellini*—required numerous rehearsals which I could not give into the hands of anybody else.'[1] In a letter to Wilhelm Fischer, chorus-master at the Dresden Opera, dated Weimar, 4th January 1854, Liszt wrote:

> I am convinced that when you have looked more closely into the score, you will be of my opinion, that *Cellini*, with the exception of the Wagner operas—and they should never be put into comparison with one another[2] —is the most important, most original musical dramatic work of art that the last twenty years have to show.

In more recent times *Benvenuto Cellini* has been successful in Germany, especially under Felix Mottl[3] at Karlsruhe. This famous conductor was, like Liszt, a great admirer of Berlioz's operas and performed them all. Perhaps it may afford matter for reflection among a few of those who read this book that it has always been musicians of a very superior order who have loved and performed Berlioz's music.

[1] It is worth noting by musicians that Liszt wrote to Gustav Schmidt, Kapellmeister at Frankfort-on-Main: 'The effect of Berlioz's works can only be uncommonly good when the performance is satisfactory. They are equally unsuited to the ordinary worthy theatre and concert maker, because they require a higher artistic standpoint from the musician's side.'

[2] Because Wagner's operas were labelled 'music-dramas' and 'music of the future.' Now they seem old-fashioned as operas and music of the past; the theories on which they were written are exploded; and to-day every good musician recognizes the superiority of the pre-Wagnerian operas of Gluck and Mozart.

[3] Mottl, Felix (1856–1911).

CHAPTER VI

PAGANINI AND 'ROMÉO'

AT the concert Berlioz gave on 16th December 1838, after the failure of *Cellini*, he conducted *Harold en Italie*, and Paganini, who was present, heard it for the first time. Paganini was so moved that at the end of the concert he went to Berlioz, fell on his knees before him, and kissed his hand. Berlioz relates the incident in his *Mémoires*, stating that as Paganini was suffering from a *maladie du larynx* he communicated through his son Achille, who said: 'My father orders me to tell you that never in his life has he had such an impression at a concert, and that he cannot refrain from kneeling before you to express his gratitude.'

This was gratifying enough, but fortunately for Berlioz, two days later, he received a letter from Paganini enclosing a banker's order on Rothschild for twenty thousand francs. Berlioz relates this in a letter to his father, dated Paris 18th December, in which he quotes Paganini's letter, which he had only just received. He quotes this letter in its original Italian, as follows:[1]

MIO CARO AMICO,

Beethoven estinto, non c' era che Berlioz che potesse farlo revivere; ed io, che ho gustato le vostri divine composizioni, degne di un genio qual siete, credo mio dovere di pregarvi a voler accettare in segno del mio omaggio venti-mila franchi, i quali vi saranno rimessi dal signor baron de Rothschild.

Credete mi sempre
il vostro affettuoso amico,
NICOLO PAGANINI.

---

[1] This is the English translation: 'My dear Friend,—Beethoven being dead, there is only Berlioz who can make him live again; and I who have experienced your divine compositions, worthy of such a genius, believe it my duty to beg you to accept as a sign of my homage twenty thousand francs, which will be remitted to you by the Baron de Rothschild. Believe me always, your affectionate friend.

Berlioz, in a letter to Adèle on 20th December, quotes Shakespeare as saying that misfortunes never come singly, and tells her that he has just learned that he has been appointed assistant librarian at the Conservatoire, which will bring him in two thousand francs a year.[1]

Paganini's gift made a tremendous sensation, especially as he had a reputation for being very mean and fond of money. It has been said that Paganini made this gift to Berlioz merely to win popularity (having been severely criticized for not giving his services at a charity concert) and that the advice came from the journalist Jules Janin, a friend of Berlioz's. According to August Morel,[2] Paganini later declared:

> I did that for Berlioz and for myself—for Berlioz because I saw a man full of genius whose force and courage would perhaps have ended in being broken in this terrible fight he had to carry on daily to maintain himself against jealous mediocrity and public indifference, and I said to myself, 'I must come to his aid.' For myself, because later justice will be done to me on this subject, and when my claims to musical glory come to be reckoned not the least of them will be that I was the first to recognize a man of genius and to have pointed him out for the admiration of all.

Paganini's motives may have been mixed; even the idea may have come to him from someone else;[3] but this does not detract from the virtue of his deed. Berlioz, in a letter to his sister Adèle dated 20th December, says that most people do not understand an artist like Paganini, and relates how when calling on him to express his gratitude, Paganini spoke with tears in his eyes of the satisfaction and joy it had given him to be able to help Berlioz: 'You have given me emotions that I had not anticipated; you have advanced the great art of Beethoven.'

Berlioz's young brother Prosper had come to Paris to study in October 1838, but he died on 15th January in the *pension*

[1] Berlioz's first instinct was always optimistic; the amount never exceeded fifteen hundred francs.

[2] Writing in the *Journal de Paris*.

[3] It has been said that the money came from Bertin, proprietor of the *Journal des Débats*, but I know of no evidence for this. Also there is no reason why Bertin should not have given the money direct to Berlioz if he had wanted to. Berlioz was not a fool. It would not have hurt his pride to take twenty thousand francs from Bertin.

where he was living. In a letter to his father dated 30th November Berlioz writes that Prosper is studying hard and that his teachers are satisfied with him; also that they have been much together. Paganini left Paris about a month after his gift to Berlioz, and the two never met again.

The greater part of 1839, thanks to the generosity of Paganini, was devoted to the composition of the dramatic symphony *Roméo et Juliette.* If Berlioz had had a success at the Opéra with *Benvenuto Cellini* it is likely that he would have composed *Roméo et Juliette* in operatic form, but there was little chance of the Opéra accepting a new work by him, so he was compelled to plan a new form which would give him the opportunities he required. *Roméo et Juliette* was begun on 24th January and finished on 8th September 1839. Dedicated to Paganini, it was first performed with about two hundred executants[1] under the direction of Berlioz himself in the hall of the Conservatoire on 24th November 1839.[2] It was a success with the public chiefly owing to the effect of the second movement (Grande fête chez Capulet), the 'Queen Mab' Scherzo, and the Finale. The performance according to Berlioz was 'satisfying,' which no doubt means mediocre.

Roméo et Juliette. This work, which is included in the uncompleted Breitkopf & Härtel edition, is also available in miniature score, published by Eulenburg, Leipzig.[3] Berlioz's own title for his work is *Symphonie dramatique, avec Chœurs, Solos de Chant et Prologue en récitatif choral, composée d'après la Tragédie de Shakespeare.* Now, the first thing to be said about *Roméo et Juliette* is that it is the only adequate musical conception of Shakespeare's play in existence. What Berlioz did later with Goethe's *Faust* in his *Damnation de Faust* he did with

[1] 160 musicians, the choir made up of 12 voices for the chorus of the Prologue, 42 for the Capulets, 44 for the Montagus, the soloists being Mme Widemann, Dupont, and Alizard.

[2] Two further performances followed, for which Berlioz made some alterations; nevertheless he says in his *Mémoires* that he felt there were many retouches still to be made.

[3] There is also a pianoforte and vocal score arranged by Th. Ritter and published by Hofmeister, Leipzig, and Brandus, Paris.

Shakespeare's *Romeo and Juliet* in this work. He has not set either to music, taking the text as a libretto like an ordinary musician, but inspired by these two great dramatic poems, he has conceived two immense musical works on their subjects much as Milton wrote *Paradise Lost* on the story in the Book of Genesis and Dante his *Commedia* on Christian theology. In the history of music Berlioz's *Roméo et Juliette* and *Damnation de Faust* stand out first of all by their seriousness,[1] and secondly by their scale. They have a grandeur of conception and a quality of inspiration that removes them totally from comparison with all the operas by Gounod, Bellini, or others on these subjects.

During twenty years of constant attendance at concerts in London and frequent visits on the Continent, I have never heard *Roméo et Juliette* performed.[2] Bits of it, of course, are frequently played, and some musicians, I am sure, even take the fourth of its seven parts, the 'Queen Mab' Scherzo, to be the complete work; it lends itself, being for orchestra alone, to separate performance and to the foolishness of ignorant critics who use it to digress on the familiar theme of Berlioz's genius for instrumentation. Nearly all Berlioz's works are mutilated in performance, because the musicians responsible are generally inferior persons without respect for Berlioz who ignore totally the very careful and precise instructions he has laid down. It is only a Liszt or a Mottl, or a Gustav Mahler, who can even conceive the idea that Berlioz may have known more than they do and that his instructions deserve attention.

Berlioz lays down exactly how *Roméo et Juliette* should be performed. I shall not quote these elaborate instructions because they chiefly concern conductors who wish to perform this work and are printed in the Breitkopf & Härtel edition and in the miniature score edition. It suffices to say that any conductor who does not try to observe these instructions is a scoundrel or a fool. As for those who cut *Roméo et Juliette*

[1] Not solemnity, but true seriousness in the sense that they are not written as an entertainment.

[2] It is played in Germany fairly regularly. The Germans respect (and have always respected) Berlioz, but I am not sure how far they understand him.

instead of giving it in its entirety, they are just blackguards. The seven sections of this dramatic symphony are as follows:

(1) Prologue. (Combats, tumults—Intervention of the Prince.)

This begins with an instrumental introduction (*allegro fugato*); then follows the Prologue proper, contralto solo and small chorus (fourteen or twenty) (*moderato*); after this Strophes (*andante avec solennité*), contralto and small chorus; a tenor solo is now added (*moderato*), followed by a Scherzetto with tenor solo; then the choir (*andante*) sings of the sovereignty of death. Thus, in this Prologue, Berlioz ingeniously sets forth the whole programme of his symphony and almost a thematic exposition of its contents.

(2) Romeo alone—Sadness—Concert and Ball—Grand fête at the Capulets'.

This is the musical incarnation of youthful love and gaiety. There is nowhere in music such a young and ardent hymn to love, which, like Shakespeare's verse, becomes ever richer and more complex; but even the words of the greatest poet cannot give the brilliance and gaiety of the concluding fête as music can and as Berlioz with his Shakespearian plenitude of orchestral invention does. Some might say the ball ends in a cataclysm. Not at all; it is just an almost inconceivable splendour and uncontrollable gaiety.

(3) Love-scene — Serene night — The Capulets' garden silent and deserted.

One cannot describe this section without seeming to use too many superlatives. After a short introduction (*allegretto*) (flutes and strings, to which horns are presently added), a double chorus (tenors and basses) is heard in the distance, 'ladies of Verona dream of dancing and of love,' it ends *ppp* and the *adagio* begins. In this love-scene the voices of Romeo and Juliet do not appear; their music is given to the instruments. This exquisite tactfulness of Berlioz was not unconscious; he himself said:

> If in the famous scenes of the garden and the cemetery this dialogue of the two lovers . . . is not sung; if, in short, the duets of love and despair

are given to the orchestra, the reasons are numerous and obvious. . . . Duets of this kind having been treated a thousand times vocally and by the greatest masters, it was prudent as well as interesting to attempt a different mode of expression.

So Berlioz has recourse to the instrumental language, 'a tongue,' he says, 'richer, more varied, less limited, and by its very vagueness incomparably more powerful in such a case.'

One can only say that Berlioz's experiment is completely successful. In the whole of music there is nothing to compare with this scene. Here is not simple melody, but the very perfumes of melody and the moonlit ecstasy of passionate first love.

As usual with Berlioz's finest conceptions, it was adversely criticized. In his *Mémoires* Berlioz mentions this fact. 'A critic, speaking of the love-scene,' he says, 'of the *adagio*, that piece which three-quarters of the musicians of Europe who know it put nowadays above everything else I have written,[1] declared that I had not understood Shakespeare!!!' Then he adds bitterly: 'TOAD, SWOLLEN WITH STUPIDITY, HOW WILL YOU PROVE THAT TO ME!'

Let me add that the conductor who dares to perform this scene without the introductory chorus, that is to say who dares to mutilate it, deserves to have his ears cut off.[2]

(4) Queen Mab, or the Dream-Fairy.

This celebrated piece of musical imagination needs no praise; its originality and fantasy are admitted by every musician, although the clodhopper type, like Edward Dannreuther, thinks that 'the fantastic element predominates to such an extent that the effect is more curious than beautiful; indeed, borders upon the ludicrous.' Dannreuther was a Wagner fanatic and, as such, his finer auditory sensibility was shattered by the crudity

[1] This was before the composition of *L'Enfance du Christ*, *Les Troyens*, and *Béatrice et Bénédict*.

[2] It is amusing to find Edward Dannreuther (that deafened Wagnerian) writing in the *Oxford History of Music* of this *Scène d'amour* that it 'contains some two hundred bars of the richest and most delicately passionate music in existence. There is nothing in the whole range of French music to approach it, and nothing but *Nacht der Liebe* in the second act of Wagner's *Tristan* to surpass it.' The comparison is a bad one. Berlioz's is pure passion like Shakespeare's, while Wagner's is morbid eroticism like Swinburne's. The difference is most striking!

of his idol. That this is still the case with most musicians is proved by the fact that there is hardly a conductor living who can get an orchestra to play this *scherzo prestissimo* with the necessary sensitiveness, delicacy, and exactitude. The nineteenth-century attitude to this piece was the same as the eighteenth-century attitude to Shakespeare's Queen Mab passage; they thought it barbarous and bordering 'upon the ludicrous.'

(5) 'Convoi funèbre de Juliette.'

This is described by Berlioz as a 'fugal march, at first instrumental with a psalmody on a single note in the voices; then vocal with the psalmody in the orchestra.'

One of the ridiculous catchwords of the nineteenth century was that Berlioz did not understand or, at least, was not a master of fugue and counterpoint. Such nonsense reminds me of a book by the late T. W. H. Crosland on the English sonnet. It shows that all the great poets—Shakespeare, Milton, Wordsworth, Keats—were imperfect sonneteers, and quotes many perfect and completely dull and worthless sonnets by schoolmasters and others. I have already proved[1] that Berlioz had under Reicha the best and most thorough teaching in fugue and counterpoint that was available in Europe in his time, a scholastic training that Wagner, for example, never underwent. In this 'Convoi funèbre' you will find Berlioz using the fugal method with the imagination and mastery that Beethoven brought to it. Like Beethoven, Berlioz did not care for writing formal fugues, but he used fugue as a means of expression with a consummate mastery that no composer since Beethoven has ever equalled.

(6) Romeo at the tomb of the Capulets.

This is a scene in which the music may be described as representative; or, rather, Berlioz expected his auditors to imagine the tomb scene of Romeo and Juliet while his music depicted the emotions of the protagonists and the gloom of their environment. But, he said: 'The public has no imagination.

[1] Reviewers, please take notice, and do not let yourselves give further currency to this lie about Berlioz's inadequate training.

Pieces addressed to the imagination have therefore no public. The following instrumental scene is in this situation and I think it is better to suppress it . . . ninety-nine times out of a hundred.'

(7) Finale—The crowd at the cemetery; strife between Capulets and Montagues—Recitative and air of Father Laurence —Sermon of reconciliation.

This finale is on a grand scale with choirs, bass solo, and orchestra, and brings this great work to a noble and splendid conclusion.

It is well known that Balzac and Théophile Gautier were great admirers of Berlioz's music. Gautier wrote a most eulogistic article on *Roméo et Juliette* in the *Presse* of 11th December 1839, in which he says: 'He has given a soul to each instrument of the orchestra, an expression to each note; he has wished that every phrase should have a precise sense; this idea, foreshadowed by some masters, used by Beethoven, has been well developed by M. Berlioz. . . .'

In a letter to his father dated 26th November 1839, Berlioz says: 'This morning Balzac said to me: "Your concert-hall was indeed a brain-pan." And truly all the intelligentsia of Paris was there.'

CHAPTER VII

'I AM GOING DOWNHILL'

THREE performances of *Roméo et Juliette* at the end of 1839 exhausted the public interest in this work. It was now becoming quite clear that for Berlioz, as for every true creator, there was no livelihood in his artistic creations. His genius, working for a year, might produce a symphony or an opera; but after three performances, each taking a few hours, the small public interested was satiated, and to regain its interest a new work must be provided. While the first flush of his early manhood endured, Berlioz could provide a stream of great and original creations, but also he had to earn his living, support his family, and withstand the misrepresentation, malice, and envy of those in whom a great man arouses not respect but hatred. He really needed a Paganini every year, as Beethoven had his annual allowance from the Archduke Rudolf; but this was not to be.

On Friday, 31st January 1840, he wrote to Ferrand:

> . . . For the three evenings (of *Roméo et Juliette*) I had to pay the performers twelve thousand one hundred francs; the receipts amounted to thirteen thousand two hundred, so . . . I get only eleven hundred francs. Is it not a melancholy thing that so splendid a result . . . should turn out to be so paltry when one looks to it for means of subsistence? Serious art is decidedly incapable of maintaining its disciples, and it will continue to be so until a government arises that can appreciate how unjust and horrible such a state of things really is.

Here is an example of Berlioz's inveterate youthfulness, optimism, power of self-illusion—call it what you will! No government will ever arise that will support the true creator, for the simple reason that every government will be either a dictator or a committee, and always, inevitably, of inescapable necessity, every dictator and every committee will choose to support pliant and comprehensible, if not flattering, mediocrities and will ignore, because they cannot perceive, genius. As

Berlioz grew older he became more and more gloomy. The words *crétins*, *gredins*, *crapauds* were always on his lips. It is true that he was surrounded by them and suffered exceedingly from them. These toads, villains, blockheads were to the right of him, to the left of him, in front of him, and behind him. Every year they seemed to grow more numerous or to be replaced by thousands of fresh ones, while his few friends grew older and feebler: 'I see Gounet very seldom, and he is generally very melancholy. He is becoming really old, more so than you would believe.' [1]

Also he was losing his youthful taste for diplomacy, for manipulating his career; he was becoming more aware of the reality around him and how little it corresponded with what lived in his imagination; he was, in other words, an artist, not a careerist:

> I was asked by the Opéra to write the music for a libretto in three acts by Scribe. I took the manuscript, but I afterwards changed my mind and sent it back ten minutes afterwards without reading it. It would take up too much time to tell you my reasons. The Opéra is a school of diplomacy. I am improving. But, joking apart, my dear Ferrand, this sort of thing wearies, disgusts, shocks me and makes me indignant. Fortunately we shall very possibly have a change soon; the management is ruining itself. . . .

In that last sentence we have an indication of Berlioz's irrepressibly sanguine temperament. Almost to the end of his days he lived in expectation of 'a change.' Only rarely did it dawn on him that 'a change' never comes. Certain sensitive persons are likely to be estranged in reading Berlioz's *Mémoires*, and even this biography, by this alternation of spleen and optimism. In this he is more akin to Beethoven than to any other composer, and quite unlike Mozart, who suffered just as much as Beethoven or Berlioz but took it as a matter of course. Mozart somehow understood that inferior musicians must naturally be more generally appreciated than he was, that it was his lot as a great genius to be considered merely a gifted musician like any other; but Beethoven even in his last days

[1] Letter to Humbert Ferrand, 31st January 1840.

was full of bitterness and vituperation for the Viennese public running after novelties, and Berlioz writes: 'I am so dreadfully melancholy that nothing makes the slightest difference to me; what is going to happen to me? Most probably nothing. Well, we shall hear all about everything some day or other. Come what may, I love you sincerely; never doubt that.'[1]

Nevertheless, he was only thirty-six, and energy poured out of him. He obtained the commission for a work to be performed on the occasion of the inauguration of the Column of July, erected on the place de la Bastille in honour of the tenth anniversary of the July Revolution of 1830. This work, composed during the first part of 1840 and duly performed on 28th July 1840 at the public ceremony, was the:

Grande Symphonie funèbre et triomphale, pour grande harmonie militaire avec un orchestre d'instruments à cordes et un chœur ad lib. The symphony is divided into three parts: Funeral March, Funeral Oration, Apotheosis; the choir takes part only in the last movement. This work is published in the Breitkopf & Härtel edition, but the only reason I can give for its total and undeserved neglect is that hardly anybody nowadays knows of its existence. Instead of appraising it myself I will quote Wagner's opinion of it.

Wagner arrived in Paris towards the end of 1839 via London, having left Riga in July 1839. During the whole of 1840 he was living in Paris, finishing *Rienzi* and writing the libretto of *The Flying Dutchman*. In *Mein Leben* he says that he wrote for Schlesinger a short story, *Une Visite à Beethoven*, which appeared in the *Gazette musicale* and, as a sequel, *Un Musicien étranger à Paris*, which Heine praised; he then continues:

> Even Berlioz was touched by it and spoke of the story very favourably in . . . the *Journal des Débats*. He also gave me signs of his sympathy, though only during a conversation, after the appearance of another of my articles entitled 'Ueber die Ouvertüre' (On the Overture), mainly because I had illustrated my principle by pointing to Gluck's overture to *Iphigénie en Aulide* as a model. . . .
>
> During the previous winter I had often heard his grand instrumental

[1] Letter to Ferrand, 31st January 1840.

pieces played under his own direction and had been most favourably impressed by them. During that winter [1839–40] he conducted three performances of his new symphony, *Roméo et Juliette*, at one of which I was present.

All this, to be sure, was quite a new world to me, and I was desirous of gaining some unprejudiced knowledge of it. At first the grandeur and masterly execution of the orchestral part almost overwhelmed me. It was beyond anything I could have conceived. The fantastic daring, the sharp precision with which the boldest combinations—almost tangible in their clearness—impressed me, drove back my own ideas of the poetry of music with brutal violence into the very depths of my soul. I was simply all ears for things of which till then I had never dreamt, and which I felt I must try to realize. . . .

During the same winter Berlioz produced his *Symphonie fantastique* and his *Harold en Italie*. I was also much impressed by these works; the musical genre pictures woven into the first-named symphony were particularly pleasing, while *Harold* delighted me in almost every respect.

It was, however, the latest work of this wonderful master, his *Grande Symphonie funèbre et triomphale*, most skilfully composed for massed military bands during the summer of 1840 . . . which had at last convinced me of the greatness and enterprise of this incomparable artist. But while admiring this genius, absolutely unique in his methods, I could never quite shake off a certain feeling of anxiety. His works left me with a sensation as of something strange, something with which I felt I should never be able to be familiar, and I was often puzzled at the strange fact that though ravished by his compositions, I was at the same time repelled and even wearied by them. It was only much later that I succeeded in clearly grasping and solving this problem, which for years exercised such a painful spell over me.[1] It is a fact that at that time I felt almost like a little schoolboy by the side of Berlioz. . . .

A little later, 4th February 1841, Wagner got his *Columbus* overture performed; he had no great opinion of it, but he had nothing else suitable; he says:

'Berlioz, who was present at the rehearsal, remained silent throughout. He gave me no encouragement, though he did not dissuade me. He merely said afterwards, with a weary smile, "that it was very difficult to get on in Paris." '

During the whole of 1841 Berlioz composed nothing; he did not even give a concert. He was toying with the idea of an

[1] It is a pity that Wagner never communicated to the world this solution. Or is this a gigantic piece of Wagnerian bluff? I think that probably Wagner's solution was only good for himself but quite genuine.

opera, *La Nonne sanglante*, which came to nothing, and he wrote the recitatives for the new production of Weber's *Der Freischütz* at the Opéra. In a letter to Ferrand dated 3rd October 1841, he writes:

. . . Spontini has just returned. . . . He has been, so to speak, driven out of Prussia and that was my reason for writing to him. In such a case one is bound to give utterance to every protest, however trivial, which can bring balm to the wounded heart of a man of genius, whatever may be his mental defects and however great his egoism. The temple may possibly be unworthy of the deity who dwells therein, but the deity is a deity for all that. . . .[1]

I should so like to see you! It seems to me that I am going downhill with fearful velocity. . . . This year, among other things, I have written the recitatives for Weber's *Der Freischütz*, which I succeeded in getting produced at the Opéra without mutilation, correction, or *castilblazade* of any kind. . . .

In addition to composing these recitatives Berlioz, a little later, orchestrated Weber's *Invitation à la valse*, which was used for a ballet in *Der Freischütz* at the Opéra. He also published a set of six songs, *Les Nuits d'été* (Summer Nights), composed at various times, the words by Théophile Gautier. These beautiful and original songs are almost entirely unknown to-day; but as they deserve—more than any songs composed since Schubert—to be prized by music-lovers I will give some details of them here:

Les Nuits d'été[2]

(1) *Villanelle*, a simple but exceedingly fresh and lovely country song (*Ländliches Lied*) for mezzo-soprano or tenor and pianoforte; in 1856 Berlioz made an exquisite orchestral version of it.

(2) *Le Spectre de la rose*, for contralto and pianoforte,

[1] Berlioz wrote on 27th August 1841 a letter of the warmest enthusiasm to Spontini on his opera *Fernand Cortez*, which he ends: 'Farewell, dear master. There is a religion of the beautiful; I belong to it. And it is a duty to admire great things and to honour great men; I feel that in clasping your hand it is also a happiness to do so.' This letter, according to Tiersot, is a superb piece of calligraphy, written with the greatest care on beautiful paper.

[2] I take these particulars chiefly from the *Collection de 33 Mélodies pour une ou plusieurs voix et chœur*, published by S. Richault, Paris. This pianoforte edition has the French text and a German text, a translation from Gautier by Peter Cornelius.

orchestrated in 1856. This is a longer and more complex song, in which Berlioz's subtlety of melodic expression is a source of inexhaustible pleasure. Those who do not understand why some claim that he is the greatest melodist since Schubert should begin by studying such songs as this and *La Captive.*

(3) *Sur les lagunes*, for baritone, contralto, or mezzo-soprano and pianoforte; orchestrated by Berlioz in 1856. This is a fine piece of mood-painting, with a very remarkable atmosphere.

(4) *L'Absènce*, for mezzo-soprano or tenor and pianoforte; orchestrated in 1843 by Berlioz. This is one of the finest and most expressive love-songs in the whole history of music. Only in Schubert and Mozart can one find anything to compare with it.

(5) *Au cimetière* (*Clair de lune*), for tenor and pianoforte; orchestrated by Berlioz in 1856. This song, with its extraordinary chromaticism, is very characteristic of Berlioz's especial melancholy vein of melody which resembles that of no other composer. It is something of a test piece. Those who appreciate its rare, expressive quality are true Berliozians.

(6) *L'Ile inconnue*, for mezzo-soprano or tenor and pianoforte; orchestrated by Berlioz in 1856. This song, unlike No. 5, requires no initiation, no study of Berlioz's genius. It is as exquisite as it is simple.

It may be thought by the reader ignorant of these songs that I have overpraised them. But this book is written not as a paean to Berlioz but merely to do Berlioz justice. In proof of which I will now quote what that Wagner-sodden musician and musicologist, Edward Dannreuther (one of the most prejudiced of anti-Berliozians), has written about Berlioz's songs:[1]

It is pleasant to find that the tendency to eccentricity rarely appears in Berlioz's *chansons*. . . . *Chanson de Paysan*,[2] *Petit oiseau*, *La Belle*

---

[1] *Oxford History of Music*, vol. VI.

[2] As far as I know *Chanson de paysan* and *Petit oiseau* are the same song. The *Chanson de paysan* is a sub-title. It belongs to the set entitled *Fleurs des Landes*, Opus 13.

Voyageuse, Elle s'en va seulette,[1] or the Villanelle, No. 1 of *Les Nuits d'été* (verses by Théophile Gautier), are gems with a real charm of their own. . . . No. 3, the so-called Lamento *Sur les lagunes* and No. 4, *Absence*, rank among the finest histrionic examples of forlorn passion. For their due effect *Les Nuits d'été* should be sung, not at the pianoforte but with a small orchestra as originally written.

Dannreuther is surely wrong in declaring the orchestral version the earlier one. I have not found a copy of the first published edition of *Les Nuits d'été*, but Richard Pohl, who had his information from Berlioz, states that this edition is for voice and pianoforte, *später instrumentiert* (instrumented later). Weingartner and Malherbe in their Breitkopf & Härtel edition agree.

Towards the end of 1841 Berlioz made the acquaintance of a Marie Geneviève Martin who called herself Marie Recio, half Spanish by birth, and about twenty-seven years old (b. 1814). She was a singer, and made her first appearance at the Opéra on 5th November 1841 as Ines in *La Favorite*. Berlioz praised her, and on 30th January 1842 wrote a favourable notice of her performance as the page in *Comte Ory*. In this he speaks of her good figure compared with many in this role, who mostly resemble 'a sack of nuts.' Many writers say that she owed her engagement to the influence of Berlioz. In any case there was, sooner or later, a liaison between them. His wife, unfortunately, had developed into a violently jealous woman. She does not seem to have had any serious provocation until this liaison with Marie Recio; but according to Legouvé,[2] an intimate friend of Berlioz, she had aged prematurely, as the plump blonde type is apt to do, and having been an actress, she was unfortunately well equipped to make scenes. She spied on Berlioz, read his letters, searched everywhere for signs of infidelity, and made such terrible scenes that their son Louis, now about seven years old, used to weep with anguish. In short,

[1] *Sic* in the *Oxford History of Music*! I do not know this song, but these are the opening words of *La Belle Voyageuse*. I am quoting from the second edition, Oxford University Press, 1931; but one does not expect English musical editors (or musicians) to know Berlioz's works. This, however, does not prevent them from decrying Berlioz!

[2] In *Soixante ans de souvenirs* by Ernest Legouvé.

Berlioz's wife Harriet turned out to be quite incapable of living with her difficult husband after the first seven happy years. She did everything she ought not to have done and made his home intolerable to him. This was a great misfortune for Berlioz; it changed what might have been a temporary liaison with a woman of mediocre character and talent into a permanent one, and compelled Berlioz at last to leave his home where he could find no peace and to maintain two separate *ménages*. This continued for the greater part of his life, until his wife Harriet died in 1854, when he married Marie Recio, who in her turn died in 1862.

In September 1842 Berlioz made a trip to Brussels with Marie Recio and gave two concerts there, which were on the whole a failure but about covered their costs. One writer, Zani de Ferranti, had the discernment to point out one of the reasons for the failure of Berlioz's music to attract the public: 'This music has the great fault of having appeared in an epoch that could not be more unfavourable—an epoch of positivism and of prose.'

This was not the only reverse of the year. In March Cherubini died. Berlioz hoped to be elected to the Institut in his place, but Onslow was appointed. Then an inspector of singing in the primary schools died and Berlioz applied for the post, but he did not get it. Back to journalism! That was his only resource to earn his living, for he was lucky if his concerts paid their expenses.

One untried resource remained—Germany! So Berlioz decided to make a concert tour there. He left Paris early in December 1842 (he was thirty-nine years old on the 11th of that month), taking Marie Recio with him, and passing through Brussels, arrived at Mayence about the 19th, where he found there was no chance of giving a concert; he proceeded to Frankfort-on-Main, where he heard *Fidelio* at the theatre, but was told that owing to the rage there for two 'prodigy' sister violinists prospects for a concert were too unfavourable. He then left for Stuttgart, where he gave his first concert in Germany on 29th December 1842.

BOOK IV

(1843–69)

CHAPTER I

BERLIOZ AMONG THE GERMANS

I do not propose to follow Berlioz's first German tour in detail; in fact in this last book I shall deal with him more generally than I have done in the three earlier books, in which I was anxious to present an abundance of facts, and copious extracts from his letters, so as to give as full a representation of him as possible. Further, as a man gets older he becomes less expressive, except in his art, and Berlioz, who was now approaching his fortieth birthday, henceforth more rarely writes letters with the fullness and abandon of his youth.

His first tour in Germany,[1] which lasted from January to the end of May 1843, was a series of vexations and trials, owing sometimes to small and inferior orchestras and to the usual difficulties of a foreigner trying to get his works performed. His first concert was due to the collaboration of Lindpaintner, Kapellmeister to the Royal Band of the King of Wurtemberg at his capital, Stuttgart. Berlioz gave his concert (including the *Francs-Juges* overture, the *Fantastique*, and the March from *Harold*) in the presence of the king and the court. Mendelssohn considered Lindpaintner (in 1831) to be the best conductor in Germany, and he had brought his orchestra to a high level, so Berlioz was able to write to Paris that the performance was 'excellent and its success considerable.'

This brought him an invitation from the Prince of Hechingen, who had a small private orchestra directed by Täglichsbeck; 'by patience and good will' parts of the *Fantastique* and *Harold* were given and the prince became an enthusiastic admirer and staunch supporter of Berlioz for the rest of his life.[2] Returning to Stuttgart, Berlioz proceeded to Karlsruhe, but the theatre

[1] Berlioz published an account of it in his *Premier Voyage en Allemagne.*

[2] This prince gave a great Berlioz festival at Löwenberg in 1863 which Berlioz conducted.

there was not free for ten days owing, says Berlioz, 'to the engagement of a flautist from Piedmont . . . full of respect for this great flautist, I hastened to Mannheim,' where he gave a concert which the Grand Duchess Stéphanie admired. He then returned to Frankfort, where he fell ill with throat trouble. This was the birthplace of his old friend Ferdinand Hiller, who in his *Aus dem Tonleben unserer Zeit* relates that on the evening following Berlioz's arrival he was giving a concert in Frankfort-on-Main:

> I asked Berlioz to assist. 'Impossible,' he replied, 'you know that I am travelling in company with a singer. She yowls like a cat; that would not be altogether a misfortune if she had not the unhappy ambition to wish to sing at all my concerts. I am going from here to Weimar, where we have an ambassador, and it is impossible for her to accompany me, so I have my plan. She believes that I am invited this evening to Rothschild's; I shall have to leave the hotel, I have taken my ticket for the post, my trunks are packed and will be taken from the hotel to the station; I shall leave, and in two hours she will get a letter announcing my flight. . . .

Unhappy Berlioz! His first wife acted—at home, when she could no longer perform on the stage—and his mistress and second wife sang. If he had lived long enough he would no doubt have married a third who would have been a *writer*! God preserve all artists from artistic women! Do not misunderstand me, reader! Nothing is finer, and nothing to-day is rarer, than a woman of culture; but women who are ambitious to *perform* in public—whether it is on the stage, in the pulpit, on the platform, at the cross-roads, or in the home—are sent for a chastisement to man as God sent the plagues to Job.

Of course Marie Recio was too much for Berlioz. She tracked him down and arrived unexpectedly at Weimar just as he was walking in the moonlight, dreaming of Goethe and Schiller, and of the sudden possibility of being once more an artist capable of love and creation.

We can imagine the scene. This was the last attempt—as far as we know—that Berlioz made to get free. On 25th January he gave a successful concert at Weimar. Marie Recio sang three times (*Absence* (!), *La Belle Voyageuse*, *Le Jeune Pâtre breton*). No doubt Berlioz thought to himself: 'What is the good of making the effort to get rid of her? I shall only fall into the clutches of another woman who may be far worse—for the unknown is always worse than the known.' The reader will excuse this solitary occasion on which I have taken the liberty of suggesting what was in Berlioz's mind; but it is based on an element in the character of Berlioz which seems to me very strong, namely his profound scepticism and fatalism with regard to life.

Berlioz hesitated to go to Leipzig, where his old acquaintance Mendelssohn reigned, so he wrote tentatively to Mendelssohn, who gave him a friendly invitation with practical information. In these days of blind fanaticism, when it is thought a virtue to hate those who differ from you in any way and still more virtuous to try to destroy them, it is pleasant to look back upon the tolerant and genial attitude of Mendelssohn towards a colleague whose music he disliked. Dislike is not too strong a word. In a letter to Mendelssohn dated 12th February 1834, Moscheles[1] writes:

> After yours [*Melusine* overture] . . . I had Berlioz's *Les Francs-Juges* to conduct. We were all curious to know what the result of French genius would be. . . . But oh! what a rattling of brass . . .! What cruel, wicked scoring! as if to prove that our ancestors were no better than pedants. . . .

To which idiotic effusion Mendelssohn replied from Düsseldorf in April 1834:

> With what you say of Berlioz's overture I thoroughly agree. It is a chaotic, prosaic piece, and yet more humanly conceived than some of his others . . . his orchestration is such a frightful muddle, such an incongruous mess, *that one ought to wash one's hands after handling one of his scores.*[2] . . .
>
> At first he made me quite melancholy, because his judgments on others are so clever, so cool and correct, he seems so thoroughly sensible, and yet does not perceive that his own works are such rubbishy nonsense.

But Berlioz liked Mendelssohn, and it is clear from the last

[1] Moscheles, Ignaz (1794–1870), a famous pianist and conductor. He disliked Chopin's music almost as much as Berlioz's. On the other hand he much admired a composer named Bennett.

[2] My italics. To what fanatical blindness mere pure-mindedness and idealism can lead a man who is decent but narrow!

sentence I have quoted from his letter that Mendelssohn was impressed by Berlioz personally. Consequently, when Berlioz arrived at the Gewaudhaus in the midst of a concert given by Mendelssohn and greeted him warmly and praised his music, Mendelssohn cordially responded. They exchanged batons,[1] and Berlioz conducted his first concert in Leipzig on 4th February 1843, including the two overtures *Francs-Juges* and *Roi Lear*, the *Fantastique*, and a piece for solo violin composed about 1839, *Rêverie et caprice*, played by the leader of the Gewandhaus orchestra, Ferdinand David. The reception was mixed and the *Allgemeine musikalische Zeitung* wrote that 'Berlioz does not write to please but to be characteristic . . . his fantasy alone is his law . . . he might be described as the 'Hell Breughel' of music[2] . . . beside the 'Sabbath' of the *Fantastique*, Weber's scene in the Wolf's Glen would pass for a cradle-song.'

On 6th February Berlioz left Leipzig for Dresden, where he spent about three weeks. Owing to the success of *Rienzi* in 1842, Wagner, at the age of thirty, had been appointed Kapellmeister to the Royal Court Theatre of Dresden on 2nd February 1843. One of Wagner's first duties was to help Berlioz give his first concert in Dresden. Wagner does not say a word about this in *Mein Leben*, but, luckily, in Praeger's *Wagner as I Knew Him* we have an account of how Berlioz and Wagner got on together, given to Praeger by August Roeckel, who was assistant musical director to Wagner from 1843 to 1849. Roeckel was a passionate admirer of Wagner and, according to Praeger, this is his description of their intercourse:

Wagner was at first attracted, but the cold, austere, though always polished demeanour of Berlioz checked Wagner's enthusiasm. He had the air of patronizing Wagner; his speech was bitter, freezing the boisterous expansiveness of Wagner. At times the conversation[3] was so strained

[1] Berlioz wrote a characteristic letter to Mendelssohn beginning: 'Grand Chief! we have promised to exchange tomahawks . . .' Fenimore Cooper was a passion with Berlioz and his friends in their youth, and it was Chateaubriand (another favourite writer of the young Berlioz) who introduced the Red Indians and the New World to literary France.

[2] Pieter Breughel the younger (c. 1564–1637), nicknamed 'Hell Breughel' from his fondness for macabre subjects.

[3] The conversations would be in French, as Berlioz understood no German. Richard Pohl relates in his *Hector Berlioz* how in 1863, in spite of his frequent and long visits to Germany (the only country where his music was appreciated

that Roeckel was of opinion that Berlioz intentionally slighted Wagner. The more they were together, the less they appeared to understand each other; and yet, notwithstanding the fastidious criticism, the constant fault-finding of Berlioz, he took pains to arrange meetings with Wagner, naturally fascinated by the vigour with which Wagner discussed art.

In an article written from Paris (1840–1) for a Dresden paper, *Europa*, under the signature 'Freudenfeuer,' after hearing some of Berlioz's works, Wagner makes some observations about Berlioz's character, stating that he alone composes 'without regard for money,' and that 'in spite of his displeasing character' he is a unique artist; Wagner also says of the *Symphonie funèbre*, that it is 'great from the first note to the last.'

Berlioz, on the other hand, hearing in Dresden for the first time *Rienzi* and *The Flying Dutchman* (*Der fliegende Holländer*), was not greatly impressed, although he found things to admire. In the *Journal des Débats* of September 1843 he writes: 'Wagner conducted his operas with an energy and precision very uncommon.' Roeckel, according to Praeger, said of Berlioz's impressions of *Rienzi*: 'Satisfied he was not; about the only number he thought meritorious was the Prayer. With the *Dutchman* he was still less contented. He complained of the excess of instrumentation.'

Praeger thinks this very curious in a composer who employs 'four orchestras with twelve kettle-drums in one work.' A technical analysis of Berlioz's works would show, however, that his scoring is much less thick than Wagner's, his sense of instrumentation far more delicate and original; also that Berlioz's orchestration is invariably clean in colour and has a transparency that more resembles Mozart's (in spite of other differences) than anybody else's.

At Dresden Berlioz conducted *Harold*, with Lipinski playing the viola, the *Fantastique*, the *Symphonie funèbre*, the cavatina

warmly during his lifetime), Berlioz understood only one word of German. At Löwenberg, the enthusiastic public wanted to encore the Love Scene from *Roméo et Juliette* and the March from *Harold*. They cried out '*Da capo!*' '*Da capo!*' ('From the beginning!') but Berlioz had learnt the word *bis*, which was used for 'encore' elsewhere in Germany, and he took *Da capo* for 'Bravo!' and gave no encore. 'Charming, true Parisian!' exclaims Pohl.

from the first act of *Benvenuto* sung by a Mme Schubert, and the *Sanctus* from the *Requiem* sung by Tichatscheck. *Le Cinq mai* was also given, for the first time in Germany. He gave two concerts and made some money, so that he was able to send his wife (Harriet Smithson) five hundred francs. Returning to Leipzig he gave another concert, but had to abandon the attempt to perform the last movement of *Roméo et Juliette* but was able to give some fragments of the *Requiem*. It was after this concert that Schumann made the often quoted remark: 'This Offertorium surpasses everything.'

Berlioz heard that it was useless to go to Munich at the moment and Meyerbeer wrote to him that it would be better to defer his visit to Berlin, so he went to Brunswick, where he found an excellent orchestra and made a real success before a large audience on 9th March with his concert at the theatre. He also gained a new adherent in Robert Griepenkerl,[1] who wrote shortly afterwards an enthusiastic pamphlet on the 'French Beethoven,' entitled *Ritter Berlioz in Braunschweig, zur Charakteristik dieses Tondichter*. A similar success followed at Hamburg, where he gave a concert at the Opera-house on 22nd March.

Berlioz then proceeded to Berlin, where he stayed some time, arriving on 28th March and giving two concerts in April. The press was unfavourable but, as everywhere, Berlioz's music aroused a lively discussion; and strangely enough the King of Prussia, father of the first Emperor William, seems to have taken a strong fancy to some of Berlioz's music, in particular the *Fête chez Capulet* from *Roméo*, and came to his second concert.

More interesting is the fact that Berlioz heard in Berlin Meyerbeer's *Huguenots*, Gluck's *Armide*, and a Bach Passion—whether the St. Matthew or the St. John he does not say. He was sympathetic to Meyerbeer's opera, partly because Meyerbeer was a friend and an ally, but his real enthusiasm was for Gluck's *Armide*.[1] Berlioz was thrilled by the fine singing of

[1] Griepenkerl, Wolfgang Robert (1810–68).

[2] The present neglect of Gluck will not last. Some years ago (about 1928–9) *Armide* was revived at Covent Garden. It was given three times and I was present on each occasion, not being able to miss this wonderful work. But the public (or rather the press) preferred Wagner, and *Armide* was a comparative failure.

Bach's Passion; of the music itself he says practically nothing, but he remarks on the almost religious veneration with which the public listens to Bach. 'Bach is Bach as God is God.' He adds in a letter to Habeneck: 'You do not expect of me an analysis of Bach's great work,' but the fact that he is not altogether sympathetic is clear. Some writers have tried to make out that Berlioz's attitude to Bach (and to Handel) was that of a musician who was not a master of counterpoint and fugue. This is nonsense. In the art of combining themes together in a sustained development, retaining their freedom and their individual expressiveness so as to make a whole that is complete and significant, Berlioz is one of the greatest masters.[1] This is the true art of counterpoint. Berlioz was not a master of the art of saying nothing at great length. If that is counterpoint then Berlioz certainly was not a contrapuntist. We may also be sure that Berlioz heard all there was to be heard in Bach's music, and if it did not move him as Beethoven's and Gluck's did, that is an idiosyncrasy which other great musicians have shared.

From Berlin Berlioz went to Hanover, where he gave a concert on 6th May. An account of this concert is given by Georg Fischer;[2] he says the success was considerable but the receipts poor; he expresses his astonishment at the audacity of Berlioz's ideas and his profound knowledge of instrumentation, and gives a description of him: 'A high forehead, very deep-sunk eyes, an aquiline, slightly hooked nose, a mass of bright brown hair, an extraordinarily mobile face with a fiery expression, thus Berlioz appeared at the conductor's desk.'

A final concert was given at Darmstadt, and Berlioz returned to Paris at the end of May 1843. As far as the outside world went, he still resided with his wife and child at 31 rue de Londres, having his correspondence addressed there, but he

[1] The first movement of *Harold* is a sufficient example of this, but Berlioz's music is full of examples of his mastery in this respect; in fact he was rather a contrapuntal musician like Bach than a vertical, harmonic musician, if we may make this distinction.

[2] *Opera und Concerte im Hoftheater zu Hannover bis* 1866, published in Hanover in 1899.

also lived with Marie Recio and her mother, and in time the whole financial burden of these two women was borne by him. A significant passage occurs in a letter to a Doctor Burke of Leipzig in September 1843, in which he says he is tied to Paris 'like Gulliver at Lilliput by a thousand imperceptible bonds; I suffer from lack of air and space, and I cannot even compose. . . . I have not the time to be a musician; I must waste all my hours working to live because music brings me nothing until long after it is written. . . .'

His voyage to Germany supplied him with plenty of matter for articles and he was now preparing his *Treatise on Instrumentation* for publication. On 3rd February 1844 the *Carnaval romain*[1] overture was performed for the first time, at the Salle Herz, and was well received. In August 1844 a selection of articles by Berlioz was published in two volumes by Labitte, entitled *Voyage musical en Allemagne et en Italie*;[2] most of the matter in these two volumes was used for later prose works and for his *Mémoires*. His book was well received and brought him in a little money; also he combined with Strauss (the Vienna waltz-king) to give a festival concert at the industrial exhibition in 1844 at Paris, but this caused him an immense amount of organizing labour.[3] His old professor of anatomy in his medical student days met him, and was so startled by his appearance that he bled him and packed him off for a holiday to Nice, during which he revised his *Corsair* overture. From this time up to August 1845 Berlioz led the same life of journalistic drudgery and domestic discomfort; he also made the acquaintance of the Russian composer Glinka,[4] who considered him 'the first composer of the day—in his line.' Glinka came to Paris in 1844; some of his music was performed there and Berlioz wrote an appreciative article in the *Débats* on him. In a letter to a friend, quoted by Octave Fougue, Glinka writes:

[1] A four-handed arrangement by Pixis was played at a concert in Paris on 11th May by Pixis, Heller, Hallé, and Liszt.

[2] This was quickly translated into German and published by Lobe at Leipzig and Gathy at Hamburg.

[3] He also found time to write a short *Hymn à la France* for this occasion.

[4] Glinka, Michael Ivanovitch (1803–57).

I have become the friend of Berlioz so far as it is possible with a character as eccentric as his—I have heard some of his music, and this is my opinion. In the realm of fantasy nobody has such tremendous inventions; on the other hand, led away by his fantastic temperament, he lacks naturalness and falls into error.

His life in Paris had now settled down to what it was to remain almost until his death, a monotonous struggle for money and a series of attempts to give concerts and make known his new works. But this monotony was broken by his trips abroad, which became—with occasional setbacks—more and more successful and stimulating to him as an artist.

In 1845 his *Traité de l'instrumentation et d'orchestration modernes*, already published in Paris by Schonenberger, was translated into German and was published by Grünbaum (Berlin, 1845) and Dörffel (Leipzig, 1864). It was this work that spread his name through Europe and made it impossible, for Germans especially, to treat his music otherwise than with respect even when they did not understand it. An English translation of this, together with the later treatise, *Le Chef d'orchestre*, translated by Mary Cowden-Clarke and edited by Joseph Bennett, is published by Novello and Co.[1] A few words are necessary about this work, which is the outstanding classic on the subject.

The article on orchestration in Grove's *Dictionary* (latest edition), written by William Wallace, is a shocking example of the blindness of later nineteenth-century musicians, owing—one may largely presume—to the Wagner madness which has prevailed in Europe almost to the present day. Mr. William Wallace makes the following statements:

Modern orchestration may be said to date from the *Symphonie fantastique* of Berlioz. In the 63 bars of the opening *largo* there are more expression marks and indicated nuances than in a Mozart symphony. This shows that he attached the utmost importance to tone and phrasing, and left nothing to the caprice of the individual player.

. . . .

Berlioz, who had the flair for the capabilities of instruments more than any of his predecessors or contemporaries . . . he had mastered the

---

[1] There are modern revised editions in German by Felix Weingartner and Richard Strauss, and in Italian by Ettore Panizza.

mysteries of the brass instruments, of which those who used them constantly had not even dreamed.

. . . .

His *Traité de l'instrumentation*, published in 1844, came as an awakening and a message which no one in the world of music could afford to disregard.

. . . .

It will ever be a mystery that with his analytical ear, surely the most sensitive to sound, he did not listen more to what his instruments could give forth. There are few of his bars that do not enshrine a secret; other composers, if they did not capture it wholly, at least learned from it. . . . In the history of music there is no figure more pathetic than that of Berlioz, who, in despite, lacked the crowning gift.

I quote these extracts, not to attack Mr. William Wallace, but to confound him out of his own mouth. I maintain that you cannot put these extracts together to make coherent sense. There is the same discrepancy here as we find in Mr. Wallace's book on Wagner, in which he says no stone may be thrown against Wagner the musician, but every stone may be thrown against Wagner the man. This is to reduce the artist to a mere mouthpiece for some musical spirit; but even a mouthpiece (as every brass-instrument player knows) alters every sound blown through it, according to its material and its shape. So the music blown by the spirit[1] through Berlioz and Wagner was inevitably Berliozized and Wagnerized.

Now, what is it to have genius for instrumentation but not for music? I maintain you cannot separate music from instrumentation since no music can be made audible without an instrument.

What do such musicians as Mr. Wallace mean when they say that Berlioz was the greatest master of instrumentation but not a great composer? Do they imagine that Berlioz first scientifically studied instruments and then laboriously pieced together bits of music to show all their capacities? But we know this is exactly the opposite of how he composed.[2] Berlioz became a great master of instrumentation in the search for the right expression of his musical ideas. There was an affinity between

[1] Let us call her Saint Cecilia; both Berlioz and Wagner would have preferred a feminine spirit.

[2] See p. 243, note 6.

BERLIOZ IN 1845
Prinzhofer

them as there is an affinity between the richness of Shakespeare's thought and the richness of his vocabulary. I maintain that it is impossible to read through Berlioz's *Traité de l'instrumentation* without realizing that the writer must have been a great composer, because it is the work of an artist who knows his craft from A to Z, and not the work merely of a scholar learned in acoustics. Also Mr. Wallace says not a word about the examples from his own works which Berlioz gives. The author of the *Traité de l'instrumentation* was either a great composer or the most remarkable scientific, analytic, and musical scholar that has ever lived. But do scholars when analysing, say, the prosody of Milton or the sonatas of Beethoven, give passages written by themselves not only as good as Milton or Beethoven but embodying original ideas that Milton or Beethoven never had?

It is because every cheapjack throughout the musical world of England and America repeats this untenable thesis of Mr. William Wallace (because, being ignorant, they all go to Grove's *Dictionary* as a standard authority to know what to say) that I have given some space to criticizing it.

A three days' festival on 10th, 11th, and 12th August 1845 took place at Bonn for the inauguration of the statue of Beethoven, which had been erected by public subscription owing chiefly to the efforts of Liszt. It was an elaborate affair, the King of Prussia and other royalties being present.[1] Berlioz was sent by the *Journal des Débats*. During the festival Berlioz heard the *Missa solennis*, the Ninth Symphony, the C minor Symphony, the Concerto in E flat played by Liszt, and a part of *Fidelio*. This must have been a great joy and inspiration to him; he writes that to all intelligent and sensitive souls Beethoven is a 'benefactor and a friend.' On his return to Paris he arranged for his first journey to Austria, and it is legitimate to suppose that he was stimulated by the Bonn festival to fresh creation, for he was meditating a new work on a grand scale, based on his youthful *Huit Scènes de Faust*. Before leaving Paris for Austria he had several fresh scenes written according to his instructions by M. Gaudonnière, and, while travelling, he composed

[1] Including Queen Victoria and Prince Albert.

the words for others. In this way the text of the *Damnation de Faust* was prepared. The first part to be written was the Invocation to Nature, which, he says in his *Mémoires*, he did:

seeking neither to translate nor to imitate [Goethe's] masterpiece but to be inspired by it and to extract from it the musical substance. Thus I made this piece, which gave me the hope of being able to write the rest:

Nature immense, impénétrable et fière!
Toi seule donnes trêve a mon ennui sans fin!
Sur ton sein tout-puissant je sens moins ma misère,
Je retrouve ma force et je crois vivre enfin.
Oui, soufflez, ouragans, criez, forêts profondes,
Croulez, rochers, torrents, précipitez vos ondes!
A vos bruits souverains ma voix aime à s'unir.
Forêts, rochers, torrents, je vous adore! mondes
Qui scintillez, vers vous s'élance le désir
D'un cœur trop vaste et d'une âme altérée
D'un bonheur qui la fuit.[1]

Once started, I wrote the verses which were needed in succession as the musical ideas came to me, and I composed this score with a facility that I have rarely experienced in my other works. I wrote when and where I could; driving in a carriage, in railway trains, on steamboats, and even in towns, in spite of the various tasks imposed on me by the concerts I had to give in them. Thus in an inn at Passau . . . I wrote the introduction: *Le vieil hiver a fait place au printemps.*[2] At Vienna, I wrote the scene on the banks of the Elbe, the air of Mephistopheles, *Voici des roses*,[3] and the *Ballet des sylphes* . . . in one night, also at Vienna, I wrote the march on the Hungarian Rakoczy theme. The extraordinary effect it produced at Pesth induced me to introduce it in *Faust* by taking the liberty of placing my hero in Hungary at the beginning of the action. . . .

---

[1] 'Nature, immense, impenetrable, unaware!
Thou alone givest relief to my endless fatigue!
On thy all-powerful breast I forget my despair,
I recover my strength, once again hope to live.
Yes, blow hurricanes, cry forests profound,
Avalanches descend, ye cataracts of sound
To unite with your voices my own shall dare.
Woods, rocks, cascades, I love you! Spheres
That scintillate, to you upsprings the desire
Of a heart too great and a soul athirst
For happiness which escapes.'

[2] 'Old Winter has given place to Spring.'

[3] 'Here are roses.'

Berlioz goes on to say that many German critics have attacked him for the modifications he has made in Goethe's drama for his text, as if, he says, 'one could put the whole of such a poem into music.'[1] Then he adds:

I have often asked myself why these same critics have never reproached me on account of the plan of my *Roméo et Juliette* symphony, which also departs from that immortal tragedy! Doubtless it is because Shakespeare *is not a German.* Patriotism! Fetishism! Idiotism![2]

At Pesth by the light of a shop gas-lamp, as I wandered one evening through the town, I wrote the refrain of the chorus *Ronde des paysans.* At Prague I got up in the middle of the night to write a theme I was afraid of forgetting, the chorus of angels of Marguerite's apotheosis:

Remonte au ciel, âme naïve
Que l'amour égara.[3]

At Breslau I wrote the words and the music of the Latin song of the students, *Jam nox stellata velamina pandit.*[4] On my return to France, having gone to spend some days near Rouen at the house of M. le baron de Montville, I composed there the trio, *Ange adoré dont la céleste image.*[5] The rest was written in Paris, always at odd moments, at home, at a café, in the Tuileries garden, and even on a milestone of the boulevard du Temple. I did not seek out ideas, I let them come and they presented themselves in the most unexpected order. When at last the whole sketch of the score was finished I set myself to work over the whole, to polish the various parts, to unite them, to fuse them together with all the passion and all the patience of which I am capable, and to finish the scoring which was only indicated here and there.[6] I regard this work as one of the best I have produced. . . .[7]

I do not intend to relate the details of this second visit of Berlioz's to German-speaking countries; he has given many particulars of it in his *Mémoires.* He left Paris on 22nd October 1845, with Marie Recio, gave concerts in Vienna, Prague,

[1] A composer without genius or instinct might certainly do this.

[2] I must use this word for Berlioz's favourite expression, *crétinisme!*

[3] 'Return heavenwards, O gentle soul whom love distracted.'

[4] 'Now night spreads out her starry garments.'

[5] 'Adored angel whose celestial image.'

[6] This completely disposes of Mr. William Wallace's statement: 'It is not certain when composition with him ended and orchestration began. He was so deeply read in all that concerned instruments that it is likely that he had them in mind more than any finely conceived theme.' See p. 240.

[7] This was written some time before February 1854.

Budapesth, Breslau, and Brunswick and returned to Paris at the end of April 1846. But it is worth quoting the impression he made on the famous German critic, Hanslick, who says that as Berlioz could not speak a word of German he was often his interpreter, and thus saw a good deal of the 'celebrated master':

What increased and strengthened our admiration for Berlioz was the impression made on us by his agreeable and intelligent (*spirituelle*) personality, artistic to his finger-nails. His artistic ideals possessed him entirely, and the realization of whatever in his never-satisfied desire he found great and beautiful was the sole aim of all his efforts. In his art, on which one may have whatever opinion one chooses, he showed an astonishing integrity. Everything practical, egoistic, calculated, or premeditated was quite foreign to this man with the head of a Jupiter.[1]

Hanslick also relates an incident which throws some light on Berlioz. He and Ambros called on Berlioz at his hotel.

As Ambros at the first meeting expressed his joy at seeing with Berlioz the original of the *idée fixe* of the *Symphonie fantastique*, Miss Smithson, he replied to us with a menacing look: 'This is my second wife; Miss Smithson is dead.' In reality his wife still lived, and lived for a long time after. . . .

In June 1846, at the inauguration of the Chemin de fer du Nord, a composition entitled *Le Chant des chemins de fer* (The Song of the Railways), with words by Jules Janin, was performed at Lille. Otherwise Berlioz was busy preparing for the first performance of the *Damnation de Faust*, which took place in Paris on 6th December 1846 before a half-empty hall. He was supported by all his friends, but at the second performance on 20th December the hall was three-quarters empty. The expenses of copying the parts of his score and of giving these two concerts left him with a deficit of from eight to ten thousand francs and no money to pay it. 'I am like a bird of prey,' he says in a letter, 'compelled to seek my life afar.' Where could he go next? He borrowed money from his friends and arranged for a visit to Russia, from which country Balzac predicted he would return with a fortune. We shall see. In the meantime I will close this chapter with some remarks on the *Damnation de Faust*, which is one of the outstanding masterpieces in

[1] Hanslick, Eduard (1825–1904), *Aus dem Concertsaal* (Vienna, 1870).

the history of music. The *Damnation de Faust* is described by Berlioz as a 'Dramatic Legend in Four Parts'; it may be performed as a cantata, an *opéra de concert* in a concert-hall, but it is so essentially dramatic that its right place is in a theatre, and there is little doubt that Berlioz would have written it for performance as an opera if he had then had the entry to any opera-house in Europe. It demands stage representation [1] and makes an opera that is musically to be classed only with Mozart's *Don Giovanni* and dramatically must be ranked with Beethoven's *Fidelio*, Gluck's *Alceste*, *Orpheus*, and *Iphigénie en Tauride*, and Verdi's *Otello*.

This selection may surprise some musicians and music-lovers, but I have already drawn a distinction,[2] which I think useful, between the lyrical and dramatic elements in a creative artist, whether he be a poet or a musician. Berlioz, I maintain, combined both elements more largely than any composer but Mozart in the history of music. That is why I say that, musically, the *Damnation de Faust* can only be compared with Mozart's *Don Giovanni*, for nowhere else in opera [3] will you find musical invention, beauty, and variety of expression, dramatic and lyrical, of such fine quality and in such abundance. I must insist on the word 'quality' because there is a certain abundance in Wagner and Verdi, but the quality is not nearly so rare as in Mozart and Berlioz. This pure musicality is not so abundant in *Fidelio* or in Gluck's operas as in Berlioz's. On the other hand, in dramatic expressiveness Beethoven's *Fidelio* and Verdi's *Otello*, and in tragic grandeur Gluck's *Iphigénie en Tauride* remain peak achievements in the history of opera. You cannot compare with them Wagner's 'Ring' or *Tristan und Isolde*, because dramatically effective and thrilling *in parts* as these works of Wagner's are, their quality is on a much lower level of human experience and consciousness. Berlioz's *Faust* [4] is on a higher dramatic as well as musical level. It combines

[1] And nowadays is usually performed as an opera, requiring extremely little adjustment.

[2] See p. 63.

[3] Except again in *Les Troyens*.

[4] And the same is true of *Les Troyens*.

the dramatic qualities of Gluck and Beethoven with the lyrical qualities of Mozart, but has a complete originality and integrity of its own. To close one's eyes and listen attentively to the music of Berlioz's *Faust* is to have one of the greatest experiences that a musician can enjoy; every performance reveals fresh subtleties and beauties. This score is really an inexhaustible treasury of the highest and rarest musical invention.[1]

When the *Damnation de Faust* was performed at Covent Garden in 1933,[2] Sir Thomas Beecham, needing some music (which is not supplied by Berlioz) to carry on during the change of scene from the plains of Hungary to Faust's study (from Scenes 1, 2, and 3 to Scene 4 in Berlioz's score), took the strange and beautiful march, *Marche nocturne*,[3] from Berlioz's sacred trilogy *L'Enfance du Christ*, which was extraordinarily appropriate and produced just the right mysterious atmosphere. Nevertheless I think it is wrong to rob one masterpiece for a theatrical convenience in another; and it is only possible because *L'Enfance du Christ*, of which I shall write in due course, is in England a totally unknown work. Therefore I suggest to Sir Thomas Beecham, and to any conductor who may read this book, that a search should be made among Berlioz's imperfect early or fragmentary compositions for a piece of instrumental music that would be suitable here.

One of the striking virtues of the *Damnation de Faust* is its utter lack of theatrical padding. A masterly concision prevails everywhere. Berlioz says what he has to say (and it is always to the point and enough) and then passes on; but to ears accustomed to Wagner's habit—and it is a common habit with people of the theatre, who think every point has to be under-

[1] It is only Mozart's *Don Giovanni* and *Così fan tutte*—not even *Figaro* and *The Magic Flute*, wonderful works as they are—that give me a similar intensity of purely musical experience.

[2] Like Gluck's *Armide*, some years previously, it was only given three times, but unlike *Armide* before quite good houses.

[3] This is a good example of Berlioz's contrapuntal mastery. If this piece were brought forward under the name of J. S. Bach it would be hailed as a particularly fine and expressive example of his art.

lined and driven home with almost infinite repetition—of saying everything over and over again, using a minimum of ideas and a maximum of notes (and words), the most extraordinary beauties of Berlioz's are gone before they have grasped them. It is true of Berlioz, as of Mozart, that to listen to his music needs a rather strict mental training; you cannot lie under it in a half-comatose state, letting it flow over you like bath-water, as you can with Wagner and many other composers.

As an example of the range and quality of Berlioz's musical imagination, one only has to cite such different parts in his *Faust* as the 'Invocation to Nature,' a sublime and profound piece, of a breadth of conception which in itself would justify so many German musicians' description of Berlioz as 'the French Beethoven,' and the *Danse des sylphes*. The whole of Scene VII, 'By the banks of the Elbe,' is of a dream-like enchantment, for a parallel to which you may seek in vain throughout the whole of music. The word 'poetic' may be legitimately used figuratively to describe a quintessential beauty which is but rarely achieved in any artistic form—whether it be verse, painting, or music—and only this word will suffice to describe the scene 'By the banks of the Elbe' in *Faust*. Berlioz's own title for this scene is, *Bosquets et prairies au bord de l'Elbe*, which rings fragrantly in our English ears, since all these French words are our own English words with the charm of a different accent. This scene has the magic of Shakespeare's finest evocations of nature and of love. It is one of Berlioz's creations in which we feel his affinity with Shakespeare most intensely and, although it is the delight of all musicians, nevertheless I would say of it, with Cleomenes:

> The climate 's delicate; the air most sweet;
> Fertile the isle; the temple much surpassing
> The common praise it bears.

I will not linger to point out the other manifold and varied beauties of *Faust*. I will only add that the music given to Marguerite is of the purest and most exquisite feeling, and that her last scene, 'Romance,' with its close, 'Il ne vient pas, il ne vient pas,' seems to me to be the most poignant expression of absolute and eternal loss that exists in music.

But it was not to be expected that a work of such originality and power should find immediate appreciation, and on 14th February 1847 Berlioz left Paris alone for his first visit to Russia, with the object of repairing the losses he had suffered over *Faust*.

CHAPTER II

THE MIDDLE YEARS (RUSSIA, ENGLAND, AND GERMANY)

HAVING the right introductions and being taken up by the court, Berlioz's first concert in St. Petersburg, at which he gave extracts from *Roméo*, *Faust*, and the *Symphonie funèbre*, drew a large audience, including the Tsarina; the concert was a great success, the audience being overwhelmed by the novelty and audacity of the music. After paying expenses, Berlioz found himself with a profit of twelve thousand francs. 'I was saved. . . . Ah, dear Parisians!'[1] he exclaimed in a letter. On 25th March 1847 he gave a second concert, again with excellent results. His champion there, Prince Odoïewsky, served him well in the press, writing:

> At the rehearsal I nearly stifled through intense concentration . . . this is music one has to *study* as we have studied Beethoven . . . but what a joy to hear a second time this music of genius!
>
> In truth, in view of the general exaltation of our public there must be a particular sympathy between the music of Berlioz and the inmost feeling of Russia.[2]

In Moscow he gave a similar concert on 3rd April. The *Gazette de Moscou* wrote:

> . . . In this extraordinary music lies the germ of an unknown future. . . . Even the melody in his works has an instrumental character. It is rarely confided to one voice, to one instrument; most frequently it is distributed over the whole surface of the orchestra. Certainly this gives it a wholly original character but deprives it of the charm which belongs to it. . . .

The profit in Moscow was eight thousand francs. Returning to St. Petersburg, Berlioz gave a concert on 23rd April of

[1] Bertin had lent him 1,000 francs, Friedland 1,200 francs, Sax 1,200 francs, Hetzel 1,000 francs, and other friends various amounts.

[2] To-day Berlioz's music is almost unknown in Russia, as Shakespeare's work was in France during the eighteenth century.

Harold, with Ernst playing the viola, and the whole of *Roméo et Juliette*. At a second concert on 30th April he repeated fragments of *Faust*, and on 10th May left for Berlin. At Riga he went to a performance of *Hamlet*, which inspired him with the idea for two new compositions: *La Mort d'Ophélie* and the *Marche funèbre pour la dernière scène de Hamlet*.[1] He also gave a concert there which brought in only twelve francs. On 19th June he gave *Faust* in Berlin, but with little success and a mediocre attendance, in spite of the support of Meyerbeer and the King of Prussia and the court. It is interesting to find that the *Roi de Thulé* ballad was hissed, and that the press attacked him for disfiguring Goethe's poem.

Berlioz returned to Paris in July 1847 with enough money from Russia to pay his debts and a little over. He had made about fifteen thousand francs, but Balzac had prophesied 150,000. 'This great mind,' says Berlioz, 'had the weakness of seeing fortunes everywhere, fortunes which he would have unhesitatingly asked a banker to cash, so certain did he think them. . . .'

But a new prospect opened for him. The famous Jullien,[2] musician, speculator, entrepreneur, had become director of Drury Lane Theatre in London, and on 19th August a six years' contract was signed, making Berlioz conductor of the opera at Drury Lane for forty thousand francs a year, but terminable at the end of each season at the discretion of Jullien. 'I have been obliged,' wrote Berlioz to d'Ortigue, 'to abandon beautiful France for perfidious Albion.'

And Albion, or rather Jullien, proved perfidious, as we shall see.

Before going to London he decided to pay a visit to La Côte-Saint-André and take his son Louis, now aged thirteen, to see his grandfather, Dr. Berlioz. It was fifteen years since Berlioz himself had seen his father, who was now alone, for Berlioz's

[1] The manuscripts of these two fine pieces bear the dates: 'Londres, 4 juillet 1848' and '22 septembre 1848' respectively; but Berlioz's own announcement of forthcoming performances in the *Gazette musicale* in February 1848 proves that they were both sketched out before those dates.

[2] Jullien, Louis Antoine (1812–60), best known as the author of Jullien's Quadrilles.

mother was dead and both sisters were married.[1] He returned to Paris in September, and in November, taking his son Louis from his mother to a school at Rouen, where he had two friends, the Baron de Montville and Amédée Mereaux, proceeded to London, where he arrived on 5th November 1847,[2] Jullien having engaged a fine apartment for him at 76 Harley Street. Jullien did everything on the grand scale, like the excellent adventurer he was, but his operatic ventures were not lucky. He had engaged Gye as manager, Sir Henry Bishop as superintendent of rehearsals, a good orchestra, and a less good chorus. On 6th December Drury Lane opened with Donizetti's *Lucia di Lammermoor*, Berlioz conducting, with Sims Reeves[3] as the principal tenor, but it did not cover expenses owing to Jullien's extravagance and recklessness. *Lucia* was followed by Balfe's *Maid of Honour* and Donizetti's *Linda di Chamouni*, but Jullien's financial situation became more and more desperate. In a series of letters to his friend Auguste Morel, Berlioz describes his gradual disillusionment:

To Auguste Morel

London, *14th January* 1848.

. . . My occupation here is that of a mill-horse, rehearsing daily from 12 to 4 and conducting nightly from 7 to 10. Only since the day before yesterday have we been without rehearsals, and I begin to recover from the *grippe* which threatened me, due to fatigue and the icy winds of the theatre. You have doubtless heard already of the horrible position into which Jullien has dragged himself and all of us. However, as one must damage his credit in Paris as little as possible, don't speak to any one of what I tell you. It is not his Drury Lane enterprise that has ruined him. He was already ruined before it started, and counted doubtless

---

[1] He writes from Côte-Saint-André on 10th September 1847 to Ferrand: 'I am very much annoyed at not having seen you. If I do not see you at Lyons I will write you a less laconic epistle from Paris.'

[2] On 1st November he writes to Ferrand: 'God only knows when we shall see each other again. . . . My eyes now turn to England. France is becoming more and more profoundly stupid in all that relates to music. The more I look abroad the less I love my country. Pardon the blasphemy. But art in France is dead and mortification has set in. . . .'

[3] Reeves, John Sims (1818–1900) a famous English tenor. Berlioz had a high opinion of him.

on heavy receipts to restore his position. Jullien is always the same fool as you have known; he hasn't the least idea of the needs of a *théâtre lyrique*, nor of the most elementary requirements for a good musical performance. He opened his theatre without possessing a single score and, with the exception of Balfe's opera, which he has had to have copied, we live at present on the good will of Lumley's agents, who lend us the orchestral parts of the Italian operas we produce.

Jullien is now touring the provinces, making a good deal of money with his promenade concerts; here the theatre has good takings every night but, finally, after having consented to a reduction of a third in our salaries, *we have not been paid at all.* Only the chorus, the orchestra, and the workmen are paid every week, so that the theatre may continue. . . .

Berlioz goes on to say that he will give a concert on 7th February:

As for France, God preserve me from yielding to temptations such as you proffer me in your last letter, of returning to give a concert in Paris in April. If ever I have enough money to *give* concerts to my friends in Paris I will do so; but don't think me so simple any more as to count on the public to get back my expenses. I will make no more appeals to its attention, to be merely received with indifference while losing the money I earn with such labour in my travels.

It will be a great grief to me, because the sympathies of my French friends are always dearest to me. But there are the facts: the difference in the impression my music makes abroad forces me to conclude that it is the public of Paris that understands me least. Have I ever seen at Paris in my concerts, fashionable people, men and women, *moved* as I have seen them in Germany and Russia? Have I ever seen princes of the blood rising at eight o'clock in the morning to come to a cold and deserted hall to hear a rehearsal, as the Princess of Prussia has done in Berlin? Have I ever been invited to take the least part in the concerts of the court? The Société du Conservatoire is hostile to me, or at least, its directors are. Is it not grotesque that at its concerts works by every one who has any name in music are played, except mine? Is it not wounding for me to see the Opéra always resorting to musical botchers, and its directors always armed against me with prejudices which I would blush to have to fight against even if their hand was forced? Does not the press become more ignoble every day? Do we see in it (except rarely) anything but intrigue, baseness, and *crétinisme*? Those people whom I have so often obliged and helped by my articles, have they ever shown me the least real gratitude? Do you believe that I am the dupe of the crowd of people who smile and hide from me their nails and teeth only because they know that I have claws to defend myself with? To see everywhere nothing but imbecility, ingratitude, or fear—that is my lot in Paris. If even my friends were happy there! But far from that, you are almost all slaves, in trying positions, and troubled. I can do nothing for you, and your efforts for me are powerless.

Thus France is wiped off my musical map, and I have determined to turn my eyes from it and to think of it as little as possible. I am not to-day in the least degree melancholy; I have no spleen; I speak to you with the greatest sangfroid and lucidity of mind. I see things as they are . . .

Berlioz's actual situation in his own country could not have been more justly described, but a detached vision is one thing and a detached behaviour is quite another. Berlioz could never overcome his desire to be appreciated in his own country, in his beloved Paris, among his dearest friends! Naturally, also, he was to discover that foreign countries had their bad as well as their good points, even although they welcomed him and (certainly in the case of Germany, Austria, and Russia) understood his music better than the Parisians. To General Lwoff he wrote from London on 28th January 1848:

Talking of idiots, if you only knew into what a nest of them I have fallen here! God only knows who directs the director of this unfortunate theatre! It is called the Royal Academy of Music, the Grand English Opera, and ever since it opened, that is for two months, I have done nothing but conduct Donizetti and Balfe. We had a superb orchestra, but the director has taken the cream of it into the provinces, where he is giving popular concerts. . . . I hear arguments about music, the public, the artists, which would make the four strings of your violin break in a rage if they could hear them; I have to listen to English singers, ladies, who would break and twist into a knot the hair of your bow.

I am engaged for four concerts . . . we have not yet been able to get the whole orchestra together once for rehearsal. These gentlemen come when they please, and go about their business, some in the middle of a rehearsal, others before it is a quarter over. The first day I had no horns at all, the second I had three, the third I had two, who left after the fourth piece. . . . The chorus alone is devoted to me, almost as much as that of St. Petersburg. . . . I have been ill in bed with violent bronchitis for five days, brought on by the anger, disgust, and grief all this has caused me. However, there is much to be done here, for the public is attentive, intelligent, and really loves serious works.

I have heard poor Mendelssohn's last oratorio, *Elijah*. It is magnificently grand and indescribably sumptuous in harmony.

On 7th February 1848 Berlioz gave his first concert in

London, including in his programme *Harold*, the overtures *Carneval romain* and *Cellini*, fragments of *Faust* and the *Requiem*; and the 'Apotheosis' from the *Symphonie funèbre*. The concert lasted four hours and had an excellent reception in the press the next day. Davison in *The Times*, Chorley in the *Athenaeum*, Hogarth [1] in the *Daily News*, Holmes [2] in the *Atlas*, C. L. Gruneisen in the *Illustrated London News* [3] were all warmly favourable.

Presently Drury Lane Theatre closed down and Berlioz in March began to fill up his spare time by writing his *Mémoires*. In a letter to d'Ortigue, dated London, 15th March 1848, he writes:

Life in London is even more absorbing than in Paris; everything is in proportion to the immense size of the place. I get up at noon; at one o'clock come visitors, friends, new acquaintances, and artists with introductions. Whether I like it or not I thus lose three hours a day. From four to six I work; then if I have no invitation I dine some distance away. I read the papers, after that comes the hour for theatres and concerts. I listen to some sort of music until half-past eleven. Then three or four of us artists go together to sup and smoke in some tavern until two o'clock. . . . The directors of Covent Garden want me to arrange a Shakespearian concert. . . . I told them I would not consent . . . unless they guaranteed me fifteen days' study for the voices and four rehearsals for the orchestra. They are now seeing how they can manage this.

The Philharmonic Society began its season yesterday. They played a symphony by Hesse (organist, of Breslau) very well made, very cold, and very useless; another by Mendelssohn in A . . . much superior in my opinion to the other in A that is played in Paris. . . . As far as my musical career is concerned, I have only England and Russia to consider. I gave up France for lost long ago; the last revolution makes my determination firmer and more necessary.[4] Under the old regime I had to fight against hatreds sown by an article, against the ineptitude of those directing our theatres and the indifference of the public; now I shall have also to contend with a mob of great composers evoked by the republic and against popular, philanthropic, national, and economic music. . . .

---

[1] Charles Dickens's father-in-law.

[2] Author of the well-known *Life of Mozart*.

[3] *The Illustrated London News* published a photograph of Berlioz on 12th February 1848.

[4] 1848 was the year of revolution in Europe. In France King Louis Philippe had to fly in February, and the second republic took his place.

France, from a musical point of view, is a country of fools and rogues; one would have to be deucedly chauvinistic not to see that. Is it true Perrot has lost his place? I don't know whether anybody has condescended to keep mine for me at the library of the Conservatoire, which brought me in 118 francs a month. I have written to the Minister of the Interior on the subject, but he has not replied.

To Auguste Morel on 24th April he writes:

Paris appears to be growing more tranquil. God grant that it may last and that the Assembly may really represent the nation. Then, indeed, we might hope for great things. You have no idea how much the situation of you, Morel, and that of other friends of mine disquiets and preoccupies me. How can you emerge in safety from the midst of this triumphant debacle?

Unlike Wagner, Berlioz was not a political partisan. He looked upon revolutions when they came as unavoidable but perhaps necessary evils—a sort of sociological earthquake or eruption; but he would have no more thought of active participation for or against them than he would have thought of standing on the side of Mount Vesuvius and gesticulating for or against an eruption. And, being human, he would always hope that a fresh flow of lava might prove fruitful after it had ceased to be destructive.

On 29th June he gave a second concert in London, at Hanover Square. The receipts were poor but the press good. This was the end of the season, and a writer in the *Musical World* deplored the fact that the Philharmonic had not invited Berlioz to take part in any of its concerts. This gave Berlioz an opportunity to write, on 10th July, a letter to the editor, which was also reproduced elsewhere, in which he says:

. . . I return to that country which is still called France and which, after all, is mine. I am going to see in what way an artist can live or how long it will take him to die in the midst of the ruins under which the flower of art is crushed and buried. . . .

The personal question is . . . only secondary, because you may believe me that I love music much more than *my* music, and I would wish that I had more often the occasion to prove it. . . .

Adieu, then, all you who have so cordially treated me; I am downhearted at leaving you and I repeat involuntarily the sad and solemn words of the father of Hamlet:

Farewell, farewell, remember me.

But he returned to Paris without money. Jullien had failed him, and although the artists, the press, and the public had been friendly and even enthusiastic, his two concerts brought little more than their expenses. His wife Harriet was now paralysed; he had to support her and his son, also Mlle Recio and her mother. He had to resume his journalism and to borrow from his brother-in-law, Adèle's husband, Camille Suat.

On 26th July his father died, and about the middle of August Berlioz went to La Côte-Saint-André to meet his two sisters and settle his father's affairs.[1] In Chapter LVIII of his *Mémoires* he describes most poignantly this visit to his home. Of his father he says:

> His mind was highly idealistic. He was full of a sensibility, a goodness, a benevolence, both complete and natural. He was so happy to have been wrong in his forecasts about my musical future. . . . To the affection which exists between a father and son was added in our case a friendship independent of this sentiment and perhaps stronger. . . .

Before returning to Paris he had a desire to see Grenoble again and the house of his grandfather at Meylan:

> I wished (singular thirst for suffering) to see the place of my first passion: I wished to embrace my whole past, to intoxicate myself with memories, however devastating the resultant sadness. My sisters, knowing that I wanted to be alone on this pious pilgrimage, remained at La Côte. I feel my arteries throb at the idea of relating this excursion. I want to do it, nevertheless, were it only to show the persistence of certain ancient feelings, seemingly irreconcilable with new ones, and the reality of their co-existence in a heart which is incapable of forgetting.
>
> This inexorable action of the memory is so strong in me that I cannot even to-day look without pain on the portrait of my son at the age of ten. His aspect makes me suffer as if I had had two sons and there remained to me only the grown-up young man, death having taken from me the charming child.[2] . . .

---

[1] Berlioz's share of his father's estate was nominally about one hundred and thirty thousand francs, but this was its value if realized. To realize a scattered agricultural property was quite another matter, and the management of it was left in the hands of Adèle's husband, who was a lawyer.

[2] It seems to me this is a most significant statement, giving one a more vivid conception of Berlioz's extreme sensibility than almost anything else. Berlioz wrote this passage between December 1848 and the year 1854. His son Louis was twenty years old in 1854.

He then describes how he arrived at Grenoble at eight o'clock in the morning and walked to the village of Meylan on 'one of those beautiful autumn days, so full of poetic charm and serenity.' Having arrived, he went to his grandfather's house, which had been sold to a farmer, opened the door and found nobody there, the new proprietor having installed himself in a new building.

I entered the *salon*, where formerly the family gathered . . . it was untouched with its grotesque pictures and its fantastic paper birds of all colours. . . . Here is my grandfather's seat, where he slept after noon, there his old game of tric-trac; on the old buffet I saw a little willow cage that I had made as a child; here I saw my uncle waltz with Estelle . . . I hurried out.

. . . I seek a seat on which, in the evening, my father would rest for hours in reverie, his eyes fixed on Saint-Eynard . . . the bench is broken, there remain only the two worm-eaten feet.

There is the field of maize where I wandered at the time of my first love to hide my sadness. It is at the foot of this tree that I began to read Cervantes.

Now to the mountain. It is thirty-three years since I last visited it. I am like a man who has since died and is now resurrected. And I find again in resurrection all the feelings of my inner life, as young and as ardent. . . .

I climb these rocky and deserted paths towards the white house, seen only afar on my return from Italy sixteen years ago, the house where shone Stella.

I climb, I climb, with the continuation of my ascent I feel my palpitation increase. I believe I recognize on the left an avenue of trees; I follow it, but it leads to an unknown farm. . . .

I return to the path; it had no exit and ended in vineyards. . . .

I decide to inquire at the farm. . . . I enter the barn, where I interrupt the work of the threshers . . . and ask if they can tell me the way to the house where Mme Gautier used to live.

One of the threshers scratches his head: '. . . Mme Gautier, there is nobody of that name in these parts.' 'Yes, an old lady, she had two young granddaughters who came to visit her every year in the autumn.'

'I remember,' said the wife of the thresher, intervening. . . . 'Mam'-zelle Estelle, so pretty that everybody stopped at the church door on Sundays to see her pass. . . . The house is now let to a merchant from Grenoble . . . it 's up yonder; you must follow the fountain-path, here, behind our vineyard, and then turn to the left. . . .'

'The fountain is there! Ah, now I know where I am. . . . Thank you, thank you. . . .'

Soon I hear the fountain. . . . I am there. . . . There is the path, the avenue of trees like the one that misled me. . . . God, the air intoxicates me . . . my head turns. . . . I arrive at the entrance to the avenue. . . . A gentleman in a jacket, no doubt the prosaic master of the sanctum, is on the threshold lighting a cigar. He looks at me in astonishment.

I pass without a word and continue to climb. I must reach an old tower . . . from which I shall be able to see everything. . . .

The tower! the tower! I don't see it . . . is it destroyed? No, there it is, the top has been pulled down and the trees, which have grown, prevented me from seeing it. . . .

Near here, where now these young beeches are green, my uncle and I sat while I played for him on the flute the air of the *Musette* from *Nina*.

There Estelle used to come . . . perhaps I occupy in the air the exact space her charming form once filled. . . . Let us look now. . . . I turn and see the whole picture . . . the sacred house, the garden, the trees and, lower, the valley, the winding Isère, far off the Alps, the snow, the glaciers, all she had seen, all she had admired, and I breathe this blue air which she breathed. . . . Ah! . . .

A cry which no human tongue could translate is repeated by the echo of Saint-Eynard. . . . Yes, I see, I see once more, I adore . . . the past is present, I am young, I am twelve years old! Life, beauty, first love, that infinite poem! I kneel and I cry into the valley, to the mountains, to the sky: 'Estelle! Estelle! Estelle!' and I clasp the earth in a convulsive embrace; I bite the moss . . . a spasm of isolation grips me . . . indescribable . . . raging. . . . Bleed, my heart, bleed, but leave me the strength to suffer still! . . .

. . . .

Adieu! . . . vieille tour, adieu! . . . vieux Saint-Eynard, adieu! . . . ciel de mon étoile, adieu! Farewell, my romantic youth, last reflections of pure love! The stream of time carries me on; adieu, Stella! . . . Stella!

And sad, like a spectre re-entering its tomb, I descended the mountain. I repassed the avenue of Estelle's house. The gentleman with the cigar had disappeared. . . . I went slowly, slowly, stopping at each step, with anguish taking my gaze off every object. . . .

I had no further need to constrain my heart. . . . It seemed to beat no more. . . . I was as if dead. . . . And everywhere around the soft sunlight, solitude, and silence.

. . . .

The next day . . . at Grenoble . . . I had, one may well believe, a preoccupied, strange air. Left alone with my cousin Victor for a moment, he could not help saying:

'What is the matter? I have never seen you like this. . . .'

'What is the matter! Well, you will mock me, but I will answer. . . . Besides, it will relieve me, for I choke . . . yesterday I was at Meylan. . . .'

'I know; what is to be seen there?'

'There is, among other things, the house of Mme Gautier . . . do you know her grandchild, Madame F * * *?'

'Yes, the one we used once to call the beautiful Estelle D * * *.'

'Well, I was desperately in love with her when I was twelve and . . . I love her still.'

'But you idiot,' replied Victor, bursting into laughter, 'she is now fifty-one, her eldest son is twenty-two . . . he studied law with me.'

And his laughter redoubled and mine joined his, but convulsively, distorted, desolate like the rays of the April sun through rain.

'Yes, it is absurd, I feel it, and nevertheless it is so; it is absurd and it is true . . . it is puerile and it is immense. . . . Do not laugh or laugh if you will, what does it matter? Where is she now?'

'Since the death of her husband she is living at Vif.'[1]

I have quoted this long passage from Berlioz's *Mémoires* for a double reason. Firstly, because we have come to the period of his life when he wrote his *Mémoires*, and I have thought it best to deal with them by giving a long and extremely characteristic extract rather than by describing or criticizing what is, in any case, the most extraordinary and gifted literary work ever written by a musician. Secondly, to prepare the reader for the strange relationship with Estelle which he entered into in the latter part of his life.

On 17th November 1848 the National Assembly of the French Republic rejected the economies proposed by the fanatics which threatened the school at Rome, the Conservatoire, the libraries, the subsidized theatres, the museums, etc. This was largely due to the eloquence of Victor Hugo, supported by others with longer views, such as Charles Blanc and Félix

[1] Berlioz did not go to see her, but he wrote her a letter dated Grenoble, 6th December 1848, though this date has been questioned and the suggestion made that it should be 6th September because in December Berlioz was back in Paris. But he may have written from Paris. This letter will be found on p. 441 (chap. lviii) of his *Mémoires* (1st ed., Lévy, Paris, 1870).

Pyat.[1] Berlioz retained his post of librarian and even received a gratuity of five hundred francs 'to encourage him as a composer.' On 10th December 1848 Prince Louis Napoleon was elected president of the republic, and a long period of tranquillity was to set in, but not for a year or two; not until he was proclaimed emperor in 1851.

During this period Berlioz was harassed by his double *ménage*, by poor receipts from the farms at La Côte, as the times were bad, and by the incessant need to write articles to provide for himself and his dependants. Nevertheless, he managed during 1849 to compose his *Te Deum*. In 1850 his elder sister Nanci died, and during that year he composed, under the fictitious name of Pierre Ducré,[2] the chorus *L'Adieu des bergers*, which was the germ of his future sacred trilogy *L'Enfance du Christ*. In 1850 he also founded a Philharmonic Society, which lived for a short period and then collapsed for lack of support.

The *Te Deum*. This work, although written in 1849, was not performed until 1855, at Saint-Eustache on 30th April. It consists of eight sections, two of which are instrumental, as follows:

(1) *Te Deum*. Hymn.
(2) *Tibi omnes*. Hymn.
(3) *Prelude* (orchestra alone).
(4) *Dignare, Domine*. Prayer.
(5) *Christe, rex gloriae*. Hymn.

[1] In a letter to Lenz at St. Petersburg, dated 22nd December 1848, Berlioz with his usual clarity and hatred of humbug wrote about the revolution: 'Universal suffrage has given us an overwhelming majority for Louis Napoleon; the peasants do not anticipate having any taxes to pay for a long time and base great expectations on the good advice the emperor will give his nephew, for they know exactly what value to attach to the lie about the emperor's death. . . . Attention is speedily to be paid to the distribution of the thousands of millions brought back by Napoleon the Great from Egypt, an inexhaustible treasure dug from the Great Pyramid. We are going to spin out days of gold and all be on velvet. . . . How you must laugh at us—us who call ourselves an "advanced" people! Do you know what we call woodcocks when they are high? We call them also *avancées*' (advanced).

[2] Berlioz pretended that Pierre Ducré was Master of Music at the Sainte-Chapelle in Paris and that the piece had been first performed in 1677. Many were deceived, although Léon Kreutzer in the *Gazette musicale* said that the piece 'was very happily modulated for a period when they scarcely modulated at all.'

(6) *Tu ergo quaesumus.* Prayer.
(7) *Judex crederis.* Hymn and prayer.
(8) *March for the Presentation of the Colours* (orchestra and organ).

It is composed for three choirs, orchestra, and organ. Berlioz gives precise directions as to composition of the choirs and their placing, and insists that the orchestra and choirs should be at the other end of the church to the organ. These directions are almost invariably ignored and the third choir is often omitted, although Berlioz says that it 'greatly enhances the general effect.' This is the sort of work which, in England, should be performed at the annual Three Choirs Festival, which is at present wholly in a groove, running on Handel, Mendelssohn, and Elgar.

(1) *Te Deum.* This is a magnificent double fugue, treated in the most spacious way.

(2) The *Tibi omnes* is a beautiful melodic movement; like most of Berlioz's lyrical movements it is polyphonic and flows smoothly and inevitably.

(3) *Prelude.* This was intended by Berlioz to be played only when the occasion of the *Te Deum* had some military connection. It is a masterpiece of dramatic suggestion.

(4) Prayer, *Dignare*, another beautiful lyrical movement, notable for its fine polyphony.

(5) Hymn, *Christe, rex gloriae.* A piece of epic force and simplicity.

(6) Prayer, *Tu ergo.* This movement, full of long-breathed, wandering melody, is rich in subtlety and beauty.

(7) *Judex crederis.* This is one of the most tremendous pieces of its kind Berlioz ever composed. Its effect is overwhelming and no doubt influenced Verdi's *Requiem.*

(8) *March for the Presentation of the Colours.* This is a fine heroic march without any of the usual banality of such compositions.

Two points may be mentioned about Berlioz's *Te Deum.* Firstly, his superb and original use of the organ, which is not used to reinforce the orchestra, to add more volume of sound

—as nearly all composers who combine the organ with the orchestra use it—but antiphonally and dramatically. The second point is the military character of the work, which means it would make its utmost effect when used for a special occasion.[1]

In July 1851 he received a piece of good news, a request from Liszt for the score (manuscript) of *Benvenuto Cellini*, which Liszt wished to produce at Weimar: 'However infantile my joy may appear, my dear Liszt, I will not hide it from you.'

He spent some time retouching it, and wrote to Morel on 10th February 1852:

> I was going to leave to-morrow for Weimar, the first performance of *Benvenuto* being due on the 16th of the month. . . . Now Liszt writes to tell me of the illness of two of the principals. . . . That will delay it for fifteen or twenty days. Now, as I have to be in London on 1st March I will probably not go to Germany. . . .
>
> I am vexed not to be going to hear *Benvenuto*. Liszt says it goes marvellously; they have been working at it for four months. I had well cleaned, tidied up, and restored the score before sending it. I had not looked at it for thirteen years; it is diabolically lively, I shall never again find such a shower of youthful ideas. What ravages those fellows of the Opéra made me make in it!

On 20th March 1852 Liszt gave the first performance of *Benvenuto Cellini* in Weimar; on 24th March Berlioz conducted at the Exeter Hall in London the first concert for the New Philharmonic Society, which had been founded by Cramer, Beale, and others in rivalry to the Old Philharmonic conducted by Costa. At the first concert the first four parts of *Roméo* were performed in a translation by George Linley; Mme Pleyel[2] played Weber's *Concertstück*, and there was a selection from *La Vestale*.[3] At the fourth concert, on 12th May, Berlioz gave a remarkable performance of the Ninth Symphony, with Clara Novello, Martha Williams, Sims Reeves, and Staudigl as soloists; this performance made such an impression that it was

[1] Actually it originated in an early work for a victorious celebration of Napoleon entitled *Le Retour de la campagne d'Italie*.

[2] Berlioz's former fiancée, Mlle Moke.

[3] Spontini's widow, the daughter of J. B. Erard, came from Paris for this occasion and presented Berlioz with the baton with which Spontini used to conduct the operas of Gluck and Mozart.

demanded again, and at the sixth and last concert on 9th June Berlioz repeated the Ninth Symphony and gave some fragments of his *Faust*.

But, as usually happened, the artistic success was greater than the financial results,[1] and Berlioz returned to Paris at the end of June in a not very cheerful mood to take up again his task of writing articles. About this time, or a little earlier, is a letter to his son Louis:[2]

MY DEAR LOUIS,

Your mother is a little better, but she has to keep to her bed and refrain from talking. Besides, the slightest emotion would be fatal to her. So do not write to her a letter like the last you have sent me. Nothing is more depressing than to see you yourself condemned to inaction and sadness. You will reach your eighteenth year without being able to enter any career. I have no fortune; you have no position: on what shall we live?

You are always talking of becoming a sailor. . . . If I were free, entirely independent, I would go with you, but . . .

Whatever happens I shall always be your best friend and the *sole* one entirely devoted and full of unalterable affection for you . . . however, it will be sad indeed if you remain at *twenty* a young man useless to yourself and to society.

In September 1852 Michel Lévy published Berlioz's book *Les Soirées de l'orchestre*, a collection of articles adroitly connected so as to make a whole. This book was a success and in about a year went into a second edition. Its success must have been bitter for Berlioz, since it was a thoroughly devastating attack on the bad musical conditions of Paris and a championship of honesty of purpose and sincere love in art. The public approved and enjoyed what he wrote; the bad conditions remained unchanged. To Alexis Lwoff in Russia he writes:

Here . . . the mediocrities feed upon each other and I regard the struggles and the meals of these dogs with almost as much anger as disgust.

The judgments of the press and of the public are of a foolishness and frivolity unexampled among other nations . . . the feeling for truth in art is as extinct as that for right in morality. . . .

[1] The cost of the rehearsals for the Ninth Symphony alone took up one-third of the subscriptions (letter to d'Ortigue, 22nd May 1852).

[2] Incorrectly dated in *Correspondance inédite* as 'samedi 25 . . . (vers 1846).'

Suddenly a temporary relief came; he was invited by Liszt to Weimar to take part in a Berlioz Week to begin on 17th November 1852. Liszt had already produced *Tannhäuser* and *Lohengrin* (in 1851) at the Court Theatre in Weimar; *Cellini*, at the first performance on 20th March 1852, had also been successful and was to be repeated. The performance of *Cellini* on 17th November, conducted by Liszt, with Berlioz and the Grand Duke and Duchess in the audience, made a great impression. On 20th November Berlioz conducted his *Roméo* (entire) and the first two parts of *Faust*. Musicians came from all parts to this festival, including Hans von Bülow, Klindworth, Pruckner, and others. On 22nd November Berlioz was given a banquet and presented with the order of the Falcon of the Grand Duke.

One effect of the success of Weimar was that *Benvenuto Cellini* was produced at Covent Garden on 25th June 1853, in Italian. Unfortunately its title suggested to the public that it was a conventional Italian opera *à la* Donizetti, and since it was so utterly unlike what was expected it was a complete failure and Berlioz withdrew his score the next day.

With this failure Berlioz's hopes of making any large sum of money were demolished. He had already sold the score of his *Faust* for seven hundred francs, and now returned to his daily fight in Paris, with his wife Harriet permanently ill and his other *ménage* with Mlle Recio and her mother more of a burden than a refuge. It is about this time that we may place the incident related in his *Mémoires* of the unwritten symphony which he heard in a dream:

When I woke the next morning I recalled almost all the first section which (it is the only thing I now remember) was in two-four time, *allegro*, in A minor. I went to my table to write it, when I suddenly thought: If I write this piece I shall be compelled to write the rest. The scale on which my mind now always tends to work will give to this symphony enormous proportions. I shall have to give up three or four months exclusively to this work (I took seven to write *Roméo et Juliette*). I shall write no articles or almost none. My income will diminish accordingly. Then, when the symphony is finished I shall be weak enough to have it copied. I shall have it copied, which will put me in debt for a thousand or twelve hundred francs. Once the parts are copied I shall be harassed by the temptation to have it performed. I shall give a concert of which the receipts will scarcely cover half the expenses; that is inevitable to-day. I shall lose what I haven't got; I shall lack means for the necessities for my invalid wife, I shall not be able to meet my personal expenses nor have anything to pay for my son's allowance in the boat which he has to join soon.[1] These ideas made me shudder and I threw down my pen, saying: 'Bah! to-morrow I shall have forgotten the symphony.' The following night the symphony obstinately came back into my mind and stuck in my head; I heard distinctly the *allegro* in A minor—more, I seemed to see it written. I woke in a feverish agitation, I sang the theme, whose character and form pleased me extremely; I was about to get up . . . but the reflections of the day before returned to me; I stiffened myself against the temptation, I clung to the hope of forgetting it. At length I fell asleep, and the next day on waking all recollection of it had indeed vanished for ever.

Berlioz goes on to say that he will no doubt be called a coward by the young fanatic who loves art; he admits that when he was younger and his wife was in health and able and willing to encourage him and share his privations he would have taken the risk and written the symphony; but in his then situation, he says:

I have the consciousness of having been only human and, while believing myself as devoted to art as you or any one else, I believe I am honouring it by not treating it as a monster avid for human victims, and in proving that it has left me with the capacity to distinguish between courage and ferocity.[2] If I have yielded little by little to my musical desires in writing recently my sacred trilogy, *L'Enfance du Christ*, it is because my position is no longer the same, such imperious duties are no longer imposed upon me. Besides, I have the certainty of easily getting this work frequently performed in Germany, where I am invited to return by several important towns. I go there frequently now; I have made four trips there during the last eighteen months. . . .

At the end of 1853 Berlioz visited Brunswick, Hanover,[3] Bremen (where Joachim played the alto solo in *Harold*), and Leipzig, where he gave two concerts on 1st and 10th December in the Gewandhaus, conducted by himself. Numbers of

[1] Louis Berlioz entered the French mercantile marine.

[2] A lesson to all idealists, whether political, religious, or artistic!

[3] In this town Beethoven's and Goethe's Bettina von Arnim, now seventy-two years old, came, 'not to see me but to look at me,' says Berlioz in a letter.

eminent musicians came to these concerts, including Liszt, Raff, Cornelius, Mason, Pruckner, Pohl, Reményi, and Klindworth, and his music begins to win more and more supporters and greater and greater general enthusiasm.[1] Liszt and most of the younger musicians were fervently for him, and with repetition his music was being better understood.[2]

He returned to Paris at the end of 1853 and on 3rd March 1854 his wife, Harriet Smithson, died, after a long and painful illness. On 11th March he writes to Liszt announcing her death:

We have not been able to live together nor to separate for twelve years. These lacerations have rendered the last and final separation more grievous for me. She is delivered from a horrible existence and from atrocious sufferings which she endured for the last three years. My son had just been spending four days here and was able to see his mother before her death. Happily I was not away. It would have been frightful for me to hear in my absence of her death all alone. . . .[3]

To his son Louis, who was serving his apprenticeship on board the dispatch-boat *Le Corse*, he wrote on 6th March:

I have just come from the cemetery; I have left on her tomb two wreaths, one for you and one for me. . . . The servants are here for several days more to put everything in order. I have kept her hair; do not lose the little pin which I gave you. You will never know what we have suffered from one another, your mother and I . . . at any rate, she saw you before her death. . . .

I shall be able to help you more than in the past, but I shall take every precaution against your squandering money.

Berlioz's extremely French family sense comes out strongly in a letter written a week or so later to his son:

. . . Write and tell me if you can get back the watch, which I fear you pawned at Havre when you were behaving so foolishly. It was given to you by my father. . . . I have had a watch-chain made of your poor mother's hair, and I should like you to preserve it religiously. I have also had a bracelet made which I shall give to my sister, and I shall keep the rest. . . .

[1] During his absence in Germany, although Berlioz was a candidate, the French Academicians elected in the place of Onslow, who had died, a musician named Clapisson as a member of the Institut.

[2] Brahms, then aged twenty, was also at Berlioz's concert on 1st December at the Leipzig Gewandhaus and met Berlioz a few days later. See p. 330.

[3] It is significant that he never mentions his second wife in his *Mémoires*.

In April 1854 Berlioz made another visit to Germany and gave concerts in Hanover and Dresden. Joachim in Hanover and Hans von Bülow in Dresden were among his warmest supporters. He returned to Paris in May, and the rest of 1854 was spent in the composition of *L'Enfance du Christ*. He also completed his *Mémoires*, to which, however, he added, later, several short postscripts. His concluding words, dated Paris, 18th October 1854, were:

> Here I make an end . . . thanking with overflowing warmth holy Germany, where art is preserved pure; and thee, generous England; and thee, Russia, who hast saved me; and you, my good friends of France; and you, noble hearts and minds of all the nations I have known. To know you was for me a happiness; I keep, and I shall keep faithfully, the most precious memory of our relationship. As for you, maniacs, stupid bulls and mastiffs, as for you, my Guildensterns, my Rosencranzes, my Iagos, little Osrics, serpents and insects of every kind, *farewell, my . . . friends*;[1] I despise you and I hope I shall not die without having forgotten you.

[1] In English.

CHAPTER III

THE 'SECOND SIMPLICITY'

On 19th October 1854[1] Berlioz married Marie Recio, thus regularizing, as he says in a letter to his son, a relationship which had lasted 'fourteen' years. On 10th December he gave in Paris the first performance of his *L'Enfance du Christ*, which met with a success 'revolting,' writes Berlioz to Liszt's Princess Sayn-Wittgenstein, 'to his elder brothers.' Berlioz was rightly indignant at the way some critics wrote of this work:

> They say I have mended my ways, that I have changed my manners . . . and other idiocies. . . .[2]
>
> I must tell Liszt, as a piece of information useful for . . . my concert at Weimar, that *L'Enfance du Christ* lasts only an hour and a half. . . .

His new work was performed again in Paris on 28th January, and at the Opéra-Comique at Easter, 7th and 23rd April; also three times (18th, 22nd, and 24th March) at the Théâtre-Royal du Cirque, Brussels.

Fétis, who heard it there, wrote to Liszt about its success and added: 'I have found him [Berlioz] much changed and aged.[3] He gave me the pleasure of dining with me and my wife; he is a man of intellect and of great intelligence, musical and otherwise. . . .'

Something must now be said of this work, which was recognized as a masterpiece—a very rare occurrence, especially for Berlioz—on its first appearance.

L'Enfance du Christ. This trilogy consists of three parts:

(1) *Le Songe d'Hérode* (Herod's Dream).
(2) *La Fuite en Égypte* (The Flight into Egypt).
(3) *L'Arrivée à Saïs* (The Arrival at Saïs).

[1] The day after the conclusion of his *Mémoires*, which, as he carefully points out, are not confessions.

[2] There is no end to this sort of nonsense. It is written by nearly all critics, literary and musical, who never seem to recognize the elementary rule that different means are used by an artist when the purpose is different. There is nothing more characteristically Berliozian than *L'Enfance du Christ*.

[3] In January 1855, Berlioz had just passed his fifty-first birthday (11th December 1854).

The middle section, *La Fuite en Égypte*, was composed first and part of it put forth as a newly discovered work by an imaginary Pierre Ducré.[1] He then added the last section, *L'Arrivée à Saïs*, writing to Liszt on 24th January 1854: 'I have been stopped in the middle of my work . . . by a thousand prosaic affairs and by the proofs of *Faust* which are unending. I need another two full months. Impossible to find a day free!'

When he wrote this, he had not yet conceived the first part, *Le Songe d'Hérode*, which he first mentions to Liszt in a letter dated 4th April 1854: 'I begin to see dawn in the plan of the "massacre,"[2] for which Chorley has also given me some ideas.' The section *La Fuite en Egypte*[3] was first performed and published separately, in Paris, and in Germany with a translation by Peter Cornelius. On 28th July 1854, in a letter to Hans von Bülow thanking him for his pianoforte arrangement of the overture to *Cellini*, Berlioz says:

I have worked hard since my return from Dresden; I have written the first part of my second trilogy: *Le Songe d'Hérode*. This score precedes the embryo which you know under the name *Fuite en Égypte*, and will form with *L'Arrivée à Saïs* a whole of sixteen sections, lasting an hour and a half. . . .

I have tried several new effects: the air of *L'Insomnie d'Hérode* is written in G minor on this scale, described in plainsong under some Greek name which I do not know:[4]

2

[5]

[1] The chorus, *L'Adieu des bergers*. See p. 260.

[2] Massacre of the Innocents.

[3] I possess a copy of the early pianoforte edition of *La Fuite* published by Richault, Paris; it bears the inscription 'Attributed to Pierre Ducré, imaginary Chapelmaster, and composed by Hector Berlioz'; it consists of the overture, the chorus *L'Adieu des bergers*, and legend and pantomime for tenor and choir of angels, *Le Repos de la Sainte Famille*.

[4] Berlioz was much interested in the study of the music and the versification of the Greeks and Romans. He writes to M. B. Jullien, author of a work, *De quelques points des sciences dans l'antiquité*, on 23rd January 1854, saying he had cleared up for him several points in Latin prosody.

[5] This is how the scale is printed in the original French edition of the letters, but it must be wrong. If the flat before F were a sharp, this would give the feeling

This gives rise to some very sombre harmonies and cadences of a special character which seem to me to fit the situation. . . .

L'Enfance du Christ was the first of Berlioz's works for which he himself wrote *all* the words. The text is of a beautiful simplicity and directness worthy of a distinguished writer in a country where the general literary standard has always been extremely high. The music is written for a soprano, a baritone, three basses, two tenors, and a chorus.

(1) *Le Songe d'Hérode.* It begins with a tenor solo with a small orchestra of wood-wind (flutes, clarinets, bassoons) and strings. The charm of this piece is to be found even in the words:

Dans la crêche, en ce temps, Jésus venait de naître,
Mais nul prodige encore ne l'avait fait connaître;
Et déjà les puissants tremblaient,
Déjà les faibles espéraient,
Tous attendaient. . . .
Or, apprenez, chrétiens, quel crime épouvantable
Au roi des Juifs alors suggéra la terreur,
Et le céleste avis que, dans leur humble étable,
Aux parents de Jésus envoya le Seigneur.[1]

This is followed by the wonderful *Marche nocturne*,[2] representing a street in Jerusalem, and Roman soldiers on patrol at night. I remember showing this in the full score to Artur Schnabel, and I watched him read it with concentrated attention. 'What a strange piece!' he exclaimed; and it is true that although

of the scale of G minor (harmonic minor) as Berlioz states; although the E natural and the A flat do not belong to that scale but are due to the Greek (dorian) mode. It is obvious that F sharp, not F flat, is correct from the piece itself, which is written in two flats. Berlioz made great use of Greek modes in his music, but this is the only occasion I know of when he has mentioned the fact, and even then his music is too complex to be put in any one mode.

[1] 'In his cradle, about this time, Jesus was born,
Though no wonder as yet had made it known;
But already the strong feared,
Already the weak hoped . . .
Now, learn Christians, what terrible crime
His terror suggested to the King of the Jews,
What advice from on high to their humble stable
The Lord sent to the parents of Jesus.'

[2] See bk. IV, chap. i, p. 246.

PAGE FROM THE FINALE TO THE FIRST PART OF 'L'ENFANCE DU CHRIST'

in a sense simple, this is an exceedingly strange piece, full of fantasy. The soldiers exchange greetings and the patrol continues and dies away. The whole atmosphere of that ancient time, of that strange Judaeo-Roman history, and of that birth of the Christian myth or religion is evoked in this music of genius with a simplicity that only the greatest masters possess.[1]

Next comes the air of Herod in his palace, which has a sombre gravity retaining the sense of mystery already created. Then comes the announcement of Polydorus that the soothsayers have arrived by command of the king. The dialogue between them and Herod is full of ingenious touches; next come the cabalistic evolutions of the soothsayers in a strange rhythm with alternations of three beats and four beats to the bar; then the soothsayers announce:

La voix dit vrai, seigneur. Un enfant vient de naître
Qui fera disparaître
Ton trône et ton pouvoir,
Mais nul ne peut savoir
Ni son nom ni sa race.[2]

The next scene is the stable of Bethlehem, in which, after a duet between Mary and Joseph (soprano and baritone), a choir of angels warn them to depart. This scene is full of poetry and ends the first part of the work.

(2) *La Fuite en Égypte* begins with a short instrumental overture, followed by the famous chorus, *L'Adieu des bergers* (Farewell of the Shepherds), which is like Fra Angelico in its delicate naivety and freshness of colour. Then follows the exquisite tenor solo, *Le Repos de la Sainte Famille*, concluding with an invisible angelic chorus (sopranos and altos) *Alleluia*. This *Repos* is one of the most exquisite pieces of music in existence. No analysis, no description can give the reader any

[1] It is characteristic of the general incapacity to understand the imaginative ideas of genius that even J. G. Prod'homme in his special work on *L'Enfance du Christ* has not understood this orchestral piece.

[2] 'The voice speaks truth, sire. A child has been born
Who will make disappear
Thy throne and thy power,
But none can declare
Or his name or his race.'

idea of its transcendental beauty. In the whole of the nineteenth century, since the death of Schubert, there has been no composer but Berlioz capable of writing such celestial music.

(3) *L'Arrivée à Saïs* opens with the recital (tenor) of the arrival of the Holy Family at Saïs. This is followed by a duet between Mary and Joseph:

Dans cette ville immense
Où le peuple en foule s'élance,
Quelle rumeur!
Joseph! J'ai peur!
Je n'en puis plus . . . las . . . je suis morte . . .
Allez frapper à cette porte.[1]

The house is inhabited by Romans, and six bass voices dramatically reply to Joseph:

Arrière, vils Hébreux!
Les gens de Rome n'ont que faire
De vagabonds et de lépreux.[2]

They knock at another house, and twelve bass voices (first and second basses) of Egyptians reply even more brutally. They then apply elsewhere, and are received by the father of a family of Ishmaelites. The section that follows is beautiful in its simplicity and sublimity. The Ishmaelite asks who they are; Joseph replies:

Elle a pour nom Marie,
Je m'appelle Joseph,
Et nous nommons l'enfant Jésus.[3]

---

[1] 'In this city immense
Where the people crowding gather,
What a din!
Joseph! I tremble!
I can go no further . . . I die . . .
Knock and they may let us in.'

[2] 'Be off, vile Hebrews!
The people of Rome have no use
For vagabonds and lepers.'

[3] 'Her name is Mary,
I am called Joseph,
And the child we call Jesus.'

When the Ishmaelite hears that Joseph is a carpenter, which is his own trade, he says:

Ensemble nous travaillerons,
Bien des deniers nous gagnerons,
Laissez faire.
Près de nous Jésus grandira,
Puis bientôt il vous aidera
Et la sagesse il apprendra.[1]

Then follows a charming instrumental piece played by the young Ishmaelites, a trio for two flutes and Theban harp; there is then an ensemble with chorus:

Allez dormir, bon père,
Doux enfant, tendre mère,
Bien reposez.[2]

The narrator (tenor) follows:

Ce fut ainsi que par un infidèle
Fut sauvé le Sauveur. . . .[3]

This is followed by a mystic chorus, beautiful, aerial, floating away into space on the words:

O mon âme, pour toi que reste-t-il à faire,
Qu'à briser ton orgueil devant un tel mystère! . . .
O mon cœur, emplis-toi du grave et pur amour
Qui seul peut nous ouvrir le céleste séjour.
Amen!
Amen![4]

---

[1] 'Together we shall labour,
Earning our livelihood,
So let it be.
Close to us Jesus will grow,
Then soon he will help you
And he will acquire wisdom.'

[2] 'Retire to sleep, father,
Infant and mother
Soundly repose.'

[3] 'Thus it was that by an infidel
The Saviour was saved.'

[4] 'O my soul, for thee what remains now to do,
But to bend thy pride before such a mystery!
O my heart, fill now with a love deep and pure
That alone can guide us to a heavenly abode.
Amen!
Amen!'

Thus concludes one of the purest and most exquisite works of its kind in music. It is no doubt true that Berlioz could not have written it when he was young. There are the creations of youth and the creations of maturity; but only the greatest artists can achieve what has been called and is best described as the 'second simplicity,' and they only achieve it when they themselves through experience have attained to that 'second simplicity.' But otherwise nearly all the characteristics of Berlioz's musical genius are there. In this 'second simplicity' *L'Enfance du Christ* does resemble the mature Mozart, while Berlioz's earlier works have rather more affinity with Beethoven.

It is also a witness to the maturity of Berlioz that he does not treat the subject either as a believer or a non-believer in Christianity. His approach is not at all rationalistic. He accepts the story as part of his human environment and attempts no sophistical attitude towards it. He is content to treat it as one of the mysteries with which he is surrounded, and his approach to it is as simple and direct as his approach to the love of Romeo and Juliet, to the story of Faust, and to Nature. This gives a unique quality to *L'Enfance du Christ* which separates it from the bulk of so-called 'religious' music. It is the work of a free, grown-up man, not the work of a Protestant or a Catholic or a Rationalist or an Atheist.

I will now leave *L'Enfance du Christ*, after quoting the opinion of only one celebrated musician upon it out of all the reams of praise this work has received since it first appeared. And I will choose for this purpose an out-of-the-way composer who is neglected to-day, but who had great talent and was not likely to be deceived by the quality of a work. Offenbach [1] wrote in *L'Artiste* of 4th January 1855:

'We cannot extend ourselves to-day as much as we could have desired on this great composition, in which science of harmony and of orchestration seem to parallel beauty and originality of melody.'

[1] Offenbach, Jacques (1819–80), composer of *La Belle Helène* and *Les Contes d'Hoffmann.*

CHAPTER IV

LISZT, WAGNER, BERLIOZ

In February 1855 Liszt invited Berlioz to a double Berlioz-Week of a fortnight, from 10th to 27th February, at Weimar. During this festival *Lélio; ou le Retour à la vie*[1] and *L'Enfance du Christ* were performed, as well as extracts from *Roméo*, *Cellini*, and *Faust*. The success was great, but the greatest achievement of this visit was Berlioz's promise to Liszt's friend, the Princess Sayn-Wittgenstein, to write a great opera on the subject of the Trojans from Virgil's *Aeneid*.

The 'music of the future' had now arrived in Germany, and Liszt was its protagonist. His two great exponents of this music were Berlioz and Wagner, and he himself was a contributor. He had made Weimar a temple dedicated to music, where the great works of the past were performed and where all that seemed good in the present was also offered to the public. Sustained as he was by the Grand-Ducal family, and having a court theatre under his control, he was able to do more for music than almost any other man in Europe. At least he did more, and it was due to him that Wagner's *Lohengrin* had become known and that Berlioz's *Cellini* had been resuscitated. Berlioz was a much older friend of his than Wagner, but about this time his contact with Wagner (living in exile from Germany since the revolution of 1848–9) by correspondence had become closer. It was natural that he should have wished to bring together the two composers who were, in his opinion, the great leaders of the time. He was immersed in Wagner's written theories and was stimulated by Berlioz's disgust with the conditions of the opera in Paris to think there was common ground between them. So there was—up to a point! But between Wagner and Berlioz there was a fundamental discrepancy which no community of suffering, no similarity of fate, no diplomacy

[1] See bk. III, chap. ii, p. 158 *et seq.*

or benevolence of Liszt could bridge. Also, Berlioz did not think very highly of Wagner's music, but he had allowed Liszt to write a most eulogistic article on *Tannhäuser* in the *Journal des Débats* in May 1849, and he had been fair and open in his own criticism of Wagner. Not so Wagner. He, on the contrary, with his usual duplicity, mixture of motives, and utter disregard for truth, had adversely criticized works by Berlioz *which he had neither heard nor seen in score.*

Only very intelligent persons exceptionally well acquainted with the details of Wagner's life have any notion of the depth of cunning in this man who has added to our conceptions of genius; but before dealing with his subtler duplicities, I shall give now chapter and verse for the statement I have just made about his criticism of works of which he was entirely ignorant.

In a letter to Liszt, dated 13th April 1852, he writes:

> What is this you have heard about me in connection with your performance of *Cellini*? You seem to suppose that I am hostile to it. Of this error I want you to get rid.[1] I look upon your undertaking as a purely personal matter, inspired by your liking for Berlioz; what a beast I should be if I were to criticize that liking and that undertaking! . . . But where a pure matter of the heart is submitted to speculative reason I must find that mistakes creep in which a third person can perceive. In the consequences which, as I am told, you expect from the performance of *Cellini* I cannot believe; that is all. . . .
>
> I am sorry you have not produced *Lohengrin* again. . . .

Wagner did not know a single note of the score of *Cellini* when he wrote this letter. The proof of this is that Wagner did not arrive in Paris until September 1839, and the last performance of *Benvenuto Cellini* (and that was only a fragment of it) took place in February 1839 in Paris. Not a note of Berlioz's opera was in print and not a note of it was seen or heard again until Liszt asked Berlioz for the score (in manuscript) in 1851 for the first performance at Weimar (the first and only performance since the original Paris production in

[1] Is it not extraordinary, Wagner's complete lack of self-awareness or self-criticism? In the sentences that follow what he says amounts to this: To produce *Cellini* is a tribute to your good heart (as Berlioz is a friend of yours) but a sad error of judgment.

1838–9) on 20th March 1852. Wagner was then an exile from Germany living in Zürich, and he did not hear either the Weimar performance of his own opera *Lohengrin*, or the Weimar performance of *Cellini*.

Worse, if worse is possible, is to come. In a letter to Liszt a few months later, on 8th September 1852, Wagner writes from Zürich, and, after some remarks about Berlioz wasting his time in recasting *Cellini*, adds:

> Believe me, I *love* Berlioz, although he keeps apart from me in his distrust and capriciousness: he does not know me, but I know *him*. If I expect anything from a composer it is from Berlioz, but not if he follows the path which has led him to the platitudes of his symphony of *Faust*, because if he continues to follow these tracks he can only become quite ridiculous. If ever a *musician* wanted *the poet* it is Berlioz, and his misfortune is that he always prepares this poet for himself, according to his musical fancy, arbitrarily handling now Shakespeare, now Goethe. He wants a poet who would completely penetrate him, who would *conquer* him by delight, who would be to him what man is to woman.[1] I see with dismay that this exceedingly gifted artist is perishing in his egotistic solitude. Can I save him ?

The first comment to be made on this letter is that Wagner, although he speaks of 'the platitudes of *Faust*,' had also neither heard nor seen a note of the score of *Faust*, in spite of his judgment upon it. *Faust* was first performed in Paris in December 1846. Fragments of it had been given in Russia and in Germany, but not where Wagner was, and since 1849 Wagner had not been in Germany. Wagner was not in Paris in December 1846 when *Faust* was first performed there, and it had not been performed there since, owing to its initial failure, when Wagner wrote. Also, the score was not published. Berlioz sold it in March 1853, and we know that he was correcting the proofs early in 1854.[2]

What are we to think of this? I do not think that Wagner is lying consciously; he is merely jumping to conclusions from prejudices which he does not bother to analyse. His conclusions are dearer to him than the supposed facts upon which they

[1] How revealing this is *of Wagner*! And how utterly inapplicable to Berlioz!

[2] Wagner set the habit—now second nature to almost all critics and musicians—of judging Berlioz's music without having heard it.

pretend to be based. As for his 'I *love* Berlioz,' it is—like most asseverations of love—mere words. His other remark, that Berlioz 'does not know me, but I know *him*,' is just the opposite of the truth. Everything goes to show that Wagner knew nothing about Berlioz, whereas Berlioz always distrusted Wagner, in spite of his gifts and his voluble lip-service to the highest artistic ideals.

Liszt continued his attempts to make his two 'lions' friends, and in a letter to Wagner in 1853 he writes:

A few days ago I received a letter from Berlioz in answer to my last, in which I had said several things about you. I quote the following lines (from Berlioz's reply):

'Our art, as we understand it, is an art of millionaires—it requires millions. As soon as these millions are found every difficulty disappears; every dark intellect is illumined; moles and foxes are driven back into the earth; the marble block becomes a god, and the public human; without these millions we remain clodhoppers after thirty years' exertion.

'And yet there is not a sovereign, not a Rothschild, who will understand this. Is it not possible that, after all, we, with our secret pretensions, should simply be stupid and insolent fools?

'Between Wagner and me smooth gearing would not be impossible if only he would put a little oil in his wheels. As for the few lines of which you speak, I have never read them, and therefore feel not the slightest resentment on their account. I have fired too many pistol shots at the legs of passers-by to be astonished at receiving a few pellets myself.'

In a letter to Wagner, dated 31st October, Liszt returns to the subject of *Cellini*.

We have arranged a Wagner week; and the *Flying Dutchman*, *Tannhäuser*, and *Lohengrin* have taken firm ground and cast deep roots here. All the rest is moonshine to me with the sole exception of Berlioz's *Cellini*.[1] For this work I retain my great predilection, which you will not think uncalled for when you know it better.

In a letter dated Zürich, 12th September 1853, Wagner writes: 'Paris begins almost to be unpleasant to me in my imagination; I am afraid of Berlioz. With my bad French I am simply lost.'

In a letter to Wagner dated Weimar, 21st February 1854,

[1] Liszt is only referring to operas.

Liszt says that the failure of *Cellini* in Paris and London 'must be attributed to low villainy and misapprehension.'

Before leaving Weimar at the end of February 1855, Berlioz wrote to Fiorentino in Paris that he was being spurred, goaded, and stung into writing 'a great theatrical machine.'

In the last chapter of his *Mémoires*, written about October 1854 and dated, at the end, 18th October 1854, after speaking of the death of his wife (3rd March 1854), Berlioz goes on to speak of his career:

> Now I am arrived, if not at the end of my career, at least on the slope which conducts more and more rapidly to it; fatigued, burnt but always burning, and filled with an energy which awakes sometimes with a violence that almost frightens me. I begin to understand French, to write passably a page of a score and a page of verse or of prose, I know how to conduct and to inspire an orchestra, I adore and respect art in all its forms. . . . But I belong to a nation which to-day is no longer interested in any of the noble manifestations of intelligence, for whom the calf of gold is the only god. . . .
>
> For three years I have been tormented by the idea of a vast opera of which I would like to write the words and the music as I have just done with my sacred trilogy *L'Enfance du Christ*. I resist the temptation to realize this project and I will resist, I hope, until the end.[1] The subject appears to me grand, magnificent, and profoundly moving, which manifestly proves that the Parisians would find it flat and boring. . . .

There is further evidence that Berlioz had been meditating for some time a great opera on Virgil's *Aeneid*, and that he had been re-reading Virgil. In a letter to Hans von Bülow dated 1st September 1854, he writes:

> What a grand composer was Virgil! What a master of melody and harmony! He ought to have said with his dying breath, *Qualis artifex pereo!*[2] instead of that buffoon, Nero, who only had one single inspiration in his whole life. And that was on the evening he set fire to the four corners of Rome—a brilliant proof that a mediocre man may occasionally be possessed of a grand idea.

---

[1] Berlioz puts a footnote, added in 1858, to this remark which reads as follows: 'Alas! no, I have not resisted. I have finished the poem and the music of *Les Troyens*, an opera in five acts. What will become of this immense work? . . . 1858.'

[2] 'What an artist is passing away!'

However, he was not able to set to work immediately on this 'great theatrical machine,' but had to leave Paris in June 1855 for London, where he was engaged again to conduct for the New Philharmonic Society. The Old Philharmonic Society had meanwhile engaged Wagner to conduct their concerts that season, and naturally there was great rivalry between the two organizations. Berlioz and Wagner, however, met amicably, and this time appeared to get on fairly well together. 'I felt much stimulated,' says Wagner,[1] 'on the two or three occasions when Sainton invited me to dine with Berlioz . . . [he] seemed to be pleasantly affected by the attitude of gay spontaneity I adopted with him. His usual, short, almost reserved manner thawed visibly during the friendly hours we passed together. . . .' Praeger,[2] who was in London at the time and was a close friend of Wagner's, has left a description of the intercourse between the two men: 'Hector Berlioz,' he says, 'was of an excitable temperament, too, but could repress it. Not so Wagner. He presented a striking contrast to the polished, refined Frenchman, whose speech was almost classic through his careful selection of words.'[3]

On 5th July 1855 Wagner wrote to Liszt:

> I bring back from London one real benefit; it is a cordial and profound friendship that I have conceived towards Berlioz . . . he has revealed himself to me under quite a different light to that in which I had previously seen him; each suddenly recognized in the other a companion in misfortune. . . . After my last concert he came to see me . . . we remained together until three o'clock in the morning and we separated with a fervent embrace. . . .

On 25th June 1855 Berlioz wrote to Liszt:

> We have spoken much about you with Wagner lately, and you may imagine with what affection, since, on my word of honour, I believe he loves you as I do.

[1] In *Mein Leben.*

[2] Author of *Wagner as I knew him.*

[3] There are a number of people—it would be an insult to decent men to call them mediocrities—who hate to think that great men exist. And in spite of this book they will continue to spread the lie that Berlioz was a 'romantic' madman, without discipline or sense of proportion.

He will no doubt tell you of his stay in London and of all he has had to suffer from prejudiced hostility. He is superb in his ardour and warmth of heart, and I confess that even his violences delight me. It seems that a fatality prevents me from hearing anything of his latest compositions. . . .

But Wagner's phrase about companions in misfortune gives the clue to this cordiality; also the fact that, after all, they were both artists with a *métier* in common. But even in this temporary agreement their divergencies appear. Wagner heard Berlioz conduct the New Philharmonic and wrote to Liszt: '. . . I have been indifferently edified by the manner in which Berlioz conducted the Mozart symphony (G minor). . . .' In *Mein Leben* he says: 'I . . . heard him conduct some classical works, and was amazed to find a conductor who was so energetic in the interpretation of his own compositions sink into the commonest rut of the vulgar time-beater.'

Berlioz was less 'amazed' at Wagner's conducting, but equally critical, and more precise in his criticism; he wrote to Liszt: 'Wagner conducts in a free style, the way Klindworth plays the piano . . . such a style is like dancing on a slack-rope . . . *sempre tempo rubato*.'

Liszt, however, still did his best to bring them closer together. In reply to Wagner's letter of 5th July, written on his return to Zürich, Liszt wrote from Weimar on 11th July:

. . . I am delighted at your friendly relations with Berlioz. Of all contemporary composers he is the one with whom you can converse in the simplest, most open, and most interesting manner. Take him for all in all, he is an honest, splendid, tremendous fellow; and together with your letter I received one from Berlioz in which he says . . .

Liszt then repeats to Wagner all the nice things Berlioz said about him, not mentioning, of course, his reservations about Wagner's conducting. The activity of Liszt on behalf of the music of Berlioz and Wagner about this time and for years to come was tremendous. Not only did he perform their works at Weimar constantly, but he wrote enthusiastic articles for French and German papers,[1] urged other conductors to perform their music and lent the whole weight of his authority

[1] Liszt wrote in French, and his musical articles were generally translated into German by P. Cornelius.

with young musicians on their behalf.[1] Further, it was largely through Liszt that Dr. Karl Franz Brendel, who edited Schumann's *Neue Zeitschrift*[2] from 1845, became the champion of the music of Berlioz and of Wagner. But up to about 1855 it had been Berlioz who was, as Richard Pohl puts it, the true 'Bahnbrecher.'[3] And between Berlioz and Wagner there was absolutely no community of ideas and no affinity of gift; they were united only in their opposition to the routine of the opera-house and to the venality and commonplaceness of their musical environment. It was because what brought them together was negative, not positive, that the bond had no permanence. Wagner was always a one-party man, and his party was himself. Even his expressed admiration for Berlioz's music is drawn out of him, as it were, by astonishment, and, as soon as he recovers from his astonishment, is immediately qualified; and Berlioz is the only one of his contemporaries whom he ever praises. We may dismiss his compliments to Liszt—whatever we may think of Liszt's music—because, firstly, Liszt not only constantly helped him with money but was his chief musical supporter, and secondly, the very tone in which Wagner praises Liszt's music rings of insincerity.

Berlioz did not seem to have shown much interest in Liszt's compositions,[4] but Liszt, if hurt by this, did not allow it to affect his attitude to Berlioz; but after Berlioz's visit in 1856, when *Cellini* was again produced at Weimar, conducted by Liszt, and the whole of *Faust* was performed, Liszt became more and more closely bound up with Wagner, although he continued his activity on behalf of Berlioz. He had failed to win over Berlioz to Wagner's music, so the triumvirate of the advance-guard of music was non-operative as far Berlioz was concerned.

[1] For example, he reproves Anton Rubinstein in a letter dated 21st February 1855 for having missed a concert at which Berlioz's *Fuite en Égypte* and *Fantaisie sur la Tempête de Shakespeare* were performed.

[2] *Neue Zeitschrift für Musik*, the most influential German musical review, founded in 1834 by Robert Schumann.

[3] Path-breaker, or route-maker, i.e. the pioneer.

[4] Liszt dedicated his 'Faust' Symphony to Berlioz and his 'Dante' Symphony to Wagner.

After conducting a performance of *Lohengrin* which Berlioz heard, Liszt wrote to a friend: 'He has for *Lohengrin* a regard and an affection analogous to that which Nélida has for the Princess W * * *.'[1]

Also to Hans von Bülow Liszt wrote: 'Berlioz took little pleasure in *Lohengrin*. We have scarcely spoken of it together, but he has expressed himself to others in unguarded terms, which has vexed me.'

Berlioz himself wrote to Auguste Morel from Paris on 23rd May:

> We have had at Weimar incredible scenes on the subject of Wagner's *Lohengrin*. . . . It would take too long to tell you. The result has been all sorts of stories which are now appearing in the German press. . . .
>
> I am tremendously busy and to tell you the truth very ill, without knowing what is the matter . . . perhaps it is the spring. I have undertaken an opera in five acts, of which I am writing both words and music. I am at the third act of the poem; I finished the second yesterday. This is between ourselves; I will polish it at leisure after having modelled it as well as I can.

In a remarkable letter, written from Baden[2] on 12th August 1856 to the Princess Carolyne Sayn-Wittgenstein, thanking her for her long letter about the poem of *Les Troyens* which he had sent her, Berlioz, after explaining several points of the libretto, continues:

> Thank you, then, for all the encouragement your exquisite goodness has given me. On my return to Paris I will try to free myself from all other occupations and begin my musical task. It will be severe; may all the gods of Virgil come to my aid or I am lost! What is immensely difficult in it is to find the musical *form*, that form without which music does not exist, or is no more than the humiliated slave of the word. This is the crime of Wagner;[3] he wishes to dethrone it, to reduce it to *expressive accents*, exaggerating the system of Gluck (who very happily *has not succeeded* himself in following this impious theory). I am for music which you yourself have called *free*. Yes; free, proud, sovereign, and conquering; I want it to attempt everything, to assimilate everything, that there should

---

[1] 'Nélida' stands for Daniel, Daniel Stern being the pen-name of the Comtesse d'Agoult, who was replaced in Liszt's affections by the Princess Wittgenstein.

[2] Where he conducted Gluck, Mozart, and Beethoven.

[3] It has taken nearly a hundred years for musicians to discover that Berlioz was right on this point.

be for it neither Alps nor Pyrenees; but for its conquests it must fight in person and not through lieutenants. . . .

To find the means to be *expressive*, *true*, without ceasing to be a musician, and to give in fact new means of action to the music, that is the problem. . . .

Another rock before me in composing the music of this drama is that the feelings which it is a question of expressing move me too much. That is no good. It is necessary to try to make burning things coolly. That is what hindered me so much in writing the *adagio* of *Roméo et Juliette* and the scene of reconciliation of the finale; I thought I should never emerge from it.

Time! Time! that is the great master! Unfortunately, like Ugolino, he devours his children. . . .

This letter is an interesting example of the truth that a great artist knows exactly what he is doing. It makes clear also that, to a musician like Berlioz, the methods of Wagner could not but be alien. The principles he expresses in this letter are those of Mozart, for whom the music was the principal essential of an opera. It may also be said that there are degrees of musicality even in musicians. Berlioz, in a letter to Th. Ritter dated 12th January 1856,[1] after reminding him that he had on that day begun the study of the marvels of great dramatic music . . . the sublimities of Gluck,[2] says: 'There are two great superior gods in our art, Beethoven and Gluck . . . although the former may be much above the latter *as musician*.'[3]

In the same way we may say that *as musicians* Mozart was much above Gluck and Berlioz much above Wagner; it is this fact which inspired their different approach to opera.

The attitude of a genius like Berlioz to the best of his contemporaries in his art must necessarily be complex. That is to say, he will regard them from different planes, according to whether he is considering them from the pinnacle of his genius or from some lower slope. This explains what might appear as a discrepancy in his attitude. For example, he writes a long,

[1] I do not know if this date is correct. It occurs in the *Correspondance inédite*, in which there are many errors.

[2] Berlioz was often astonished at the ignorance of Gluck shown by German musicians.

[3] My italics.

BERLIOZ IN 1856

After a photograph

cordial, and extremely interesting letter to Hans von Bülow, dated Paris, 20th January 1858, in which he says:

> Your faith, your ardour, your hatred even, enchant me. I, like you, have terrible hates and volcanic ardours; but as for faith, I believe firmly that there is nothing true, nothing false, nothing beautiful, nothing ugly.[1] . . . Don't believe a word of it, I slander myself. . . . No, no, I adore more than ever what I find beautiful, and death has, to my mind, no crueller disadvantage than this: to love no more, to admire no more. It is true that one is not aware that one loves no more. But no philosophy! in other words, no nonsense!
>
> You have undertaken, then, a series of concerts, and at Berlin again! A glacial town (no, not glacial, a block of ice is beautiful, it radiates, it has character), a town which thaws, cold, humid. And then the Lutherans —people who never laugh, blond without gentleness—you see how I digress, I have been blond and I have not been gentle. . . . Laugh, I permit it, it is all the same to me.
>
> Your programme was very fine; you have done me the injustice to suppose that only the fate of my two pieces would interest me in the account you have given. . . . You have spoken to me neither of your overtures nor of the pieces by Liszt; you calumniate me. But I forgive you. . . .

Now, beside this letter (which has other matters of great interest which I have not quoted) let us put the following extract from a letter written about this time to his son Louis:

> Several days ago I received a long letter from M. de Bülow, one of the sons-in-law of Liszt, the one who married Mlle Cosima. He tells me that he has given a concert at Berlin and has performed with great success my overture to *Cellini* and the song *Le Jeune Pâtre breton*. This young man is one of the most fervent disciples of that senseless school which is called in Germany the school of the *future*. They won't give in and will absolutely have me as their leader and standard-bearer. I say nothing, I write nothing, and I can only let them go their way; people of good sense will be able to see what truth there is in it.

In 1858 Wagner came to Paris to prepare for possible productions of his operas there. There was a fresh wave of propaganda, and Berlioz had the humiliation of seeing some of his friends and young musicians (Reyer, for example) lend themselves to this. Wagner saw Berlioz in Paris, but their relations were lukewarm, at least on Berlioz's side. One of the last

[1] Berlioz has some ideas in common with Spinoza.

written communications between them was the following note from Wagner:

Dear Berlioz,

I am delighted to be able to offer you the first copy of my *Tristan*. Accept it and keep it out of friendship for me.

Yours,

21st January 1860. Richard Wagner.

And on the score Wagner wrote: 'To the dear and great author of *Roméo et Juliette*, the grateful author of *Tristan und Iseult*.'

Wagner gave a concert in Paris on 25th January 1860, to which Berlioz went.[1] Wagner gave two more concerts, and everybody waited to see what Berlioz would write in the *Journal des Débats*. On 9th February 1860 his article appeared.[2]

This article has been much misrepresented; it is detached, but fair and sympathetic, if not enthusiastic, in its attitude to Wagner's music. Berlioz begins by stating the difficulties Wagner has had to contend with to give these concerts. He then refers to the lack of open-mindedness and the partisanship and biases which prejudge works when it is a question of music that differs from that which 'runs the streets'; and says he will only give his personal impressions without taking any notice of the diverse opinions about Wagner. *Der fliegende Holländer* (Flying Dutchman) overture made the same impression on him as in 1843, when he heard the opera in Dresden:

'The opening is magnificent . . .' the work is 'vigorously instrumented,' its sonority 'has a strange character that makes one shudder,' but 'the development appears to me excessive' and it 'manifests already the tendency of Wagner . . . not to mind the *sensation*,[3] to see only the poetic or dramatic idea to be expressed without bothering whether this idea obliges the composer to go outside musical conditions or not.'

[1] At this concert extracts from *Tristan* were first played. The concerts were not a success with the public.

[2] This article was reprinted by Berlioz in his book *A travers Chants* (chap. xxiv), from which I take the extracts quoted.

[3] I take it that Berlioz means the musicality, the pure sound-structure. It appears to me that he is on dangerous ground here and that it is not a position he could have defended without further elucidation.

The *Tannhäuser* extracts he praises highly, and he is still more eulogistic of the *Lohengrin* extracts, which he says 'have more salient qualities than the preceding works; also more novelty than is in *Tannhäuser*.' The Prelude to *Tristan*, he says, has much the same plan as the Introduction to *Lohengrin*; it has 'no other theme than a sort of chromatic moan,' and he confesses that here he does not understand the author's meaning.[1] He then concludes:

This sincere account puts sufficiently in evidence the great musical qualities of Wagner. One must conclude, it seems to me, that he possesses that rare intensity of feeling, that interior ardour, that strength of will, that faith which subjugates, moves, and carries one away; but that these qualities would have much greater effect if they were united to more invention, to less straining, and to a juster appreciation of certain constituent elements of art. So much for the practice.

I think that is a fair and accurate judgment and one that has stood the test of time. Berlioz then turns to the theory of this so-called 'Music of the Future,' and here he reveals his isolation and his complete refusal to be classed as one of this group.

For a long time opinions on this subject have been attributed to me in Germany and elsewhere which are not mine; consequently I have often been the subject of praises which appeared to me to be insults; I have kept a strict silence. To-day, summoned to explain myself categorically, can I be silent any longer or ought I to make profession of a false faith? Nobody, I hope, will be of this opinion. Let me then speak, and speak with complete frankness.

Now if the school of the future says:

(1) Music to-day in the full force of its youth is emancipated, free, does what it wishes.

(2) Many old rules no longer hold good; they were made by inattentive observers or by routine minds for other routine minds.

(3) New needs of the spirit, of the heart, of the sense of hearing, impose new efforts and even infractions of old laws.

(4) Many forms are too worn to be still allowed.

(5) Everything is good or bad according to the use made of it and the motive behind the use.

---

[1] He objected to Wagner's abuse of enharmonic modulation and of appoggiaturas. He had found the same faults in Hérold's *Zampa* in 1835. This harmonic deliquescence of Wagner's is akin to his rhythmic laxity—*sempre tempo rubato*.

(6) In its union with drama, or only with the sung word, music ought always to be in direct relation with the feeling expressed by the words, with the character of the personage singing, often even with the accentuation and vocal inflection which one feels would be the most natural in the spoken language.[1]

(7) Operas ought not to be written for singers, but, on the contrary, singers ought to be formed for operas.

(8) Works written merely to show off the talent of virtuosos can only be compositions of a secondary order and of inferior quality.

(9) Executants are only more or less intelligent instruments intended to set forth the form and the intimate meaning of works: their despotism is ended.

(10) The master remains the master; it is for him to command.

(11) Beauty of sound and sonority rank below the idea.

(12) The idea ranks below the feeling and the passion.

(13) Long rapid vocalizations, ornaments, vocal trills, a multitude of rhythms are irreconcilable with the expression of the greater part of serious, noble, and profound feelings. It is thus senseless to write for a *Kyrie eleison* (the most humble prayer of the Catholic Church) in a character which resembles the vociferations of a troop of drunkards in a cabaret.

It is perhaps not less so to apply the same music for an invocation to Baal by idolaters and a prayer addressed to Jehovah by the children of Israel.

It is still more odious to take an ideal figure, the creation of the greatest of the poets, an angel of purity and love, and to make her sing like a harlot.

. . . .

If such is the musical code of the school of the future, we are of that school, we belong to it body and soul with the profoundest conviction and the warmest sympathy. . . .

Berlioz then tries to draw up what might be a musical code he would not agree with; but, it must be confessed, without much success; for he does not wholly escape the danger, which always awaits the independent but unwary artist who attempts to do this, of seeming to limit the freedom of his art [2] and thus give a weapon into the hands of his opponents. Nevertheless, he has a case, which he expresses best, finally, in quoting a remark he made to a lady who said to him, after hearing a piece of music such as to-day we also should call 'futuristic': 'You,

[1] Berlioz's well-known severe criticism of the *allegro* of the last aria of Donna Anna in Mozart's *Don Giovanni* is based on this ground.

[2] And the one thing that Berlioz certainly believed in was freedom in art. See his confession of faith, Appendix I, p. 351 *et seq.*

at any rate, should like that.' Berlioz replied: 'Yes, madam, I like it as I like drinking vitriol and eating arsenic.'

Wagner replied to Berlioz's article and his reply, expressed in extremely friendly terms, was printed in the *Débats* of 22nd February 1860. His most significant sentence is: 'Permit this hospitable France to give an asylum to my lyric dramas; I await on my side with the most lively impatience, the representation of your *Troyens* . . .' but Wagner reproaches him, as a friend, for fastening on Wagner's work 'this ridiculous label, *music of the future*.' Nevertheless, it must be remembered that the propaganda for Wagner's music under this banner, 'music of the future,' was enormously influential, as anything which suggests a new departure in art always is. Through it and through the growing vogue for Wagner, Berlioz's reputation was deprived of its normal growth and his real superiority became obscured. Some months later Wagner wrote Berlioz a fervent letter, thanking him for an article on *Fidelio*, and in a letter to Liszt, dated Paris, 22nd May 1860, Wagner writes:

> I have not seen Berlioz since my concerts, it was always I who had to run after him and invite him; he has never troubled himself about me. That has saddened me greatly: I didn't resent it but I asked myself if the good God would not have done better to omit women from His work of creation. . . .[1]
>
> The article of Berlioz (on *Fidelio*) has made me see clearly once more how lonely the unhappy are. . . . I have recognized . . . that the man who is richly endowed can only find a friend who understands him in a man above the ordinary, and I have arrived at the conclusion that to-day we form a triad exclusive of any other . . . because we are three equals: this triad is composed of you, him, and me. But one must take care not to say so to him. . . .

I must confess that the last sentence I have quoted is to me particularly revealing. We, Liszt, Berlioz, and Wagner, says Wagner to Liszt, are three equals, but 'we must take care not to say so to *him*.' No, indeed, for what real affinity had Berlioz

[1] A reference to the known jealousy of Marie Recio, Berlioz's second wife, of Wagner; she naturally saw in him only a rival flattering Berlioz to get his support as critic of the *Journal des Débats*.

either with Liszt or Wagner? His affinity was with Shakespeare,[1] Beethoven, Mozart, and Gluck. These he loved passionately because he understood them and felt at one with them. But Liszt he liked as a friend and esteemed as a man and an artist. Nowhere does one find one warm word about Liszt's music. As for Wagner, he liked his enthusiasm, he recognized his talent, but never does he show anything of that intense sympathy so characteristic of Berlioz towards the artists who really move him. Personally I am convinced that Berlioz was quite aware that as an artist he was with Shakespeare and Beethoven and Gluck and Mozart, but not with Liszt or with Wagner.

And slowly musicians are coming to realize this. Busoni was indignant at a French critic's admiration of Wagner. 'Was he so blind as not to see that it was Berlioz who had pointed the way for unknown generations?'[2]

That strange man Liszt, however, had extraordinary flashes of insight, and I will end this chapter with a quotation from a letter of his, written to Marie Lipsius, dated 3rd February 1876:

'In the third edition of *Musikalische Studienkopfe* I lately read "Berlioz"—an excellent characterization and recognition of this extraordinarily great master, who perhaps hovers more in the untrodden regions of *genius* than anywhere else.'

[1] 'Father,' as he calls him in his *Mémoires*.

[2] Professor Edward J. Dent's *Ferrucio Busoni*, p. 280. Busoni foreshadowed the attitude of the twentieth century towards Wagner, whom he loathed and referred to as Bandinelli. Bandinelli was a rival of Benvenuto Cellini, and his works are now considered coarse and pretentious.

CHAPTER V

CULMINATION

BERLIOZ's opera *Les Troyens* (The Trojans) was written, words and music, between 1855 and 1858, the last page is dated April 1858; but after that date he himself undertook the pianoforte arrangement in order to get the opportunity to revise the work in the process of making the pianoforte edition of it. In 1859 he made a further revision, put into a favourable mood for it by the revival in November 1859 of Gluck's *Orpheus*, at the Paris Théâtre-Lyrique, which Berlioz was asked to supervise and the success of which (the score having been protected by him from mutilation) gave him great pleasure.

Circumstances were rather favourable for the composition of this great work. The death of his first wife, Harriet Smithson, had eased the strain of his financial situation, and the repeated success of *Benvenuto Cellini* at Weimar, the steady growth of his reputation in Germany, the great increase in the performances of his works there, were all favourable factors. Also his election in June 1856 to be a member of the Institut was a natural source of pleasure to him. Berlioz, with the true modesty of a great man who is conscious of his genius, may have been naïvely surprised and contented at any recognition of this sort, but he sought for it not only with the humanity of a man who likes to be linked honourably with his fellow-men, but with the knowledge of its usefulness in his fight for existence.

In July 1856 he sent the completed text of the poem of *Les Troyens* to the Princess Carolyne Sayn-Wittgenstein, and I have already quoted from his reply to her acknowledgment of it. His letters to the princess between 1856 and 1859 give an extraordinarily interesting account of the genesis of the work, and deserve quotation at much greater length than I am able to give here. I must, however, make a few extracts.

Before quoting these, however, in order to show the mixed

Shakespearian and Virgilian origin of *Les Troyens*, I will mention the fact that on 11th June he wrote to Bennet, the father of the pianist Theodore Ritter (the arranger of the pianoforte score of *Roméo et Juliette*), that he had just finished the third act of his poem and, further, that:

Yesterday I completed the words and *the music* of the great duet of the fourth act, a scene stolen from Shakespeare and Virgilianized, which puts me into ridiculous states.

I have only had to bother with the editing of this immortal raving of love, which makes the last act of the *Merchant of Venice* the worthy pendant of the sublime hymns of *Romeo and Juliet*. It is Shakespeare who is the veritable author of the words and the music. It is strange that he should have intervened, he, the poet of the north, into the masterpiece of the Roman poet. Virgil had overlooked this scene. What singers these two are!!!

Writing to the princess on 24th June 1856, Berlioz says much the same thing. I shall now quote from his letters to her:

24th June 1856.

A thousand pardons, princess, for only replying to-day to your last two letters. You may guess that the *Aeneid* and the Academy are the cause of this delay; but the *Aeneid* much more than the Academy.[1] Every morning I got into a carriage with my album in my hand, and during the whole of my peregrination I thought, not of what I was going to say to the Immortal [2] I was visiting, but of what I was going to make my characters say.

At last this double preoccupation is over. The Academy has elected me, as you know; and the opera [3] is nearly finished. I am at the last scene of the fifth act. I get more passionately excited over this subject than I should, and I resist the enticements to start the music which from time to time tempt me. I want to finish everything properly before starting the score. Last week I could not resist, however, writing the duet from Shakespeare:

In such a night as this
When the sweet wind did gently kiss the trees.[4]

And the music for these litanies of love is written.

---

[1] Berlioz was again a candidate for the French Academy and was elected on 21st June 1856.

[2] Members of the French Academy are known as the Immortals, but the immortality of many of them has been very short.

[3] The poem, or 'book,' only, of course.

[4] Act V, Scene i, *The Merchant of Venice*. Berlioz, of course, in this duet between

PARIS, *July* 1856.

. . . When I say *Les Troyens*, it is not that this title is settled. But it is the one which seems the best at the moment. All the others *Énée*, *L'Énéide*, *Didon*, *Troie et Carthage*, *Italie!* have been successively adopted and rejected. . . .

You mock my projects of retreat, my desire for deserts, etc.; none the less it is true that for eight days I have not been able to find one solid hour of freedom of mind to ruminate my project, and that the whole of next month will be stolen from me. . . .

And yet . . . and yet . . . and yet . . . Will you believe that I have fallen *in love*, but utterly, with my Queen of Carthage? I love her madly, this beautiful Dido! . . . You will find many borrowings from Shakespeare in the midst of my Virgilian poetry. I have laced my wine of Cyprus with brandy. I should like Mlle Rachel to have the complaisance to read to me one of these days the fifth act and the Cassandra scenes in the first and second acts. There are accents there to be discovered, silences to measure, inflections to grasp. . . . But she is too much the *diva* and above all just now *diva jurens*. The great success of Ristori has put her in a state of concentrated rage that makes her unapproachable. . . .

PARIS, 14*th November* [1856].
4 RUE DE CALAIS.

. . . I have not ceased for one day from my Phrygian task in spite of the miserable moments of disgust with which my *malaise* inspired me. Then I have found all I have done, cold, flat, stupid, tasteless; I wanted to burn it. . . .

The human mechanism is indeed strange and incomprehensible. Now I am better, I re-read my score and it seems to me that it is not as stupid as I thought.

I am still at the big ensemble:

Châtiment effroyable! Mystérieuse horreur!

after Aeneas has related the catastrophe of Laocoön. I compose one piece in two days and sometimes in one, and I then take three weeks to ruminate on it, polish it, and instrument it. . . .

An article written to-day has interrupted me, another will interrupt me the day after to-morrow. And it will be like that to the end.

How good you are to interest yourself as you do in the crystallization

---

Aeneas and Dido cannot use the finest of Shakespeare's lines; he invents others not unworthily in place of:

'In such a night
Stood Dido with a willow in her hand
Upon the wild sea-banks and wav'd her love
To come again to Carthage.'

But the consciousness of these lines both in Berlioz's mind and in the minds of the audience (especially an English audience) during this wonderful scene of *Les Troyens* gives a marvellous depth of effect.

of this long work! I thank you again. That gives me patience and courage. But when I go, by misfortune, to the Opéra, patience and courage fly from me. The last thing they have given is a *Rose de Florence* . . . music by one named Billetta . . . when the public listens without a murmur to such a *conception* it is worthy of the company of Bushmen and the Hottentots of the Cape of Good Hope.

4 RUE DE CALAIS.
25th or 26th December 1856.

. . . You ask of me news of Troy. . . . Yesterday I was at Carthage, I completed the instrumentation of the finale of the fourth act and the great duet of the lovers. Which does not mean that the preceding pieces are done. I work now at the end of the first act (the scene of the procession of the horse); all the rest of this act is finished. I retouch the poem again and again. It lately seemed to me that the allusion of the dying Dido to the French dominion in Africa was a pure chauvinistic puerility and that it was much finer and worthier to keep to Virgil's idea. . . .

Then a crowd of changed words, of remade verses . . . then I am set on polishing, cleaning, weeding. But when I think of what this work will become I go cold at the heart. . . . The taste of the majority is so different from ours! What touches us leaves the great public so cold! What enchants it disgusts us so greatly! And where shall I find my virgin daughter of Priam, Cassandra? And Dido?

It is above all at night that weariness overwhelms me; in the morning courage, or rather indifference to the future, returns to me with the light, and I begin again to roll my rock; and I say to myself: There are so many other Sisyphuses! . . .

4 RUE DE CALAIS (*undated*).

. . . The last piece I have written, which I hope will please you, is the ensemble preceding the duet of the lovers in the fourth act:

> Tout n'est que paix et charme autour de nous,
> La nuit étend son voile et la mer endormie
> Murmure en sommeillant les accords les plus doux.[1]

It seems to me that there is something new in the expression of this happiness at *seeing the night, and hearing the silence* and lending sublime accents to the sleeping sea. Further, this ensemble links with the duet in a totally unexpected fashion brought about by chance because I had not thought of it when writing each of the pieces separately. . . .

PARIS, *Wednesday*, 18*th March* 1857.

. . . It is eleven days since I have been able to find an hour to work at my score. . . . I am working at the scene of the *Chasse royale* which

[1] 'All is but charm and quiet around us,
The night outspreads its veil and the sea asleep
Murmurs in slumbering the fragilest music.'

opens the fourth act (all the rest of this fourth act is finished). I have still to write the second, third, and fifth acts. . . .

I thus go on with my long task without bothering myself about the fate reserved for the work when finished. I see so many horrible absurdities come and stir our musical world that I feel from day to day a stronger desire to withdraw from the mêlée. . . .

Tuesday, 24th March 1857.

. . . I leave Ascanius and the Trojans in the African forest with the trumpets sounding and the thunder rolling, to give myself the pleasure of talking with you. For the scene of the spectres (there is only one) on the subject of which you question me . . . I believe you said that it was feared that four shades advancing successively to the middle of the scene to say in turn: 'I am Priam, I am Coroebus,' etc., might in procession produce a dangerous effect. But I have found another *mise-en-scène* if this presents a real danger, which I don't believe.

The most important changes I have lately made in the book are to prepare this apparition, to give it more weight. And I have begun the fifth act of a scene in which occurs this chorus of the Trojan chiefs:

Chaque jour voit grandir la colère des dieux,
Des signes effrayants déjà nous avertissent;
La mer, les monts, les bois profonds gémissent;
Sous d'invisibles coups nos armes retentissent.
  Comme dans Troie en la fatale nuit,
  Hector, dont l'œil courroucé luit,
  En armes apparaît; un chœur d'ombres le suit;
  Et ces morts irrités, ô terreur infinie!
La nuit dernière encore ont crié par trois fois . . .

LES OMBRES INVISIBLES.

Italie! Italie!

LES CHEFS.

Dieux vengeurs! c'est leur voix! etc.[1]

---

[1] 'Every day increases the anger of the gods,
And signs appalling already prepare us;
The sea, the mountains, deep forests are murmuring;
From invisible blows our arms are resounding.
  As in Troy on that fatal night
  Hector, whose flaming eye shone,
  In arms appears; a group of shades follows,
  And these dead ones provoked, O endless fear!
Again last night have cried three times

INVISIBLE SHADES.

Italy! Italy!

THE CHIEFS.

Avenging gods! 'tis their voice!'

Then the entrance of Aeneas, his monologue, and the arrival of the spectres.

There is another great *tirade* for Cassandra added towards the end of the first act at the moment when the procession of the horse disappears after crossing the back of the stage. . . .

It would take too long to tell you the numerous small changes I have made here and there, when the score is finished I will be able, but only then, to consider the book as finished. . . .

30th November 1857.

It was not very meritorious of me to refuse the American engagement of which you speak. Should I not remain at my task? . . . Money, however, is very necessary for making music, but on condition that the music first exists. I should be in a nice situation now had I accepted. The talk everywhere in America is of nothing but bankruptcies, and the theatres and concerts are rushing down the falls of Niagara. Ours are not in this danger. There is no cataract with us because there is no current. We row on a very calm swamp, full of frogs and toads, enlivened by the flight and the song of ducks . . . but I am living in my score like the rat of Lafontaine in his cheese—pardon the comparison.

27th December 1857.

Excuse me, princess, for not having yet replied to your last letter. I was taken up with the last monologue of Aeneas and would not have been capable of putting two ideas together until it was completely written. In such a case I am like those bulldogs who let themselves be cut in quarters rather than give up what they have seized with their teeth. . . .

20th February 1858.

For the last fortnight I have owed you an answer, princess. It is also a fortnight since I have had two hours of leisure. I go to bed almost every night at three o'clock and rise at midday. Then the unavoidable journeys in Paris, the penal servitude of my articles, the buzzing of blockheads who pursue me even into the foyers of the theatres to ask for an appointment so as to acquaint me with their *inventions*. . . .

What you tell me of the revival of *Alceste* at Weimar does not surprise me. What astonishes me is only that one lets the bourgeois into the theatre when such works are presented. If I were the Grand Duke I would send on such an evening to each of these good folk a ham and two bottles of beer requesting them to remain at home. . . .

You say such flattering things to me, princess, that I confess frankly it seems I ought to guard myself against your letters. At times they make me vain, at other times, uneasy, as if you were making fun of me. And I say with Montaigne: 'What do I know?' You are not unaware of my Pyrrhonism. I believe in nothing: that is to say, I believe that I believe in nothing. Then I do believe in something. See what words do and where logic takes one . . . there is nothing real but feelings and passions.—What nonsense I talk to you? What about death? and fools? and imbeciles? and a thousand other too real realities? . . .

6th May 1858.

It is always with excuses, princess, that I must begin my letters. This time it seems more inexcusable than ever not to have replied sooner to all the charming things you have had the kindness to write to me recently. When I am ill, in mind, body, heart, and head, as I have been for almost a month, I take care to abstain from writing to those to whom I fear to appear in an unfavourable light. I am then like a wounded wolf and I can do nothing better than retire into my corner and let my wounds bleed. I have not sent you the manuscript of *Les Troyens* because I know of your intention to come to Paris with Liszt in July. Then I will ask your permission to read my five acts, giving you some indications of what I have attempted in the music of certain scenes. . . .

It makes a devil of a stir, and the more fuss there is, the colder I show myself to the officials . . . and the less desire I show to have it produced. This desire is indeed not strong; I know too well the state of our musical world. I do not wish to offer up for insults either Cassandra, or Dido, or Aeneas, or Virgil, or Shakespeare, or you, or me!

10th March 1859.

. . . I do not think it would be fitting to have the book of *Les Troyens* printed, still less translated. That would show on my part literary pretensions which I cannot have. . . .

20th June 1859.

. . . As to our *Troyens*, I have not said a word, not made a step, not seen even a minor official to get them to concern themselves with it. I lick it and lick it into shape as bears lick their cubs. The pianoforte score is finished; I get an act or two played from time to time to have a clear idea of the details. It will be very difficult for the two grand creatures, Cassandra and Dido; it is a question of getting the proper diction of the principal scenes, for without that in an epic passion all significance is lost.

I wish you were convinced of my gratitude, princess, for the insistence with which you have made me undertake and finish this work. Whatever destiny awaits it I am to-day thoroughly happy at having brought it to a conclusion. I am now perfectly cool and able to judge it, and I believe I can say that in this score there are things worthy to be offered to you. There are also new things. The second act contains, of this sort, a chorus of Trojan women constructed on this strange scale:

and the tone of desolation which results from the continual predominance of the G related to the D flat has a singular effect. . . . The account of the catastrophe of Laocoön, and especially the ensemble piece which follows, are, it seems to me, two tremendous horrors which will make your heart beat. . . .

To these quotations from Berlioz's letters to the Princess Sayn-Wittgenstein I will now add an extract from a letter to his son Louis,[1] dated Paris, 9th February 1858:

DEAR LOUIS,

The Indian mail leaves to-morrow and I have only a few moments to-day to talk to you. I am very impatient to hear from you. How did you bear the long voyage? How are you? Are you comfortable on board? Do not forget any of these details. . . . As far as I am concerned I am tolerably well at the moment; but my wife is almost always in bed, in great suffering and fretting very much. . . .

I work as much as I can to finish my score and I advance little by little. I am now at the last monologue of Dido: 'Je vais mourir dans ma douleur immense submergée.'

I am more satisfied with what I have just written than with all my former works. I believe that the terrible scenes of the fifth act will be in music of heartrending reality.

But I have again modified this act. I have made a large cut and have added a piece of character designed to contrast with the epic and passionate style of the rest. It is a sailor's song; I thought of you, dear Louis, when I was writing it, and I send you the words. It is night, the Trojan ships are visible in the harbour: Hylas, a young Phrygian sailor, sings from the masthead:

Vallon sonore
Où, dès l'aurore,
Je m'en allais, chantant, hélas!
Sous tes grands bois chantera-t-il encore
Le pauvre Hylas?
Berce mollement sur ton sein sublime,
O puissant mer, l'enfant de Dindyme! [2]

I think I have told you all my news, my dear boy. I went to a ball at the Tuileries last Wednesday; there was such a crowd one couldn't even see

[1] Louis Berlioz was now an officer in the French merchant service.

[2] There are three stanzas; I have only quoted the first to show its character:

'Echoing valley
Where I would dally,
Singing as I wandered, alas!
'Midst thy deep woods will he e'er sing again,
O poor Hylas?
Rock gently on thy breast sublime,
O mighty sea, the child of Dindyme!'

the emperor or empress and I left at eleven only too happy not to have been stifled and to have recovered my overcoat. . . .

Jules B * * * came back the day before yesterday from a tour in the provinces. He is now fixed in Paris in a very humble position which gives him terribly hard work and hardly a living. And with his intelligence and talent—such is life!

On 3rd November 1858 Berlioz wrote to Humbert Ferrand:

Oh, my poor dear friend, how your letter has upset me! . . . And yet, according to your account, one ought to rejoice over the slight improvement in your health. You can think, you can write, you can walk. God grant that the severe winter with which we are threatened, whose stings are already making themselves felt, may not retard your recovery.

As for me, I am a martyr to neuralgia which for the last two years has settled in my intestines, and except at night I am in constant suffering. . . .

We write to each other so seldom now that I have to give an account of my life during the last two years. This long time has been employed in the composition of an opera in five acts, *Les Troyens*, of which, as in the case of *L'Enfance du Christ*, I have written both the words and the music. . . .

Again, on 8th November, he wrote:

My very dear Friend,

. . . Oh, how I wish I could read and sing my *Troyens* to you! There are some very curious things in it; at least they seem so to me.

Heu! fuge nate deae, teque his, ait, eripe flammis;
Hostis habet muros, ruit alto a culmine Troja!
. . . . .

Ah! fuis fils de Vénus! l'ennemi tient nos murs!
De son faîte élevé Troie entière s'écroule!
La mer de flamme roule,
Des temples au palais, ses tourbillons impurs . . .
Nous eussions fait assez pour sauver la patrie
Sans l'arrêt du destin. Pergame te confie
Ses enfants et ses dieux. Va! . . . cherche l'Italie
Où pour ton peuple renaissant
Après avoir longtemps erré sur l'onde,
Tu dois fonder un empire puissant,
Dans l'avenir dominateur du monde,
Où la mort des héros t'attend.[1]

[1] This extract, giving two of the original lines of Virgil which Berlioz expands into twelve lines for his libretto, offers an admirable example of the difference between poetry (which must never be set to music) and verse which is intended for music. Virgil's two lines are poetry, totally unfitted by their very nature for music; Berlioz's twelve lines are perfect verses for musical setting. We have here examples of the two, wholly opposite, ideals.

This recitative of Hector, brought to life for a moment by the will of the gods, but who gradually sinks into oblivion again as he accomplishes his mission to Aeneas, is I think, a strangely solemn and mournful musical idea. I quote this passage to you, because the idea in it is precisely one of those to which the public pays no attention.

It has been my secondary object in quoting these extracts to give the reader a general notion of Berlioz's opera, *Les Troyens*, because I do not propose to make a detailed analysis of what is, in my opinion, the greatest opera that has ever been written. I will content myself with a brief description:

Les Troyens. Berlioz's original work is an opera in five acts as follows:

Act I, Scene I. The camp abandoned by the Greeks on the plain of Troy. In the background on the tomb of Achilles three shepherds playing double flutes (oboes); in the foreground the joyous crowd of Trojans singing the chorus *Après dix ans* (After ten years) and dancing. The Wooden Horse is discovered, whereupon they rush off stage to see it. Cassandra enters, proclaiming the approaching doom of Troy (recitative and air), and bewailing the fate of herself and her lover Coroebus. A scene between Cassandra and Coroebus follows, in which she vainly implores him to leave the doomed city. The scene ends with her resignation: 'Jealous Death prepares our nuptial bed for to-morrow.'

Scene II. Another part of the plain, near the walls of Troy; on one side a throne, on the other an altar. It is a fête in celebration of their deliverance from the Greeks. A march and a hymn, during which the principal Trojans enter the scene, are followed by Homeric games. Andromache (widow of Hector) and her son Astyanax come and place flowers upon the altar, after which they take their place before Priam on his throne. Cassandra passes with a warning; Andromache and Astyanax retire, the crowd sighs in sympathy. Suddenly Aeneas enters, announcing the extraordinary death of Laocoön. This is followed by an octet and chorus when, to appease the goddess Pallas, the Trojans hasten to bring the Wooden Horse to her temple, interrupted by the cries of Cassandra: 'Malheur! malheur!'

Left alone on the stage, she gives way to an expression of her despair. A March (*Marche troyenne*) leads to the entry of the Wooden Horse, accompanied by the crowd, on its way to the temple. The tragic voice of Cassandra, alone on the stage, is heard prophesying ruin as the Wooden Horse enters the city.[1]

Act II, Scene I. The apartment of Aeneas in the palace. Night. Aeneas is asleep. The shade of Hector appears to him, tells him that Troy is taken and in ruins, and instructs him to fly with his son and the images of the gods: 'Cherche l'Italie.' Trojan soldiers enter, seeking Aeneas, and all depart together.

Scene II. Before the altar of Cybele, a chorus of Trojan women lamenting. Cassandra enters and announces that Aeneas and his companions, having preserved the gods of the country, have reached the sea; also that Coroebus is dead and the Greeks will soon arrive to take them all as slaves. She tells them to die rather than submit. As the Greeks enter Cassandra stabs herself, crying: 'Italie! Italie!'[2]

Act III, Scene I. An amphitheatre in the garden of the palace of Dido in Carthage. It is a fête and the Carthaginians are singing in praise of peace. A national hymn to Queen Dido follows. (Berlioz asks here for a choir of men, women, and children, numbering two or three hundred, seated on the steps of the amphitheatre.) Dido enters with her sister Anna, and her minister, Narbal, and takes her seat on the throne. Dido recalls to her people the events of the last seven years in a declamation and aria of serene dignity and beauty, punctuated by the acclamations of the Carthaginians. The fête is over and Dido and her sister are left alone; a duet follows, when Iopas enters, announcing the arrival of deputies from a strange fleet asking for harbourage. Dido orders them to be admitted. Aeneas with his son and followers arrive. Aeneas is disguised, and it is his son Ascanius who speaks. According to Virgil,

[1] This act lasts an hour and ten minutes and is of an incomparable tragic grandeur.

[2] The tragic figure of Cassandra dominates the first two acts as Queen Dido does the next three acts. Berlioz has delineated both with magnificent clarity and power.

Venus makes her son Cupid take the place of Ascanius during this interview, and Dido's heart is lost as soon as Aeneas reveals himself. This happens almost immediately, when Narbal enters, announcing that Numidia has declared war. Aeneas throws off his disguise, and tells Dido who he is and that he will fight for her. The scene ends with a chorus of Trojans and Carthaginians preparing for war.

Scene II. An African forest, morning. (*Pantomime.*)

This is one of Berlioz's finest and most daring inventions. While the orchestra plays the famous *Chasse royale et orage*,[1] naiads flit about the stage and listen to the far-off hunting horns; huntsmen arrive, the sky grows dark, the rain falls; Ascanius crosses the scene with other huntsmen; Dido and Aeneas enter and take refuge in a grotto. Wood-nymphs appear, making strange cries; fauns enter dancing; there are shouts of 'Italie! Italie!' A flash of lightning destroys a tree; the fauns and wood-nymphs seize the branches and dance. Then they all disappear. The scene is slowly covered with clouds; it is now entirely dark:

Hic Hymenaeus erit. . . .

Only the orchestra is heard; the storm passes. Silence! Curtain![2]

Act IV, Scene I. The gardens of Dido on the edge of the sea. Anna and Narbal (duet) are speaking together of Dido and Aeneas. Dido and Aeneas enter; there are dances for the entertainment of Aeneas. At the end of the dances Dido asks the poet Iopas to sing. After this begins a beautiful quintet, then a septet. Through all this marvellous music the sea is

[1] This is fairly familiar to European audiences as a concert piece, but it loses immensely, taken from its proper place in the opera.

[2] At the first production at the Théâtre-Lyrique, Paris, in November 1863, this marvellous scene was found totally incomprehensible and went for nothing. Berlioz, sad and disgusted, wrote upon his score this note: 'In case the theatre is not big enough to permit the staging in a grand and animated way of this interlude, if one cannot get women choristers to run with dishevelled hair and men as fauns and satyrs doing grotesque dances and crying "Italie!", if the firemen are afraid of fire, the stage-hands afraid of water, and the director afraid of everything, then one had better suppress this symphony, which in any case needs an orchestra such as is rarely found in a theatre.'

murmuring. Then Dido and Aeneas are left alone, the duet follows: 'Nuit d'ivresse et d'extase infinie.' Of this scene one can only say that Berlioz has equalled in music the purest poetry of Shakespeare:

On such a night . . .

But as the lovers pass off the stage there is a sudden interruption. Mercury appears in a beam of moonlight near a column on which the arms of Aeneas are hung, and strikes with his caduceus two blows on the shield; then, crying in a sombre voice: 'Italie! Italie! Italie!' disappears, and the curtain falls.

Act V, Scene I. The seashore, covered with the tents of the Trojans. It is night. Two sentinels are on guard. The young sailor, Hylas, sings from the masthead *Vallon sonore*, then falls asleep. The Trojan priest Pantheus enters with some Trojan chiefs. They deplore Aeneas's love for Dido and their consequent delay in Carthage: 'Chaque jour voit grandir la colère des dieux,'[1] and from the shadows the cry of 'Italie!' is heard. They enter their tents declaring that they must leave Carthage the next day. Then follows a duet between the two sentinels.[2] After this Aeneas enters in great agitation and expresses his despair. Now follows the scene of the spectres —Hector, Cassandra, etc. Aeneas wakes the chiefs and tells them they must sail at once, before dawn. Dido enters and attempts to stop him, but in vain.

Scene II. Interior of Dido's palace. Anna tries to console Dido, telling her that Aeneas loves her but his departure was inevitable. 'No,' says Dido, 'he does not love me. I know love, and if Jupiter himself forbade me to love him, I would

[1] 'Every day increases the anger of the gods.'

[2] This is a thoroughly characteristic Berliozian grotesque scene. It is cut out of the most common pianoforte and vocal edition published by Choudens. The French public of the time could not appreciate this scene. Berlioz notes on his score: 'The soldiers' duet, a little rude in character, produces a vivid contrast with the melancholy song of the sailor which precedes it and the passionate air of Aeneas which follows. In France the mixture of tragic and comic is dangerous and impossible in the theatre—as if the opera *Don Giovanni* were not an admirable example of the good effect to be produced by this mixture . . . as if Shakespeare did not exist. It is true that for the majority of Frenchmen Shakespeare is less than the sun is for moles. Because moles can at least feel the warmth of the sun.'

brave his anger.' Iopas describes the departure of the Trojan fleet. Dido has a moment of rage. She then calls upon the gods of the underworld, and makes a solemn farewell to her sister and to Carthage.

Scene III. The gardens by the sea, with a burning pyre and the belongings of Aeneas by the side of it. The priests of Pluto make a sacrifice; Anna and Narbal join in their prayers. Dido enters; she falls convulsively on the bed of Aeneas, then takes his sword and proclaims prophetically the coming of an avenger, Hannibal! She then stabs herself with the sword of Aeneas and dies. The chorus of priests and Trojans sings as the Capitol is seen shining in the background: 'Rome! Rome!' [1]

Les Troyens is not an opera in the ordinary sense; it is something much rarer, described by Berlioz himself as a *tragédie lyrique*. Just as Beethoven completed the great symphonic edifice of Haydn and Mozart, so Berlioz crowned and completed the search through centuries from Monteverde to Gluck for the musical-dramatic form of tragedy. Berlioz's *Les Troyens* is, in a certain sense, in relation to the great operas of Gluck (*Orpheus*, the two *Iphigénies*, *Armide*, *Alceste*) what Beethoven's Ninth Symphony is to Mozart's and Haydn's symphonies. This is not to make a valuation of their essential qualities, but merely to declare their affinity, and a certain similar increase and culmination of musical resources. The operas of Wagner are on a lower, more popular, plane. They should be judged, in fairness to Wagner, only in comparison with those of Marschner, Weber, Meyerbeer, and Boito—although Wagner was much inferior to Weber in natural musical genius.

In 1862 [2] Liszt wrote to Dr. Franz Brendel:

Berlioz was so good as to send me the printed pianoforte edition of his opera *Les Troyens*. Although for Berlioz's works pianoforte editions

---

[1] The similarity between this finale and the closing scene of *Götterdämmerung* will be obvious to all. But *Les Troyens* was completed in 1859 and partly performed in 1863. *Rheingold* was begun in 1853; the first and second acts of *Siegfried* were written about 1857, the third act about 1869, and *Götterdämmerung* was begun in 1870.

[2] Rome, 10th August 1862.

are plainly a deception, yet a cursory perusal of *Les Troyens* has nevertheless made an uncommonly powerful impression on me. One cannot deny there is enormous power in it, and it is certainly not wanting in delicacy—I might almost say subtlety—of feeling.

But the greatness of *Les Troyens* has been almost entirely obscured for more than fifty years by the vogue of Wagner and the corruption of musical feeling during the last part of the nineteenth century. It is just as if Shakespeare's *Hamlet* had been obscured (as it was) by Colley Cibber's [1] *Love's Last Shift* or *The Careless Husband.*

When *Les Troyens* is given in its complete original form with an adequate production and cast, under a musical director and conductor who understands the work and can realize his conception, the effect will be overwhelming and there will be no possible doubt among artists of its unique position. No matter how music develops in the future, *Les Troyens* will remain one of those few great creative achievements of the human mind which persist through all psychological and artistic changes, much as the Alps and the Himalayas persist through the minor geographical changes of Europe and Asia. And the reason for this persistence, the inexhaustibility of this fount of beautiful and profound impressions, is the same. In mankind, as in nature (of which obviously man is a part), there are these great eruptions of power (we have no exacter word) which leave behind their monuments. Berlioz was such an eruption; instinctively he is always using the word 'volcanic' about himself; and among the monuments of his volcanic power left to us none is higher, more massive, more wonderful than *Les Troyens.*

Played in its original form, *Les Troyens* takes about six and a half hours to perform. It has, to my knowledge, never been performed as Berlioz intended. As it was impossible for him to get it performed at the Paris Opéra, owing to the hostility and fear of the directorate, he accepted the offer of Carvalho to perform it at the Théâtre-Lyrique. But the resources of this theatre were not equal to tackling the work as a whole.

[1] Cibber Colley, (1671–1757), poet laureate, famous dramatist, adapter of Shakespeare's plays.

Berlioz reluctantly consented to divide the work into two parts:

(1) *La Prise de Troie* (The Taking of Troy), an opera in three acts.

(2) *Les Troyens à Carthage* (The Trojans at Carthage), an opera in five acts, with a Prologue. The Prologue is an addition, made in 1863 to give some idea of the events preceding those enacted in *Les Troyens à Carthage*; that is to say, it is a substitute for the first part, *La Prise de Troie*.

It was *Les Troyens à Carthage* which Carvalho produced at the Théâtre-Lyrique in Paris on 4th November 1863.

Do not inflict any regrets on me [wrote Berlioz to Ferrand on 8th July 1863], I must resign myself to my fate. There is no Cassandra[1] now; the *Prise de Troie* will not be given and, for the time being, the first two acts are suppressed. I have been obliged to replace them by a prologue and the scene will open in Carthage. The Théâtre-Lyrique is neither rich enough nor large enough; in addition, the entire work would last too long. Besides, I could not find a Cassandra.

Mutilated as it is, the work divided into five acts and prologue, will last from eight o'clock until midnight on account of the complicated scenery of the virgin forest and the final tableau, the funeral pile, and the apotheosis of the Roman Capitol.

To Alexis Lwoff in Russia he wrote on 13th December 1863:

It is four years since *Les Troyens* was finished and the second part only has just been produced. . . . I will never write anything again except for a theatre where I am obeyed blindly without comment, where I am *absolute master*. And that will probably never happen.

The theatres . . . are the low resorts of music and the chaste muse that one leads there can only enter them shuddering . . . the *théâtres lyriques* are to music *sicut amori lupanar*.[2]

And the imbeciles and idiots who pullulate there!

Adieu, cher maître; God protect you from contact with that race. What I write you on the subject of theatres in general is strictly confidential;

---

[1] 'O my noble Cassandra, my heroic virgin, I must resign myself never to hear thee! . . . and I am like the young Coroebus: *Insano Cassandrae incensus amore*,' Berlioz writes in his *Mémoires*, Postface, p. 475, original edition.

[2] 'What brothels are to love.' This expression may seem strong to some innocent readers. I find it merely exact. The theatres in my day in London, with rare exceptions and on rare occasions, offer to the public not only the negation of all art but the lowest substitute for it.

especially as I have met with devotion and good will at the Théâtre-Lyrique from the director to the last musician in the orchestra.

And yet . . .

And nevertheless . . .

But it has made me ill.

The mutilated *Troyens* ran at the Théâtre-Lyrique, Paris, for twenty-one performances.[1] Even in its truncated form it made a profound impression, and musicians like Meyerbeer were to be seen there night after night.[2] This is the occasion of one of Berlioz's most famous remarks. A friend, to console him for all he had to endure in the mutilation and imperfect rendering of his work, pointed out to him that after the first night the audiences were increasing: 'See,' he said encouragingly to Berlioz, 'they are coming.' 'Yes,' replied Berlioz, 'they are coming, but I am going.'[3]

Nevertheless, he was able to sell his score of *Les Troyens* for fifteen thousand francs to the publisher Choudens, who promised to print the full score; but he did not keep his word:[4]

My publisher [writes Berlioz to the Princess Sayn-Wittgenstein, in August 1864], who was to have published the full score of *Les Troyens* this summer, has not kept his word—as all, as always. Dedicate it to the emperor, who has not deigned to come to one performance! No, no, why should I? That would be a platitude. *Divo Virgilio solo.*[5] How-

---

[1] Twenty-two, counting the *répétition générale.* The extraordinarily novel and impressive pantomime scene, *La Chasse royale*, was suppressed after the first performance. This scene, which is one of the most imaginative conceptions in the history of opera, was completely incomprehensible to the Parisian audiences of the time.

[2] Adophe Jullien gives the receipts for each night, which were comparatively good for the time.

[3] 'Ils viennent, mais moi, je m'en vais.' He was sixty years old on 11th December 1863.

[4] I am informed that there is an old edition (full score) of *Les Troyens* in existence and that it is excessively rare. I have never seen it in any foreign catalogue. I possess the old pianoforte and vocal score published by Choudens of Paris in two volumes. There is no modern full score, as Breitkopf & Härtel's collected edition of Berlioz had not been completed by 1914 and has not been finished since the war.

[5] The score bears the dedication: *Divo Virgilio* (To the divine Virgil), and a supplementary dedication in the form of a letter to the Princess Sayn-Wittgenstein.

ever, the emperor has made me an officer of the Legion of Honour. . . .

I have to inform you, and you will learn it without astonishment, that the population of Paris has become completely crazy. An inexplicable frenzy has seized all, men, women, and children, to cry in the streets, the gardens, on foot, in vehicles, on horseback: 'Eh! Lambert! ohé Lambert! avez-vous vu Lambert?'[1]

. . . I learn that the cry of 'Lambert' is repeated already at Havre, Rouen, Versailles. All France begins to repeat it.

My God! my God! The human brain is liquefying.

I have a word to say before I finish with *Les Troyens*, which I consider to be in music a work comparable to Milton's *Paradise Lost* and Virgil's *Aeneid* in literature.

We are promised by Sir Thomas Beecham a production of *Les Troyens* at Covent Garden[2] in 1935 or 1936. It will be extremely difficult to obtain an adequate cast; if Sir Thomas achieves this he will be doing for *Les Troyens* in London what Liszt did in Weimar for *Benvenuto Cellini*. But it is essential that this revelation of an unknown masterpiece should be complete. The work must be performed in its entirety, as Berlioz wrote it. The public in London is now accustomed to going to *Die Walküre* and *Siegfried* at 5 o'clock or 5.30 and to *Die Götterdämmerung* at 4.30 or 5, with an interval for dinner; it is therefore quite possible as well as proper to give the whole of *Les Troyens*, beginning at 5 o'clock or 5.30. As *Les Troyens* is in every way a superior work to Wagner's trilogy, the public can be relied upon to pay it due respect if the artists themselves respect it as they should. On the first night of *Les Troyens* in London every musician who loves his art will be there. Among them—unless health prevents—will be the group of Berlioz's best-known English enthusiasts. Nothing is to be expected of us, if this great work is mutilated, but mild protests. We are all too disillusioned, too exhausted from the rubbish we have had to listen to for twenty years. I hope, however, there will be in the younger section of the audience something of Berlioz's

[1] The words of a popular song of the time.

[2] The 'Royal Opera' House, London, built in 1856–8.

own spirit. I don't expect much from England's young musicians yet; but from England's poets and writers, who *have* a great tradition, I do expect something. I hope, if there is any attempt to present us with a mutilated version of Berlioz's work at Covent Garden, that there will be young artists in the auditorium who will tear the house to pieces in their spontaneous and righteous rage. I will say no more.

CHAPTER VI

LAST WORK

Les Troyens was not Berlioz's last work. He was only fifty-five years old in 1859 when it was completed, and as vigorous as ever, in spite of his intense sufferings from intestinal neuralgia. Now that *Les Troyens* was completed, the Princess Sayn-Wittgenstein wanted him to start a new work, and in a letter dated Paris, 13th December 1859, Berlioz replies:

. . . Your letters agitate me terribly, princess; your ideas, your dreams, fall on me like powder on a fire. If I were twenty years younger you would make something of me. But what would you have? tranquillity, serenity of mind, health, all are lacking for undertaking or achieving. . . . Besides, if you knew how I waste my time . . . I scarcely manage to get one hour in forty to work as an artist. What projects can one make in such conditions, with such a distracted life? Of these forty hours, quite twenty are taken up in some form of suffering, at least twelve in sleep, seven in the devilish work at which I earn my living.

Lately entering the *salon* of Mme Viardot (there was music there), the sounds coming to me gave me a shock accompanied by a flash of lightning,[1] and I seemed to see our Cleopatra wreathed in a strange aureole. Ah, yes, it seems to me I could make a seductive creature of this torpedo, that would be so different from all I have done! There is so much room there for the unexpected, the strange, the unbounded! I feel I should confine myself to borrowing certain details from Shakespeare and that I should do best by letting my fantasy range unbridled. Firstly, I must have the interior of a pyramid, the priests of Isis, their mysteries, their juggleries; for Cleopatra I need the greatest audacity; I must have the scene on the Cydnus; a secret orgy of women with the eunuch Mardian, as a pendant to the public orgy of the triumvirs on the galley of the young Pompey. Perhaps it would be possible to present the wise and cold Octavius and the mad Egyptian; what a contrast! Ah, yes, that would be curious . . . but it needs time and life. I consider myself only too happy to have had more than a year to finish and revise my Trojan score; it is a favour whose worth I value fully. And the proverb is not wrong: 'Qui trop embrasse mal étreint.'

---

[1] This reminds one of Schumann's saying that Berlioz's Mephistophelian passages left behind them the smell of burning sulphur.

No further mention is made of a new work on this subject of Cleopatra. It was destined never to be written. Berlioz's life during the next few years was harassed by the advent of Wagner to Paris and the propaganda of Wagner and his friends. Owing to the influence of Princess Metternich, Wagner was able to get *Tannhäuser* produced at the Paris Opéra in March 1861,[1] but Berlioz could not get *Les Troyens* produced there. However, he received a commission from Benazet, the Casino King of Baden, who was also connected with Berlioz's paper the *Journal des Débats*, to compose an opera for the opening of the new theatre Benazet was having built at Baden. For this he returned to an early project of writing a comic opera on the subject of Shakespeare's *Much Ado about Nothing*.

A few extracts from various letters will give the best idea of his life at this time:

To Humbert Ferrand

26th November 1858.

. . . The oppression of my heart decreases as I write to you; do not let us be, as we have been, years without writing to each other, I beseech you. We are dying with fearful rapidity; think of that. Your letters do me good. You have received the score of *L'Enfance du Christ*, have you not? There are no means of composing music here, where one ought to be rich like your friend Mirès. I was dreaming of it last night (of music, not of your friend Mirès).[2]

This morning my dream has come back to me; I performed it mentally, just as, three years ago at Baden we performed the *adagio* out of Beethoven's Symphony in B flat . . . and growing wide awake by degrees, I fell into an unearthly ecstasy, and I shed all the tears of my soul as I listened to the sonorous smiles which shine from angels alone. Believe me, my dear friend, the being who wrote such a marvel of celestial inspiration was not a man. So must the archangel Michael sing, as he dreamingly contemplates the worlds uprising to the threshold of the empyrean. . . .

Let us come down to earth again. I am going to be disturbed—triviality, vulgarism, this stupid life! . . . I should like to have a

---

[1] This was the occasion of its historic failure. Berlioz did not write about this production of *Tannhäuser* in the *Journal des Débats* but got his friend d'Ortigue to write the review in his place.

[2] Cp. bk. IV, chap. ii, p. 264.

hundred pieces of ordnance wherewith to shoot down all such things at once. Good-bye. I am somewhat comforted. Forgive me!

To Auguste Morel

Paris, 18*th March* 1859.

I do not like to take on myself the responsibility of bringing you to Paris to have your eyes attended to; the cures of Dr. Vriès in this line are unknown to me; besides, he is more and more unapproachable; you have to wait four or five hours in a queue without then being sure of seeing him and he would insist on your following his treatment for several months.

As for me, I have had a return for the last ten days of my infernal colic, which does not leave me for one hour in twenty-four. Nothing to be done!

To Ferrand

Paris, 28*th April* 1859.

Ill as I am, I have still strength enough to rejoice greatly when I hear from you. Your letter has put new life into me. It took me by surprise, nevertheless, in the midst of a concert which I gave . . .

L'Enfance du Christ was performed better than it has ever been . . . the mystic chorus at the end, *O, mon âme* . . . was played for the first time with the requisite shades and accent. The entire work is summed up in this vocal peroration. It seems to me to contain a feeling of the infinite, of divine love.[1] I thought of you as I listened to it. My very dear friend, I cannot, as you can, give expression in my letters to certain sentiments common to us both, but I feel them, believe me. Besides, I dare not give myself up to them to too great an extent; there is so much flattery in what you write so far as I am concerned. I am afraid of allowing myself to be influenced by your sympathetic words. . . .

To Louis (his Son)

Paris, 14*th February* 1861.

Thank you for your letter, which I was hoping for every day. I see, however, you are still in a state of mind that causes me great anxiety. I do not know what dreams you have been indulging in to make you feel your present position appear painful; all I can say is that at your age I was far from being as well treated by fate as you are.

Further, I did not expect that when you had been promoted captain you would so soon have found even a modest employment. Your impatience to succeed is natural but exaggerated. I must impress that upon you again and again. . . .

What can I say to make you more patient? You torment yourself

---

[1] Compare with Berlioz's abstention from any profession of religious beliefs.

about trifles and you have a mania for matrimony which makes me laugh. . . .

At twenty-six years of age you have a salary of 1,800 francs and the prospect of perhaps rapid advancement. When I married your mother I was thirty years old, I possessed only the 300 francs my friend Gounet had lent me and the remainder of my Prix de Rome pension—for eighteen months only. Beyond that nothing but a debt of your mother's for 14,000 francs (which I paid little by little), and I had to send money from time to time to her mother in England. I was on bad terms with my family . . . and in the midst of these embarrassments I had to make my first breach in the musical world. . . .

And even now, do you think it is a lively existence to be forced, compelled to remain bound by this infernal chain of article-writing? . . . I am so ill that the pen falls from my hand every minute, and yet I have to constrain myself to write in order to gain my miserable hundred francs and to hold my position armed against the crowd of rogues who would annihilate me if they were not afraid. And my head is full of projects, of works which I cannot carry out because of this slavery. . . .

During the last month I have not been able to find a single day to work at my score of *Béatrice*. Happily I have ample time for it.

. . . That is my present position. . . . Everybody for himself and God for nobody! That is the true proverb. You at all events have a father, a friend, a comrade, a devoted brother, who loves you more than you appear to think but who would gladly see your character strengthen and become more clear sighted.

To Louis

Paris, 21*st February* 1861.

You tell me it is useless to write to you at Marseilles before the end of March; then at the end of your letter you ask me to write again. . . .

Well, I am writing; I have just got up, it is three o'clock in the afternoon. As I cannot work, what can I do better than talk to you. . . .

Scribe died yesterday in his carriage. Mirès has been arrested in connection with some paltry millions. M. Richemont, a receiver compromised in the affair, hanged himself yesterday. Murger[1] is dead, Eugène Guinot is dead, Chélard is dead at Weimar. This is a flourishing state of things. . . .

How provincial and childish you are to be astonished that the newspapers do not mention me! What would you have them say? Do you think the world bothers itself about my doings? . . . Wagner is driving the singers, the orchestra, and the chorus of the Opéra mad. One cannot get away from this music of *Tannhäuser*. The last general rehearsal has been, so I am told, atrocious and finished only at 1 o'clock in the morning.

[1] Author of *La Vie de Bohème*.

Nevertheless they will have to go through with it. Liszt is coming here to support this *charivari* school. I will not write the article on *Tannhäuser*; I have asked d'Ortigue to do it. That will be better from every point of view and will disappoint them more. Never have I had so many windmills to fight as this year; I am surrounded by idiots of every kind. There are moments when rage suffocates me.

Adieu; I must try to go out and to walk; if I cannot I shall go to bed again.

To Louis

4th May 1861.

. . . Last night there was a reading of some of the scenes of *Les Troyens* at M. E. Bertin's; splendid success, everybody was astonished at the world of opposition to me at the Opèra. . . .

The minister of state has invited me to dine with him next Monday; it will be like dining with the emperor; they will talk to me of the rain and of fine weather! One must endure this outrageous indifference. And I am sure that I have made a great work, greater and nobler than anything that has gone before it! Yet one must die in silence, crushed beneath the feet of these ponderous animals!

Ah! you are discouraged! What can I do?

I can only suffer and be silent.

Life is very hard and burdensome. I still cannot get to work on *Béatrice et Bénédict*; but it must be finished somehow, and at least, it will be performed. But I am ill and plagued with so many diverse occupations, many boring affairs of all kinds.[1]

Good-bye. I embrace you with all my heart.

To Louis

2nd June 1861.

I see that you are very much worried; I can give you no reassuring news. Alexis is trying to find you a position in Paris and it is precisely because he is trying that he will not succeed. I, also, am incapable of altering your position. It is for you to make your own fate and not to get yourself into any mess from which it will be impossible for any one else to extricate you.

---

[1] On 16th May 1861 Liszt wrote from Paris to the Princess Sayn-Wittgenstein: 'Our poor friend Berlioz is depressed indeed and full of bitterness. His life at home is like a nightmare, and outside he meets with nothing but vexations and mortifications. . . . He speaks in a low voice and his whole being inclines towards the tomb. I don't know how he has managed to get so isolated here. Truly he has neither friends nor partisans—neither the sun of public favour nor the sweet shade of intimacy. The *Débats* still supports and protects him. . . .'

By way of compensation I have been asked to superintend the production of *Alceste* as I did that of *Orphée* at the Théâtre-Lyrique, offering me full author's rights; for musical reasons, too lengthy to explain to you, I have refused. People think in this world of ours that an artist will do for money things quite opposed to his conscience. I have proved to them it is not so. . . .

My refusal to produce *Alceste* has created a sensation and annoyed many people. It would be better to put on *Les Troyens* at once than to waste time and money on insulting one of Gluck's masterpieces. But as good sense indicates that course it will not be adopted. Liszt has made a complete conquest of the emperor: he played at court last week and yesterday he was nominated Commander of the Legion of Honour. Ah! what it is to play the piano!

I have not finished the score of *Béatrice*; I can work at it so seldom. However, it is getting on by degrees.

To Louis

Monday, 28th October 1861.

If I did not know what a detestable influence disappointment can have on the best characters, I should be capable of replying to you with some sad home-truths; you have wounded me to the heart, and with a coolness that shows deliberate choice in your expressions. But I excuse you and embrace you. . . .

Honestly, is it my fault that I am not rich, that I have not sufficient means to allow you to live quietly and in idleness in Paris with a wife and children? Can you with any shadow of justice reproach me on that account? You wrote to me at Baden in the middle of August—since then not a word. . . . Now you write to me in a tone of irony—ah, my poor, dear Louis, this is not right.

Don't worry about what you owe to your tailor; I will pay the bill when it is presented to me. . . . It is true that I thought you younger than you are; are you going to set down my lapse of memory as a crime? I cannot tell you the ages of my father, my mother, my sisters[1] when they died; does this mean that I did not love them? Ah! truly . . . but I seem to be trying to justify myself. I repeat that disappointment has made you beside yourself, and for that reason I can only love and pity you the more. You talk to me of soliciting for you, but from whom? and for what? You know very well that I am the worst in the world at begging favours. But tell me clearly what I can do and I will do it. . . .

[1] His favourite sister, Adèle, was seriously ill early in 1860. Berlioz visited her and she seemed to improve. He returned to Paris and received a telegram announcing her death (2nd March 1860).

To Louis

17th June 1862.

You will have received a telegram and, this morning, a letter from me. I write again to-day to tell you that I am pretty well and that there is no necessity for you to come.[1] . . .

I should like you to meet me in Baden on the 6th or 7th of August; I know you would enjoy the final rehearsals and the first performance of my opera. At all events you would be my companion in my leisure and I could present you to my friends and, in a word, we should be together. . . .

I do not know yet what money I shall be able to send you . . . and I am afraid of bringing you to this nest of gambling and gamblers. However, if you give me your word of honour that you will not risk a florin I will trust you and resign myself to the grief of our separation when you leave, a grief I shall feel all the more keenly in my altered circumstances. . . .

To Ferrand

Paris, *30th June* 1862.

I am writing merely a few lines in my desolation. My wife has just died with awful suddenness from heart disease. No words of mine can describe the fearful isolation which has resulted from this sudden and violent separation. Forgive me for not writing more.

To Princess Sayn-Wittgenstein

Paris, *22nd July* 1862.

Your letter, so sweetly cordial, made me happy for several hours. The misfortune is that these assuagements last such a short time. I am none the less grateful for all the comfort you have wished to give me. Like you, I have one of the theological virtues, Charity; but, unlike you, I have not the other two.[2] . . .

To Ferrand

21st August 1862.

I have just returned from Baden, where my opera *Béatrice et Bénédict* has achieved a marked success. . . . The performance which I conducted was excellent. . . . Well, you will scarcely believe me when I tell you that I was suffering so terribly from my neuralgia that I took no interest in anything, and took my place at the desk before that Russian, German, and French crowd . . . without the slightest emotion. The result . . . was that I conducted better than usual. I was far more uneasy at the second performance. . . .

---

[1] Berlioz's second wife, Marie Recio, died on 13th June 1862.

[2] Hope and Faith.

You would laugh if you could read all the silly praises bestowed upon me by the critics. They are discovering that I have the gift of melody, that I am gay, and even comic. The history of the astonishment caused by *L'Enfance du Christ* is repeating itself. They have come to the conclusion that I am not noisy because they do not *see* any blaring instruments in the orchestra. What an amount of patience I should need if I were not so indifferent!

My dear friend, I suffer martyrdom *every day* now from 4 a.m. till 4 p.m. What is to become of me? I do not tell you this to make you bear your own sufferings patiently; I know full well that mine do not afford you any compensation. I cry aloud to you as one is always tempted to cry to beings loving and beloved.

The first performance of *Béatrice et Bénédict* took place at Baden on 9th August 1862. It was a decided success, and this, together with the pleasure of hearing his opera, stimulated Berlioz, as we shall see, to make an addition of two numbers to the second act on his return to Paris. *Béatrice et Bénédict* is a comic opera and is undoubtedly the finest contribution that France has made in a style which, after its Italian origin, was more highly developed in France than in Germany or elsewhere. Historically, a distinction is generally made between the Italian *opera buffa* and the French *opéra-comique*. The chief difference being that in the Italian form the dialogue is carried on in *recitative secco* (literally 'dry recitative,' i.e. with no orchestral accompaniment, only a preliminary or punctuating chord), while in the French form it is spoken. *Béatrice et Bénédict* conforms to the French type in having spoken dialogue. To such an extent are we all slaves of our period and of fashion that even a good musician like Felix Mottl, when he revived *Béatrice et Bénédict* at Karlsruhe in 1887, thought it necessary to set the connecting dialogue to music (written by himself). This was one of the accursed results of Wagner's influence and of the mania which, after him, set in all over Europe for operas which are what the Germans call *durch-komponiert*.[1] Even to-day musicians have not got free from this cramping and wholly idiotic obsession that every opera must be cast in the same form, which means that there are no longer any forms. This

[1] Composed throughout.

pernicious Wagnerian idea, that there is only one form, the 'music-drama,' with every word set to music, and that the ideal is music flowing in a completely amorphous stream (in which singers, actors, musicians, and audience all *swim*), has almost destroyed opera, and it has prevented the performance of such masterpieces as *Béatrice et Bénédict.*

In English it is best to use the one term 'comic opera' for any opera that is a comedy and not a tragedy. The most typical and the best comic operas known to me are Mozart's *Figaro* and *Così fan tutte*, Rossini's *Barbiere di Siviglia*, Berlioz's *Béatrice et Bénédict*, and Verdi's *Falstaff.*[1]

Berlioz's exquisite work resembles Mozart's more than it does Rossini's, both in its finer and more developed musicianship and in its richer sentiment. I will give a short description of it.[2]

Béatrice et Bénédict. A comic opera in two acts, after Shakespeare.

The overture is a gay, charming, and piquant piece, deftly constructed from material out of the opera.

Act I. A park, the garden of the Governor of Messina, Leonato. The people are rejoicing at the raising of the siege of the town by the Moors—a vigorous chorus, *con fuoco*. This is followed by spoken dialogue between Leonato, Hero, and Beatrice which is taken almost word for word from Scene 1, Act I, of Shakespeare's *Much Ado about Nothing*. The people again begin singing. Beatrice would stop them but Hero encourages them and the chorus concludes. It is followed by a national dance, *Sicilienne*, with *tambours de basque*. This fascinating piece is of so individual a character, says Richard Pohl, 'as was probably never danced in Sicily.' The crowd then disperses and Hero, left alone, sings an aria: *Je vais le*

[1] Many will be surprised at the omission of Wagner's *Die Meistersinger* from this list. But after a long acquaintance with this work I have come definitely to the conclusion that it is a masterpiece of craftsmanship and not of genius. It seems to me that it possesses neither great nor beautiful conceptions and completely lacks gaiety and spontaneity. Although its fine craft is not to be denied it has neither sparkle nor depth. Wagner in this work is as pedantic and over-elaborate as any of his mastersingers.

[2] This is the one opera of Berlioz's which exists in a modern full score. It is published in the Breitkopf & Härtel collected edition.

voir. In form this may not seem to differ from operatic arias by Verdi and other good Italian composers, yet it has not only an absolutely individual Berliozian character but also a refinement of artistry, a purity of taste and quality that, in the absence of a more suitable word, one may call French, as the verses of Racine and La Fontaine are French.[1]

Don Pedro with Benedict and Claudio now arrive and the Shakespearian dialogue follows, leading into a duet between Beatrice and Benedict, full of vivacity and charm. This duet is a difficult but superb piece in which the Shakespearian duel of words is delightfully enhanced. A short dialogue precedes a trio of the three men, Don Pedro, Benedict, and Claudio. It begins with Benedict's words:

Me marier? Dieu me pardonne![2]

This trio is rather free in form, of ample scale, and a masterpiece of ensemble writing of which no musician could ever tire. Only in Mozart and in Verdi at his best can one find anything comparable.

But neither of these composers has given us anything like the next piece. Here Berlioz introduces a character, Somarone, a *Kapellmeister* or *maître de chapelle*, who is not in Shakespeare's play. He brings a choir and instrumentalists to rehearse an epithalamium; *Epithalame grotesque*, Berlioz calls it. The words and music of this scene are most amusing. Somarone begins with a famous saying of Spontini's: 'Ladies and gentlemen, the piece you are about to hear is a masterpiece.' The words of the Epithalamium begin:

Mourez tendres époux
Que le bonheur enivre!
Pourquoi survivre
A des instants si doux?[3]

---

[1] This applies to the whole score of *Béatrice et Bénédict*. It is a quality that Verdi only touched in *Falstaff*. Even the fineness of the best of *Traviata* and of *Un Ballo in maschera* is not quite the same thing.

[2] 'I, marry? God preserve me!'

[3] 'Tender lovers, now die
While still drunken with joy!
Why wait to sigh
When these sweet pleasures cloy?'

The words of this scene are by Berlioz.

Somarone also explains to Don Pedro that the piece is a fugue, because the word *fugue* means *flight*, and he has made a fugue on two subjects to make the two lovers think of the *flight* of time.

After a long dialogue taken from Shakespeare which carries on the action, Benedict says: 'When I said I would die a bachelor I did not think I would live till I were married,' and sings *Ah, je vais l'aimer*, a lively rondo.

Evening is now approaching; there is a brief dialogue between Hero and Ursula, and then a duet (*notturno*) between the two women as the moon rises: *Nuit paisible et sereine* (Night peaceful and serene). This duet is a marvel of indescribable lyrical beauty in which Berlioz's feeling for nature is wonderfully expressed. The instrumentation is of extraordinary delicacy and charm. It is night, the two young women cross the scene arm in arm, and the curtain falls on this piece of the purest Shakespearian enchantment.

Act II. *Salon* of the governor's palace. An interlude based on the *Sicilienne*, brilliant and gay, precedes a dialogue between servants. Somarone improvises a remarkable Drinking Chorus with guitars, trumpets, and tambourines; a truly original instrumentation. This piece, in two sections, is a superb example of Berlioz's fantasy. The crowd depart into the garden and Beatrice enters. She knows Benedict loves her but struggles against her own inclination. For her Berlioz writes an aria (*recitative*, *andante*, *allegro*) on a grand scale: *Il m'en souvient* (I remember), *Je l'aime donc?* (I love him, then?), which is one of the finest numbers in the opera and requires a most accomplished singer. Ursula and Hero now enter and the three women sing a trio, which is a pendant to the trio of the three men in the first act and is one of the most fascinating pieces in the opera.[1] It is followed by a charming chorus (in the distance) of sopranos, altos, and tenors with an accompaniment of guitars. Benedict enters and there is a dialogue between him and Beatrice in which they both try to hide their love. Leonato and the others enter, and there follows a general

[1] This and the following number are the pieces added by Berlioz when he returned to Paris after the production of the opera in Baden.

Phot. Pierre Petit

BERLIOZ IN 1863

ensemble piece, *Marche nuptiale*, with a fine sextet and chorus. A short dialogue, a last skirmish between Beatrice and Benedict, then precedes the signing of the two marriage contracts between Hero and Claudio, and Beatrice and Benedict. This is followed by the *scherzo duettino*, *L'Amour est un flambeau*, with chorus, a piece of sparkling grace and brilliance, which brings the opera to a close.

It is typical of the prevailing ignorance of Berlioz's music that this incomparable masterpiece is to-day completely unknown in England and America and almost unknown on the continent of Europe.

CHAPTER VII

LAST YEARS

On his return from Baden at the end of August 1862 after the successful production of *Béatrice et Bénédict*, Berlioz wrote to Ferrand (26th August 1862):

Your letter, my dear friend, has done me a world of good. Thank Mme. Ferrand for the pressing invitation to me to be near you. I stand in so much need of seeing you that I should have set out at once, did not a mass of paltry matters keep me here at present. My son has resigned his post on a ship belonging to the *Messageries impériales*, and from what my friends in Marseilles say he was right in doing so. He is now cast adrift, and it is necessary to look out for some fresh employment for him. I have other matters to attend to, consequent on the death of my wife.

In addition to these I have to see after the publication of the score of *Béatrice*, as I am slightly enlarging the musical portion in the second act. I am writing a trio and a chorus, and I cannot leave the work in suspense. I am in a hurry to untie or cut all the bonds which chain me to art, so that I may be ready at any time to say to death: 'Whenever you please!' I dare not complain when I think of your intolerable sufferings, and the aphorism of Hippocrates may fitly be applied to our case, *Ex duobus doloribus simul abortis vehementior obscurat alterum.*

Are such sufferings the compulsory consequences of our organizations? Must we be punished for having throughout our lives adored the beautiful? Probably so. We have drunk too deeply of the intoxicating cup; we have run too far after the ideal. . . .

You, my dear friend, have an attentive and devoted wife to aid you in bearing your cross! You have no knowledge of the terrible duet sung in our ears during the busy whirl of day and in the silence of the night by weariness and isolation! God keep you from the knowledge of it, for it is sorry music!

Good-bye; the tears which well up in my eyes would make me say things that would only render you more melancholy still. . . .

To Princess Sayn-Wittgenstein he wrote from Paris ('Toujours rue de Calais, 4') on 21st September 1862:

. . . First, I must ask you for news of Liszt. . . . Is it true that he has again taken up his religious ideas?[1] If it is, so much the better, he will be stronger against the torments ('les torments et les tourmentes') of this world. As for me, I am not at all in the state to reply to the affectionate and consoling reasonings which your goodness and the elevation of your mind has made you address to me. You know that for a long time now I have taken a dislike to philosophy, and all that resembles it, religious or not; and if such reflections could make me weep there would fall from my eyes (as Shakespeare says) only millstones.

You ask for news of my opera at Baden. All went well, several numbers produced tempests of applause. . . . There was a pack of Tartuffes there who overwhelmed me with demonstrations, whose *sincerity* I know perfectly well. . . . I had to assume a stupid look and pretend to believe them. . . .

Now I have finished; yesterday I wrote the last note with which I shall ever in my life blot a sheet of paper. *No more of that. Othello's occupation 's gone.*[2]

I want to have nothing more to do, nothing, absolutely nothing. I have arrived at that point, and I can say at any time to death, that abominable fellow: 'When you will!' I have only one ambition, to become rich enough to be able to resign my position on the *Journal des Débats*, which brings me in twelve hundred francs a year. I have the ambition to cease to be a servant, to mount no longer behind the carriage of fools and idiots, to be able, on the contrary, to throw stones at them if it pleases me. But Macbeth's witches have predicted nothing for me, I shall never be either Thane of Cawdor or Thane of Glamis or king; and I shall still for a long time have to praise men and things which I despise. God wishes it!

You see how dangerous it is to caress wild beasts! I am on the point of roaring an ode of impieties, which would make you blush. But I refrain. I do not understand what you can do at Rome;[3] one can have

---

[1] In 1861 Liszt left Weimar, which in twelve years he had made the centre of musical life in Germany, and went to Rome. Liszt's religious ideas met with understanding but no sympathy from Berlioz. In a letter to Dr. Franz Brendel dated 8th November 1862, giving him advice on a musical organization, the Tonkünstler-Versammlung, Liszt writes: 'But enough of my insignificant self. Let us pass over at once to the subject of those two brave fellows who, in your opinion, ought to play a chief part in the next Tonkünstler-Versammlung: Berlioz and Wagner. . . . Considering what has occurred and what has appeared in print, it strikes me as more than doubtful whether Berlioz would . . . undertake the musical conductorship of the Tonkünstler-Versammlung. . . . Besides which, his moral influence at the festival and the negotiations would be hindering and disturbing.'

[2] In English in the original.

[3] The Princess Sayn-Wittgenstein preceded Liszt to Rome.

faith and hope everywhere. You practise charity at a distance so well, why cannot you preserve the other two virtues even in Paris? When you write me letters of such cordiality, so affectionate, so indulgent, it is charity that makes you speak. Thank you, princess, you are not unaware that of all the fine qualities of the human heart, it is goodness that I prefer, and to goodness you add so much *esprit*! . . . Let me kneel before you and kiss your *man pietosa*.

In April 1863 Berlioz went to Weimar, where *Béatrice et Bénédict* was produced with great success. As the Grand Duke was unable to produce a work on such a scale as *Les Troyens* at Weimar he asked Berlioz to read the poem at the court. Liszt and the Princess Sayn-Wittgenstein were no longer in Weimar, but Berlioz had good musical friends there in Richard Pohl and his wife, who was a professional harpist. Pohl translated into German some of Berlioz's French texts, and Berlioz writes to Ferrand from Weimar on 11th April 1863:

In the midst of my rejoicing last night I took the liberty of embracing my Béatrice, who is charming. She was rather surprised at first, but afterwards she looked me full in the face and said: 'Oh! I must embrace you too! . . .'

I have heard much praise bestowed on the translator's work, but in spite of my ignorance of the German language, I have detected a great want of faithfulness in very many places. His excuses are very lame, and irritate me. He is the same man who translated my book *A travers Chants*. For instance, in the passage: 'This *adagio* seems to have been breathed forth by the Archangel Michael one evening when, in a melancholy mood, he contemplated the worlds uprising to the threshold of the empyrean,' he has taken the Archangel Michael to mean Michelangelo, the great Florentine painter. . . . Is not that enough to make one hang such a translator? But, after all, he is so thoroughly devoted to me, and such an excellent fellow. . . .

Louise, the wife of Richard Pohl, has left an account of Berlioz at the time of this visit to Weimar, from which I quote:

In spite of the honours and the success with which he was overwhelmed at Weimar, Berlioz—then in great suffering—was profoundly melancholy, almost always silent, and shut up in himself. The sole being who could win a smile from him was a large, beautiful Newfoundland belonging to one of the friends he frequently and willingly visited. . . . Berlioz suffered to such a degree that he would stay in bed without moving. . . . His nature was delicate and distinguished, 'French' in the best sense of the word. Without any affectation he was irritable to excess. This man of superior organization was a martyr to his music,[1] but had absolutely nothing of the showman, as his enemies have so often pretended.

Berlioz's habitual melancholy may have been accentuated by an incident of which I shall say no more than is revealed in the following quotation from a letter to Ferrand dated Paris, 3rd March 1863, a few weeks before he left on this visit to Weimar:

Your conjectures on the subject of my distress are, happily, erroneous. Alas! my poor Louis has tormented me cruelly, but I have forgiven him so completely! . . .

It is a question of love once more, a love which came upon me in smiling guise, which I never sought, but, on the contrary, resisted for some time. The state of isolation in which I live, and the inexorable need of tenderness which kills me, conquered in the end. I allowed myself to love, my love increased a hundredfold, and a voluntary separation on both sides became necessary and compulsory—a separation complete, without compensation, absolute as death itself. There you have the whole story. I am being gradually restored to health, but health under the circumstances is so sad. Do not let us talk about it any more.

After Weimar, Berlioz visited for the last time Löwenberg, where the Prince of Hohenzollern-Hechingen had always welcomed him and now prepared a special festival of his music.[2] This was the occasion when the prince asked him which he thought was the greatest of Beethoven's overtures, and Berlioz replied, '*Coriolan*.' According to Richard Pohl, who was there and served as interpreter, Berlioz was in a happier mood, and at the farewell supper party made a lively and warm-hearted speech in French. Berlioz, writing to Ferrand on 9th May 1863, says:

On the morning of my departure the good prince said, as he embraced me, 'You are going back to France, and you will meet there people who love you. Tell them I love them.'

I was completely upset the day of the concert, when, after the *adagio*, the love-scene in *Roméo et Juliette*, the chapel-master, who was in tears, exclaimed in French: 'No, no, no, there is nothing more beautiful than

---

[1] 'Do you think I listen to music for my pleasure!' Berlioz once remarked to a friend. Liszt quotes this remark in a letter to Ludwig Bösendorfer dated 12th July 1877.

[2] This prince had a private orchestra of sixty musicians. He was an invalid and died shortly after this visit and the orchestra was dispersed.

that!' Then the orchestra stood up. There was a flourish of trumpets, and a shout of applause. I seemed to see the smiling countenance of Shakespeare looking upon me and I longed to say: 'Father, are you content?'

Throughout the rest of the year 1863 Berlioz was occupied in rehearsing for the production by Carvalho of part of his opera *Les Troyens*.[1] Again, a few extracts from his letters will give the best picture of his life about this time:

TO FERRAND

PARIS, *4th June* 1863.

MY DEAR FRIEND,

I fear I have overtaxed your strength, for I see very clearly by your tremulous handwriting that your hand is not as steady as it used to be. Let me beg of you, therefore, to refrain from sending me lengthy remarks about my musical efforts. You might as well write articles, and I know what that means, even when you are in good health and spirits. . . . I shall be satisfied if I can distract your attention for a moment from your sufferings.

TO FERRAND

28th July 1863.

What a splendid institution the post is! For four *sous* we can have a chat, however far away we are from each other. Can anything be more charming?

My son arrived yesterday from Mexico, and as he has managed to get leave of absence for three weeks, I shall take him with me to Baden. . . .

Berlioz visited Baden with his son in August 1863, when *Béatrice et Bénédict* was revived with success, Berlioz himself conducting two performances. On his return to Paris he was busy again with rehearsals of *Les Troyens*. He wanted to consult Flaubert, of whose writings he was one of the earliest and most enthusiastic admirers, about the Carthaginian costumes, but whether he did or not I have not been able to find out.[2]

The strain of the production of part of *Les Troyens* in Paris

[1] In a letter to Ferrand dated 27th June 1863 Berlioz says: 'Madame Charton-Demeur is so enraptured with the part of Dido that she lies awake at night thinking of it. . . . But I never cease repeating to her: "Do not be afraid of any of my bold flights, and do not cry."' The production, as we have seen in chap. v, took place on 4th November 1863.

[2] The writer of the article in the *Encyclopaedia Britannica* says that Flaubert 'must have known by heart' the scene of Berlioz meeting Estelle, as described by Berlioz in his *Mémoires*, when he wrote its parallel in *L'Éducation sentimentale*.

at the end of 1863 must have taken a great deal out of Berlioz. The last performance took place on 20th December 1863, and on 23rd December Berlioz writes to the Princess Sayn-Wittgenstein:

Your letter has just revived me. Since midnight I have been suffering the torments of hell . . . a return of my neuralgia. I hasten to reply, and begin by asking a favour. You have seen at the head of my pianoforte score of *Les Troyens* these two words, *Divo Virgilio.* It is as though I had written these sacramental words: *Sub invocatione Divi Virgilii.* Now I am having engraved the full score of both parts . . . *La Prise de Troie* and *Les Troyens à Carthage*, which would not exist without you; permit me to dedicate them to you. If you consent I shall be doubly grateful. The *Divus Virgilius* does not prevent this dedication, and thus I shall have a double patronage. This publication can hardly be finished in less than a year. The publisher is a blunderer whom I have to watch very closely; he will commit a thousand idiocies if I let him. . . .

I am very happy to learn that life at Rome does not weigh upon you, and that your health is passable. . . . Tell me, if you go by chance to Subiaco, whether you have seen a pyramid of stones which I made on the top of a mountain near the village thirty-two years ago. Some French painters assured me last year that it still existed. . . .

'*Seul,*' '*solo,*' 'alone,' '*allein,*' in every language this word sounds ill. Your religious exhortations have no effect upon me, or indeed, they make me think of the sublime words of my poet describing the death of the Queen of Carthage: 'Oculisque errantibus alto quaesivit coelo lucem ingemuitque reperta' (With eyes wandering over the heavens she sought the light and finding it, groaned).

It is better not to see than to see what is.

Addio, bell' alma. The rest is silence.[1]

I shall continue to quote from letters to give a picture of his life during 1864.

TO FERRAND *12th January* 1864.

MY DEAR HUMBERT,

Do not be so impatient. I have not yet been able to get hold of a copy of the full score of *Alceste.*[2] The other day I had the pianoforte arrangement sent me, but the arranger (the villain!) has taken the liberty of altering the progressions. However, you shall have your chant in a few days.

---

[1] In English.

[2] Berlioz supervised the revival of *Alceste* at the Paris Opéra on 12th October 1866. We may see here what care and forethought he would give to it. Ferrand was writing a hymn to music by Gluck.

I must tell you once more that your lines do not go exactly with the music. You must not let French prejudices weigh with you to the extent of adapting perfect lines to this sublime music; the first line should consist of nine syllables with a feminine ending; the second of ten syllables with a masculine ending; the third like the first and the fourth like the second.

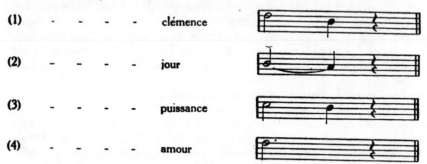

(1) - - - - - clémence 

(2) - - - - - jour 

(3) - - - - - puissance 

(4) - - - - - amour 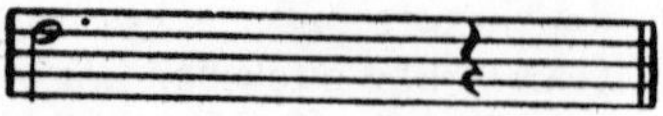

But I will point all this out to you more clearly when I send the manuscript. The words should fit the music, so perfectly beautiful, like a drapery sculptured by Phidias on a nude statue.[1] Seek it patiently and you will find it. Words have been put to the same chant in England for use in the Protestant churches. I would rather not know them. . . .

MY DEAR FRIEND, *17th January* 1864.

You have hit upon the very thing. It is ineffably sublime and enough to make the very stones of the temple weep. There is no need of a second couplet, as each repetition should be sung twice. It would be too long and the effect would be marred considerably. You will notice two or three alterations of syllables which you can arrange as you think best. As the parts are not parallel it was necessary in the case of the tenors and basses to make these alterations.

I must tell you that, in certain passages, the counter-tenor part is very badly written by Gluck; no pupil would ever dare show his master a lesson in harmony so clumsy in some respects. But the bass, the harmony, and the melody make the whole composition sublime. If you are going to depend upon women and children I think you might leave the chant in G, but they must not scream; it should be breathed forth like a sigh of celestial love. . . .

TO A. M. BENNET (FATHER OF THÉODORE RITTER)

PARIS, *22nd February* 1864.

. . . Remember me to your amiable and affectionate little world. I clasp Théodore's hand with the serious wish that he should forget Parisian manners, Parisian conversation, and everything Parisian in style. Nothing

[1] This is to be remembered when *Les Troyens* is performed in a translation.

is more stupid than this eternal dull *blague* that is applied to everything in Paris; let him forget it for ever! He is too good an artist to bother about it. Let him not write too much, nor too quickly, nor for too big a public, and let him wait for people to come to him without troubling them with advances. Adieu.

To the Same

PARIS, 15*th March* 1864.

. . . I have resigned my position on the *Journal des Débats*.[1] Nothing could be more comic than the disappointment and rage of those who for the last three months have been paying court to me; they have lost their advances; they are robbed. . . .

To Ferrand [2]

PARIS, 4*th May* 1864.

How are you, my dear friend, by night and by day? I am taking advantage of a few hours' respite from my pains to ask after yours.

It is cold and raining; some prosaic sadness or other is hovering in the air. One portion of our little musical world, the one I belong to, is melancholy; the other is gay, because Meyerbeer is dead. We were to have dined together last week, but he failed to keep the appointment.

Let me hear if you have come across a composition called *Tristia*, with this motto from Ovid:

Qui viderit illas
De lacrymis factas sentiet esse meis.[3]

If you have not it I will send it to you, because you like to read lively things. I have never heard the work. I think the first chorus in prose, *Ce monde entier n'est qu'une ombre fugitive*,[4] is worth hearing. I composed it in Rome in 1831.

If we could only have a chat together and I could be quite close to your arm-chair, I think I could make you forget your sufferings. The voice and the eye have a certain power which is not possessed by paper. Have you flowers and newly bursting foliage outside your windows? I have nothing but stone walls outside mine. Out in the street a cat has been howling for the last hour, a parrot is screaming, and a parakeet is imitating the twittering of the sparrows; in a courtyard some washerwomen are

---

[1] The money he received from Choudens for *Les Troyens* enabled him to do this. He had been writing regularly for the *Débats* since 1835. His last article, on 8th October 1863, was in praise of Bizet's opera *Les Pêcheurs de Perles*, which was, like *Carmen* later, a failure on its first appearance.

[2] This is an extremely interesting letter.

[3] 'Whoever sees them will know they have been made by my tears.' Ovid, *Tristia*, I. i, 13.

[4] *Méditation religieuse*, No. 1 of *Tristia*, Opus 18.

singing, and another parrot is shrieking incessantly 'Carry—arms!' What can one do? The day is very long.

My son is on board his ship again and will sail from Saint-Nazaire for Mexico a week hence. He was reading some of your letters the other day, and he congratulated me on being your friend. He is a good lad, and his heart and mind have developed richly, though tardily. Fortunately for me I have some musical neighbours close at hand who are very kind to me. I go to their house frequently in the evening, and I am allowed to lie full length on the sofa and listen to the conversation without being expected to take any great part in it. No fools ever intrude there, but in the event of such a catastrophe happening it is understood that I may go away without a word.[1]

I have not had an attack of musical fever for a long time, but Th. Ritter is giving Beethoven's five concertos with a delicious orchestra at his fortnightly concerts, and I go and listen to those marvels. Our *Harold* has just been performed for the second time in New York with great success. What have these Americans got into their heads?

Good-bye. Do not tire yourself by writing more than half a dozen lines.

On 3rd August 1864 Berlioz wrote to the Princess Sayn-Wittgenstein: 'Do you imagine that I am composing anything! Well, I have long given up such foolery; the most I do is to laugh at the Meyerbeer comedy and the role played by this great abscess of a Rossini.' On the other hand, he writes on 30th August 1864, reproving her for an apparent lack of disinterestedness in music:

I own to you that I note with some sadness the facility with which you play the party role in the practice of art.[2] You seem to find it quite simple

---

[1] These friends were M. and Mme Massart. She was a fine pianist. Berlioz wrote: 'She is for me a consoler, a sister of charity; when I suffer excessively, when I am out of my mind and heart I go about midnight to her *salon*, usually very full at this hour. I draw her aside: "I am at the end of my strength, make a little music for me." "What do you want," she replies, "the sonata in F minor, the one in C sharp minor, the trio in B flat?" "First get rid of all these people and then play me the sonatas and the trio." Then when the *salon* is almost empty they gorge me with Beethoven until two in the morning and I go away cured for the rest of the night.'

[2] Compare Brahms's letter to Joachim in 1853 when he went to see Franz Brendel in Leipzig. He says: 'On Sunday I even went to see Brendel in spite of the wry faces pulled by the Leipzigers . . . Berlioz praised me with such great warmth and cordiality that the others humbly followed suit.' Brahms played before Berlioz a scherzo and adagio, and Berlioz embraced him and wrote to Joachim: 'He will suffer greatly.' But Brahms had a most successful life and did not 'suffer' in Berlioz's sense as an artist.

that we do not admire those who do not admire us, and reciprocally. This is terrible, and constitutes the complete negation of art. I am no more able to restrain myself from adoring a sublime work by my greatest enemy than not to execrate a horrible piece of nonsense by my most intimate friend. I swear that that is true for me; because, I am an artist, and whoever doubts it insults me.

Those who dislike the violence of some of Berlioz's expressions will find he agrees with them. In this same letter to the princess he tells her not to write flattering things to him as one does to idiots, because that saddens him. He adds that there are parts of his music in which he believes that he has expressed certain feelings in a quite exceptional way, but

these are precisely those which you do not know well, or know but little or not at all. As for my literary style, as far as I have one, it is that of a writer who seeks the word capable of expressing what he feels, and never finds it. I am too violent, I have tried to be calm, and have not succeeded; that gives to the turns of my prose something uneven, staggering, like the walk of a drunken man. . . .

Berlioz's friends and the fellow-artists of his youth were dying one by one: Meyerbeer, Wailly (librettist of *Cellini*), and that aloof poet with whom he had most sympathetic relations, Alfred de Vigny, all died in 1864. On the death of Meyerbeer, who, to do him justice, was one of the few to appreciate the greatness of *Les Troyens*,[1] there was a public funeral given to him of almost royal dimensions, and the fuss made in the newspapers of the time was extraordinary: 'Meyerbeer is one of those great lights which illuminate a whole century'; he was compared to Shakespeare and Goethe; the public was informed (and no doubt agreed) that the world of music was now 'without a master,' there was an 'interregnum.' Well, no doubt, Berlioz did not much mind being totally ignored in this way; he liked Meyerbeer, and it is more than probable that Meyerbeer's attitude to him in private was that of an artist who freely acknowledged in admiration his superior. Berlioz had always praised the good

[1] According to Adolphe Jullien, George Sand relates in her *Lettres d'un voyageur* that she once found herself next to Meyerbeer during a performance of the *Marche au supplice* (*Symphonie fantastique*) and that, strongly moved, he gripped her hand and applauded enthusiastically 'this great unrecognized artist fighting heroically against the public indifference and his bitter destiny.'

qualities of Meyerbeer,[1] but when Meyerbeer's posthumous work *L'Africaine* was produced at the Paris Opéra in 1865, Berlioz wrote: 'These are not strings but chains, and chains woven of straw and paper rags. I am happy not to have to write about it.' Nevertheless, the receipts of *L'Africaine* were enormous, breaking records. 'I have left this musical eating-house,' he writes to Ferrand on 26th April 1865, 'and I shall never enter it again.'

In an earlier letter to Ferrand, dated 28th October 1864, after speaking of his son Louis who has got a command (*La Louisiane*, *en route* to Mexico), which separates them so that they see each other only for a few days every four or five months ('our affection for each other is inexpressible'), he says:

The musical world of Paris has reached a pitch of corruption beyond conception. I am becoming more and more isolated every day. *Béatrice et Bénédict* is in preparation at Stuttgart now. I shall perhaps go and conduct the first performance. I have also had an offer for St. Petersburg . . . but I shall not accept unless the terms are sufficiently favourable, and compensate me for braving the terrible Russian climate once more. If I go it will be for Louis's sake; as far as I am concerned a few thousand francs, more or less, will not alter my existence to any appreciable extent. . . .

I do not quite know how to account for the flatteries which are now heaped upon me by so many people. I have enough compliments paid me to turn any ordinary head, and I invariably feel a desire to say to my toadies: 'But sir (or madam), you forget that I am a critic no longer, and that I have given up writing articles.'

We know that Berlioz ended his *Mémoires* originally on 18th October 1854, the day before he married his second wife. Later, he added a *post-scriptum*, dated Paris, 25th May 1858, in which he mentions, among other matters, Heine's withdrawal of his criticism of Berlioz which he made in his book *Lutèce*. Finally, in 1864 he added a *postface* in two sections; the first deals with his last works and a few intervening events; he begins by saying that it is nearly ten years since he finished his *Mémoires*, but that events sufficiently important to be noted have since occurred:

---

[1] One of Berlioz's innumerable witticisms is on Meyerbeer: 'He had not only the luck to be talented but the talent to be lucky.'

I think I ought to record some of them here in a few words, and then not return to this long task under any pretext.

My career is finished, *Othello's occupation's gone.* I compose no more music, I conduct no more concerts, I write no more, either verse or prose; I have given my resignation as a critic; all the musical works which I had undertaken are finished; I do not wish to do any more, and I do nothing except read, meditate, fight against a mortal boredom, and suffer from an incurable neuralgia which tortures me night and day.

He then writes with his usual vivacity about other matters and ultimately describes the transportation of the remains of his first wife, Harriet Smithson, to a new grave, made necessary owing to the destruction of the old little cemetery of Montmartre. Previous to this the remains of his second wife had been also removed to this new grave, which had been presented to him by a friend, Édouard Alexandre. This scene, as described in his *Mémoires*, is almost unbearable to read in its details. One wonders how Berlioz could have written it, and the horror of it is accentuated by the laconic, dry, and detached style in which he describes it. We are, here, far indeed from the rhapsodic fervour of his youthful days. He ends the deliberate narration of this event:

The two dead repose tranquilly there at this hour, waiting until I bring to this charnel-house my portion of decaying matter (*pourriture*).

. . . . . .

I am in my sixty-first year; I have no longer any hopes, illusions, or great thoughts; my son is almost always far from me; I am alone; my contempt for the imbecility and dishonesty of men, my hatred for their atrocious ferocity, are at their height; and hourly I say to death: 'When you will!' Why then does it wait?

This chapter was evidently written in extreme depression. In fact, he begins the second section of this *postface* to his *Mémoires* by stating: 'Rarely have I suffered from depression so much as during the first days of September last, 1864. Almost all my friends, as is the custom at this time of the year, had left Paris. . . .'

A little later, however, his son Louis paid him a visit of several days on leave and, after his departure, Berlioz had the desire to make another trip to his home in the Dauphiné. He wished to see once more Vienne, Grenoble, above all Meylan, visit his nieces (the daughters of Suat and his favourite sister Adèle) and 'someone else, if I could discover her address.'

He describes his second visit to Meylan[1] in similar terms, but more briefly, to those employed in his description of his first visit. Again he visits the home of Estelle:

I had controlled myself, so far, to murmuring in a low voice: 'Estelle! Estelle! Estelle!' but then an overwhelming oppression made me fall on the ground, where I remained for a long time, stretched out, hearing in terrible anguish these atrocious words which every beat of my arteries made resound in my brain: The past! the past! time! . . . never again! never! . . . never!

I got up, my feet were in the place where her feet had been; I was quite sure this time that *I occupied in the atmosphere the space that her charming form had occupied!* . . .

Ah! there is the cherry tree, how it has grown! I break a piece of its bark, and I put my arms around the trunk and press it convulsively against my breast. You certainly remember her, beautiful tree! and you understand me!

He then describes how he enters the garden, and an old lady and her daughter, to whom he explains that the place has old memories for him, invite him to look round. . . . He enters the little room from which Estelle when he was twelve years old had often spoken to him. It is just the same as it was; even the furniture has not been changed:

I bit my handkerchief to pieces. The young girl watched me with almost a frightened look.

'Don't be surprised, mademoiselle, all these objects that I see again . . . it is just that I . . . that it is forty-nine years since I was last here.' And I fled bursting into sobs. What must the women have thought of such a strange scene whose meaning they will never know?

'He repeats himself,' the reader will say. It is only too true. Always memories, always regrets, always a soul that clings to the past, always a pitiful desperation to retain the present which is flying, always this useless fight against time, always this madness of wishing to realize the impossible, this terrible need of immense affection! How should I not repeat myself? The sea repeats itself; all its waves are alike.

. . . .

The same evening I was at Lyons. I passed a strange night there, thinking of the visit projected for the next day. I was going to see Mme.

[1] For the description of the first see pp. 257 et seq.

F ***.[1] I decided to visit her at midday. While awaiting that hour, so slow in its approach, and thinking it very likely that at first she would not wish to see me, I wrote the following letter so that she might read it before knowing the name of her visitor:

'MADAME,

'I come once more from Meylan. This second pilgrimage to the places inhabited by the dreams of my childhood has been more sorrowful than the first, made sixteen years ago, after which I dared to write to you at Vif, where you were then living. To-day I dare more, I ask you to receive me. I shall know how to restrain myself, do not fear any outbursts from a heart rebellious in the embrace of a pitiless reality. Grant me some moments, permit me to see you again, I beg of you.

'HECTOR BERLIOZ.

'*23rd September* 1864.'

The interview took place and it led, after much hesitation and reluctance on the part of Mme Fornier, who was six years older than Berlioz, to a correspondence between them which lasted for some years. Her letters were a source of much consolation to Berlioz, although they were in striking contrast to his. He prints some of this correspondence in the last pages of his *Mémoires*,[2] and adds that he begins already to feel the amelioration she has brought into his life.

The past is not entirely past. My sky is no longer empty. With a softened eye I contemplate my *star*,[3] who seems from afar to smile sweetly on me. . . .

I must be reconciled to her having known me too late, as I am reconciled to not having known Virgil, whom I should have loved so much, or Gluck, or Beethoven . . . or Shakespeare . . . who, perhaps, might have loved me. (It is true that I am not reconciled.)[4]

. . . .

Which of the two powers can raise man to the most sublime heights, love or music? It is a great problem. However, it seems to me that one ought to say this: Love cannot give any idea of music, music can give an idea of love. . . . Why separate one from the other? They are the two wings of the soul.

. . . .

---

[1] The former Estelle, now a widow.

[2] He destroyed the remainder of her letters at her request and wrote to her on 26th February 1866: 'It is done! Everything is burnt, I have nothing but the envelopes.'

[3] *Stella montis*, Estelle.

[4] This is one of the most characteristic and revealing utterances of Berlioz.

Seeing in what way some people understand love, and what they look for in the creations of art, I always involuntarily think of pigs who . . . dig the earth in the midst of beautiful flowers, and at the foot of great oaks, in the hope of finding there the truffles of which they are fond.

But let us try to think no more about art. . . . Stella! Stella! I shall be able to die now without bitterness and without rage.

The above paragraph are the last words of Berlioz's *Mémoires* and are dated 1st January 1865.

Berlioz in his letters to the Princess Sayn-Wittgenstein at first told her vaguely about his last pilgrimage to Meylan, but, later, on her writing to him sympathetically, he explained the whole affair and begged her to tell *nobody*, meaning especially Liszt, who was at that moment in Paris. He says he has seen Liszt twice and that they passed some good hours together: 'He is indeed charming, as always. I do not think that he would find me ridiculous if you spoke to him of my confidences; however, I prefer not to appear so childish to him.'

In this same letter, dated Paris, 19th October 1864, he says to the princess:

I write to you to-day, dear friend, in a kind of tranquil dejection. I received lately from *her* a letter I did not expect; this letter, which promises me others, has calmed me. Nevertheless I shall not go to Lyons this month. I should upset and embarrass her, I feel sure of it. To-day her son is getting married, later she will be preparing to go with the newly married pair to live at Geneva. No doubt the strange intensity of my feelings astonishes her, but she understands up to a certain point, and she has not thought that I was mad. But, indeed, the child of twelve who loved her terribly inspired no response, and could not inspire any response in the wonderful girl of eighteen who scarcely guessed at his anguish. She has no very lively recollections, she thinks like you that my imagination plays a great part, and no doubt she is not unaware, any more than you, that the imagination *is the untrue.* But I think that, unknowingly perhaps, she begins to believe that it is the *opposite* that prevails, and that the *opposite* will remain the master to the end; because it is *the true.*

In any case I shall do all I can not to be importunate or indiscreet or frightening; I shall be as reserved as possible, and perhaps one day she will say to herself in the secrecy of her heart: 'It would be a pity not to be so loved.'

The years have almost quite destroyed everything that was hers, one must reconstruct in thought almost entirely her splendid beauty; only her

BERLIOZ IN 1867

After a photograph

figure of a goddess has remained; nevertheless I experience in seeing her a rapture so extraordinary that I lose almost entirely the sense of reality. . . . Ah! my dear sister, forgive me; see how my calmness disappears. To speak to you thus of her . . . what a misfortune! to be no longer master of oneself! Impossible! Farewell. . . .

Most of the year 1866 was spent by Berlioz in France. In spite of his sufferings from neuralgia his letters of the period are full of spirit, but his changes of mood were very rapid. He had his *Mémoires* printed privately in an edition of 1,200 copies, which were to be put on sale only after his death. When informing Princess Sayn-Wittgenstein of this fact he says: 'From a philosophic point of view, what a storm in a teacup!' and tells her of the recent discovery near the Mississippi of a valley named Les Mauvaises Terres, where a mountain of bones of antediluvian animals was discovered, species of which none to-day exists except that of the rhinoceros. 'Who,' he adds, 'among us can flatter himself that he will be a rhinoceros?' Later (11th May 1865), answering some queries of hers, he says: 'Your suppositions with regard to the *postface* of my *Mémoires* are equally [1] gratuitous. There is *not one* word in the account of my last ten years which deals with Wagner, or Liszt, or the music of the future.'

A letter from Mme Fornier (Estelle) or from one of his intimate friends was sometimes enough to restore Berlioz temporarily to a state of well-being. Music also could have this effect. On 17th January 1866 he writes to Ferrand that he has been asked to supervise the production of Gluck's *Armide* at the Théâtre-Lyrique:

Mme Charton-Demeur, who plays the trying part of Armide, comes every day to rehearse with M. Saint-Saëns, a great pianist, a great musician, who knows his Gluck almost as well as I do. It is curious to see this poor woman groping in the sublime, and to witness her gradual enlightenment. This morning, in the Hatred scene, Saint-Saëns and I shook hands. We were speechless. Never did any other man discover such *accents*. And to think there are people who blaspheme this masterpiece. . . .

---

[1] This 'equally' refers to her having asked him not to write mockingly to her in reply to her letter informing him that Liszt had decided to take orders in the Roman Catholic Church. Berlioz says: 'I knew of Liszt's decision. I do not make fun of it. Your recommendation was superfluous.'

Since I have been thus plunged again into music my pains have gradually disappeared.[1] I get up every day now, just as the rest of the world does.

This congenial work coincided with another agreeable event. On 30th January 1866 Berlioz informs Princess Sayn-Wittgenstein, in a letter, that the salaries of all officials of the Conservatoire have been raised and that his (as librarian) is now increased from 1,400 francs to 2,800 francs a year:

Ah, well, you laugh, but that helps me a great deal. It replaces, and more, the damned feuilleton which I gave up. Ah! if one could only live for two hundred years one would finish by becoming rich, wise, glorious, perhaps even *young*, who knows?

It is only sincere and deep affections which do not increase, because that is impossible.

Unfortunately the production of *Armide* was abandoned. In March 1866 Liszt came to Paris, and a performance of his Mass [2] was given at Saint-Eustache. Berlioz writes to Ferrand: 'There was an immense crowd, but alas, what a negation of art!' The subject of music had now become almost taboo between Liszt and Berlioz.

Berlioz took great pleasure in the last few years of his life in reading Shakespeare and Virgil to a few intimate friends. He writes to Mme Massart in the early autumn of 1865 complaining of the dreariness of Paris, 'nothing but provincialisms right and left,' tells her of his visit to Geneva to see Mme Fornier, where he was well received, fêted, and grumbled at a little. Mme Fornier had already reproached him for having printed three of her letters in his *Mémoires*, of which he had sent her a copy; but her daughter-in-law had taken Berlioz's part, and in a letter to his dear friends M. and Mme Damcke, he says he does not think *she* is very angry about it. But on his return to Paris he had hoped to see the Massarts, and he adds:

When you come back, some evening or other, we must gather together

---

[1] On 26th April 1865 Berlioz writes to Ferrand: 'The famous German violinist Joachim is here on a visit of ten days . . . I have heard Beethoven's pianoforte trio in B flat, the sonata in A, and the quartet in E minor played by him and other first-rate artists—the music of the starry spheres. You may well imagine—more than that, you understand how impossible it is after . . . such miracles of inspiration to endure ordinary music. . . .'

[2] *Messe de Gran.*

once more our small male audience, and we will read *Coriolanus*.[1] Nothing gives me a greater sense of being alive than the sight of the enthusiasm of men who are not used up, but intelligent, and gifted with sensibility and imagination. I took pleasure at Vienne [2] in making my nieces weep their eyes out. They are charming girls, whom I love as though they were my daughters; they receive the impressions of poetry as a photographic plate receives the sun. . . .

Another of his amusements was reading at the library of the Institut on the days of its meetings—to which he habitually goes early for this purpose, he tells the princess, adding (12th July 1866):

Of the celebrated men (*Biographie universelle*) who are not artists I begin to be weary. These poor scoundrels who are called great men inspire me with an irresistible horror. Caesar, Augustus, Antony, Alexander, Philip, Peter,[3] and so many others are merely bandits. Then the biographers contradict themselves, one sees clearly that they are sure of nothing, that they know nothing.

When I think that I myself have forgotten certain characteristic details of my life I ask myself how a stranger would be able, at a distance of two thousand years, to retrace the lives of men the writer has neither seen nor known. History is a fraud, like many other accepted things.

Towards the end of 1866 Berlioz had the great pleasure of being asked to superintend the production at the Opéra of Gluck's *Alceste*. He writes to Ferrand:

The rehearsals of *Alceste* have reanimated me to a certain extent. . . . An entire generation is now hearing this marvel for the first time. . . . Ingres is not the only one among our compères at the Institut who habitually attends the performances of *Alceste*; the majority of painters and sculptors are gifted with a love of the antique, a love of the beautiful which no amount of suffering can transform. . . .

The success of this production of *Alceste* meant a great deal to Berlioz, and evidently under his direction the work was made manifest in its true light (always a much rarer event than the public realizes!), for Fétis wrote to him: 'You have entered profoundly into the mind of the great author of *Alceste*. . . .

[1] *Hamlet* and *Othello* were two of his favourite works for reading at Mme Girard's and at the Massarts' before small selected audiences.

[2] Not Vienna in Austria, but in Dauphiné.

[3] Probably Peter the Great of Russia.

In such a production one recognizes not only a great musician but a poet and a philosopher.'

Berlioz's faithful friend and successor on the *Journal des Débats*, d'Ortigue, died on 20th November 1866. In December Berlioz left for Vienna, where his *Faust* was being prepared by Herbeck[1] for performance by the famous Gesellschaft der Musikfreunde. In spite of these activities, Berlioz was really perpetually ill and spent most of his time in bed. The best description of his illness is given by himself in a letter to Ferdinand Hiller on his return from Vienna dated 8th February 1867:

> You are the most excellent friend one could find. I shall do what you ask: I will try to gather some strength and on the 23rd of this month I shall leave for Cologne and shall be at the Hotel Royal that evening. But do not reserve *rooms* as you mention; *one* little room will suffice. If I am incapable of travelling I shall send you the orchestral parts of the duet and you will be free to conduct the whole performance. You talk to me like the doctors: 'It is neuralgia.'
>
> Thus Madame Sand having remarked to her gardener that a garden wall had fallen down: 'Oh, it is nothing, madame, the *frost* caused it.' 'Yes, but it must be rebuilt.' 'Oh! it is nothing, it is merely the frost.' 'I don't deny it, but the wall has collapsed.' 'Don't worry, madame, it is the frost.' . . .

Faust had been well prepared by Herbeck when Berlioz arrived in Vienna, but Berlioz, who was always insatiable for rehearsals, found plenty to do. Adolphe Jullien relates that he was informed by Oscar Berggruen, who followed the rehearsals with enthusiasm, that Berlioz was in a very irritable state: 'A 'cellist made a false entry: "Be quiet!" cried Berlioz in French, white with anger. The cor anglais made a mistake in Marguerite's air. Berlioz uttered a cry of rage and hurled his baton at the man's head; Herbeck recovered it and returned it to Berlioz: "Oh, I am ill to death," exclaimed Berlioz in inexpressible pain, and Herbeck relieved him of the rehearsal.'

Berlioz conducted the performance on 16th December in the famous hall (Redoutensaal) and its success was tremendous, as even the hostile section of the press admitted. He was given a banquet by the famous old society in the Hotel Munsch on

[1] Herbeck, Johann (1831–77), a famous Austrian conductor.

the following day. Prince Czartoriski gave his toast in a speech in French and was followed by Herbeck, who said:

I am happy to raise my glass, in the hall where Mozart gave his concerts, to drink to the health of this eminent—no, the word is too hackneyed—of the man who has opened up new paths in art, who in 1828, a year after the death of the musical genius whose birthday we celebrate to-day [Beethoven, b. 16th or 17th December 1770], gave us the *Symphonie fantastique*, by which he has destroyed all narrow-minded and bourgeois musicians. I drink to the health of Hector Berlioz, who has been fighting for half a century against the petty miseries of existence; I drink to the genius of Hector Berlioz.

Writing to his friend, the well-known French composer Ernest Reyer, from Vienna, Berlioz describes the satisfaction Herbeck and his excellent musicians gave him, and adds:

. . . It is the greatest musical joy of my life. You must forgive me for speaking at length about it. People have come from Munich and Leipzig. . . . Well, there is one of my scores saved. They will play it now in Vienna under Herbeck, who knows it by heart. The Paris Conservatoire can continue to leave me outside! Let it stick to its ancient repertory!

Berlioz was able to go to Cologne, where he saw his old friend Ferdinand Hiller and conducted *Harold* and the duet *notturno* from *Béatrice*. On 11th January 1867 he writes to Ferrand, telling him that the journey to Vienna has nearly put an end to him, and adds:

The cold of our frightful climate is fatal to me. My dear Louis wrote to me the day before yesterday describing his morning rides in the forests of Martinique, the tropical vegetation, and the sun, the real sun. I am inclined to think that it is the very thing we both need, you and I. Of what use is mighty Nature if we die far away from her and in ignorance of her sublime beauties? My dear friend!—the stupid rumbling of carriages disturbs the silence of the night—Paris, damp, cold and muddy! Parisian Paris! now everything is quiet—sleeping the sleep of the unjust—well, sleeplessness *sans phrases*, as one of the brigands of the revolution said. . . .

On 11th June 1867 he wrote to Ferrand:

Thank you for your letter, which has done me much good. . . . I am ill in every way; I am tormented by anxiety. Louis is still on the shores of Mexico and I have not heard from him. I dread those Mexican brigands. . . .

I was writing these few lines to you from the Conservatoire, where the jury, of whom I am one, for the competition in musical composition at the Exhibition had to assemble. . . . On the preceding day we heard a hundred and four cantatas and I had the pleasure of witnessing the crowning (unanimous) of my young friend Camille Saint-Saëns, one of the greatest musicians of the present day. . . .

I am altogether upset by this meeting of the jury. How happy Saint-Saëns will be! I went straight to his house to tell him of his success. . . . Well, our musical world has at last done a sensible thing; it has given me fresh strength. If it had not been for the pleasure I have derived from it I could not have written you so long a letter.'

Nineteen days later, on 30th June 1867, Berlioz writes to Ferrand:

My dear Humbert,

A terrible blow has fallen upon me. My poor son, captain of a large ship and only thirty-three years of age, has just died at Havana.'

The day before (29th June) he wrote to Mme Fornier:

Dear Madam,

Forgive me for turning to you at this moment when I am suffering from the worst grief of my life. My poor son is dead at Havana, aged thirty-three.

Your devoted,
H. Berlioz.

Louis Berlioz died of yellow fever. Berlioz now had to remake his will. One day he brought to his apartment one of his assistants at the library of the Conservatoire, and between them they took back to the library all the wreaths, trophies, prsentations, newspaper reviews, articles, testimonials, etc., that Berlioz had accumulated from abroad and at home during his lifetime and slowly burned the lot. To Mme Fornier he left a life annuity of 1,800 francs; a suitable provision was made for his second mother-in-law, Mme Martin Recio, who still kept house for him; his manuscript scores were left to the Conservatoire and his books and other personal belongings of value to his intimate friends.

The temperament of Berlioz was such that the destruction of all these mementoes must have revived him considerably for the moment, but he writes to Ferrand on 15th July 1867:

MY DEAR, INCOMPARABLE FRIEND,

I am writing a few lines to you since you wish, but it is not right of me to sadden you. I suffer so frightfully from the increase of neuralgia in the intestines that I do not know how I remain alive. I have scarcely enough intelligence to attend to the affairs of my poor Louis. . . .

His doctor sent him to take the waters at Néris. On his return to Paris he writes to Mme Damcke:

. . . Arrived at Néris, I took five baths; at the fifth the doctor, hearing me speak and feeling my pulse, said: 'Come out, quick, the waters don't suit you; you will have laryngitis. . . .'

I left the same evening. I just missed suffocating from a fit of coughing in the train. Then I arrived at Vienne [Dauphiné], where my nieces overwhelmed me with attentions. I remained nearly the whole time in bed. At last my voice slowly returned, my bad throat was cured; but my neuralgia also returned, more ferocious than ever. . . .

Now I am at Paris, and nearly always in bed. A few days ago the Grand Duchess Hélène of Russia got round me to promise to go to St. Petersburg; she wanted to see me and at length I consented. I will leave on 15th November to conduct six concerts at the Conservatoire, one of which will be entirely of my music.

The princess pays my travelling expenses there and back, places one of her carriages at my disposal, lodges me in her palace, and gives me fifteen thousand francs. If I die of it, at least it will have been worth the trouble. . . .

To Madame Massart he writes similarly, adding: 'You come too; I will make you play your jolly harpsichord concerto in D minor by S. Bach and we will have a hearty laugh together. . . .'

To the Massarts Berlioz used to write in a lively chaffing style, of which the following letter dated 2nd November 1867, just before his departure to Russia, is an example:

How are you, master and mistress?
How is your château?
Do you still know French?
Do you still know music?
Do you still know how to live?
Do you know that you don't know anything?
Do you know that you are forgotten?
Do you know that the world has passed you by?
Do you know that you have passed out of fashion?

Good evening!

2nd November, Day of the Dead.

And when one is dead it is for a long time.

It was twenty years since Berlioz had visited Russia, and his success was even greater than before. The programmes of his concerts were changed, so that more of his own works could be performed. The famous Russian composer and critic, César Cui, has left the following account of these concerts and of Berlioz's conducting:

> How he understands Beethoven! What serenity, what austerity in the execution! And what effect without tinsel and with no concession to bad taste! I much prefer Berlioz to Wagner as a conductor of Beethoven. In spite of all his excellent qualities Wagner often shows affectation and introduces in the time of his *ritardandos* a meretricious sentimentality. . . . As for his own works, Berlioz in conducting them opens a new world to us which the most assiduous reading of his scores had not revealed. . . . Of all the conductors we have known at St. Petersburg, Berlioz is certainly the greatest. . . .

The quality of the Russian orchestras and choirs, the enthusiasm of the Russian musicians for his works, and the general atmosphere of temporarily intelligent appreciation that surrounded him reawakened Berlioz to life. He writes on 15th December 1867 to Édouard Alexandre:

> . . . Everybody, from the Grand Duchess down to the meanest performer in the orchestra, overwhelms me with attention and applause.
>
> They found out, I know not how, that 11th December was my birthday [sixty-four]. I received charming presents and in the evening had to be present at a dinner laid for a hundred and fifty persons, and there was no lack of toasts, as you may imagine. . . .
>
> At the second concert I was recalled six times after the *Symphonie fantastique*, which was performed in a startling manner. . . .
>
> What an orchestra! What precision! What ensemble! I do not know if Beethoven ever heard himself performed in such a way. Also, I must tell you that in spite of my sufferings, when I get to my desk and see myself surrounded by all this sympathetic world, I feel myself reanimated and I conduct as perhaps I have never conducted before. Yesterday we had to play the second act of *Orphée*, the Symphony in C minor (Beethoven), and my *Carnaval romain* overture. . . .
>
> These Russians only knew Gluck by the horrible mutilations made here and there by incapable people!!! Ah! it is for me an indescribable joy to reveal to them the masterpieces of this great man. There was no end to the applause yesterday. In a fortnight we shall give the first act

of *Alceste.* The Grand Duchess has ordered that I am to be obeyed absolutely. I do not abuse her order but I use it. . . .

Berlioz gave two concerts in Moscow with, if possible, even greater success. Then he returned to St. Petersburg and gave his final concert on 10th February 1868.

The tremendous efforts he had made in Russia and the intensity of his enjoyment there left him absolutely exhausted. To Mme Massart he writes on 18th January 1868 from St. Petersburg: 'I suffer so terribly, dear madame, my agony is so unremitting that I do not know what is to become of me. . . .' To Stassoff he writes from Paris on 1st March 1868:

I have not written to you since my return because I have been in such terrible suffering. To-day I am a little better. . . . I leave this evening at 7 o'clock for Monaco. I do not know why I do not die. But since I do not I am going to revisit my beloved Nice, the rocks of Villefranche and the sun of Monaco. . . . Oh, when I think I am going to lie full length on the marble seats at Monaco in the sun, on the seashore!!!

Do not be too exacting; write to me in spite of my brevity. Remember that I am ill, that your letter will do me good, and do not speak to me of composing or any such nonsense. . . .

It has been frequently repeated by one writer copying another, without any attempt at verification, that in his last years Berlioz's faculties were weakened and his vitality exhausted. The proof that his mind was as clear and vital as ever is to be found in his letters, quite apart from the evidence of his Russian trip. But it is undoubtedly true that for a number of years before the time of which I am now writing, Berlioz—except to a few very intimate friends—was extremely reserved and distant. Gustave Bertrand, who saw Berlioz during his last visit to St. Petersburg, says in his *Nationalités musicales étudiées dans le drame lyrique* (Didier, 1872) that there was not the slightest eclipse of intelligence in Berlioz as many believed, but that he deliberately delighted in silence, awaiting his approaching annihilation. He had still some time to wait, but the end was not far off. In April 1868 he writes to Stassoff, describing his two falls down the rocks at Monaco—both occasioned by his trying to descend to the sea—and of his subsequent week spent in bed at Nice and his return, much damaged, to Paris. He ends: 'I cannot write any more. If I wait until I feel better I may perhaps wait a long time. Write to me all the same. It will be an act of charity.' In this letter he begins with a very characteristic touch: 'My dear Stassoff,—Both you and Cui called me *Monsieur* Berlioz in your last letters, but I forgive you both.' However, he recovered even from this double accident sufficiently to resume, though considerably enfeebled, his ordinary life. He paid his regular visits to the Institut and went out occasionally to the houses of a few friends. On 25th November 1868 he got up from bed to vote for the election of Charles Blanc, to whose efforts he owed the retention of his post as librarian of the Conservatoire after the revolution in 1848.

One of the last visits he paid was to Ernest Reyer, assisted by his faithful servant, whose name, oddly enough, was Schumann. As he was leaving, Reyer asked him to autograph a score of *Benvenuto Cellini* which Berlioz had given him. Berlioz took a pen and began mechanically to write:

'A mon ami' (To my friend). . . . Then he stopped, looked up at Reyer vacantly: 'Tiens, comment vous nommez-vous?' 'Reyer.' 'Ah! . . . oui . . . Reyer. . . .'[1]

Soon after this he was confined to his room. A few friends used to visit him during the winter of 1868–9. He would receive them, stretched out on his bed, with a sad smile but without saying a word. If the visitor, after a little while, got up to go Berlioz would retain him with a friendly gesture, as if to say that he enjoyed his presence and that last evidence of affection.

On 8th March 1869, at half-past twelve, Berlioz died in the presence of his mother-in-law, Mme Martin, Mme Damcke, Mme Charton-Demeur, and Mme Delaroche. In his will he left personal souvenirs to all his friends, forgetting only Auguste Morel and Stephen Heller. The residue of his property (which was not inconsiderable), after a life's interest to Mme Martin and the annuity already mentioned to Mme Fornier, went to his nieces.

[1] 'Wait, what is your name?' 'Reyer.' 'Ah! . . . yes—Reyer.'

Confucius has said that a superior man is never satisfied but easily served, while inferior men are easily satisfied but difficult to serve. Berlioz behaved like a simple, decent, profoundly affectionate and just man in all his personal relationships. As a man and as an artist he stood fighting upon his own feet as long as he could stand, and when he could no longer stand, then, without any fuss he died. 'Pas de philosophie!' he once wrote to Princess Sayn-Wittgenstein, 'c'est une bêtise!'

APPENDIX I

BERLIOZ AS CRITIC

I HAVE deliberately refrained from inserting any quantity of Berlioz's critica writings in the main text of this book, because their importance is secondary to that of his music, and it would have been disproportionate to treat his literary works chronologically in the same way as his musical compositions.

Berlioz hated writing. So he says. But if a man has a gift he enjoys using it, and what Berlioz hated was the compulsion of the journalistic task through which he earned his livelihood for thirty years. The quantity and the gusto of Berlioz's writings prove that he did not write without pleasure; but his own account of his position as a critic is as follows:

'This always recurring task poisons my life . . . to what miserable precautions am I not delivered! what circumlocutions to avoid telling the truth! what concessions made to social connections and even to public opinion! what bottled-up rage! what swallowed shame! Yet I am considered unbalanced, ill-tempered, contemptuous! Ah, you scoundrels who speak of me thus, you would see, if I disclosed all my thoughts, that the bed of nettles on which you pretend to be stretched by me is merely a bed of roses compared with the gridiron on which I would roast you.'

He then adds that, nevertheless, he has never failed to express freely his enthusiasm for fine things, having often praised warmly people who had done him mischief, and with whom he was not on friendly terms, 'because it is sweet to me to praise an enemy of merit, besides being a duty which any honest man must fulfil.' This is completely true, the candour of Berlioz's writing is one of its most attractive qualities. Berlioz's feelings were too strong to be disguised, and nothing is more characteristic than his remark that to write a word in favour of a friend without talent caused him the utmost torture. The lying words simply refused to be written, and he confesses that the violent effort he has had to make to praise certain works is such that 'the truth oozes through my lines as, in the extraordinary efforts of the hydraulic press, the water sweats out of the sides of the machine.'

It is difficult for a man who is not an artist, however intelligent and sympathetic, to understand the sufferings of an artist. I do not say that he suffers more than other men. In fact, one might imagine that if an artist has of necessity to suffer intensely as an artist he can hardly have his full share of other men's sufferings. I do not say it is so, but it may be so. What I want to emphasize is the fact that in Berlioz's account of his torture in writing an article, which I am about to quote, there is not a word of exaggeration. The reader must believe this, and though he is free to laugh at the violence of Berlioz's expressions (which, no doubt, made Berlioz himself smile grimly when he wrote them), he is a miserable blockhead if he does not realize that what made Berlioz smile was not the strangeness of his expressions, but the extravagance of his feelings, *which he could not help*.

'I once remained three whole days shut up in my room in order to write an article on the Opéra-Comique without being able to begin it. I no longer remember the *work* about which I had to write (one week after its first performance I had forgotten its name for ever), but the torture I suffered during those three days before writing the first three lines of my article; well, I still remember that. The lobes of my brain seemed ready to separate. My veins seemed full of burning cinders. Sometimes I leant on my elbows over my table, holding my head in my hands; sometimes I paced with long strides like a sentinel in twenty-five degrees of frost. I looked out of the window at the surrounding garden, the hills of Montmartre, the setting sun. . . . In a reverie I was transported a thousand miles from my hateful Opéra-Comique. When, returning to my surroundings, my eyes fell again on the cursed title written at the top of the cursed paper, still white and obstinately awaiting the other words with which I had to cover it, I felt overwhelmed with despair. I had a guitar leaning against my table; with one kick I broke its belly. . . . On my mantelpiece two pistols regarded me with their round eyes. . . . I considered them for a long time. . . . Then I began to batter my head with my fist. At last, like a schoolboy who cannot cope with his task, I wept with indignation, tearing my hair. The salt water coming from my eyes relieved me a little. I turned against the wall the barrels of my pistols that were always looking at me. I took pity on my innocent guitar, and, taking it up, I plucked several chords which it gave me without bitterness. My son, aged six, came at this moment to knock at my door; in my bad humour I had unjustly scolded him that morning. But as I did not open it:

'"Father," he called out, "are we friends?"

'And running to open it:

'"Yes, my boy, let 's be friends! Come in!"

'I took him on my knees, I drew his blond head against my breast, and we both went to sleep. I had given up the attempt to find a beginning to my article: it was the evening of the third day. The next day I succeeded, I don't know how, to write I don't know what, on I don't know what. . . .

'It is fifteen years since this happened! And still my torture endures. . . .'

Berlioz often speaks of weeping. It is thought that nobody weeps nowadays, but I confess that often in the course of writing this book, when transcribing Berlioz's own words, the tears have come into my eyes.

The mingled rage and hatred which Berlioz felt for writing was due to the fact that he wanted to be doing something else.

'Let me have scores to write, orchestras to conduct; let me stay eight, or even ten hours on my feet, baton in hand . . . until I spit blood and cramp binds my arm; make me carry desks, double-basses, harps, move platforms, nail planks, like a commissionaire or carpenter; compel me then, instead of resting, to correct throughout the night the errors of printers and copyists; I have done it, I do it, I shall do it; that belongs to my musical life, and I bear it without complaint, without even thinking of it, as a hunter endures cold, heat, hunger, thirst, sun, showers, dust, mud, and the million discomforts of the chase! But eternally to write articles for a living! to write nothings on nothing, to give lukewarm praise to unbearable insipidities! to speak to-night of a great master and to-morrow of a *crétin*, with the same seriousness, in the same language! . . .'

I intend to give the reader some notion of Berlioz's critical writings by quoting a few characteristic passages on diverse subjects. First of all I will give some of his general ideas on music. The reader of this book is aware that Berlioz makes no profession of any religious beliefs, that he gently chided the Princess Sayn-Wittgenstein for trying to persuade him to them when she and Liszt turned to Rome for consolation and faith. Possibly in his heart he despised Liszt a little for resorting to any religious faith as a prop, but if so he did not mock him. It is certain that he would have had no sympathy with the gospel of renunciation and the Parsifalism of Wagner.

But in December 1853, when he was in Leipzig, Professor Lobe asked him to write for his paper, *Fliegende Blätter für Musik*, a statement of his musical creed. This little-known document was reprinted by Richard Pohl, from whom I take it, as *Berlioz's Glaubensbekenntnis* (Berlioz's creed). It reads as follows, but it must be remembered that I am translating from the German what was originally written by Berlioz in French:

'You have invited me to write down for your journal a short statement of my ideas on the art of music and its present and future condition, but have exempted me from speaking of its past. For this dispensation I am grateful. But to undertake the treatise you demand would need a rather thick technical book, and your 'Flying Leaves' (*Fliegende Blätter*) if burdened with it would fly no longer.

'In fact, you ask me for my confession of faith.

'Thus virtuous electors proceed with candidates who request the honour of representing them in the Chamber. But I have not the least ambition to *represent*; I will be neither deputy nor senator, neither consul nor burgomaster.

'If indeed I sought consular rank I believe I could not do better in order to win the voices—not of the people, but of the patricians of art—than, like Coriolanus, take myself to the Forum, bare my breast, and show the wounds that I have received in defence of the fatherland.

'Is not my creed to be found in all that I have had the misfortune to write? In what I have done and in what I have not done?

'What to-day music is, you know, and you cannot think that I do not know it. But what it will be—of that neither you nor I have the slightest idea.

'So what shall I say to you about it? As a musician much, I hope, will be forgiven me, because I have loved much. As critic I have been, and still am, harshly enough attacked because all my life long I have expressed pitiless hatred and boundless scorn. That is a just requital. But this love, this hatred, this scorn is, doubtless, also your own. Is it necessary then for me to point to the objects of it?

'*Music is the most poetic, the most powerful, the most vital of all arts. It should also be the most free, but unfortunately it is not. Hence our sufferings as artists, our misunderstood sacrifices, our disgust, our hopelessness, our longing for death.*

'Modern music, the real music (not the courtesan stuff which one meets with everywhere under this name) is like the classical Andromeda, whose divine beauty and flaming look transfused through tears radiates in many-coloured beams.

'On the shore of the immeasurable sea—whose waves ceaselessly flow over her beautiful feet and cover them with dirt—chained to a rock she awaits the victorious Perseus, who shall break her chains and annihilate that monster Routine, whose jaws with pestilent breath threaten her.

'But I believe this monster is old. His limbs are lame, his teeth loose, his claws blunt. His clumsy paws slip from Andromeda's rock. The monster begins to perceive that his utmost efforts to climb this rock are vain; he sinks back; at times one may hear his death-croaking.

'When, however, this hateful chimera has succumbed to its fate the lover speeding to the godlike prisoner breaks her chains, bears her in happiness through the waves, and restores her to Greece at the risk of being treated by Andromeda with indifference and coldness for all his devotion.

'The satyrs among the rocks laugh at his fiery impetuosity to free her. In vain they call to him: "You fool, leave her in her chains. Are you sure that she will devote herself to you when she is free? The majesty of her misery is less vulnerable if she lies in chains."

'The true lover, however, hates violation; he would receive, not compel a favour. With chaste hand he frees Andromeda; with warm tears of love he bathes her wave-chilled feet; yes, he would even, if he could, give her wings in order to make her freedom still less restrained.

'There you have my whole faith, all that I can avow to you. And I give it only and solely to show you *that I have a faith.* So many professors have none! Unluckily I have one; I have for so long preached it from the housetops, faithful to the teaching of the Evangel.

'The saying: "Faith brings happiness" [Blessed are the faithful], is, however, false. On the contrary: Faith is our destruction. And it will destroy me also. That is my conviction.

'I conclude, as my Galilean friend Griepenkerl concludes all his letters, *E pur si muove.*[1]

'But don't betray me to the Inquisition!'

Such was Berlioz's *credo.* Nothing is more characteristic of Berlioz, nothing distinguishes him more sharply from the millions of ordinary decent believers than his statement that faith does not make blessed, but destroys. Here we touch his profound sense of reality. It is assumed that all men in love are under an illusion. Berlioz has been described as the arch-romantic because of his extraordinary capacity for love. It seems inconceivable to the majority of his critics that a man can love with his eyes wide open; but it is true of Berlioz. When he wrote this *credo* in his fiftieth year Berlioz was a man without illusions, but not a man without love. Is it possible to give higher praise than that? I think not, for it can be said only of the greatest of men.

Apart from his *Mémoires*, which is a book without parallel or rival, Berlioz's writings may be divided into two classes, the technical and the non-technical. In the first class comes his *Traité de l'instrumentation* with his *Art du chef d'orchestre.* This is a classic for the use of musical students, and I have already dealt with it as far as was necessary in this book. His non-technical writings consist of musical criticism and what the French call *feuilletons*—a kind of light, witty, and entertaining articles on any subject. Of these there are five collections:[2]

(1) *Voyage musical en Allemagne et en Italie*, 1844.

(2) *Les Soirées de l'orchestre*, 1852–3.

---

[1] The reputed saying of Galileo when arraigned by the Catholic Church for saying the earth went round the sun. He recanted but under his breath added: 'Nevertheless it moves.'

[2] For further information see list of literary works in Appendix II.

(3) *Les Grotesques de la musique*, 1859.

(4) *A travers Chants*, 1862.

(5) *Les Musiciens et la musique* (posthumous), 1903.

The first of these originally appeared in 1844, and was not kept in print, the bulk of the material being incorporated later by Berlioz in his *Mémoires*, or elsewhere; his second literary work, *Les Soirées de l'orchestre*, is the only series of critical essays known to me that is cast into an artistic form and is not a mere miscellany.[1] It is not surprising, therefore, to find that *Les Soirées* is not a book of analytical criticism, but a piece of creative fantasy which has more in common with Voltaire's witty ironic stories, such as *Candide* or *Zadig*, than with philosophical or 'scientific' criticism. It would not be too much to claim that Berlioz is one of the greatest wits that France, the motherland of wit, has produced. It is impossible therefore by any short extract to give an adequate idea of the abundance of invention and humour in such a book as *Les Soirées de l'orchestre* ('Evenings in the Orchestra').

It is divided into a prologue, twenty-five evenings, and two epilogues. It is a mixture of dialogue and narrative, and the speakers are as follows:

The Conductor of the orchestra
Corsino, first violin, a composer
Siedler, principal of the second violins
Dimski, first double-bass
Turuth, second flute
Kleiner (senior), kettle-drummer
Kleiner (junior), first 'cello
Dervinck, first oboe
Winter, second bassoon
Bacon, viola (no descendant of the man who invented gunpowder [2])
Moran, first horn
Schmidt, third horn
Carlo, orchestra attendant
A Gentleman, a frequenter of the orchestra stalls
The Author

The book is made up of conversations among these characters which take place during the performances of bad operas, and it is full of amusing and fantastic stories, skits, serious reflections, ferocious critical attacks, and other matters from Barnum to Beethoven. The 'Evenings' vary enormously in length; the best of them are much too long to quote here, but to give the reader a slight notion of the tone of the book I will mention that there are six evenings when the musicians do not speak. I leave the reader to guess what operas are being performed on those nights. I will, however, quote the whole of the first of these six nights of devoted silence, namely, the

'THIRD EVENING

'Performance of *Der Freischütz*

[1] Coleridge in his *Biographia Literaria* attempted something of the sort but hardly succeeded as far as the form is concerned.

[2] One of Berlioz's innumerable puns is hidden here; in the original *inventer la poudre* also means: 'to set the Thames on fire.'

'No one in the orchestra speaks. Each musician is occupied with his task, which he carries out zealously and lovingly. During an interval one of them asks me if it is true that at the Paris Opéra a real skeleton had been used in the infernal scene. I reply in the affirmative, and promise next day to relate the biography of this poor fellow.'

In addition to the wit, wisdom, irony, and passion this book contains, there are stories, such as that of Vincent Wallace and Tatéa, that are unforgettable.

In *Les Grotesques de la musique* we have more of the witty, malicious side of Berlioz, the Berlioz who scribbled on the walls of the Paris Conservatoire in his youth: '*C'est défendu de faire la musique contre ces murs*' (Do not make music here!) It contains the stories of the 'cellist who never washed his face after having once been kissed on the forehead by Rossini; of the dumb clarinettist; of the pianoforte with only white keys; of the ballet-dancer who could not dance in the key of E major; and a hundred other drolleries.

A travers Chants, a title which it is difficult to translate, is a collection of more serious and critical articles on Beethoven, Gluck, Weber, Wagner, etc. Berlioz was one of the first musicians to say those things about Beethoven's music which have since become the platitudes of criticism. The tardiness with which Beethoven's music won its way is now generally forgotten; it is therefore worth pointing out that as late as 1853 a famous book by Wilhelm von Lenz was published entitled *Beethoven et ses trois styles*, which Grove describes (and justly) as 'full of knowledge, insight, and enthusiasm,' in which the author subscribes to a common belief that there was an engraving mistake in the scherzo of the C minor Symphony. Berlioz, writing about Lenz's book in *Soirées de l'orchestre*, says:

'As to the alleged mistake . . . consisting, according to the critics supporting that thesis, in the inopportune repetition of two bars of the theme at its reappearance in the middle of the movement, this is what I have to say: First, there is no exact repetition of the four notes C E D F, of which the melodic design consists; the first time they are written as minims, followed by a crotchet, and the second time as crotchets, followed by a rest, which changes its character.

'Besides, the addition of these two bars is not in the least an anomaly in the style of Beethoven. There are not a hundred but a thousand examples of similar caprices in his works. That these two added bars destroy the symmetry of the phrase was not enough to cause him to abstain from them if the idea came to him. Nobody disregarded more boldly than he what is called "squareness" . . .'

I do not intend to reproduce here any of the analyses made by Berlioz of Beethoven's symphonies in *A travers Chants*, but I must add the interesting fact that Berlioz's analysis is at times not a little scholastic, one might even say that it is occasionally pedantic; also, that Berlioz has the high opinion of the sixth and eighth symphonies which the best musicians since him have also, sooner or later, come to hold. A definition of music, given in his first chapter, ought, however, to find a place here:

'Music is at once a sensation and a science; it requires of those who cultivate it, executant or composer, a natural inspiration, and a knowledge only to be acquired by long study and profound meditation. The union of the knowledge and the inspiration constitutes the art.'

Les Musiciens et la musique contains some interesting early appreciations of Mozart, and two fine biographical essays on Cherubini and Lesueur. The essay on Cherubini is an excellent example of Berlioz's freedom from pettiness or bias. In his *Mémoires* he makes very good fun out of Cherubini as his director when a pupil at the Paris Conservatoire; but with his usual sense of justice and well-balanced judgment he pays him a noble tribute as a musician and composer. The other essays are chiefly interesting for Berlioz's contemporary opinions on Meyerbeer, Glinka, Gounod, Offenbach, Bizet, etc.

It now remains to say a word about Berlioz's letters. This word shall be left to the great French writer Flaubert, since my opinion of these letters is contained in the fact that I have quoted so many of them. Writing to his niece in a letter dated 10th April 1879, Flaubert says:

'Reading the *Correspondance inédite* of Berlioz has reanimated me. Read it, I beg you. There was a man! And a true artist! . . . It surpasses the correspondence of Balzac by thirty-six thousand arms' lengths! I am no longer surprised at the sympathy there was between us. If only I had known him better! I would have loved him!'

The French have never yet appreciated fully the real status of Berlioz. In the preface to a recent book a French academician, M. Louis Barthou, says, 'Berlioz is the greatest name in French music between Rameau and Debussy.' Now, this is as if an English critic were to write baldly: 'The greatest English dramatist between Kyd and Oscar Wilde is Shakespeare.' It is perhaps the last irony of Berlioz's career that a complete collected edition of his music should have been undertaken only by a German firm; [1] but, from the beginning, German musicians were wont to call him the 'French Beethoven.' It is inappropriate as applied to one of the most original of composers, but it does show some sense of the dimensions of Berlioz's creative power.

---

[1] Begun in 1900 by Felix Weingartner and Charles Malherbe for Messrs. Breitkopf & Härtel of Leipzig, but unfortunately not yet completed.

APPENDIX II

CHRONOLOGICAL LIST OF WORKS

MUSIC

(*a*) *Unpublished, lost, or destroyed*

1.	Potpourri sur des thèmes italiens pour Flute, Cor, et instruments à cordes	1815
2.	Deux Quintetti pour Flute et instruments à cordes	1816
3.	Romances pour Estelle de Florian	1816
4.	Le Cheval arabe (Cantate pour basse et orchestre)	1822
5.	Béverley ou le Joueur (Scène pour basse et orchestre)	1823
6.	Messe solennelle	1824-5-7
7.	Le Passage de la mer Rouge (Oratorio)	1825
8.	Erigone (Scène lyrique)	1826
9.	La Mort d'Orphée (Scène lyrique)	1827
10.	Marche religieuse des Mages [1]	1828
11.	Les Franc-Juges (Opéra)	1828–30
12.	Sardanapale (Scène lyrique) (This was the composition with which Berlioz won the Grand Prix de Rome in 1830)	1830
13.	Le Chasseur de chamois (Chœur pour voix d'hommes)	1833
14.	Hymne vocal arrangé pour six instruments Sax	1843
15.	La Nonne sanglante (Opéra)	1841–7

(*b*) *Published Works, with and without Opus Number*

	Title	*Opus No.*	*Remarks*	*Date of Composition*
1.	Resurrexit	None	Arranged by Berlioz 1827 and 1831, first published by Breitkopf & Härtel in collected edition begun Leipzig, 1900	1825
2.	Le Dépit de la bergère	None	Romance, with pianoforte accompaniment	before 1826
3.	Toi qui l'aimas verse des pleurs	None	Romance, with pianoforte accompaniment	before 1827
4.	Le Maure jaloux	None	Romance, with pianoforte accompaniment	before 1827
5.	Scène héroique (La Révolution grecque)	None	First published by Breitkopf & Härtel	1828
6.	Waverley	1 *bis*	Ouverture	1827–8

[1] I do not know if this work was transformed or not into the *Coro dei Maggi* written in Rome in 1832. See No. 35.

Title	*Opus No.*	*Remarks*	*Date of Composition*
7. Les Francs-Juges	3	Ouverture	1827–8
8. Herminie	None	Scène lyrique with orchestra, first published by Breitkopf & Härtel. This cantata won the second Prix de Rome in 1828	1828
9. Amitié, reprends ton empire	None	Song, with pianoforte accompaniment	before 1828
10. Le Montagnard exilé	None	Chant élégiaque with pianoforte accompaniment	before 1828
11. Canon libre à la quinte	None		before 1828
12. Pleure, pauvre Colette	None	Romance, with pianoforte accompaniment	before 1828
13. Hélène (No. 2 Mélodies irlandaises, Op. 2)[1]	None	Ballade, with pianoforte accompaniment (orchestrated 1844)	1829
14. La Belle Voyageuse (No. 4 Mélodies irlandaises, Op. 2)	None	Légende, with pianoforte accompaniment (orchestrated 1834)	1829
15. Ballet des Ombres	None	For chorus and pianoforte, afterwards incorporated in *Lélio*	1829
16. Chant guerrier (No. 3 Mélodies irlandaises, Op. 2)	None	For chorus and pianoforte	1829
17. Chanson à boire (No. 5 Mélodies irlandaises, Op. 2)	None	For chorus and pianoforte	1829
18. Chant sacré (No. 6 Mélodies irlandaises, Op. 2)	None	For chorus and pianoforte	1829
19. Fugues à 4 et 8 parties	None	First published by Breitkopf & Härtel	1829
20. Cléopâtre	None	Cantata (first published by Breitkopf & Härtel)	1829
21. Huit scènes de 'Faust'	1	Cantata	1829
22. Le Coucher du soleil (Rêverie) (No. 1 Mélodies irlandaises, Op. 2)	None	For voice and pianoforte	1830
23. L'Origine du harpe (Ballade) (No. 7 Mélodies irlandaises, Op. 2)	None	For voice and pianoforte	1830
24. Adieu, Bessy (No. 8 Mélodies irlandaises, Op. 2)	None	For voice and pianoforte (arranged 1850)	1830
25. Élégie (No. 9 Mélodies irlandaises, Op. 2)	None	For voice and pianoforte	1830

[1] The nine songs were published as *Neuf Mélodies irlandaises*, Op. 2, in 1830.

Title	Opus No.	Remarks	Date of Composition
26. Le Pêcheur	None	For voice and pianoforte (incorporated in *Lélio*)	1827–31
27. Symphonie fantastique	14	First published in 1846 as Op. 14, dedicated to Liszt, whose pianoforte arrangement was published in 1834)	1830
28. Fantaisie sur la 'Tempête' de Shakespeare	None	For choir, orchestra, and pianoforte (four hands); this was incorporated in *Lélio*	1831
29. Le Roi Lear	4	Overture	1831
30. Le Corsaire	21	Overture, revised and published in 1855 as Op. 21	1831
31. Méditation religieuse (Ce monde entier n'est qu'une ombre fugitive)	None	For choir and orchestra (No. 1 of *Tristia*, Op. 18)	1831
32. Lélio; ou le Retour à la Vie	14 *bis*	Mélologue	1831
33. Rob Roy	None	Overture. (This is claimed by the editors of Breitkopf & Härtel's edition to be first published by them, but I believe an earlier edition exists)	1832
34. Le Cinq mai	6	For chorus and orchestra	1832
35. Coro dei Maggi	None	For chorus and orchestra (first published by Breitkopf & Härtel)	1832
36. La Captive	12	Song with pianoforte accompaniment (Versions 1, 2, and 3), arranged 1834	1832
37. Sara la baigneuse, Orientale de Victor Hugo	11	First form for four men's voices, arranged later for three choirs with orchestra, and also for two voices with pianoforte accompaniment	1834
38. Harold en Italie	16	Symphony with alto solo	1834
39. Le Jeune Pâtre breton	None	For voice and pianoforte. No. 4 *Fleurs des Landes*, Op. 13 (orchestrated in 1835)	1834
40. Je crois en vous	None	Romance, words by Léon Guérin, for voice and pianoforte	1834

Title	Opus No.	Remarks	Date of Composition
41. Villanelle	None	For voice and pianoforte (arranged 1841, orchestrated 1856). No. 1 *Nuits d'été*, Op. 7	1834
42. Le Spectre de la rose	None	For voice and pianoforte (arranged 1841, orchestrated 1856). No. 2 *Nuits d'été*, Op. 7	1834
43. Sur les lagunes	None	For voice and pianoforte (arranged 1841, orchestrated 1856). No. 3 *Nuits d'été*, Op. 7	1834
44. Absence	None	For voice and pianoforte (arranged 1841). No. 4 *Nuits d'été*, Op. 7	1834
45. Au cimitière (Clair de lune)	None	For voice and pianoforte (arranged 1841, orchestrated 1856). No. 5 *Nuits d'été*, Op. 7	1834
46. L'Ile inconnue (Barcarolle) [1]	None	For voice and pianoforte (arranged 1841, orchestrated 1856). No. 6 *Nuits d'éét* Op. 7	1834
47. Les Champs (Aubade)	None	For voice and pianoforte (arranged 1850). No. 2 *Feuillets d'album*, Op. 19	1834
48. Benvenuto Cellini	23	Opera in two acts by Léon de Wailly and Auguste Barbier, performed at the Paris Opera in 1838; divided in four acts and translated into German by Riccius, and produced by Liszt at Weimar in 1852; revised into three acts and retranslated by P. Cornelius and produced by Liszt at Weimar in 1856. Published with dedication to Grand Duchess of Weimar as Op. 23 in 1856	1835–8

[1] The six songs were published in 1841 as *Les Nuits d'été*, words by Theophile Gautier, for voice and pianoforte, Op. 7.

Title	*Opus No.*	*Remarks*	*Date of Composition*
49. Grande Messe des morts (Requiem)	5	First edition published at Paris in 1838; second edition, containing important changes, published by Ricordi at Milan	1837
50. Premiers transports	None	For voice and pianoforte	1838
51. Roméo et Juliette	17	Grand dramatic symphony with chorus, dedicated to Paganini, and first performed in Paris in 1839. First published in 1848, Op. 17. Revised in second edition, and published in 1857	1838–9
52. Rêverie et caprice	8	(*a*) For violin and pianoforte (*b*) For violin and orchestra	1839
53. Symphonie funèbre et triomphale	15	In three parts for large military band, performed in the open air in Paris, 28th July 1840; revised with addition of a string orchestra and choir *ad lib.*, and published in this form, dedicated to the Duc d'Orléans	1840
54. Recitatives for Weber's *Der Freischütz*	None	Specially composed by Berlioz for the revival of Weber's opera at the Paris Opera House	1841
55. Hymne à la France	None	Words by Auguste Barbier, for chorus and orchestra (No. 2 of *Vox Populi*, published 1851)	1844
56. La Tour de Nice	None	Overture (this appears to be another version of the *Corsaire* overture which was published in 1855 as Op. 21. It was performed in Paris on Jan. 1845, and destroyed afterwards)	1844
57. Le Carnaval romain	9	Overture (first performed 3rd Feb. 1844)	1844

Title	Opus No.	Remarks	Date of Composition
58. La Belle Isabeau	None	For voice and pianoforte, words by Alexander Dumas (No. 5 of *Feuillets d'album*, Op. 19)	1844
59. Zaïde (Boléro)	None	For voice and pianoforte (No. 1 of *Feuillets d'album*, Op. 19)	before 1845
60. Le Chasseur danois	None	For voice and pianoforte (No. 6 of *Feuillets d'album*, Op. 19)	1845
61. Sérénade agreste à la Madone	None	For organ or harmonium	1845
62. Hymne pour l'Élévation	None	For organ or harmonium	1845
63. Toccata	None	For organ or harmonium	1845
64. Le Chant des Chemins de fer	None	For chorus and orchestra (No. 3 of *Feuillets d'album*, Op. 19)	1846
65. La Damnation de Faust	24	Opéra de concert	1846
66. Page d'album	None	For voice and pianoforte	1847
67. La Mort d'Ophélie	None	For chorus and orchestra (No. 2 of *Tristia*)	1848
68. Marche funèbre pour la dernière scène de Hamlet [1]	None	For chorus and orchestra (No. 3 of *Tristia*)	1848
69. L'Apothéose (Chant héroïque)	None	For chorus with pianoforte accompaniment	1848
70. La Fuite en Égypte	None	The first part of *L'Enfance du Christ* to be composed	1850
71. Le Chant des Bretons	None	For chorus and pianoforte (No. 5 of *Fleurs des Landes*, Op. 13)	1850
72. Le Trébuchet	None	Scherzo for two voices and pianoforte (No. 3 of *Fleurs des Landes*, Op. 13)	1850
73. Le Matin	None	For voice and pianoforte (No. 1 of *Fleurs des Landes*, Op. 13)	1850
74. Petit oiseau	None	For voice and pianoforte (No. 2 of *Fleurs des Landes*, Op. 13)	1850
75. La Menace des Francs	None	For chorus and orchestra (No. 1 of *Vox Populi*, Op. 20)	1851

[1] On the only two occasions I have heard this performed in London it has been without the chorus; although the chorus has only one word to sing the effect is novel and important.

Title	Opus No.	Remarks	Date of Composition
76. L'Enfance du Christ	25	Oratorio	1854
77. Te Deum	22	For solo voices, chorus, and orchestra	1849–54
78. L'Impériale	26	Cantata	1855
80. Prière du matin	None	For women's and children's voices and pianoforte (No. 4 of *Feuillets d'album*, Op. 19)	1855
81. Les Troyens	None	Opera in five acts	1856–63
82. Hymne pour la consécration du nouveau Tabernacle	None	For three-part choir	1859
83. Le Temple universel	None	For double choir with organ, in two languages (French and English)	1860
84. Béatrice et Bénédict	None	Opéra-comique in two acts	1860–3
85. Veni Creator	None	Motet for solo voices and choir	
86. Tantum ergo	None	Motet for solo voices and choir	

(c) *Arrangements*

Title	Remarks	Date of Composition
1. La Marseillaise	Orchestrated	1830
2. Weber's Invitation to the Waltz	Orchestrated	1841
3. Recitatives for Weber's *Der Freischütz*	Composed. (These are hardly arrangements, but I have included them here also, for convenience)	1841
4. Pater Noster and Adoremus, by Bortniansky	Adapted	1843
5. Plains-chants de l'Église grecque	Arranged for quadruple choir in six parts	1843
6. Marche marocaine, by Leopold de Mayer	Orchestrated	1845
7. Plaisir d'amour, romance by Martini	Arranged for small orchestra	1849
8. Schubert's Erlkönig [1]	Orchestrated and performed at Baden-Baden	1860
9. Invitation à louer Dieu, by Couperin		

[1] This was never published and is not mentioned in Breitkopf & Härtel's list of Berlioz's arrangements. It may still be among his MSS. belonging to the Paris Conservatoire.

LIST OF BERLIOZ'S WORKS PUBLISHED IN HIS LIFETIME WITH OPUS NUMBER

Op. 1. Huit scènes de 'Faust'
„ 1 *bis*. Ballet des Ombres
„ 2. Irlande, neuf mélodies:
(1) Le Coucher de soleil
(2) Hélène
(3) Chant guerrier
(4) La Belle Voyageuse
(5) Chanson à boire
(6) Chant sacré
(7) L'Origine de la Harpe
(8) Adieu, Bessy
(9) Élégie
„ 2 *bis*. Ouverture de 'Waverley'
„ 3. Ouverture des 'Francs-Juges'
„ 4. Ouverture du 'Roi Lear'
„ 5. Grande Messe des morts (Requiem)
„ 6. Le Cinq mai
„ 7. Les Nuits d'été, six mélodies:
(1) Villanelle
(2) Le Spectre de la rose
(3) Sur les lagunes
(4) Absence
(5) Au cimetière
(6) L'Ile inconnue
„ 8. Rêverie et caprice pour violon
„ 9. Ouverture du Carnaval romain
„ 10. Traité d'instrumentation
„ 11. Sara la baigneuse
„ 12. La Captive
„ 13. Fleurs des Landes, cinq mélodies:
(1) Le Matin
(2) Petit Oiseau
(3) Le Trébuchet
(4) Le Jeune Pâtre breton
(5) Le Chant des Bretons
„ 14. Episode de la vie d'un artiste:
(1) Symphonie fantastique
(2) Lélio; ou le Retour à la Vie
„ 15. Symphonie funèbre et triomphale
„ 16. Harold en Italie
„ 17. Roméo et Juliette
„ 18. Tristia:
(1) Méditation religieuse
(2) La Mort d'Ophélie
(3) Marche funèbre pour la dernière scène de 'Hamlet'
„ 19. Feuillets d'album, six mélodies:
(1) Zaïde
(2) Les Champs
(3) Chant des Chemins de fer
(4) Prière du matin
(5) La Belle Isabeau
(6) Le Chasseur danois

Op. 20. Vox populi, deux chœurs:
(1) La Menace des Francs (2) Hymne à la France
„ 21. Ouverture du 'Corsaire'
„ 22. Te Deum
„ 23. Benvenuto Cellini, opera
„ 24. La Damnation de Faust
„ 25. L'Enfance du Christ
„ 26. L'Impériale
„ 27. —
„ 28. Le Temple universel

LITERARY WORKS

1. *Voyage musical en Allemagne et en Italie, études sur Beethoven, Gluck, et Weber, mélanges et nouvelles.* 2 vols., 8vo. Published by Labitte, Paris, 1844. Much of this material was included in later publications.
2. *Traité de l'instrumentation et d'orchestration modernes.* Published Paris 1844, republished in 1856, with a preliminary chapter on *L'Art du chef d'orchestre*, Op. 10.
3. *Les Soirées de l'orchestre.* Dedicated 'A mes bons amis les artistes de l'orchestre de X ***, ville civilisée.' Published by Michel Lévy, Paris, 1853. 2nd edition, 1854; 3rd edition, 1861.
4. *Les Grotesques de la musique.* Dedicated 'A mes bons amis les artistes des chœurs de l'Opéra de Paris, ville barbare.' 1 vol. Published by Michel Lévy, Paris, 1859. 2nd edition, 1861.
5. *A travers Chants, études musicales, adorations, boutades, et critiques.* 1 vol. Published by Michel Lévy, Paris, 1862.
6. *Mémoires, avec un portrait de l'auteur.* 1 vol. Published by Michel Lévy, Paris, 1870.
7. *Les Musiciens et la musique.* A posthumous collection of miscellaneous articles written by Berlioz. Edited, with an introduction, by André Hallays; published by Calmann-Lévy, Paris, 1903.

Note. A list of the editions of Berlioz's letters will be found in the bibliography.

To the above list of literary compositions must be added the poem *L'Enfance du Christ*, the poem for *Les Troyens*, much of the text of *La Damnation de Faust*, the arrangement from Shakespeare's *Much Ado about Nothing*, for *Béatrice et Bénédict*, and the prose sections of *Lélio*.

INDEX